CONTEMPORARY TELEVISION

COMMUNICATION AND HUMAN VALUES

Series Editors

Robert A. White, Editor, The Centre of Interdisciplinary Studies in Communication, The Gregorian University, Rome, Italy
Michael Traber, Associate Editor, World Association for Christian Communication, London, UK

International Editorial Advisory Board

Binod C. Agrawal, Development and Educational Communication, Space Applications Centre, Ahmedabad, India
Luis Ramiro Beltrán, La Paz, Bolivia
S.T. Kwame Boafo, Culture and Communication Sector, UNESCO, Paris
James W. Carey, University of Illinois, USA
Marlene Cuthbert, University of Windsor, Canada
William F. Fore, Yale Divinity School, USA
George Gerbner, University of Pennsylvania, USA
James D. Halloran, University of Leicester, UK
Cees Hamelink, Institute of Social Studies, The Hague, The Netherlands
Neville D. Jayaweera, Stockholm, Sweden
Emile G. McAnany, University of Texas, USA
Walter J. Ong, St. Louis University, USA
Breda Pavlic, Culture and Communication Sector, UNESCO, Paris
Miquel de Moragas Spa, Autonomous University of Barcelona, Spain
Anabelle Sreberny-Mohammadi, Centre for Mass Communication Research, University of Leicester, UK

Other Volumes in this Series

Designing Messages for Development Communication: An Audience Participation-based Approach
Bella Mody

Communication, Culture and Hegemony: From the Media to Mediations
Jesús Martin-Barbero

The Politics of World Communication
Cess J. Hamelink

Women in Grassroots Communication: Furthering Social Change
Edited by **Pillar Riaño**

Participatory Communication: Working for Change and Development
Edited by **Shirley A. White** *with K. Sadanandan Nair and Joseph Ascroft*

CONTEMPORARY TELEVISION

Eastern Perspectives

EDITED BY

David French
Michael Richards

Sage Publications
New Delhi • Thousand Oaks • London

First published in 1996 by

Sage Publications India Pvt Ltd
M-32 Greater Kailash Market I
New Delhi 110 048

Sage Publications Inc
2455 Teller Road
Thousand Oaks, California 91320

Sage Publications Ltd
6 Bonhill Street
London EC2A 4PU

Published by Tejeshwar Singh for Sage Publications India Pvt Ltd, phototypeset by Pagewell Photosetters, Pondicherry and printed at Chaman Enterprises, Delhi.

Library of Congress Cataloging-in-Publication Data

Contemporary television: eastern perspectives / edited by David French, Michael Richards.
p. cm.—(Communication and human values)
Includes bibliographical references and index.
1. Television broadcasting—Asia—Case studies. I. French, David, 1946– . II Richards, Michael, 1945– . III. Series: Communication and human values (Newbury Park, Calif.)
HE8700.9.A78C66 384.55′095–dc20 1996 95–46609

ISBN: 0–8039–9282–3 (US-hb) 81–7036–516–3 (India-hb)
0–8039–9283–1 (US-pb) 81–7036–517–1 (India-pb)

Sage Production Editor: Sumitra Srinivasan

TO
Sue and Jeanette

Contents

List of Tables and Figures

Tables

Figures

I

The Global Context

1

Studying Television: New Worlds and Contemporary Debates

David French and *Michael Richards*

This book is about the importance of television in a number of countries in South and Southeast Asia. Among the various aspects to which attention is directed are the role of television as an increasingly dominant form of leisure pursuit, television as a source of news and information for its viewers and as an important influence upon the cultural life of those societies in which it is available. Although dealt with here in different ways, the topics are ones which are familiar to any reader acquainted with the various traditions of the study of television around the world.

Such studies have acquired a particular salience in recent years as a number of new issues have come to the fore in international debate about public policy. The agenda now features prominently the confrontation between the concern to preserve the distinctiveness of existing cultural identities at the national, regional and other levels, and the apparently irresistible pressure of 'global' forces. It also gives an important place to the role of broadcasting as a major public forum in which informed debate can take place. This has often been construed in terms of Habermas's concept of the 'public sphere'; this issue is taken up in Chapter 2 of this volume (also see Baynes, 1994; Hallin, 1994, for useful recent discussions of it).

Another major issue is the significance of the increasing importance in the world of the ideologies of free-trade, finding its strongest expression in the setting up on 1 January 1995 of the World Trade Organisation, following the successful resolution of the Uruguay Round of the General Agreement on Tariffs and Trade (GATT) negotiations over the previous decade. The growth in acceptance of this approach is in some real conflict with another important set of themes; those concerned with matters of information inequalities in the world marketplace. These continuing concerns are reflected in the debate over the New World Information and Communication Order (NWICO) and in the notion of actual or potential media imperialism (see Chapters 3 and 18 of this volume).

In all of these debates the role of television is crucial, particularly so in countries where the growth of ownership of television sets has been fast, as it has been in those covered in this book. But the context within which discussions of television have itself taken place has changed radically in the recent past.

From the earliest days of the medium (dating back to its introduction in the 1930s in the UK and USA) until the mid 1980s, the nature of 'television' as a cultural and social form was essentially determined by its nature as 'technology'. The television set enabled a multitude of individual households to receive sound and pictures all at the same time transmitted by a single broadcasting organisation, or at most very few broadcasting organisations. In response to the limited opportunities to broadcast made available by the old technology (the problem of 'spectrum scarcity'), governments generally took care to ensure some substantial measure of public regulation of television services. In order to satisfy their regulators and mass audiences, and because of the high cost of making original programmes, broadcasters in most countries settled for similar kinds of schedules (Carrie and Ehrenberg, 1992); with a mixture of popular entertainment and more serious news and information programmes, generally drawing substantially from the vigorous international market in television products.

This is still the dominant picture world-wide. There is often still strong support for the 'old' terrestrial services, even where television is received and is widely available through the new technologies of satellite or cable. However, is the relationship between the viewer and the provider of the service so very different from that of the more popular versions of traditional television?

The enormous change is in the perception of the future of television. With the widespread and fast-growing introduction of cable and satellite delivery, television now shares its distribution technology with the whole field of telecommunications, and thereby with the explosion of interest in the opportunities offered by information technology. To quote the Singapore Minister of Information and the Arts (Yeo, 1994, p. 104):

> A technological revolution is sweeping the world. No aspect of life is left untouched. All societies are affected and some are shaken to the core. The revolution in communication, information technology and transportation has weakened the power of governments and integrated the world economy in a way never seen before. It broke up the Soviet Empire and forced open countries like China and Vietnam. All borders are now porous. National wealth is increasingly based more upon knowledge than on land and natural resources.

This echoes the widely known views of the American Vice-President, Al Gore (Gore, 1994, p. 22), in support of:

> . . . the creation of a network of networks, transmitting messages and images at the speed of light across every continent, is essential to sustainable development for the human family.
>
> It will bring economic progress, strong democracies, better environmental management, improved healthcare and a greater sense of shared stewardship of our small planet.

There is of course a good deal of argument about the accuracy of these views (see for example Golding, 1994, especially pp. 469–77). Gore, in particular, is open to the charge of utopianism. But they remain as very clear indicators of the extent to which debate about television is having to open its frontiers to encompass a far wider range of applications and usages.

So where can this debate take place and, in particular, what role are the universities, in Asia and across the world, taking in this changing intellectual context? This is a question which will be of particular interest to those readers of this book who work and study in academic institutions. In order to answer the question, the functions of universities will be considered in three categories: as educators of students; as sources, through their research activities, of informed contributions to public debate; and as venues within which such debate can take place.

Undergraduate Education[1]

One group that does seem to recognise the increasing importance of the subject are those who wish to become students of it. It is a universal characteristic of courses in this area that they are besieged by enormous student demand. In those European countries, such as Spain, in which the door to university is open to all those achieving pass standard in the school leaving examinations, the dimensions of student numbers are staggering. For example, Alvarez (1994) reports that in 1991–92, 25,872 Spanish students matriculated in Information Sciences, and the numbers are increasing.

This increase is reflected in the experiences in other countries also, although selective systems restrict the number of students to courses; but only at the expense of leaving many other well-qualified applicants in a state of frustrated rejection or in the expensive pursuit of places to study abroad. It is also leading to the rapid expansion and reorganisation of undergraduate education in the field, one of many examples of which is the establishment of the new School of Communication Studies at Nanyang University in Singapore (Hukill, 1994). But in most countries, the study of communication is still a new feature of the university system. Nowhere else does it yet parallel that of the United States, where the biggest teaching and research association, the Speech Communication Association (SCA), claims a membership running into thousands.

In terms of course content, the communication and media departments of the world have faced a common set of dilemmas (see French and Richards, 1994; Hukill, 1994). To be specific, pressure is often experienced from students, and some potential employers, for vocationally-oriented training. But, even if such narrow inculcation of skills could be reconciled with the broader aims of university education, it is difficult for generally cash-starved universities to keep up with state-of-the-art, broadcast-standard, technology.

This is one of the areas in which the changing nature of the communication industry is highly relevant. In some countries, at an early stage of nation-building, the perceived need may overwhelmingly be for trained professionals. Hadlow (1993) provides some tantalising evidence in this regard concerning the newly independent, former Soviet states. If all countries are confronting a future of continued flux in their communication industries (see Hadden and Lenert, 1995, for a relevant discussion), their need is not for recruits with a narrow practical training but for those capable of thinking more broadly, with an understanding of communication processes that will enable adaptation to new situations.

It is a major imperative for communication education not to shrink from engagement with practical issues, but to put them in a larger context, informed by the proper academic study of structures and their operation.

The Role of Research and of the University as Forum of Debate

Questions about the nature of changes in the information networks that we use, the ways in which they relate to established cultural forms such as television, and the approaches that can help us to understand all this and their relationship to the rest of society, are complex, demanding and of acute interest to those with commercial and public policy interests in the subject. There is very big money to be made in the communication industry, and the business importance of good information has ensured the growth of a whole sector of highly-priced consultancy, which only occasionally leaks through to the outsider in the columns of the business press. A good example of this is a study casting doubt on the real potential of the world super-highway, carried out by SRI International (described as one of the world's leading private research institutes), but quoted in the British press as available only to sponsors able to pay a two-year fee of £23,000 (Snoddy, 1994).

The place of the university in this is straightforward, but none-theless important.[2] Universities need to deal with these issues in order to fully educate their students, and to permit this they have to also be a source of independent, freely available, information. As such a source they will have a vital part to play in contributing to public debate. Without them the danger is that decisions may be taken either in ignorance or on the basis of information which will only be fully available to those who can afford to pay for it.

In other words, through their research and publications, universities have a vital role to perform in enabling societies to confront and consider their futures in what many argue is a time of fundamental change. In a curious sense, undergraduate study provides the infrastructure of the public sphere within which debate can take place.

Realities and Dangers

The rapid development of a new field of study is always problematic and it would be naive to expect that existing vested interests in traditional universities would readily accept the newcomer (see Winkin, 1994), and academic legitimacy would be ascribed only with extreme reluctance. But these are teething problems. Far more serious is the need to recognise that the academic study of communication cannot be assumed, simply because it takes place within the bounds of respected universities, to be value-neutral or independent of vested interests.

In Chapter 2 of this book, a brief account is given of the debate surrounding NWICO, which became the subject of intense controversy during the 1980s. The claims behind establishing NWICO are based upon observed inequalities in the patterns of trade with respect to the flow of information and communication output between the countries of the world and specific proposals have been made to address their consequences. The controversy was fuelled by organisations representing groups with commercial interests opposed to the acceptance of NWICO; it even eventually led to the withdrawal of the United States from UNESCO.

The story of NWICO is an extremely interesting piece of intellectual history, now fairly well documented (see Gerbner, Mowlana and Nordenstreng [eds.], 1994, which provides a full set of further references). Roach analyses its representation in American university textbooks, demonstrating the extent to which the apparently objective accounts actually incorporate the partial and selective views of American commercial and governmental lobbies, reaching the conclusion that one author had 'undoubtedly never laid eyes on the actual text [of NWICO]' (1994, p. 43), and that overall its portrayal was characterised by 'caricature and distortion'.

The present authors have not been able to check the accuracy of Roach's conclusions. But her arguments that the prejudices of political conflict about the international media have spilled over into its academic treatment point to a very important issue. If that section of culture, which is called the communication media, is characterised by substantial inequality in the scale of provision between countries and in information flows, then the same is true of that other cultural area which is known as communication education. If there is any convincing reason to be concerned about the cultural domination in any one of these, then why not in both? Furthermore, how much greater is the danger if there is even prima facie evidence that the two are inter-related?

To put the point more directly, the academic study of communication is dominated, at least if measured by quantity, by the United States. There are far more researchers there than in any other country, with far more students and tutors providing the biggest market for academic publication in the forms both of books and journals. As noted above, the SCA is enormous in comparison to any other academic society in the field, even the American based (and largely American run) International Communication Association (ICA). Vijay Menon (1993) reports direct evidence on this point, showing that, for example, 60 per cent of the mass communication and journalism textbooks recommended for use in Asian institutes 'were of North American origin, with a further 6 per cent being from European sources' (p. 30). He also notes the importance of America as a training ground for Asian students.

If there are rivals to the United States, they are much smaller, and similarly located in the developed economies of the West; all indeed seeking trade abroad as a way of covering costs at home. This mirrors the position of the media and echoes long-term debates about cultural imperialism. But is it plausible to assume from this that academic output should be treated with the same scepticism as may be appropriate for that about CNN, Rupert Murdoch's Star TV and other Western media?

It would be smug indeed for two British authors not to advise the readers of this book to treat the output of the Western academic business with some caution. But equally it is important to recognise that its output can be of value, particularly as it has increasingly responded to commercial reality. The markets in Asia, Latin America and elsewhere for studies of this subject are growing fast, but it is one which is particularly demanding and sensitive to issues of cultural subordination. The responsibility, which the editors of this volume have accepted, is to facilitate a process of making available what Beng refers to, in another context, as an 'Asian reading of Asia' (1994, p. 70).

Notes

1. The authors are particularly grateful to Mark Hukill, Zaharom Nain, Terence Lo, John Vilanilam and Keval Kumar for supplying material to draw upon in the preparation of this chapter; the responsibility for any errors remains, of course, entirely with the authors.
2. For a wider discussion see Philip Elliott's classic paper (Elliott, 1986).

References

Alvarez, M. (1994). 'Communication studies in Spain: An individual perspective'. In French, D. and Richards, M. (eds.). *Media education across Europe*. London: Routledge.

Baynes, K. (1994). 'Communicative ethics, the public sphere and communication media'. *Critical Studies in Mass Communication*, 11(3), 315–326.

Beng, Y.S. (1994). 'The emergence of an Asian-centred perspective: Singapore's media regionalisation strategies'. *Media Asia*, 21(2), 63–72.

Carrie, D.G. and **Ehrenberg, A.S.C.** (1992). 'Is television all that important?' *Intermedia*, 20 (4–5), 18–20.

Elliott, P. (1986). 'Intellectuals, the "information society" and the disappearance of the public sphere'. In Collins, R. et al. (eds.). *Media, Culture and Society: A Critical Reader*. London: Sage.

French, D. and **Richards, M.** (eds.). (1994). *Media education across Europe*. London: Routledge.

Gerbner, G., **Mowlana, H.** and **Nordenstreng, K.** (eds.). (1994). *The global media debate: Its rise, fall and renewal*. Norwood, NJ: Ablex. (First printing 1993).

Golding, P. (1994). 'Telling stories: Sociology, journalism and the informed citizen'. *European Journal of Communication*, 9(4), 461–484.

Gore, A. (1994). 'Plugged into the world's knowledge'. *Financial Times*, 19 September.

Hadden, S.G. and **Lenert, E.** (1995). 'Telecommunications networks are not VCRs: The public nature of new information technologies for universal service'. *Media, Culture and Society*, 17(1), 121–140.

Hadlow, M. (1993). 'Where new nations need new media'. *Intermedia*, 21(1), 41–45.

Hallin, D.C. (1994). *We keep America on top of the world: Television journalism and the public sphere*. London: Routledge.

Hukill, M. (1994). 'Communication education in Singapore: Responding to media needs'. *Media Asia*, 21(4), 205–9.

Menon, V. (1993). 'Tradition meets modernity on the path to the global village'. *Intermedia*, 21(1), 29–31.

Roach, C. (1994). 'American textbooks vs NWICO history'. In Gerbner et al. (eds.). *The global media debate: Its rise, fall and renewal*. Norwood, NJ: Ablex.

Snoddy, R. (1994). 'SRI denounces superhighway claims'. *Financial Times*, 31 October.

Winkin, Y. (1994). 'When the faculty meets on April Fool's Day: Arts and sciences of communication at the University of Liege'. In French, D. and Richards, M. (eds.). Media education across Europe. London: Routledge.

Yeo, G. (1994). 'The technological revolution poses threats or opportunities?' *Media Asia*, 21(2), 104–6.

2

From Global Development to Global Culture?

Michael Richards and *David French*

> . . . globalisation as used here refers to the worldwide trend towards the increasing interconnectedness of people, goods, places and capital. Globalisation has deeply impacted notions of sovereignty, national identity, class identity and the public sphere . . . (Sahin and Aksoy, 1993, p. 31).

> . . . satellite television would, he said, 'be an unambiguous threat to totalitarian regimes everywhere' (Rupert Murdoch, quoted in Rusbridger, 1994, p. 8).

Understanding Change in World Television: A Stimulus and a Challenge

Discussions of the process referred to as globalisation have become a central feature of all considerations of the future of television. The issues are prominent in the pages of academic journals, business magazines and in the political section of newspapers. But such discussions include a wide variety of themes and issues. These two quotations capture some important contrasts. In addressing globalisation, scholars are vigorously having to redefine and integrate a number of previously disparate concepts in order to grapple with the changing field. At the same time, entrepreneurs are operating in that field and forever trying to manipulate it in the hope of making even more money. On the other hand, governments and other policy-makers are coming to terms with the processes which, often quite correctly, they perceive as threatening and are sorting out various definitions of the process offered to them by competing vested interests.

The task which all three groups confront is a difficult one; the picture of change in world television becoming ever more hectic. Television is, for most of the world, a recent cultural introduction and has grown rapidly in new markets, offering new challenges to governments and other existing cultural institutions and presenting a range of sometimes unfamiliar images to viewers; all of this at a time when many of the societies into which it has come have themselves anyway been undergoing radical changes associated with post-colonial nation-building, urbanisation, and industrialisation, among many other things.

But television is now changing very fast and its fate is becoming ever more interwoven with factors beyond those which, even in the recent past, would have been regarded as the domain of television. With the convergence of its technology and that of computing and telephony, the industry finds itself at the heart of all kinds of commercial and industrial strategies.

This is, of itself, a difficult enough picture to decipher in terms of individual episodes and single processes. There are continually new events to be taken account of: scenarios behind which the concealed presence of Mr Murdoch or the Sony Corporation can be observed, new constellations of audience interests to be evaluated, and new challenges to national regulatory regimes to be considered. The task is even more demanding when viewed on a global scale. Its background has evolved over a period of more than forty years.

There is some value in seeing it as a story with a number of episodes. First, there was the 'media and development' phase, of which Daniel Lerner and Wilbur Schramm were the main exponents. Their concern was with how the mass media could be used to speed up the process of 'development', primarily by facilitating direct access for largely rural populations to Western values, Western ideas and Western technologies, all of which were deemed necessary for the process of 'modernisation'. In this episode, the role of the media was perceived as essentially benign and technocratic, a neutral instrument capable of being used effectively, in what was then seen unproblematically as a 'good' cause.

The next phase was very different; just as notions like 'development' and 'modernisation' came to be viewed as processes covering hidden agendas on the part of those claiming to be 'developed' and 'modern', so the role of the media in these processes became more suspect. The link of Western media dominance to questions of neo-colonialism and cultural imperialism came to the fore, partly through the work of the American Herbert Schiller. Very closely linked concerns were taken up by those associated with the struggle for the New World Information and Communication Order (NWICO), which sought to address, in more practical ways, the task of doing something about the evident world inequalities in the exchange of news, information and entertainment.

The third episode is about globalism, or more fully, the often alleged globalisation of world culture. Within this part of the story must be included a mass of new organisations, delivery technologies and audiences, as well as older institutions, struggling to adapt to changing circumstances. It is a story of resistance, as well as one of coercive change, and it is very clear that it is a story onto which different viewpoints have attempted to impose different meanings. The interests of those who seek to make the most profits from it are best served by the acceptance of the view that nothing can be done to resist the process. In this they are supported by those academics and governments who, whatever their ideological starting point, conclude that submergence of national differences in global culture is inevitable.

On the other hand, if an attempt to deny the power of globalism is based on the need to avoid giving succor to Mr Murdoch, rather than upon evidence and argument, then it is sure to fail. The need for analytical precision is crucial in finding a way through this hotly contested terrain.

What makes the task particularly stimulating is that this is what might be called a postmodern story; the episodes overlap and interweave, rather than following any simple progression through a list of contents. While the naivety of Lerner's simple association of the media and development has long been blown apart, some aspects of the same mission were appropriated and redefined in the Indian Satellite Instructional Television Experiment (SITE) programme (see articles by Vilanilam; and Sinha in this volume). In responding to the 'threat' of global culture, many have returned (see Gerbner, et al. [eds.], 1993; Schiller, 1992) to redefined versions of the language of media imperialism and the instruments of NWICO.

So the story is one which has been written through the contributions of characters with different perspectives, very often with particular and strongly-held policy objectives. It is replete with the polemic that comes from the clash of fundamental paradigms, analogous to those defined by Thomas Kuhn as the key to an understanding of the history of science (Kuhn, 1970, Chapter 1), as much as that of vested interests. It is also a story that is yet far from finished. Its plot is one which is being produced by human actors and to dismiss its outcome as inevitable would indeed be simplistic and risky as a step in social scientific methodology.

This chapter does not risk the danger of simplistic prediction. Rather its purpose is to provide something of a map of the emerging structure of the plot. Chapter 3 will locate the various national contributions on that map. Chapter 18 will look at some very recent major developments. But it is ultimately the reader who will have to bear the burden of understanding the future as it continues to unfold.

The Media and Development: The Early Years

The title of Lerner's classic study (Lerner, 1958) is highly revealing. *The Passing of Traditional Society* implies a one-way process, an inevitable transition from tradition to modernity.

> What is required there to 'motivate' the isolated and illiterate peasants and tribesmen who compose the bulk of the area's population is to provide them with clues as to what the better things of life might be . . . . There is no suggestion here that all Middle Easterners should learn to admire precisely the same things as people in the Western society. It is suggested, much more simply, that before any enduring transformation can be started in the Middle East, people there will have to learn about the lifeways evolved in other societies. What they subsequently accept, adapt or reject is a matter which each man [sic] will, in due course, decide for himself . . . (p. 411). [And a little later] The media teach people . . . by depicting for them new and strange situations and by familiarizing them with a range of opinions among which they can choose. Some people learn better than others, the variation reflecting the differential skill in empathy . . . the basic skill required of modern men (p. 412).

For Lerner the crucial factors which induced modernisation were individualistic, rational and materialistic. The media were seen as ideally placed in this respect, reaching the individual citizen directly, by-passing the cultural institutions of the traditional society and providing examples of the rewards that a commitment to change could bring. While it was open to such individuals to refuse the pursuit of such benefits, the cost would be the sacrifice of the prospect of achieving changes to which the leaders of such countries were, as Lerner pointed out, committed.

Another key figure in emphasising the role of the media in development was Wilbur Schramm. While Lerner was more generally interested in broad cultural consumption, seeing the viewing of 'movies', for example, as an important factor in extending his subjects' cultural horizons, Schramm focused upon the need for information. Hartmann and his colleagues identify a particularly telling quotation:

> How fortuitous, how almost miraculous it seems that, at this moment of greatest need for swift and widespread information in the developing countries, modern mass communication should be available to multiply informational resources (Schramm, 1964, p. 271; quoted in Hartmann et al. 1989, p. 27).

In retrospect, the inadequacies of this position are all too clear. Lerner, Schramm and other authorities, such as Everett Rogers (see Lerner, 1963; Rogers, 1963) were fully aware of the dangers of ascribing to the media the power of persuasion, as is hardly surprising, given that they had both worked closely with Lazarsfeld and his group in America. But they were dealing with very broad-brush processes on a scale which went far beyond that of the cautious American empirical researchers. Hartmann and his colleagues, for example, quite properly charge Lerner with naive psychologism, ethnocentrism, and crucially, with failing to recognise the complexity of the process of social change (Hartmann et al., 1989, Chapters 1 and 8). To attribute such a central role to the media, independent of more structural factors, can now clearly be seen as inadequate. It should also be recognised that some of the leading figures in the approach changed positions; for example, Everett Rogers in 1978 argued for a revision of the old 'dominant paradigm' of top-down, Western-oriented development (Rogers, 1978).

However these authors had brought the role of the media in relation to social change very much to the centre of attention, a position which it has never relinquished. All too often one can find politicians, ever in search of the quick fix, returning to the media as a key factor in development (see Curtin, 1993, for an interesting sidelight on this), and current concerns with new broadcasting technology are often related to the potential of television for positive change.

In the context of later developments, it is also important to note that the implication of these works was that the interests of developing economies would best be served by opening themselves to the world media. In this way, they would enable their most forward-thinking members to draw upon the stimulation of Western culture, thus liberating themselves from the shackles of tradition. Any dangers in this process were very much in the background. Schramm's work in this respect was supported by UNESCO, firmly locating that body, in the 1960s, as a supporter of the view that the free flow of information, using existing media structures, would be a good means of facilitating the process of world development. This is not insignificant, given what was to happen twenty years later.

Media Imperialism

The globalisation debate is not a recent phenomenon but the latest in the expressions of concern about the cultural impact of transnational flows of information and entertainment programmes from the West, usually the United States, to the East and the South. It has its antecedents in the controversy about media imperialism where concern was expressed at the growing dominance of Western, largely American, originated media practices and products, which were held to create Western-oriented elites in developing countries, therefore, reinforcing Western modes of practice on an ever increasing global scale. This process includes: the growth of interconnected infrastructures of reception, and increase in multinational ownership, the dissemination of particular types of media genre and content, and a downgrading of cultural specificity by the use of programmes originally intended for the home market. The result of all this is claimed to be an undermining and eventual displacement of the indigenous cultures of receiving countries.

During the 1970s and 1980s many viewers in developed, and then developing, countries found themselves receiving new television channels. They experienced an overall increase in the number of conventional television channels, video channels and channels provided by cable, whether from near neighbours or via satellite from further afield. This increase in channels and the number of hours of transmission available, usually led to an increase in the proportion of American originated content in television schedules.

Global flows are influenced by many factors: language relationships can encourage or discourage flows; the production capacity of domestic systems can influence the closure or openness of the domestic market to foreign media products; national media and cultural policies can erect barriers for example, by prohibiting access to certain technologies, most commonly domestic satellite dishes.

This form of transnational flows has its critics, whose doubts about the internationalisation of culture stems from a concern for what was perceived as a growing world-wide United States imperialism. The phenomenon became known as media imperialism, the cultural dimension of political and economic imperialism, and many studies of world information flows have confidently claimed that imperialistic relationships exist and that everywhere the 'media are American'. There is undoubtedly a heavy, one-way traffic in cultural products from the United States to its trading partners around the world. This is partly driven by escalating production costs in the United States and the traditional imperialistic pressure to find markets abroad (see Schiller, 1969; Smith 1980; Tunstall, 1977).

However, Collins has pointed out that evidence of the trade in television programming between the United States and the United Kingdom does not substantiate the media imperialism thesis, in either its economic or cultural sense, and that the tasks for advocates of the thesis are to demonstrate that:

> an adverse balance of trade in one sector, cultural goods, correlates with a general economic, political or cultural subordination . . ., that consumption of US cultural goods produces

> the feared threat to cultural integrity and independence of consumers and a disadvantageous homogenisation and Americanisation of audiences (Collins, 1990a, pp. 164–165).

The issues in this debate were also discussed among others, by Wells (1974), Katz and Weddell (1978), and Golding and Elliott (1979). It has continued as the new technologies of cable, and especially satellite, have on the one hand offered new opportunities to use mass communication to solve the problems of underdevelopment, whilst on the other, have increased the dependence of the poor countries on the rich, by virtue of an imbalance in the control of the new technologies.

But Tunstall and Palmer (1991) suggest that there is little evidence of an American led media industry because, while popular channels in Europe and the Far East required extra advertising revenue, both popular viewer demand and regulatory pressure persuaded those channels to invest in more domestic programming. Similarly, as Schiller himself points out, Japanese businesses continue to spend heavily on investing in Hollywood and other key parts of the American cultural tradition (Schiller, 1989).

Rather earlier, in 1977, Tunstall had argued that the television imperialism thesis was both too strong and too weak. The thesis was too strong because it accepted the optimistic rhetoric of American television promotional campaigns. Also proponents of the thesis have noted that in poor countries only the rich can afford television sets, yet television is said to subvert the whole nation. In one significant sense, which has been taken up by the globalisation thesis, the media imperialism thesis is too weak when it ignores the tendency of television, wherever the programmes may have originated, merely to repeat a previous pattern of Western dominated practices in radio and feature films.

A further limitation of the media imperialism thesis is its assumption that media imperialism equals cultural imperialism and, therefore, authentic national cultures will be swamped. The thesis claims that these cultures are undermined by the dumping of Western culture via slick media products. There are two problems with this argument: first, many programmes are bought cheaply and are old, dated, and relatively unsophisticated. They were made for a different audience at a different time in global history and, therefore, may appear inappropriate and unreal. Second, cultural identity is only part of a national identity and many countries have an ambiguous national identity. Where there are multiple languages, religions, and ethnic groupings, overlain by social class and social status differences, then the existence of any simple national and cultural identity is difficult to imagine. If it does not exist it cannot be subverted. In any case the different elements in multi-valent societies respond differently to outside media influences, whose products can be 'read' against the prevailing local culture and identity. Culture is a multi-layered phenomenon; the product of local, tribal, regional, or national dimensions, which is anything but a single international culture.

Furthermore, the media imperialism thesis often fails to recognise that there are strong regional exporters of television programmes other than the United States. For example, Mexico and Argentina have a tradition of exporting media to near neighbours and to hispanic Europe, while Indian films and records go to many countries in Africa and Asia. However, countries which are strong regional exporters of media tend themselves to be heavy importers of American media (Tunstall, 1977). This suggests that whilst rejecting some of the tenets of a simple media imperialism thesis, it would be wise also to recognise that there are open and less open markets. The door which is opened to allow exports out also allows imports to pass through it.

Finally, as Hartmann and his colleagues in their intriguing study of the impact of the mass media on village life in India and the implications for development have pointed out, assumptions about the influence of media on day-to-day life often ignore social structure and structural conflict, treating audiences as an amorphous mass. In addition, there is a tendency in the received wisdom about development and the mass media to regard consumers as essentially passive. This leads to earlier assumptions about how media effects work and, therefore, misleadingly privilege research paradigms and methodologies that operate within an effects or effectiveness framework. As these authors, and many others have noted, 'in most respects mass communications are far less important sources of information and influence than interpersonal communication' (Hartmann et al., 1989, p. 259). Peter Golding usefully links the argument about media imperialism to the earlier questions concerning development, arguing that orthodox theories of modernisation used 'the characteristics of Western European and

North American society as goal states from which calibrated indices of underdevelopment can be constructed' (Golding, 1974, p. 30). This orthodoxy, he suggested, denies the complex histories of developing countries, and imposes a set of values deemed to be crucial to development which are no more than ideological representations of free enterprise.

The New World Information and Communication Order

The increasing salience of the debate about media imperialism, supported by increasing evidence about the massive inequalities of trade in media output (see particularly Nordenstreng and Varis, 1974), provided the intellectual backdrop to the dramatic sequence of events associated with NWICO. In strong contrast to its earlier position in favour of untrammelled freedom in world media trade, in the late 1970s UNESCO became concerned with the implications of inequality. To quote from the then President of Finland:

> Globally the flow of information between states—not least the material pumped out by television—is to a very large extent a one way, unbalanced traffic, and in no way possesses the depth and range which the principles of freedom of speech require . . . . Could it be that the prophets who preach unhindered communication are not concerned with equality between nations but are on the side of the stronger and wealthier? . . . UNESCO has moved in the direction of planing down the lack of balance in international communications . . . (quoted in Gerbner et al. [eds.], 1993, p. xi).

In 1976, UNESCO set up a commission to investigate world communications, chaired by Sean McBride. The commission in due course produced a report in 1980 (McBride, 1980) which led to a resolution of the UNESCO General Assembly in 1980. The resolution reflected the quotation by the Finnish President in encouraging measures to redress the inequality of opportunities for free speech in world communication. But, in common with other international agreements produced as an outcome of lengthy negotiation and compromise, it contained tensions within it which were noted at the time by those who would normally be regarded as its supporters (see Capriles, 1981; Nordenstreng, 1981). In particular, the declaration sought to reconcile the objective of media freedom with an ascribed positive role for the media in social change and nation-building. Thus, while explicitly committed to openness and freedom of flow, to individual rights, and to a pluralistic model of the relationship of the media and the state; it also called for action against concentrations of media power, it urged that journalistic freedom should be combined with responsibility, and that developing countries should make 'their information and communication media suitable to their needs and aspirations' (Gerbner et al. [eds.], 1993, p. 5).

In several ways it was therefore engaging in a very direct confrontation with those who were benefitting out of the existing situation of inequality and it was responded to in an extremely aggressive and forceful way. This response focused overtly upon the fear that those agencies which would carry out the positive actions that were called for in the resolution would inevitably be governments, and accordingly it would, in fact, lead to a greater degree of intervention in the operation of the media, rather than any increase in freedom (see Righter, 1978).

The lengthy conflict which followed resulted in the withdrawal, in 1985, of the United States from UNESCO. The saga has been analysed from a viewpoint strongly in support of NWICO in Gerbner et al. (eds.), 1993. In a particularly useful chapter, Colleen Roach analyses the way in which the debate has developed a mythological status in American communication textbooks, with the text of the declaration being misrepresented as a direct call for government intervention, but with the manipulative actions of the American government and media conglomerates being written out of the picture (Roach, 1993, Chapter 4).

The legacy of the controversy over NWICO is not to be found in actions. There has been little by way of institutional change and UNESCO itself is now much less active in this respect (see Alleyne and Wagner, 1993; Schiller, 1992). But what it did do was to bring to the fore of consideration, particularly among the non-aligned nations, issues which previously had been contained within the preserve of academic debate. It has, in important ways, framed the context within which reactions to globalisation have sometimes been formed. On the other hand, the increasing perception of the global integration of the media and of their centrality to the futures of all national economies has encouraged a mood of fatalism in which positive action, like that proposed in NWICO, seems like blowing against a hurricane.

Globalisation and Global Culture

Peter Golding (1994) provides a very useful summary of the key principles of a global culture. He lists four aspects. First, is the supposed decline of the nation as a cultural force: people are asserted to identify more with supra-national cultural affiliations, than with those of the nation. Allied to this is the end of the nation-state as a political and economic force. Second, new levels of organisations, both 'above', at the supra-national level, and 'below', at the regional level, supposedly take over the functions previously performed by national governments. Third, is what Golding refers to as the 'syndicalisation of experience'—the emergence of major cultural and commercial symbols, in the form, most obviously, of internationally traded branded goods. Finally, he points to the role of the major international languages, particularly English, as vehicles for international culture.

In his paper, Golding's main concern is to draw attention to the patterns of inequality that lie behind such global processes and to point out that these inequalities are to be found within, as well as between, societies. If globalisation favours the information rich then the danger he points to is the exacerbation of divisions, both nationally and internationally. But it is essential to probe further the various meanings which may be encompassed within the term 'globalisation'.

Globalisation is a highly contested concept. It is useful to consider it in terms of three distinct categories. First is its corporate form as supra-national business organisations with a structure of ownership and control organised to operate on a global basis. Included within this are the activities of governments and inter-governmental organisations which provide the operative conditions under which supra-national businesses can function. Second, globalisation can be seen as corporate ideology, not in the sense that its basis lies only in the corporations, but in the sense of an ideology that has been established to serve the interests of the corporations, and which sets the terms of the debate such that the growth of global culture is accepted as a given. It may be fought against, but it is a real process which sets the terms within which action and debate has to take place. More than this, the globalisation process is something which has the force of inevitability behind it. The process will not come to fruition only if held off by the actions of resistance movements successfully defying the tide of history. In this sense, the globalisation ideology is subscribed to just as strongly by many opponents of the globalisation process as by those who support the corporate forms of globalism. The third dimension of globalisation is as a process with an empirical dimension—in other words, as a process which can be observed. Globalisation is often characterised by major social, cultural and institutional change, whose token persuasiveness demands investigation.

Ferguson focuses on what she calls the 'myths of globalisation', arguing that the meaning of the concept, the evidence for its processes and actions, and the evolution of the concept are befuddled by seven such 'myths'. These are: that big is better, that more is better, that time and space have disappeared, that a global cultural homogeneity has arrived, that globalisation has masked the real issues in saving Planet Earth, that democracy can be exported via American television, and that there is a new world order. As she points out, the categorisation of globalisation as a myth demands a critical approach to globalisation, particularly 'an examination of the resurgent economic determinism at the heart of the globalisation rhetoric emanating from postmodernists, media imperialists and corporate publicists alike' (Ferguson, 1992, p. 87). This recognition, that fundamental approaches to globalism are highly contested, is a crucial one and should lie at the heart of any attempt to understand and use the conceptual vocabulary of globalism.

Massey (1991) has examined the nature of mobility in the era of globalisation and what this means for our sense of place—the phenomenon of time–space compression. Her point echoes Golding's in suggesting that despite advances in new communication technologies and global transportation, time–space compression does not happen for everyone in all spheres of social and economic activity. Different social groups and different individuals are situated in different ways in relation to international flows and interconnections. It is to do with power. Different social groups have distinct relationships to mobility, and some are more in charge of it than others. Those distributing films, controlling the news, and selling television programmes, are really the ones in charge of time–space compression. Incidentally, in a point which is very relevant to issues raised in Chapter 1 of this book, Massey notes that this group can also include Western teachers, academics and journalists—those who write and talk most about time–space compression.

These theoretical reservations about the rhetoric of globalisation are echoed in the findings of some empirical works, a strong theme of which is the resistance by national and regional cultures to global forces.

Resistances to Global Culture

Insights into local resistance have been provided by Negus (1993), who focuses on processes of globalisation in the music industry, where usually locally produced music is depersonalised in favour of material produced by artists from Britain and USA. When local, state and community interests attempt to support musical activity, they are in opposition to the major entertainment corporations. Negus shows how transnational policies practised by music companies create local tensions and reactions, and how a complex series of nation-state, market, and zonal relationships and reactions mediate processes of globalisation, as global intentions are transformed into local activities. In that globalisation is concerned with the organisation of production and the exploitation of markets on a world scale, it signifies the continuation of a trend towards the concentration of capital and attempts by capitalist organisations to expand by breaking down geographical and political boundaries. However, Robins (1991) has argued that globalisation fractures the association between cultural and geographical territory and brings with it the potential for developing new identities. The ability to receive and act upon these new identities is, however, dependent on access to the appropriate technologies of reception. Globalisation makes the relationship between culture and geographical territory significant where products and messages are perceived as coming from the outside for, as Hall (1991) has suggested, globalisation can increase an awareness of the local and its characteristics in contrast to the global presented from the outside.

Ali Mohammadi (1990) has argued a similar case for the potential to resist global media in a case study of Iran. Acknowledging that national cultures of the Third World may be threatened by Western cultural imperialism, with media at the cutting edge of the process, he demonstrates that the Iranian experience leads us to question the powerful media/powerful effects model of communication. He argues that in pre-revolutionary Iran, the Shah could control all the media but could not procure political legitimacy; and that Iranian viewers, whilst exposed to a lot of American programming, preferred their own values to those portrayed in these programmes. But, importantly, the case study also shows that cultural identity can be an important appeal against the values of the West, for example, the social values of freedom and justice as essentially liberal Western notions.

Sahin and Aksoy (1993) demonstrate how 'the Turkish media scene was swept by powerful winds of technological change and globalisation with profound implications for national and cultural identities'. The opening of the media floodgates such as that experienced by Turkey in the late 1980s, has, according to Sahin and Aksoy, expanded the range of ideological debate, and contributed to the dissolution of official dogma and the revitalisation of Turkish culture. Thus, operating outside the official ideology, global stations like *Magic Box* brought issues such as ethnicity, religion, language and group aspirations to the fore, and in doing so have helped to redefine the national culture and identity of Turkey.

However, alongside this came the negative aspects of globalisation and the importation of cheap American and Latin American series, largely quiz shows and comedies. Global media also helped to shape the format of programmes produced in Turkey, in which professional style and production values became Westernised. Sahin suggests that global media have played a significant part in breaking up the unitary national culture by feeding the so-called small worlds of real Turkey into the larger world of imagined Turkey, whilst at the same time homogenising differences and creating imagined communities.

In this new cultural landscape 'identity by choice' (see Schlesinger, 1991) is created, where new type of communities, based around shared values such as consumption, ethnicity, religion or gender, are created. In this new landscape individuals can choose their own identities and the communities to which they wish to belong. Thus, with greater transnational communication, the identities of individuals may be determined more by economic, political or cultural communities, than by nations. Appadurai (1990) suggests that these communities are able to subvert the rival worlds of official discourse. However, choosing identities through global media is not unproblematic, for the choices may become progressively more limited where market forces of production and distribution operate in a deregulated, even delegalised, environment, and where unrestricted competition is the norm. As Morley and Robins (1989, p. 27) point out: '. . . analysis of the cultural impact of any form of domination must always be differential, concerned to establish which groups, in what places, are receptive to it'.

Globalisation and the Public Sphere

These issues are closely related to the inter-linked issues of the public regulation of the media and the concept of the 'public sphere'. The latter is defined by Habermas as 'the realm of our social life . . . in which citizens confer about . . . matters of general interest' (quoted in Hallin, 1994, p. 2). The concept of the public sphere is one about which there is a good deal of controversy, with the frequent charge that its tenor is idealistic and utopian, bearing only a limited resemblance to the realities of media organisation around the world. To quote Hallin (1994, p. 3): 'For Habermas . . . the public sphere is a realm that stands between the state, on the one hand, and the realm of private interests on the other, and it needs to be kept autonomous of both.' The public sphere is something which is in principle open to those who wish to express their views on matters of public importance and for those who wish to have access to such views.

This is not the place to engage in any lengthy attempt to summarise even the main positions in the debate, but it is clear that the concept provides a useful model to apply to the role of the media in those societies which aspire to a pluralist, participatory mode of political culture (for wider discussions see Habermas, 1989; Garnham, 1986; Baynes, 1994; in addition to Hallin, 1994). For us the key question is: in what ways does the process of increasing internationalisation in television affect those issues which arise in discussions of the public sphere and how does this relate to the future of the existing regulatory regimes and of those which may come later? Given that the pressure towards internationalisation is very much driven by the dynamics of commercial competition and the increasing dominance of the ideology of the free market, reference to Chapter 18 of this volume may be useful in approaching these questions.

But here the question will be considered in terms of two levels: first, that of the nation-state and second, the prospects of any type of supra-national public sphere.

At the national level we have already noted that theorists of globalisation stress, as a starting point, the threat to the nation-state. Insofar as this familiar thesis is correct, there is little reason to see the system of the media, and of television in particular, as in any way immune from this aspect of the process. National governments have, of course, always been particularly concerned with the 'safe' operation of the media, and indeed have been primarily responsible for the difficult task of defining the nature of the regulatory regime. Arrangements for the supervision of the media are always sensitive, whichever mode they operate in. Michael (1990, p. 40) defines two forms of supervision: 'the discretion of sound chaps' and 'the arguments of lawyers'; he might reasonably have added a third, has his frame of reference been wider, 'at the point of a gun'. The sensitivity concerning the definition of appropriate modes of regulation arises partly because of the evident subjectivity of the judgements to be made. At its simplest, the views of the regulators are unlikely to be accepted by those with different political or cultural viewpoints. It also partly derives from the very strongly competing issues of the principles that continually recur in this field: public safety and the protection of minors are forever in conflict with freedom of speech. Another frequently encountered tension is between the need for some measure of creative autonomy on the part of programme makers trying to produce successful, audience-pleasing output and the concern of regulators to be certain about the details of the programmes being passed as suitable for transmission.

Regulation by coercion and physical intimidation can be effective but, to say the least, tends to conflict with goals of modernisation and open markets. To regulate through precisely defined rules may seem more rational, but is also fundamentally problematic. First, the rules have to be agreed upon, normally not an easy process where there are conflicting views. Second, if individual incidents are often controversial, how much more difficult will the advance agreement of rules to govern all such individual incidents be? Third, rules also rapidly become outdated, another source of conflict. But the commonly adopted alternative solution to put the regulatory power in the hands of what in Britain are referred to as 'the great and the good' or Michael's 'good chaps', who can then be trusted to work out a flexible 'modus vivendi' between the broadcasters, politicians and the public, requires a good deal of stability. If the parties to the relationship are forever changing, if the prime loyalty of the suppliers of television is not to the political framework of the nation-state, and if they are attempting to sell programmes to 'mass' audiences across national frontiers, then this model of regulation can have little future.

These arguments about regulation are generalisable. If the regulation of television within the boundaries of the nation-state is going to become more problematic, then presumably so will the effectiveness of regulation as a mechanism requiring broadcasters to give access to television. Yet access is an important quality of television as a constituent of the public sphere. Can market imperatives be relied upon to deliver similarly open access? Commercial broadcasters do, of course, need to maximise audiences in order to make money; in a multi-channel environment this may be consistent with a segmentation of the market such as to produce programmes for audience sections which happen to combine political and cultural activism with commercial attractiveness. But this is little consolation. To return to Golding's arguments, made at the beginning of this section, what it does is to further reinforce a distinction between the information-rich and the information-poor, putting such power as is 'available for distribution' even more firmly in the hands of the former.

At the other level of internationalisation, i.e., the relation between the nation-state and supra-national forces, power is continually argued to be passing from the nation-state to international commercial organisations and to supra-national governmental authorities. But what will be the effectiveness of supra-national regulatory mechanisms in relation to broadcasting? There are as yet relatively few models for consideration. One of the few is the European Union, which has attempted to confront the issue both in terms of programme content and industrial structure. So far neither aspect is anything other than discouraging to the search for a successful precedent. The differences between interests of national governments have made it impossible to achieve a consensus about the protection of the European media industry, about support for new technological initiatives, or for any detailed standards concerning programme content (see Collins, 1990a, 1990b and 1994; Michael, 1990). Furthermore, there is no real evidence that even an institution as well established as the European Union has yet developed those characteristics that could be said to give its 'citizens' the shared interests appropriate to the occupation of, let alone participation in, a common public sphere. If this is so for Western Europe, how much more true is it for those haphazard assemblages of countries thrown together by the operations of the international media magnates? Whatever form the 'taste-communities' referred to by Appadurai (1990) may eventually take, it is not at all clear in what sense their members will ever 'belong' to them or what capacity for participation in any kind of joint decision-making they will offer to these members.

As Curtin points out, quoting a one-time American Assistant Secretary of State, 'satellite television could forge "new bonds of mutual knowledge and understanding between nations" because it would foster a shared symbolic system throughout the world . . . satellite television would bring together the "family of man"' (Curtin, 1993, p. 135). The similarity of rhetoric here to that of Al Gore, quoted in the first chapter of this book, is striking. It serves to remind us that to claim the creation of an international community is a good ideological cloak for the creation of an international marketplace in which the strongest will do the best. To quote Curtin again (*ibid.* pp. 140–141) 'the supposed difference between East and West rested upon the free flow of information and ideas . . .the technology of television fostered the idea of democratic dialogue', and 'even though US leaders have long argued for a free flow of programming, the strategic implications of global television have never been absent from the discourse of American policymakers'. Perhaps we should add to Ferguson's (1992) myths of globalisation, the myth of an international public sphere.

Globalisation and the Asian Television Market

The consumer market in Asia offers a seductive proposition to Western media moguls and has caused much excitement among international media companies for what they see as tremendous growth potential. In particular, the emergence of an Asian middle class, whose demands are beyond what is produced by national, often heavily state controlled systems, interests international programmers, since this co-exists with a changing continent where free market economics, some increase in democracy, and a more open policy to foreign influences and foreign capital, are becoming more common. Many countries, even those with strong central controls over broadcasting, are seeking the emergence of a clear sector of private television, often encouraged by even the most authoritarian of governments.

Evidence of the penetration of Star TV into Asia is one indication of this potential being realised; where countries such as China, India, Korea and Thailand saw increases in the number of homes receiving Star in 1993, of 533 per cent, 121 per cent, 868 per cent and 472 per cent respectively (*Screen Digest*, 1994). Malaysia, for example, has the fourth highest concentration of television ownership in Southeast Asia, with a daily reach of 85 per cent of its potential television audience (*Screen Digest*, 1994; Hashim, 1994). If their government allowed so, Malaysians, in addition to their four main terrestrial channels, could have access to a wide variety of extra-terrestrial sources including Star TV, ABN, HBV, ESPN, CNN, Sky Channel and many more. But for now ownership of satellite dishes is forbidden in Malaysia, except for hotels offering CNN International. However, the Malaysian Government is considering operating its own satellite broadcasts by 1996. Karthigesu (1994) has observed that mounting political and economic pressures have persuaded many Asian governments to review their 'monopolistic and authoritarian attitudes towards broadcasting services' (p. 75). He argues that this is more likely in countries that are politically stable and have a growing GNP, where the trend in broadcasting will become more commercialised either by governments' own initiatives or by private sector dynamism.

Whilst it is clear that the nation-state remains the primary source of regulatory frameworks for television, at the same time there is evidence of challenges to the ability of governments to regulate and control all aspects of broadcasting. The challenges come both from the possibilities for diversified viewing made available by the new communications technologies themselves and from the opportunities for market penetration provided by deregulation and privatisation (see, for example, Collins, 1994; Foster, 1992). The case of India is a clear example where a combination of satellite, cable and terrestrial transmissions combine to offer powerful 'cross-border' alternatives which media moguls are seeking to exploit (see Rusbridger, 1994). In these circumstances the structures that existed to regulate purely terrestrial broadcasting are no longer applicable.

This problem for nation-states is becoming more challenging as the number of television households in the world grow. In the past 25 years this number has grown everywhere, but the fastest growth has been in Asia. These dynamics have changed the relative importance of television regions. For example, in 1970, Western Europe and North America each accounted for 29 per cent of the world total of television households, but by the end of the century this is forecast to be 23 and 13 per cent respectively (see *Screen Digest*, 1993). Meanwhile Asia will have grown from virtually nothing to a 21 per cent share of global television households by the end of the century. At the same time, the diversity of choice between cable, satellite, and terrestrial broadcasting, a major source of difficulty for regulators, would also have grown. For example, India, a country which had 400,000 homes receiving satellite television in early 1992, had eight million by mid-1994, a figure which is expected to grow by 20 per cent per year during the rest of the 1990s (see Rusbridger, 1994).

Nation-states vary in their cultural complexity, which in turn influences the abilities of providers to satisfy audiences. India, for example, has 18 official languages and about 1,700 dialects. It has four main castes and thousands of sub-castes. It has five main religions and only about 35 per cent of the population is fully literate (see Hartmann et al., 1989). This situation gives a new meaning to the concept of segmented audiences, whose needs can be readily identified and easily met! In a multi-language nation-state, audiences may turn to the products of their language community that originate outside their country of residence—a process of space compression. The same can be true of cultural identity, at the material level, where television audiences may seek identification with cultural communities abroad, particularly if they are in a minority 'at home'. This is the case with the Chinese in Singapore and Malaysia, where Hong Kong originated programmes are popular within this section of the audience, but less so with the regulators. Again, there are European parallels (as in Drummond et al., 1993).

However, there is evidence of a national response to these challenges. This can take the form of providing, through national television, the services that minority indigenous populations seek, as for example in Singapore. Clearly, this is easier to manage where local controllable technology is available and where there are no major language difficulties, so that the programmes that audiences had been seeking across borders can now be provided locally.

Other pressures on national broadcasting structures come from more general consumer dissatisfaction with the products of existing national services. Typically audiences seek a wider range of sport and entertainment programmes than that provided locally, and so turn to alternative sources. However, the process of acceptance of these more global products, and hence a rejection of local or national programming fare, may not be as straightforward as the proponents of the globalisation thesis suggest. Whilst programmes provided 'cross border' can be attractive, they may not always meet specific cultural or linguistic needs. In several locations such needs have stimulated local television products (see, for example, Batty, 1993).

Perhaps because of its apparent status as a threat from outside, television is perceived in most of the countries referred to in this book as of particular significance, although this is often expressed in different ways. There remains a strong tendency for governments to wish to control news and current affairs programming, particularly when there is access to services such as those provided by CNN and the BBC World Service, which function as alternative means of surveillance when local sources are perceived to fail. In fact, the role of international news agencies remains strong in providing footage and global interpretations of world events, even for state television networks.

Another reason for attaching such importance to national television is that 'local', as against the 'global', can be heavily implicated in national goals; for example, when television is sometimes associated with development goals, as in India, or with the achievement of national identity, as in Malaysia. Broadcasting alone is insufficient to realise these goals despite what governments may profess and, in this sense, globalisation is not a particular impediment to the achievement of national goals, since they would have in any case not been achieved solely by a state controlled national television structure. There are of course specific instances of local agendas that override even national, and certainly international, issues. For example, the remobilisation of religious commitment in India and a desire for that to be acknowledged by and catered for in broadcast media (for a general discussion of the relationship between globalisation and religion see Beyer, 1990). There is also the local interpretation of international events which have particular significance for some communities; for example, the events of Tiananmen Square in 1989 for many of the people in Hong Kong.

But national interests can be interpreted in specific ways by particular governments. The Malaysian government has pursued its privatisation policy with vigour in its efforts to encourage the private sector to play a significant role in stimulating the domestic economy. In this context, the Malaysian government expects not only private film and television producers to play their part, but also television stations, particularly the state controlled RTM, to be 'financially viable'. In most cases this means that television stations will have to either produce or buy and then broadcast programmes that will cater for as wide an audience as possible (for a useful discussion of general issues of media economics see Picard, 1989).

So, some of the countries that provide the context for the later chapters in this book have not simply reacted to changes induced by globalisation. On the contrary, they have wished to be active participants and to take advantage of the opportunities it affords. Singapore and Hong Kong set out to be major suppliers of the services to other countries and major players in the ownership and control of televisual and telecommunications technologies. There are of course other important centres of television production around the world. A useful account of Brazil, for example, is offered by Mader (1993). This is often facilitated in the context of a relatively delayed Western global ownership of Eastern television systems.

Conclusion

At the end of the twentieth century, there is little doubt about the dominant rhetoric: it is that of supply and demand, the language of the free market. It would be consistent with this to expect the future of the television market in Asia to be a product of emergent mass market consumerism and popular television supplied by the Western media industry. But the world is, fortunately, more complex than this.

The evidence of this chapter, reinforced by the rest of the book, is that audiences in Asia are no more 'massified' than those of Europe or the United States, and indeed perhaps less so. There is a clear demand for local content, reflecting local culture and expressed in local languages. Furthermore, it is clear that national governments in Asia are no less reluctant than their Western equivalents to be active players in determining the rules under which outsiders should be allowed to enter their local media markets. Finally, there is the existence of keenly aggressive commercial interests, originating from within the ever-strengthening Asian media industry, vigorously searching out market opportunities in Asia and beyond.

The implication of this is that, whatever the forces of western global developments, there are important pressures from within Asian economies that will provide an important counter-force in the developing marketplace. The frequency with which stories appear in the Western press about the leaders of media conglomerates actively cultivating the political leaders of Asian countries is not accidental. It shows both the importance to Mr Murdoch in appealing to his corporate investors of seeming to be active in approaching the East, and that entry to the Asian media marketplace is not something which even he can take for granted. Its nature, operation and conditions of entry are, and for the immediate future will remain, deeply political matters.

References

Alleyne, M. and **Wagner, J.** (1993). 'Stability and change at the 'big five' news agencies'. *Journalism Quarterly*, 70(1), Spring, 40–50.

Appadurai, A. (1990). 'Disjuncture and difference in the global cultural economy'. In Featherstone, M. (ed.). *Global culture: Nationalism globalisation and modernity*. London: Sage.

Batty, P. (1993). 'Singing the electric: Aboriginal television in Australia'. In Dowmunt, T. (ed.). *Channels of resistance: Global television and local empowerment*. London: British Film Institute and Channel Four.

Baynes, K. (1994). 'Communicative ethics, the public sphere and communication media'. *Critical Studies in Mass Communication*, 11(3), 315–326.

Beyer, P.F. (1990). 'Privatisation and the public influence of religion in global society'. *Theory, Culture and Society*, 7(2–3), June, 373–395.

Capriles, O. (1981). 'Some remarks on the New International Information Order'. Reprinted in Whitney, D.C., Wartella, E. and Windahl, S. (eds.). (1982). *Mass communication review year book*. Beverly Hills: Sage.

Collins, R. (1990a). *Television: Policy and culture*. London: Unwin Hyman.

———. (1990b). *Satellite television in Western Europe*. London: John Libbey.

———. (1994). *Broadcasting and audio-visual policy in the European single market*. London: John Libbey.

Curtin, M. (1993). 'Beyond the vast wasteland: The policy discourse of global television and the politics of American empire'. *Journal of Broadcasting and Electronic Media*, 37(2), 127–145.

Drummond, P., Patterson, R. and **Willis, J.** (eds.). (1993). *National identity and Europe*. London: British Film Institute.

Ferguson, M. (1992). 'The mythology about globalisation'. *European Journal of Communication*, 7(1), 69–83.

Foster, R. (1992). *Public broadcasters: Accountability and efficiency*. (Hume Paper 18). Edinburgh: Edinburgh University Press.

Garnham, N. (1986). 'The media and the public sphere'. In Golding, P. et al. (eds.). *Communicating Politics*. Leicester: Leicester University Press. Reprinted in Calhoun, C. (ed.). *Habermas and the public sphere*. Cambridge, MA: MIT Press.

Gerbner, G., Mowlana, H. and **Nordenstreng, K.** (eds.). (1993). *The global media debate: Its rise, fall, and renewal*. Norwood, NJ: Ablex.

Golding, P. (1974). 'Media role in national development: A critique of a theoretical orthodoxy'. *Journal of Communication*, 24 (Summer), 39–53.

———. (1994). 'The communication paradox: Inequality at the national and international levels'. *Media Development*, 24(3), 7–9.

Golding, P. and **Elliott, P.** (1979). *Making the news*. London: Longman.

Habermas, J. (1989). *The structural transformation of the public sphere*. (Translated by Burger, T. and Lawrence, F.). Cambridge, MA: MIT Press.

Hall, S. (1991). 'The question of cultural identity'. In Hall, S., Held, D. and McCrew, T. (eds.). *Modernity and its future*. Cambridge: Polity Press.

Hallin, D.C. (1994). *We keep America on top of the world: Television journalism and the public sphere*. London: Routledge.

Hartmann, P., Patil, B.R. and **Dighe, A.** (1989). *The mass media and village life: An Indian study*, New Delhi: Sage.

Hashim, R. (1994). 'Direct broadcasting satellites and their implications for Asia'. *Media Development*, XLI(4), 14–17.

Karthigesu, R. (1994). 'Broadcasting deregulation in developing Asian nations: An examination of nascent tendencies using Malaysia as a case study'. *Media, Culture and Society*, 16(1), 74–90.

Katz, E. and **Weddell, G.** (eds.). (1978). *Broadcasting in the Third World: Promise and performance*. Cambridge, Mass.: Harvard University Press. First published, 1977.

Kuhn, T.S. (1970). *The structure of scientific revolutions*. (Second edition, enlarged). Chicago: University of Chicago Press.

Lerner, D. (1958). *The passing of traditional society*. New York: The Free Press.

———. (1963). Towards a communication theory of modernisation. In Pye, L.W. (ed.). *Communications and Political Development*. Princeton, NJ: Princeton University Press.

Lerner, D. and **Schramm, W.** (eds.). (1967). *Communication and change in the developing countries*. Honolulu: University of Hawaii, East Center Press.

McBride, S. (1980). *Many voices, one world*. Paris, London and New York: UNESCO, Kogan Page and Unipub.

Mader, R. (1993). 'Globo-village: Television in Brazil'. In Dowmunt, T. (ed.). *Channels of resistance: Global television and local empowerment*. London: British Film Institute and Channel Four.

Massey, D. (1991). 'A global sense of place'. *Marxism Today*, June 1991, 24–29.

Michael, J. (1990). 'From the discretion of sound chaps to argument by lawyers'. In Ferguson, M. (ed.), *Public communication—the new imperatives: Future directions in media research*. London: Sage.

Mohammadi, A. (1990). 'Cultural imperialism and cultural identity'. In Downing, J., Mohammadi, A. and Srebeny-Mohammadi, A. (eds.). *Questioning the media: A critical introduction*. Newbury Park: Sage.

Morley, D. and **Robins, K.** (1989). 'Spaces of identity: Communication technologies and the reconfiguration of Europe'. *Screen*, 30(4), 18–34.

Negus, K. (1993). 'Global harmonies and local discords: Transnational policies in the European recording industry'. *European Journal of Communication*, 8, 295–316.

Nordenstreng, K. and **Varis, T.** (1974). *TV traffic—a one way street*. Paris: UNESCO.

Nordenstreng, K. (1981). 'The paradigm of a totality'. Reprinted in Whitney, D.C., Wartella, E. and Windahl, S. (eds.). (1982). *Mass communication review yearbook*. Beverly hills: Sage.

Picard, R.G. (1989). *Media economics: Concepts and issues*. Newbury Park: Sage.

Righter, R. (1978). *Whose news? Politics, the press and the Third World*. London: Andre Deutsch.

Roach, C. (1993). 'American textbooks vs NWICO history'. In Gerbner, G., Mowlana, H. and Nordenstreng, K. (eds.). *The global media debate: Its rise, fall, and renewal*. Norwood, NJ: Ablex.

Robins, K. (1991). 'Tradition and translation: National culture in the global context. In Corner, J. and Harvey, S. (eds.). *Enterprise and heritage*. London: Routledge.

Rogers, E. (1963). *The diffusion of innovation*. New York: The Free Press.

———. (1978). 'The rise and fall of the dominant paradigm'. *Journal of Communication*, 28 (Winter), 64–69.

Rusbridger, A. (1994). 'The new moghul invasion'. *The Guardian*, 9 April (Weekend Supplement), 7–10 & 43.

Sahin, H. and **Aksoy, A.** (1993). 'Global media and cultural identity in Turkey'. *Journal of Communication*, 43(2), 31–40.

Schiller, H. (1969). *Mass communication and American empire*. New York: Kelley.

———. (1989). *Culture Inc.: The corporate takeover of public expression*. New York: Oxford University Press.

———. (1992). *Mass communication and American empire*. (Second edition, updated). Boulder, Colorado: Westview Press.

Schlesinger, P. (1991). *Media, state and nation: Political violence and collective identities*. London: Sage.

Schramm, W. (1964). *Mass media and national development*. Stanford, CA: Stanford University Press.

Screen Digest (1993). 'World TV households: The growth continues'. March, 61–64.

——— (1994). 'Asian television: Massive growth but uncertain opportunity'. April, 81–88.

Smith, A. (1980). *The geopolitics of information*. New York: Oxford University Press.

Tunstall, J. (1977). *The media are American*. London: Constable.

Tunstall, J. and **Palmer, M.** (1991). *Media moguls*. London: Routledge.

Wells, A. (1974). *Mass communication: A world view*. Palo Alto: National Press Books.

3

Television and Change: Comparing National Experiences

Michael Richards and *David French*

The purpose of this chapter is to draw out the contents of those individual national chapters which make up the bulk of this book, to relate these to the issues raised in the previous two chapters, and to prepare the ground for the final chapter, which looks at some contemporary developments. To begin with it is, therefore, appropriate to sketch the overall issues the book addresses.

A constant theme of the book is that the ways in which change in broadcast media is understood have profound consequences for the ways in which those media will develop. If governments feel that they will shortly become powerless to resist the demand of their television audiences for the products of the international audio-visual market, then they may decide that their best course is to abandon support for domestic public service television in favour of assertive commercial providers better able to compete in that international market. But to engage in such action is, of course, a self-fulfilling prophecy. If nations lose faith in the future of public service, then they will not provide the public financial support it requires and it will die, whatever the outcome might have been had expectations and actions been otherwise. Similarly, if policy-makers come collectively to the assumption that the future of television is international and that efforts to ring-fence national provisions are doomed, then doomed they will be.

One way of reading the arguments of the previous paragraph is that they are either a naive encouragement to conservatism, along the lines that change may not be as extreme as expected, therefore go on as before; or a perhaps equally naive counsel for perfection: act in the expectation of change, but make sure you get it right, because if you don't you may contribute to something worse. The trouble with such a reading is that there is, in fact, no alternative to the latter position. Governments have to act, because if they do not, others will. There is too much money to be made and too many entrepreneurs trying to make it for passivity to be an option. So governments have to do their very best to get it right. It is always the business of those who study the media to strive for accuracy. At the present time, when change is so rapid and decisions so crucial, it is particularly important that this goal is achieved.

Chapter 18 of this book attempts to integrate the perceptions of changes in the broadcast media and information technologies with which they are increasingly related, with recent international negotiations towards lowering tariff barriers and increasing freedom in world trade regimes. Its conclusion is very much in line with the arguments here: that changes in assumptions about the future are a key element in forming that future. That is where the book ends. But it is also very close to where the book begins, because Chapter 1 is about the vital need for an informed public discussion of this future and for universities to take a prominent part in the support of this discussion. The graduates that universities produce will be active contributors to this debate. Through research and publication, university staff will provide additions to that public stock of knowledge which will frame the terms within which the debate will take place. This is all the more important at a time when the commercial value of knowledge is increasingly being recognised, and consequently more is being produced, stored and disseminated through private, restricted channels.

This book, particularly the chapters written by authors from a wide variety of Asian countries, will play a small part in this process. In Chapter 2, a discussion of the history of research and the international media was organised into four main phases. In the chapters that follow it will be seen, as was pointed out in the introduction to Chapter 2, that the issues from these earlier phases are all still alive. This is an extremely important point. In trying to comprehend changes as large as those through which television is passing, there is a great temptation to generalise about the progression of historical periods, as if each completely replaced the concerns of its predecessor. Attractive though such sweeping generalisations may be, they are of course nonsense. We must learn from our history, and although we may now be able to pick holes in the details of the propositions put forward by our predecessors, it would be arrogant and profligate not to seek to learn from their work and to see whether some aspects of it can be used, maybe reinterpreted, perhaps simply in order to signal important issues in attempting to understand the contemporary world.

Good examples of this are to be found in the next few chapters. Studies of the role of the media in rural development did not stop with Daniel Lerner and Wilbur Schramm, concerns with media imperialism are not only to be found in the work of Herbert Schiller, and the importance of inequalities in access to information and in the pattern of control of the international media system have not disappeared in the period since NWICO left the top of UNESCO's agenda.

We argued in the previous chapter that globalisation had a number of key features. Globalisation, whilst not new, implies change. These changes are concerned with the nature of broadcasting systems globally, the massification of markets for television products, the increasing number of television outlets, the changing patterns of media ownership and control, new systems of programme distribution, the convergence of telecommunication technologies, and changes to regulatory regimes. Within these changes to the nature of broadcasting systems, the distribution of their products, and their ownership and control, attention was also drawn to the break up of the nation-state as the pre-eminent macro social unit of control and regulation and its increasing inability to resist the power of the multinational corporation to transcend national boundaries through trade and communication technologies.

Thus, if nothing else, globalisation is about change: changes to broadcasting, changes to nation-states; but globalisation is not new (see Ferguson, 1992; Golding, 1974). The papers in this collection demonstrate that irrespective of any process of globalisation many countries in South and Southeast Asia are already locked into a process of change. Broadcasting systems emerged in parallel with newly independent nation-states and were often seen as important in the creation of democracy and individual freedom. However, new nations were not easily created without birth pains and broadcasting often found its own development locked into national developments and turmoil. For example, radio, and to a greater extent television , have typically been heavily controlled by political regimes irrespective of their complexion, used to further the aims of dominant political groupings or parties, and to control areas of oppositional views. There is often an ongoing struggle which can intensify as audiences begin to demand access, either to alternative political views or to alternative styles and qualities of broadcasting.

None of this is new and it predates the so-called globalisation of television. What the consequences of globalisation may do, however, is to add another dimension to these already existing processes of change, resistance or conflict. There are cross-border territorial disputes where countries wish to resist the incursion of the media products of neighbours, there are challenges to political control where audience demand seeks alternative programming usually not readily available in the domestic market. There is no doubt that globalisation does exert real and significant pressures (see also Lerner and Schramm, 1967; Sahin and Aksoy, 1993).

Television itself is still relatively new in some countries and is specifically related to certain national priorities, whether these be national development, a desire to break post-colonial dependency, or to create a national, as opposed to, a multi-ethnic identity. Television is, therefore, a significant part of change of national development. It is both part of the national agenda and a definer of it. On the other hand, a wider range of media products is becoming available to national audiences and it is not simply a question of quantity but also of type. Crucially, programmes are on offer which offer a different set of values to a television audience. These values are of two sorts. The first is the social values that programmes espouse: the Western values of freedom, justice, individualism, the importance of commodities, monogamy, and so on. Whilst Western values aren't simply accepted and absorbed into the 'local' culture, nevertheless, new models, roles, norms and social values can be presented. In centrally controlled broadcasting systems, this is often dealt with through the process of censorship. However, censorship tends to be focused on news and current affairs programmes, with entertainment left largely untouched. Yet, it is precisely in popular programming that values are often most prominent. Light entertainment *is* popular and alternative Western values *do* achieve visibility.

The second type of 'new' value exposure relates to the nature of the programmes themselves: their production values. Programme qualities associated with those originating in the West are often perceived as superior by television audiences. BBC, CNN and other internationally recognised sources become the model of quality television which locally produced programmes often cannot match because of resource limitations and a lack of trained personnel. Viewer demand in this respect can lead to a desire for access to new cable and satellite technologies, which facilitate access to these so-called 'quality' products. Since cable and satellite systems are far more difficult to regulate than terrestrial broadcasting systems, the threat to nationally produced television is obvious. The large populations of emerging nations offer potential markets to global media organisations, even when only a relatively small proportion of those populations are urban dwellers and of a socio-economic status sufficient to afford these new technologies and the products and services delivered by them.

This is not to say, however, that the tide of globalisation is irresistable nor does it imply that national responses are uniform. Far from it. Mohammadi (1990), Sahin and Aksoy (1993), and Appadurai (1990) have all pointed to the different ways that globalisation can impact on nations and have identified the different strategies that are used to 'resist' some of the forces of globalisation. These strategies are partly dictated by the pre-existing national and media situations in the countries examined in this book. For example, India has wrestled with the problem of an ageing television service established as part of a commitment to development, with which consumers have become increasingly dissatisfied, and the 'threat' of new cable and satellite services which have no such commitment. By contrast, the more economically advanced nation-state of Singapore seeks to bolster its still developing national television service in order that it may better compete with services provided by the new technologies and rival terrestrial sources in neighbouring Malaysia. These and other variations in national broadcasting systems and 'local' responses to globalisation are demonstrated in many of the chapters in this book.

Responses then, whilst different according to national context, are not ad hoc, and one reason for this is the almost uniform attempt by governments to exercise some form of political control of broadcasting, particularly of state television. There is an almost universal desire on the part of governments to control access to, and often the content of, television, particularly in the area of news and current affairs. This produces difficulties when alternative programme genres and 'outside', or new, television sources provide attractive alternatives. The resolution of this tension is by no means uniform and in many cases is still emerging. Of particularly striking significance is the case of Thailand, where, as Ubonrat Siriyuvasak shows, the struggle over the role of television as a public space has been a central issue in recent political upheavals.

The chapters dealing with the experience of individual countries demonstrate in detail these general points. Three, those by Reddi, Vilanilam, and Sinha, deal with the challenges to Doordarshan, the national television agency in India. As Reddi demonstrates, Doordarshan was established in a very close relationship to the development policies of the Indian government and in a way which reflected the priority attached to communication in the process which led to Independence.

According to Reddi, there has been a widespread dissatisfaction with the national television structure and the programme services it provides. A powerful indication is provided by the growth in the use of video-recorders, despite their cost. VCRs liberate the viewer from the limitations of the service Doordarshan offers, opening up access to recorded films, whether from India or abroad. Similarly, and for many more practically, relatively cheap cable services provide another opportunity to escape the limitations of the state service.

But the areas of difficulty are not confined to the content of programmes and the alternatives offered by new technology. The famous Satellite Instructional Television Experiment (SITE) initiative of 1975–76 set out to test the potential of television as a mechanism for the stimulation and support of rural development, seeking by the use of satellite technology to overcome problems of distance, literacy and cultural infrastructure.

The apparent success of SITE encouraged the expectation that television should take on this developmental mission. But as Reddi, and in more detail Vilanilam, and Sinha point out, it is an ambition which is seriously problematic. Such a position can too easily import uncritical and naive beliefs about the power of television technology and dominant Western assumptions about the process of rural change, neglecting the essentially participatory nature of successful development projects (see Golding, 1974; Lerner, 1958; McBride, 1980; Sahin and Aksoy, 1993).

The challenges to Doordarshan that Reddi points out are essentially urban in location, and she suggests the possibility that its future may lie in addressing the needs of the rural population. But even here the issues are serious. Not only is there the difficulty of reconciling problematic developmental objectives with other aspects of television, there are cultural problems also. Vilanilam argues these are now widespread in India as the new communication opportunities offered by television bring together the long established religious cultures and political movements associated with them, and often take advantage of them. Furthermore, the policy of seeking a mixed economy in Indian television meets its greatest difficulties in the poorer rural areas, where, as Sinha notes, consumers are unable to purchase those goods for which advertisers are most willing to pay to promote on television. Without advertising revenue even a partially commercial television system will not reach into the Indian village communities (see Hartmann et al., 1989).

Kumar looks at a different aspect of Indian television, seeking to draw out general implications from the analysis of a particular programme. He powerfully demonstrates the difficulty of making television programmes about international news subjects while depending on the institutions of the international news business. Since these are predominantly located in Western countries and serve, in the first instance, Western audiences, their selection of stories inevitably reflects this origin. However much the local production team may attempt to compensate by adding a local commentary, it requires, as Kumar points out, a far wider revision to international journalistic practices and institutions for any fundamental change to take place (see Kariithi, 1994; Mohammadi, 1990).

Amritavalli also deals with the national experience in an international context. The concern here is with the perception of television, a particularly vital issue given the ever increasing scale of the international trade in television programmes. Amritavalli seeks to demonstrate the complexity of investigating the degrees of cultural universality and cultural specificity in the reading of televisual texts, showing the need for interdisciplinary collaboration among researchers in addressing these issues.

In Sri Lanka, by contrast, Sunanda Mahendra describes a much newer television system slowly growing under close governmental control. Here there is a very considerable dependence upon imported programming potentially operating to different standards, and there is evidence of growing tension between the two aspects. The system relies upon commercialism, but is dependent upon government support. Furthermore, as in many other systems at an early stage of development, there is real anxiety about the wider cultural effects of television.

Television is more firmly established in Pakistan, but, as Tahir shows, has had a history which reflects the varied political history of the country. As so often elsewhere, the government has mostly been concerned with overseeing the news and current affairs content of television. Only during the more restrictive periods has this control extended to entertainment programming, which has inevitably been an important feature of the growth of the system dependent upon advertising revenue. But Pakistan is a country in which the national broadcasters are coming under increasing pressure from the models offered by CNN and other international satellite services, as access to receiving dishes has spread rather quickly in Pakistan. Yet, at the same time, Pakistan has exploited the technology to extend the reach of Pakistani television way beyond its national boundaries.

Hukill reports a very different situation in Singapore. There the television service is prosperous, technologically advanced, and preparing itself to be a major player in any future global marketplace. Singapore experiences cross-border competition for its audience, particularly from Malaysia, and the government has protected the system from satellite competition whilst attempting to expand its output internationally. However, ultimately the government will have to face up to issues of reciprocity in trade in broadcasting services. The emphasis in responding to competition appears to be on improving programmes in terms of their attractiveness to local audiences. Government control of news persists, but the official emphasis is on encouraging competitiveness, taking the form of privatisation within a regime of overall government regulation (see also Beng, 1994). Shimizu (1993), writing from a Japanese viewpoint, raises questions concerning the different issues that cross-border television can represent according to whether the recipient perceives itself, in cultural terms, as powerful or vulnerable.

Malaysia, as reported upon by Nain, and Anuar and Wang, presents a contrasting picture. There is competition both within the country and from abroad and television news is subject to close government inspection. But television has also been ascribed an important role in relation to the building of a national culture in a situation of ethnic diversity. The extent to which television is able to achieve this objective is the concern of both papers. Nain deals more with structural issues and with their relationship to the international television market, where the tendency to imitate Western genres of television is increasing the pressure on local programme-makers to conform to the dictates of the market, leading to cultural conformity. Anuar and Wang address some of the implications of this in their discussion of programme-making, content and access to television when the medium is so heavily linked to policies of creating national unity.

Siriyuvasak describes a situation in Thailand in which the broadcast media, particularly television, were developed very early in comparison to many other Asian countries as a central part of the political strategy of the authoritarian government. The role of television has, however, grown and changed with the increasing wealth and sophistication of the Thai economy. But in recent years, the part which television should play in the creation of a participatory democracy has become an issue of strikingly central concern. She argues that television should be democratised, with ownership shared between the state, the private sector and other non-governmental public organisations, to encourage openness and greater cultural diversity in broadcasting. The new classes in Thailand demand greater public space which, she suggests, will not be achieved unless democracy can transcend the needs of the free market and audiences are redefined as citizens, not just as consumers.

Hong Kong, like Singapore, has a flourishing, commercial, television system. But the questions which confront it, as shown in the chapter by Terence Lo alone and in his chapter written in collaboration with Chung-bong Ng, display an intriguing mixture of the universal concerns of commercial television and the particular properties of a small country due soon to be incorporated into a huge neighbour. In the first category is the practical issue, focused upon in the collaborative chapter, of how to respond to demographic and other social changes through revision and innovation in programme schedules. The second is dealt with by an analysis of the role of television reporting in the turbulent atmosphere in Hong Kong following the events of 4 June 1989 in Tiananmen Square, Beijing. As noted earlier, this example shows very clearly how, in extreme circumstances, even a television system which is very open to international, global, influences retains crucial national characteristics (see Sahin and Aksoy, 1993, for parallels).

Finally in Korea, as Kim points out, developments in media privatisation have been locked into the experience driven by Western capitalism. Although privatisation and deregulation are distinctive features of Korean domestic media policy, a focus on the 'local' is insufficient to explain the dominance of these objectives, an explanation for which has to be sought in the movements of global capital.

References

Appadurai, A. (1990). 'Disjuncture and difference in the global cultural economy'. In Featherstone, M. (ed). *Global culture: Nationalism, globalisation and modernity*. London: Sage.

Beng, Y.S. (1994). 'The emergence of an Asian-centred perspective: Singapore's media regionalisation strategies'. *Media Asia*. 21(2), 63–72.

Ferguson, M. (1992). 'The mythology about globalisation'. *European Journal of Communication*. 7(1), 69–83.

Golding, P. (1974). 'Media role in national development: A critique of a theoretical orthodoxy'. *Journal of Communication*. 24 (Summer). 39–53.

Hartmann, P., Patil, B.R. and **Dighe, A.** (1989). *The mass media and village life: An Indian study*. New Delhi: Sage.

Kariithi, N. (1994). 'The crisis facing development journalism in Africa'. *Media Development*. XLI (4), 28–30.

Lerner, D. (1958). *The passing of traditional society*. New York: The Free Press.

Lerner, D. and **Schramm, W.** (eds.). (1967). *Communication and change in the developing countries*. Honolulu: University of Hawaii, East Centre Press.

McBride, S. (1980). *Many voices, one world*. Paris, London and New York: UNESCO, Kogan Page and Unipub.

Mohammadi, A. (1990), 'Cultural imperialism and cultural identity'. In Downing, J., Mohammadi, A. and Srebeny-Mohammadi, A. (eds.). *Questioning the media: A critical introduction*. Newbury Park: Sage.

Sahin, H. and **Aksoy, A.** (1993). 'Global media and cultural identity in Turkey'. *Journal of Communication*. 43(2), 31–40.

Shimizu, S. (1993). 'How transborder TV will alter national cultures and national broadcasting: A Japanese perspective'. *Intermedia*. 21(6), November–December, 32–350.

II

National Structures and Themes

4

The Socio-cultural Dynamics of Indian Television: From SITE to Insight to Privatisation

John V. Vilanilam

SITE and Insight

The Satellite Instructional Television Experiment, popularly known as SITE, has been the most extensive educational and social research project ever conducted in mass mediated communication. Several thousands of words have been written about it. The great educational and technological dividends and spin-offs from it have been extolled time and time again. But it took almost a decade and a half for SITE researchers to receive the 'insight' that mere 'site' was not enough. Consequent upon this insight, cultural synchronisation through privatisation of the electronic media is going on. This chapter examines the historical and conceptual background of the big changes occurring in the structure of the media in India. It also looks at the cultural impact of these changes.

The expansion of television (TV) in India took place after India's own satellite system came into operation. The Indian National Satellite (INSAT) system was put into orbit following the favourable reports based on the results of SITE. The effectiveness of TV as a medium for educating the masses in rural areas was underscored by these results, and whatever philosophical obstacles there were against the expansion of TV fizzled away. In the beginning, TV was seen as a great educator, even in the United States, but later on sociologists became concerned about its cultural consequences. 'Chewing gum for the eye', 'the idiot box', and other such endearing epithets for the electronic monster were replaced by 'mind manager', 'corrupter of the young', 'trivialiser', 'cultural bane', etc., by US and European sociologists in more recent years. But what is significant is that at the time of the introduction of TV in other countries, communication scholars always emphasised the great potential of TV in 'informing, educating and entertaining' people.

In India, when TV was introduced in a small way in Delhi on 15 September 1959, it was looked upon as a tool for disseminating educational messages in Delhi schools and agricultural messages among farmers in the suburbs of Delhi. For another decade there was no expansion of the TV network. It had yet to be proved that TV had a big role to play in the social and economic development of the villages of India, and SITE was the experiment that provided the data in support of that role. With the help of NASA, UNDP, ITU and UNESCO, the Indian Space Research Organisation (ISRO) succeeded in launching SITE, using the US supplied Applications Technology Satellite (ATS-6), on 1 August 1975. Thousands of messages on topics generally considered development oriented (agricultural modernisation through HYV seeds, better chemicals and fertilisers, better farming methods and management, family planning, public health and nutrition, social and educational improvement of women and children, better learning and teaching methods) were beamed via the satellite to community TV sets kept in 2,400 villages in 20 districts spread across six states of the Indian Union: Andhra Pradesh, Bihar, Karnataka, Madhya Pradesh, Orissa and Rajasthan. The Experiment ended on 31 July 1976.

The hardware aspects of the Experiment were found to work excellently. ISRO's success in experimenting with the applied science and technology involved in satellite communication exceeded all expectations. The system worked. And the most important hardware goal of SITE was realised on 15 August 1982, which marked a real turning point in India's TV history: the INSAT series was inaugurated, and with that the biggest expansion of TV occurred in subsequent years. It is no exaggeration to say that SITE brought India onto the world map of television.

The hardware lessons of SITE were valuable when TV was expanded at short notice for telecasting the Asian Games held in Delhi during November 1982. The import of TV sets, including colour sets, was permitted and states like Kerala, from where thousands had gone to work in the Gulf countries and who brought back TV and VCR sets with them when they came home on vacation, saw a sudden increase in the number of TV sets. The total number of TV and VCR sets in the country saw a phenomenal growth.

The proliferation of TV in India was assisted by the rapid expansion of high- and low-power transmitters (HPTs and LPTs). During the period 1983–1985, there was an LPT inauguration every other week, and soon the number of transmitters shot up to 250. Currently there are 84 HPTs and about 550 LPTs. All state capitals, other than those of the Northeastern states (except Guwahati in Assam), have an HPT Production Centre (Doordarshan Kendra). Now there are 18 such Kendras. TV signals can reach 70 to 80 per cent of the geographical area of the country, and all of these remarkable technical achievements are in no small measure due to SITE. From SITE to INSAT was a success story, and the technological dream of Vikram Sarabhai was realised.

But that was only part of Sarabhai's dream. He had a sociological dream too, which shared the dream of Jawaharlal Nehru, the architect of modern India. Their dream was to harmonise the technical advantage of the 'global village' concept with the basic needs of the local villages; advanced technology had to serve the needs of the masses—particularly mass education and development.

Inherently, technology and sociology are different. One is rapid, mindless and easily adaptable to the dictates of those who exploit it for economic objectives. The other is slow, and much less adaptable to suddenly introduced ideas that are likely to upset the status quo. When the technological steed gallops at the speed of light, the sociological mule paces at the speed of sound. Therefore, technological constants change every decade or so but sociological constants take many decades to change. What communication and media planners in poor countries (most of them erstwhile colonies) have been engaged in in the recent past was trying to make an attempt to 'leapfrog' the historical development gap between the rich and the poor nations of the world using the capabilities of the media. What they failed to observe was that in rich countries the expansion of the media took place much later than the introduction of structural changes. The media of communication by themselves cannot achieve much; they have to act as catalysts, and they do when simultaneously structural changes occur in society. Unfortunately, many poor countries of the world have invested substantial amounts of their scarce resources in the 'big' media, hoping that this would take care of development. This was tantamount to putting the cart before the horse.

The Conceptual Background of This Great Expectation

The 'big' media and their effectiveness in transforming society were treated from a purely cognitive approach by seminal communication scholars of the West, without realising the limitations and ignoring their own history and the history of the countries where they recommended the introduction of the 'big' media. Several of the ideas advanced by these scholars were based on psychological theories of development, and they looked upon the people of the poor countries as fertile ground for testing their theories. They ignored the basic fact that a merely cognitive approach would not work in countries where several hundred million people had no structure to fall back on in times of crises caused by long-drawn poverty, ignorance, unemployment, ill health, landlessness and rigid social compartmentalisation. The theorists also ignored the long colonial history of these impoverished people. Instead, they introduced the idea that the poor were poor because they were ill-informed or totally ignorant. Improve their information level and they would bring about substantial change in their own lives and lives of others, argument went.

The psychological model of development depended on the stimulus–response theory: induce change through the hypodermic injections of modernity using electronic 'needles of information and communication'. It was assumed by the communication experts of the three decades between 1950 and 1980 that such direct stimuli would create responses conducive to social change. The stages of economic growth presented by Walter Rostow was the basis of the revolutionary communication theories of those decades which established a direct link between mediated messages and socio-economic development.

From decade to decade, old paradigms were packaged in new bottles under new labels and presented by the rich sectors of the world for the consumption of the elite in poor countries, who made vital decisions on communication and media planning. In the 1950s it was 'growth through psychic mobility'; in the 1960s it was 'education for development through radio and television'; in the

1970s it was 'satellite communication for development'; in the 1980s it was 'computerised communication systems, information age, and service economy'; and now it is 'the creation of market-friendly economies through privatised micro and macro media of communication'. The sociological weaknesses of SITE could be traced to this conceptual weakness in correlating development with the cognitive capacity of communication infrastructures.

According to some SITE researchers themselves, who have been blessed belatedly by insight into the built-in conceptual deficiencies mentioned earlier, the educational objective of TV and VCR got replaced by the notion 'TV is to entertain'. Some of them have been disenchanted by 'the grip of commercialism on Doordarshan and All India Radio (AIR)'. Others have drawn attention to the limited number of TV sets generally in the country, and that of community sets in particular. There are only about 40 million sets in a country of 900 million people, or 180 million families, and only 50,000 community TV sets; a substantial number of which could be out of use or of poor quality through frequent repairs caused by sudden upsurges and downsurges in a mostly erratic and unpredictable electricity supply situation.

In 1987, the then Deputy Chairman of the Planning Commission and a former Director-General of Doordarshan endorsed the views expressed by the Working Group on Software for Doordarshan (otherwise known as the P.C. Joshi Committee) that:

1. TV was in the grip of a powerful commercial–consumerist lobby that turned it into a medium for entertaining the rich urban middle and upper classes, and
2. Nehru–Sarabhai approach of tapping the communication revolution in general, and television in particular, as a major tool for the development of the masses had been ignored.

The committee found that most of the programmes were socially irrelevant as they shut out social realities. It pointed out:

> What India lacks is neither vision nor the awareness of the role of the software, nor native talent, capable of generating relevant software. The poverty of software is explained by lack of collective national will to mobilise creative talent and to invest

resources in software planning and production on a scale suited to a country of India's size, complexity, and diversity.

TV and other media, the Report continued, had to be active instruments in promoting linkages between education, employment, local issues, local economy and local socio-cultural needs—all integrated with modern science and technology applied to local and national needs and priorities. The software planners were criticised in the Report for identifying development with affluence and the conspicuous consumption indulged in by a tiny section of the population.

The P.C. Joshi Committee, and the B.G. Verghese Committee before it, hoped that the formation of an autonomous broadcasting system would help produce more relevant localised programmes which would help even the rural people to think globally and act locally. The Joshi Committee recommended that the LPTs should ultimately become local centres for the production of locally relevant programmes and local public participation (at all socio-economic levels). Barring the Kheda TV station experiment in Gujarat, no local station could ever become a local production centre in the country. And Kheda was closed down for a while, later revived, and then closed down again in 1994. Instead of making regional and local stations into really autonomous, self-sustaining production centres under certain overall technical and ethical guidelines from a proposed Prasaar Bharati Corporation, the Government has now permitted foreign and indigenous private companies to compete with Doordarshan and AIR. There are concerns about this policy, especially among the thousands of Doordarshan and AIR employees and also among citizens who are afraid that such a policy would undermine whatever little the electronic media have been doing for economic development so far, despite their own commercialisation and heavy dependence on advertising revenue from private and public sector corporations. Some are concerned that the direct broadcasting systems, cable TV, unrestricted flow of news, features and serials through Britain's ITV, Star TV, Murdoch's FOX TV, Asiasat, etc., will pave the way for further cultural imperialism. They see the whole approach to media as part of the new economic policy of heavier dependence on international monetary agencies.

Is privatisation anything new in India? The free enterprise system has been in operation here from the time of the East India Company. And until the introduction of TV in a big way and the expansion of radio, the media users in the country depended solely on private media: the press, film, books, and sundry trade publications. The newspapers have done an exceedingly good job in all these decades; so has the film industry. Of course there is a low diffusion of newspapers and films; there is high illiteracy and poor purchasing capacity for the majority of the people. Newspapers and films are not to blamc for that situation. However, privatisation of the 'big' media (AIR and Doordarshan) had to be approached cautiously. As a first step, the AIR and Doordarshan stations had to be made more autonomous, and then private media units allowed to compete with the autonomous units, as otherwise those units would have been at a competitive disadvantage. All commercial competition had to be fair and free.

The debate about privatisation and autonomy could have dealt with the basic questions listed here, but unfortunately it did not:

1. Has there not already been privatisation in many media? How have the print and film media fared so far? What lessons could be learnt from their performance?
2. Are the private agencies handling the press, film, video, and advertising and PR agencies today prepared to recognise the development goals of the country and work towards the betterment of the information–communication–education levels of the large majority of the people who are information-poor today?
3. Will the government media be prepared to restructure their organisations and de-bureaucratise their day-to-day operations, particularly their news gathering and dissemination activities, frequencies of news presentations, etc.?
4. Will the government media introduce autonomy within their strictly 'impersonal' system so that talented programme executives can innovate for local relevance?
5. Will AIR introduce 'narrowcasting' instead of 'broadcasting'? That is, will it allocate new spectra for local stations catering to specific target groups on the basis of audience programme preferences as they do in some advanced

countries? For example, stations devoted wholly or mostly to news, sports, religious programmes, classical music, popular music, family entertainment, poetry readings, quiz programmes, educational programmes, and so on useful to different levels of students in local languages and in English?

6. Will the big media permit non-commercial stations which carry programmes sponsored by big industrial and business corporations as they do in the US (e.g., the fourth network called Public Broadcasting System)?
7. Will there be any limit (for technical and sociological reasons) on the number of TV stations or radio stations and newspapers a particular franchise can own? In the US there used to be some regulation on the number of TV stations and radio stations (12) which a media corporation could own. (Incidentally, there are some 1,000 TV stations and 10,000 radio stations in the US.) But ten years ago, this restriction was rescinded as part of the general deregulation philosophy. Even regulations stipulating the provision of Equal Time for all political parties and the Fairness Doctrine were removed in the US; but even in the US there is strong criticism against deregulation.
8. Will private owners recognise that like the air, the airwaves belong to the public? And they should broadcast 'in the public interest, convenience and necessity'; a clause that was introduced in the US when the Radio Act of 1927 was passed by Congress and reinforced when the Federal Communications Commission was constituted on the basis of the Communications Act of 1934. There are occasions when the people have to pressure the autonomous agency that looks after the compliance of stations to regulations stipulated by it for cancelling the stations' licences. All stations in the US are licensed for three years, but they can renew their licences by re-applying.
9. Will conglomerate ownership be permitted? That is, will a non-media company be permitted to own and operate print and electronic media? Will this again lead to big monopolies in the private sector as has already occurred in the US, where, according to Ben Bagdikian, a former editor and later ombudsman of the *Washington Post* (vide his famous book *Media Monopoly*), six conglomerates control more

than 50 per cent of all media in the US? For example, the General Electric Company, whose main business is electricity generation and supply, acquired the NBC network for six billion dollars a few years ago; similarly, Sony of Japan holds controlling shares in another network and several other media companies connected with that network. How will all this affect the free marketplace of ideas where competing voices have to be heard by the citizen in order to become more informed and make balanced judgments? Will it be *one voice and many worlds* instead of *many voices and one world* in the future?

10. Will vertical integration occur in the media just as it has occurred in many businesses of the world? One can see the phenomenon of the same holding company owning companies that produce everything that goes into a product, as also every channel of distribution. For example, film studios owning raw film stock production companies and a network of theatres and film distribution companies will control the entire film industry from A to Z. Or a newspaper publishing company owning newsprint factories, and even the forests that produce the timber for the pulp required for paper manufacturing, can control the entire print media industry. How will it affect the free flow of information? Will an international conglomerate be able to control national industrialists and businessmen?

Decentralisation and de-bureaucratisation should be implemented, not only in the electronic media but in all our government and public sector undertakings, universities, and science and technology organisations. Private initiative has to be encouraged. Individual enterprise has to be given full support. But the social and economic realities of the world and the nation have to be taken into account when drastic changes are introduced.

The 'big' media today are inaccessible to the large majority of the people. The diffusion rates for all media (newspapers, radio, TV, film) are extremely low in India. So is the literacy rate (see Table 4.1). The developed or rich countries could reach the fruits of the Industrial Revolution to the majority (not all) of their people through appropriate structural changes in their societies, some naturally evolved and others introduced through deliberate,

Table 4.1: The South Asian Socio-economic Scene: Mass Media, Literacy, Quality of Life, Population Density, Gross National Product and Per Capita Income

Country	*Population and Density*		*GNP (in billion $)*	*PCI ($)*	*Mass Commn./Telecommn.*				*Literacy (%)*	*Infant Mortality per 1000 Live Births*	*Annual Natural Increase in Population (%)*
	in millions	*per sq m*			*Dailies*	*Radio Sets (per 1000)*	*TV Sets*	*Tele-phones*			
Afghanistan	16.6	65	3:3	200	6	9	1	2	12	189	2.1
Bangladesh	113.0	2028	15.0	113	6	9	3	1	33	140	2.6
Bhutan	1.5	84	0.14	120	DNA	8	DNA	9	12	122	2.0
Burma* (Myanmar)	39.9	152	6.5	179	14	21	2	1	66	96	2.5
India	833.0	658	194.0	150	16	30	14	4	36	101	1.8
Maldives	0.2	1756	0.05	470	DNA	94	DNA	15	82	81	DNA
Nepal	18.8	334	2.4	160	5	106	DNA	1	29	313	2.6
Pakistan	110.5	335	32.0	360	22	47	16	5	26	125	2.6
Sri Lanka	17.5	692	6.3	340	DNA	114	DNA	6	87	28	1.7

DNA = Data not Available.

* Burma is not usually counted along with other countries of South Asia; nor is it included in the Southeast Asian geopolitical considerations, treaties, regional organisations, etc. It is included in this table since it, like the other South Asian countries, was under British rule. Burma was part of British India till 1947.

Source: *World Almanac, 1990; Far East & Australasia, 1990; Europa, 1990.*

democratic, and decentralised planning. They succeeded in achieving some distributive justice, underscoring the dictum that distribution is the prime desideratum of development. Their development resulted from the changes they introduced in their technologies of production, distribution, and management systems. It did not result from the media.

But development scholars from the rich countries spread the idea that poor countries became poor because of a cognitive drawback. Therefore, they taught, more information would bring about development to less informed people. Unfortunately, an information revolution without appropriate changes in the structure of society will be revolution at the top, and it will lead only to a few affluent islands in a vast sea of misery. There is a strong case for strengthening interpersonal communication channels in a country of illiterate and very poor millions, whose per capita income is one-tenth of the price of a TV set. There is also an equally strong case for democratising communication, through making LPTs production centres and allocating spectra for autonomous TV and radio stations in rural areas, with rural programming socially relevant to the local people.

The hope that the hardware of communication—satellite or computerised, macro or micro, private or public, controlled or autonomous—will save the millions from centuries-old poverty and ignorance is unreal. That is the insight several people have derived from SITE, *belatedly*.

Belatedly, because already major decisions have been taken by the authorities concerned—decisions that have far reaching consequences on the cultural life of the people in India and other South Asian countries.

Let us now turn to the socio-cultural impact of these major cultural decisions.

Cultural Synchronisation: Impact of Privatisation of the Electronic Media

Transnational cultural synchronisation is advancing rapidly in today's world with the full support of the rich, industrially advanced nations and the elite in poor countries that collaborate with them. Perhaps seeing this in his mental horizon far in advance of his contemporaries, Mahatma Gandhi (1921) said half a century ago:

> I do not want my house to be walled in on all sides and my windows to be stuffed. I want the cultures of all lands to be blown about my house as freely as possible but I refuse to be blown off my feet by any (p. 159).

This synchronisation is the basic philosophy of the transnational advertising, entertainment, leisure and tourism industries with headquarters in the ENAJ countries (ENAJ stands for Europe, North America and Japan; Europe includes the Russian Republic and some other Republics of the Soviet Union and countries of Eastern Europe). But their philosophy goes against the basic needs of the large majority of the world's population, whether it be of South Asia, Asia minus Japan and some oil-rich countries of West Asia, or of the highly populated and poor regions of the world, especially in Africa and Latin America.

The ENAJ countries are in a position today to look at information and media fare as commercial products. The elite in poor countries also do see the main function of the media as entertainment, and to some extent news/information of a certain kind. Moreover, they believe that in a few decades they can catch up with the ENAJ countries by achieving everything that the latter had achieved either though plain colonial exploitation or imperialist and totalitarian systems during the past century or so.

As ever, three strong forces influence global culture: finance capital, high technology and mass marketing/communication. Of these, the last mentioned is what we should examine in the context of cultural synchronisation in South Asia.

Several cultural streams that originated at different periods in South Asian history—the Indus Valley, Dravidian, Hindu, Buddhist, Jain, Aajiivaka, Christian, Islamic and their variations—are still flowing as undercurrents, nurturing the intrapersonal base of communication there. All these cultural streams are now muddied by the polluted effluents of religious fundamentalism and mammon worship. The process is facilitated by market-conquering expeditions from the West which actually started in the fifteenth century when the Portuguese landed in Calicut. In the pursuit of a mythical era of heavenly glory, the fundamentalists in South Asia are trying to dig deep into the cultural history of the region, and this leads to a deepening of the cultural crisis faced by the region. The winds of trade and acts of fundamentalism, both serve to dry up the pure fountain springs of understanding among the various sub-cultures in an unprecedented manner. The hot winds of commerce without conscience, of matter-of-fact profit and loss accounts, and inhuman economic viability (supported by the theories of social Darwinism of an earlier century), are destroying whatever humanity had remained in decision-makers and whatever concerns they had about the real causes of poverty. The fundamentalists are also unconcerned about the enormous human tragedies that can arise from raking up dead, old rivalries among followers of different religions in the region. The historical cause of poverty and the obscene economic disparities in human society do not receive the attention of either.

Electronic signals are used, via satellite and terrestrial networks, to create a magical world for the rich, who almost literally believe that the millennium of the millionaires is around the corner. The large majority of the people in South Asia are poor, illiterate, malnourished, unemployed or inadequately employed, ignorant, superstitious, ill-housed or unhoused, and easily manipulated by those elites who try to grab political power through the democratic voting machinery. In this process of influencing the poor politically, the national elite receive the monetary, material, and moral support of the international elite. The idea of both varieties of elites is to establish an economic link on the basis of a commercial culture. International monetary agencies nurture this commercial culture and the national media unwittingly repeat ideas frequently heard in the international media which support the same cultural synchronisation philosophy.

Most of the media reports and features nowadays centre on the following:

1. The technological imperative and the idea of progress force the multinational media and their new technologies to flow into new regions; and it is inevitable that the poor in those regions succumb to the rich and imbibe foreign cultural fare. The poor have no choice. They do not have the technological clout or the monetary capacity to reverse the flow. The flow has to be necessarily one way.
2. The role of the media is primarily to entertain and provide relaxation to the users. Development communication is another name for government propaganda. The sooner we

privatise, the better for media freedom, by which is meant the freedom of national private media companies to import more and more foreign media programmes, either through satellite systems (leasing transponders) or through other means (video tapes, for example).

3. The South Asian elite—the upper and middle classes—consist of at least half a billion people, potential customers who are ever ready to welcome foreign products and lifestyles propagated through foreign cultural artefacts, the most important of which is the television fare offered by the multinational entertainment (culture) industry, advertising and tourism. They should have the freedom to enjoy the fare they like. Any attempt to conscientise them about social realities is construed as an intrusion into their media freedom and freedom of information.
4. Once the TV is acquired, cable is easily accessible to the lower middle classes as well. Installation charges range from Rs. 400 to Rs. 1,000, depending on the area, and the monthly payment can be as low as Rs. 50. At such a low cost of installation and subscription, the viewer has access to at least three channels. However, the average income of the lower classes is only a fraction of Rs. 15,000 to 18,000 which they have to pay for a colour TV. Can they really afford it? Many reports orchestrated that there were 200 to 250 million potential owners of TVs in India, which is a very highly inflated figure indeed. Now there are a dozen channels (see Tables 4.2 and 4.3).
5. National TV programmes are so boring that TV users in South Asian countries will switch to cable or foreign channels when they are available.
6. Doordarshan or any other national TV is likely to go out of business soon ('time-is-running-out' proclaim headlines in newspapers), unless steps are taken immediately to improve programmes.
7. Dubbing of foreign programmes into South Asian languages is a natural corollary to the entry of foreign media companies, as otherwise they cannot stay in business on the support of the English-knowing minority. Dubbing of well-known American or British programmes which have run their natural lifespan is done in Thailand and other Southeast

Table 4.2: An Unprecedented Increase in Satellite TV Homes during 1992–93

Metropolises and Large Towns	*% of Homes with TV*	*% Increase during 1992–93*	*Remarks*
Ahmedabad	59	103	Doordarshan opened itself partially to the private sector by experimentally allotting one-hour slots on the metro channels early in 1993. It introduced five satellite channels on 15 August 1993 following the successful launching of the INSAT II-B satellite. With the launching of INSAT II-C in 1995, Doordarshan hopes to increase the number of channels to 21.
Bangalore	24	242	The five satellite channels started telecasting morning and evening English news from November 1993.
Bombay	42	133	Foreign TV companies made their appearance first through Doordarshan's own programme slots from the late 1970s, and then through Satellite TV from 1991 onwards. Star TV brings BBC programmes and also Ruper Murdoch's Fox TV fare; Star Plus entertainment, and Prime Sports. There are other foreign programmes offered through CNN, ATN and Zee TV.
Calcutta	16	300	
Delhi	30	233	
Hyderabad	20	567	
Lucknow	20	567	
Madras	9	125	

Source: *Manorama Yearbook, 1994*.

Asian countries. Why not in South Asia too? People have the right to know what is going on on their miniscreen.

8. The world is getting smaller (the global village concept) and any attempt to shut out information that flows in is not only barbaric, but a serious violation of human rights, particularly the right to be informed and entertained.
9. The new liberalised fiscal and import policies should apply to broadcast equipment too. Anyone having the means (which means the rich national media conglomerates, cross-media owners who have already got the means, and the multinational conglomerates who can operate under the name and style of NRIs) must have the freedom to import

Table 4.3: A Picture of Media Concentration in India

States	*No. of TV Sets (million)*	*Population (million)*	*Diffusion Rate**
Andhra Pradesh	2.74	66.50	41.2
Karnataka	2.15	44.97	48.0
Kerala	0.86	29.09	29.9
Maharashtra	55.43	78.70	69.7
Tamil Nadu	3.15	55.64	56.4
Uttar Pradesh	4.07	138.76	29.4
West Bengal	3.62	67.98	53.3
Total	22.02	481.64	

Note: Total No. of TV sets in India is estimated to be 47 million, including 60,000 community sets.
Almost 50 per cent of the TV sets are in seven of the 25 States of India; and more than 85 per cent of the TV sets in India are in four metropolitan cities—Bombay, Calcutta, Delhi and Madras, and a few large cities like Ahmedabad, Bangalore, Chandigarh, Hyderabad and Lucknow.

* Number of TV sets per 1000 of the State's population. TV viewership is estimated to be 150 million, including 15 million cable TV viewers and 7 million satellite TV viewers.

A similar concentration is found in newspaper and magazine (print-media) circulation.
Source: *Manorama Yearbook, 1994.*

and set up broadcasting systems. Import and other duties should be minimal; otherwise smuggling will occur on a national scale.

10. There is a new world order and a new information order after the end of the Cold War—actually, after the hot war in the desert where thousands of retreating soldiers and innocent civilians were destroyed using precision bombing with the help of computerised war machinery. Even those who claim the advent of a new world order have not been able to explain what is meant by it. For all intents and purposes, the new world information order is not based on the concept of many voices one world, but on one voice many worlds.

In none of the debates and discussions on privatisation of the electronic media, the synchronisation between the media philosophies of Doordarshan and the existing private media (books, press, film, video, etc.) appeared. Nor was any attention paid to the frequently occurring commercial messages telecast by Doordarshan. In fact, there is much congruence between the commercial philosophy of Doordarshan and that of the private media conglomerates.

What are the dominant advertisement messages reaching the elite and influencing the thoughts of the poor about the basic ingredients of culture—food, clothing, shelter?

Food: Eating natural food is no good. Buy prepared, canned food which can be cooked fast with the least amount of labour. When children return from school, noodles are prepared in a couple of minutes and both mummy and kids are happy. Eat plenty of chocolates, candies and ice creams because that will keep you healthy, active and cheerful. The colour and appearance of food is more important than its nutritional value. Drink plenty of soft drinks before, during, and after doing anything. Never bother about the contents of what you eat or drink.

Clothing: Wear ultra-modern clothes. Fly on the wings of silk with the rustle of chiffon, the flitter of polyester and the nudity of nylon. Wear the most fashionable clothes. There is plenty to choose from. Follow the style that is judged the best according to international standards. Never bother about the price.

Shelter: Housing is no problem. The problem is how to keep the mansions and bungalows already constructed by the affluent class disinfected, deodorised, shiny, sanitised, fragrant, decorated with natural or artificial flowers and foliage, covered with bright paints and polished with the best wax and varnish in the world. The lawns are to be kept trim, adorned with sprinklers and fountains. The driveway should contain, if possible, an imported sports car.

All this and much more are the essential ingredients of the reality constructed by expert TV copywriters and film makers. How will this bring about the changes essential for the betterment of the living conditions of the large majority of Indians? What is the social reality in India? Are the media, particularly the electronic media, helpful in projecting the hard reality of an average Indian's life? Will they facilitate or encourage a change in his life situation?

TV as it exists today suppresses Indian reality; it creates a world of fantasy for the rich and the poor; but the rich have access to at least some of the ingredients that construct that fantasy. This world of fantasy does not deal with the pressing problems faced by the majority.

Then what is the culture portrayed on Indian TV? It is mostly the culture of the 'global shopping centre', mixed with some dead, old customs and practices. This incongruous mixture is hated by the elite, who want everything in the mould of the rich countries with which they have cultural contacts at one time or another.

The structure of the media in today's India cannot be separated from the region's socio-economic and political structures, which have thrown open their windows and doors so wide that the upper and middle classes can be thrown off their cultural base. At the same time it reinforces the bad aspects of India's cultural past, which facilitates disintegration and disunity. The dominant new values that are reiterated and reinforced through the media for the elite and the old values (in certain South Asian countries where old fundamentalist values are better dead and buried) serve only to divide and create mutual mistrust among the masses. Both have deleterious cultural consequences, but TV in India has already embarked upon such a cultural division of the population without realising that by doing so, it is adding to the process of the destruction of the intrapersonal religious base of culture in the region.

The media underscore the elements and symbols of supranational culture which are identifiable and affordable only to the rich and socially superior groups in India, all of whom think alike and contribute to the same jet set culture sustained by the philosophy of over-consumption, consumerism and obsolescence. This transnational culture rests on cheap labour and raw materials available in different regions of the world. The workers in these regions cannot afford to own most of the consumer products and essential goods which they themselves make, something contrary to what has become the norm in the ENAJ countries.

In developing countries where TV has been introduced, the poor viewers pass through a cycle of rising expectations and frustrations and finally leave everything to fate or rise up in revolt as a last resort. Brutal suppression of dissent is what keeps the lid on the cauldron of boiling frustrations in many highly imbalanced societies.

The cultural or social role of TV in the present structure of the world is to act as the commercial messenger of 500 or so multinational corporations. The message is couched in entertainment and advertisements. It is nourished by 'optimal synchronisation of cultural values', so that individual nations do not stress their own cultural priorities but quietly conform (for economic imperatives and political survival) to international–supra-national standards set by global marketing managers. In order to show that they are 'truly national' they revive some national symbols which end up as support planks for fundamentalists.

Culture is not just religion—ritualistic or philosophical. It is not only the expression of artistic or literary talents, but the sum total of everything that sustains life and brings meaning to existence from birth to death and beyond. Therefore, it embraces technology, economics, art, literature, communication systems, and the most basic acts and facts of survival. A cultural system which ignores the majority of mankind and is ready to jettison the poor from space-ship Earth; a system that stresses consumption of material goods by the rich and advises the poor to tighten their belts or just vanish; a system that supports high technology medical services while de-emphasising the basic measures to protect the health of the majority; a system that builds five-star hotels and permits the poor to eat from the garbage bins; a system that invests billions of dollars in luxury goods, fattening foods and intoxicating drinks but brushes away the basic need of drinking water supply as irrelevant—such a system works against humanity. As Hamelink (1983, p. 15) has said: 'A cultural system which would be adequate for the poorest persons in that system would mean a set of instrumental, symbolic and social relations that helps them to survive in meeting such fundamental needs as food, clothing, housing, medical treatment and education'.

However, cultural autonomy should not lead to cultural competition of an unhealthy kind. The trend in India today, and perhaps in some other South Asian countries, is fundamentalism; ritual religion is revived not only in temples, mosques, churches and other houses of worship but on TV and radio. Every community is vying with others to show that it is the most 'religious' by reviving old customs as signs of religious fervour. Political leaders do their worshipping in public with the accompaniment of their official entourage, and the media publicise all these private and personal doings of leaders as activities of public importance. Another matter of concern for those who support a secular and scientific attitude to life is the frequent use of the media for telecasting or broadcasting purely casteist or ritual programmes as cultural programmes. The screening of two epics, *Ramayana* and *Mahabharat*, was of great significance for majority of the Indians, but a substantial number of those who watched them considered them not as epics but as religious programmes. The first was telecast in 50 weekly episodes from 25 January 1987 to 31 July 1988; *Mahabharat* was telecast from 2 October 1988 to 24 June 1990. Some people in village areas did puja to the TV set before the appearance of the screen personalities. Despite this element of irrationality associated with the reception given to the programmes by illiterate people, the two epics have done a great service to the majority of Indians in that it was the first time that so many millions were emotionally glued together through a well-known cultural phenomenon familiar to them from their childhood days. In this sense, the two programmes did a great service for national emotional integration. But there are some negative aspects of this type of programme. As long as people are illiterate, culture may be mistaken for fundamentalism; unless the literate try to conscientise the illiterate.

Chatterji (1991) discusses the problem of secularism in relation to the telecasting of the two epic serials. He says:

> Our newly founded secular state is being rocked by ugly manifestations of politicised religion such as riots, processions and *bandhs* (strikes) intended to paralyse daily life. Such activities undermine our constitutional obligation to promote harmony and the spirit of common brotherhood amongst all the people of India, transcending religious, linguistic and regional diversities; to renounce practices derogatory to the dignity of women; . . . and to foster scientific temper, humanism and the spirit of inquiry and reform (p. 209).

Although the majority of Indians enjoyed watching the epics, they watched them not as epics but as God's own religious revelation; and this has great consequences for their relationship with those who profess other faiths, particularly those faiths where the depiction of religious figures in moving or still pictures is considered sacrilegious and blasphemous.

Moreover, the Constitution of India while giving equal acceptance to all religions, does not give any sanction to any public profession, practice or propagation of any faith in a manner calculated to arouse the followers of that faith to actions that endanger public order, health or morality (Article 25). Article 28 proscribes religious instruction through an institution wholly maintained out of state funds. According to its own statements, Doordarshan has an instructional (educational) role and it is wholly government funded. Doordarshan should not become a means for propagation or reinforcement of any religious faith. Since the majority of the viewers consider the two epics as religious texts, and not secular entertainment of a literary or legendary kind (say, like the Greek epics), and since a substantial number of viewers were likely to have treated them as sacred revelations, Doordarshan was (unwittingly) propagating religious instruction.

People may draw parallels between the airing of the Indian epics and that of the *Ten Commandments* or *Jesus of Nazareth* in Western countries. There is, however, a big difference between the two. Most viewers of Biblical stories do not consider them as either literal, religious truths or sacred texts of divine revelation now. They consider programmes based on them as intensely interesting interpretations and they do not sit before their TV sets with awe and respect. They are educated enough to understand that the Judaeo–Christian films or TV serials are attempts by film makers to interpret religious works in a certain way. They consider them as any other type of TV programme sponsored by manufacturers of a series of products. Commercial interruptions further underline the fact that the viewers are very much in the real world of shampoos, soft drinks, candy bars, contraceptives, deodorants and depilatories.

These products have nothing much to do with the Ten Commandments or the last words of Jesus Christ on the Cross! In other words, Western TV viewers are reminded every five minutes that the things they watch as part of the programme should not make them forget that they live in a world where they are under pressure to buy products and be part of the marketplace of product selling ideas. They do not garland or smear sandalwood paste on their TV sets. They do not fast or pray before they sit in front of the TV to watch any Bible-based TV programme. On the other hand, what were the reactions in many Indian cities to the two epics telecast by Indian TV? Chatterji's (1991) description answers this question:

> In many towns television sets were decorated and placed in public places where large crowds viewed the programme. At the conclusion of the day's episode *prasaad* (sanctified sweets) were

> distributed to the gathering. At a bazaar in Banaras sweets weighing 125 kilograms are reported to have been distributed. Trains were delayed because passengers refused to let them off the platform till the performance was over . . . .In hospitals, nurses and other staff did not attend to patients while the programme was on. In Punjab and Haryana, terrorists placed time bombs at places where large gatherings had congregated to view the programme. On 19 June 1988 fifteen persons were killed at Kurukshetra and thirty were injured when a bomb exploded . . . . So far as Hindus were concerned, viewing was total. Anyone who had access to a TV set got there. In many cases puja timings (at temples) had to be changed so that devotees could view the programme. In reply to criticisms that too much time was being given to one community, some claimed that the epics cut across religious barriers. This is largely untrue . . . . It seems fairly evident . . .that for the vast majority of viewers, Hindus especially, the serials were religious and viewing was a form of religious participation (p. 212–213).

But, there are people who believe that such homogenisation of Hinduism will diminish the essential pluralism and internal eclecticism characteristic of the Hindu view of life through all these centuries.

According to Romila Thapar, as cited in Chatterji (1991), for example, the telecasting of *Ramayana* was:

> an attempt to project what the new culture should be, an attempt to expunge diversities and present a homogenised view of what the *Ramayana* was or is . . . . Where culture is taken over by the state as a major patron, the politics of culture is inevitably heightened. It is therefore easier for the state as a major patron to adopt a particular cultural stream as the mainstream, a cultural hegemony which frequently coincides with the culture of the dominant social group in the state (p. 215).

If there is no discussion of the religious, social, cultural, and even political messages contained in epics and of the relevance of ancient epics in modern times, the representation of the statecraft and styles of living prevalent in ancient times will be blindly accepted as relevant for modern times. The version of the *Ramayana* that was telecast had texts carrying later insertions reflecting the

Brahmanical system of caste hierarchy and subjugation of women. According to Thapar and others there are many versions of the epic—the Buddhist and the Jain versions, for example, besides the versions of Hindu writers like Valmiki, Tulsidas, Ezhuttacchan and Kamban. But the Doordarshan presentation was based on the Valmiki and Tulsidas versions, 'with significant interpolations and it reflected the Brahmanical system of caste hierarchy and the subordination of women' (Chatterji, 1991, p. 216), and the reinforcement of Manu's dictum that a woman is not a person in her own right but dependent on her father, husband or son at different stages of her life.

Moreover, the telecasting of the two religious epics became a virtual propaganda tool for ultra-right organisations like the Rashtriya Swayamsevak Sangh (RSS) and the Viswa Hindu Parishad (VHP) which looked upon Doordarshan's decision to televise the epics as an antidote to the Nehruvite model of secular development based on science and technology. Perhaps the sudden upward swing in the number of Bhartiya Janata Party (BJP) Members of Parliament (MPs), Members of the Legislative Assemblies (MLAs) and BJP-led governments in the northern states in the general elections in 1991 was due to this communal awakening and retrogressive view of development reinforced through religious telecasts. According to a spokesperson of the VHP, *Hindutva* got a fillip through the telecasting of the two epics. And some MPs are very keen to get the epics retelecast soon. Some MPs clamoured for this in a session of Parliament on 2 December 1991 (telecast of Parliament proceedings by Doordarshan on 3 December 1991, 7:15 AM to 8 AM). The young woman who played the part of Sita in *Ramayana* was elected to parliament on the BJP ticket, which is indicative of the political influence of a religious epic that was mass mediated to millions of people.

Cultural invasion, therefore, need not always be from without; it can occur from within. In an attempt to introduce uniformity in culture, the majority community's efforts to impose its cultural norms and peculiarities on the rest of the population is also cultural invasion. The ensuing changes in the socio-cultural and religious base of intrapersonal communication in India are likely to have disastrous consequences on communal harmony. This artificial division of the population on the basis of wrong internal interpretation and superimposition of that interpretation of culture on the politically weak sections is strengthened further by the external imposition of another variety of commercial cultural synchronisation to which reference has already been made.

Let us elaborate a little bit on this commercial culture. We should not be misled by the blind hatred of all foreign cultural streams indulged in by upholders of orthodoxy and fundamentalism. What we refer to here as commercial culture is that culture where everything is evaluated on the basis of profit and loss, on accountancy and book-keeping. There are many things in heaven and earth that are not dreamt of by computer experts and comptrollers of accounts. The milk of human kindness is one such item that is not favourably looked upon by commercial culture. Where there is no profit, the commercial man does not have any interest. All human relationships to him are to be converted into currency. That which does not yield profits or he who is non-productive is of no utility to the commercial man.

Those who behave differently, extol universal brotherhood and encourage human relationships based on love and kindness are dubbed unwise and inefficient in commercial culture. The supply of pure drinking water is not a priority but the manufacture and sale of mineral water is of top priority in commercial culture. Dairy farming to supply milk to all children is far less important than converting milk into chocolates, candy bars, fudges, icecreams and the like, affordable to a tiny minority in the commercial culture. Primary schools in well-constructed buildings and supplied with the basic equipment and amenities for all children in a given community are not a major concern to supporters of the commercial culture, but the special schools charging high fees affordable to a small urban or rural elite are. Huge hospitals with the latest high technology get primary attention and funding in a commercial culture, not the primary health centres with their emphasis on preventive or low technology medicine which will keep millions healthy. In commercial culture, medicine and education, knowledge and information, media and communication are all peddled for a profit. There is no profit in preventive medicine, literacy campaigns, a balanced diet or universal primary education.

Energy is another major area where the advocates of the commercial culture have influenced the media, especially the large circulation newspapers of the world and the TV networks, in favour of nuclear energy. Despite the fact that nuclear waste disposal continues to be an unsolved problem and the harmful health consequences of nuclear radiation, and despite, above all, the opposition to nuclear energy from concerned scientists of advanced nations (including some Nobel laureates), the big energy corporations of the world stress the benefits of nuclear energy because that is where the money is. Solar energy will be an inexhaustible source of energy, unlike mineral and nuclear sources which are fast disappearing. Solar energy is pollution free too, but the commercial culture does not want to promote its production.

Lastly, commercial culture measures man's values by the height of his mansion, the length of his car, the size of his office desk or the comfort of his office chair. It contemptuously tolerates scholarship, but loses no opportunity to treat scholars in a derogatory manner. 'High living and plain thinking' mark the products of commercial culture.

A culture that does not recognise the deep chasm between the rich and the poor, which refuses to acknowledge the role of some people's greed in creating many people's misery, and above all promotes mediocrity in order to keep the excellent out of the reaches of power—that is commercial culture, despite its attempt to gloss over the essential deficiencies and drawbacks of the system.

What India and other countries of South Asia, therefore, need is not a commercial culture but a culture that is based on universal brotherhood, a culture where different viewpoints about the meaning of life can co-exist in peace, a culture that permits diversity, diachronisation, autonomy and the freedom to pursue one's own spiritual fulfilment in keeping with one's own beliefs.

The advocates of privatisation often forget that the mass media of communication have had only a very brief existence in human societies and that they have been monopolised by the commercial culture. To make mass communication and the media more human and relevant to small groups of human beings, the sprawling media systems, whether belonging to private entrepreneurs or government organisations, have to be decentralised and de-bureaucratised. This is essential for local relevance. There can be national channels and a stipulation that the local LPTs set apart certain time slots for national news, entertainment programmes and educational telecasts. But the bulk of the programmes on a local channel should be locally oriented and culturally relevant. There can be popular participation in most local programmes.

To reiterate again another matter of primary importance in a plural society like India's is that cultural autonomy ought not lead to cultural competition of an unhealthy kind. The trend towards fundamentalism, intolerance and ritualism characteristic of all religious communities in India is on the rise. Religious leaders have to examine if customs are truly religious in nature or based on blind acceptance of some dead practices revived in the name of religion.

While agreeing with Hamelink (1983) and others who argue for cultural diachronisation in place of synchronisation, one has to be a little wary about too much cultural diachronisation when other social conditions are in a very backward state. Without the essential educational and cultural refinement, the largely illiterate population will become easy prey for the machinations of power wielders. Without attempting to increase the number of primary and secondary schools in each locality, this raising of cultural standards is not easy. Cultural refinement is tolerance for other points of view. Without an understanding of the basics of other religions, political and economic systems, one cannot understand the true nature of one's own points of view. Liberal education is the only way to attain such cultural fine-tuning. Therefore, what is more quickly needed today is decentralisation and de-bureaucratisation of the existing media, particularly radio and TV, for attaining local relevance. Coupled with a strengthening of educational institutions of local relevance, electronic media localisation can work wonders to make people enjoy different cultural streams in the ancient civilisations that make up the foundation of life in India.

How will the 'market-friendly' new order affect the free flow of information? Will it be free one-way flow from the media monopolies or cartels to an audience that is technologically and sociologically forced into the position of being passive/captive receivers of messages? Will it lead to suppression of dissent and inconvenient information as has been happening in many countries where the government controlled the media?

Ultimately, will it be one voice and many worlds as far as the flow of communication and information in the world is concerned? Cultural synchronisation is the one voice of greed, of building affluence for a minority on the foundation of the misery of the majority.

The McBride Commission Report drew pointed attention to the cultural domination of the poor countries by the rich by using the electronic media, and also to the big imbalance in information between the rich countries of the North and the poor countries of the South. Dubbing the Report, as well as all the efforts that went into it, as Soviet inspired, the US and UK withdrew from the UNESCO itself in 1984. In the style of Orwell's Big Brother, leaders of the rich countries indulge in 'double speak' when they talk of a new world order. There is no milk of human kindness in the so-called new world order: it is just a new slogan coined by political copywriters who have been bedazzled by the spectacular military success of some countries in the Gulf War. They have been blinded to the essential misery of the majority in this new world order which follows the same old order based on the trickle-down approach to development. As Uranga (1984) mentions:

> The domination endured by the poor of the world as a result of oppression by the powerful is a reality that degrades the whole of humankind as such. Hope for equality and justice is at the root of the struggle of every social group for the well-being of its members . . . . Human and democratic restoration of under-developed countries coincides with a basic Christian orientation: to work for the dignity of human beings in such a way that we can all see each other as brothers and sisters (pp. 13–14).

Privatisation of the electronic media cannot be isolated from the general philosophy of economic development. The demand for national TV programmes to become similar in content and technical perfection to those from CNN, BBC, or others, is a mindless, ahistorical and even unreal exercise. And the national TV's attempts to conform to foreign standards are also unrealistic. The ultimate result of the elites' demand and their own TV system's capitulation to that demand will be greater domination of national TV by the international entertainment and advertising industry. In other words, blind and hasty efforts to emulate culturally alien communication models will result in further psychological and cultural subjugation to the small group of multinational corporations for whom culture means, most of the time, what sells. As Uranga (1984) says:

> We live in a world that revolves around a small number of centres of transnational power, characterised by a concentration of economic and political power that uses culture as a means of penetrating and domesticating the peripheral sectors subject to domination by the centre (p. 5).

The new world order about which we hear so much these days is the same old world order, but without the bipolarity between the socialist and capitalist blocs following the changes in Eastern Europe. 'Culture is but another battlefield where transnational powers attempt to widen their area of domination over peripheral zones' (Uranga, 1984, p. 6).

The culture industry is a transnational industry with headquarters in London, New York, Los Angeles (Hollywood), Paris and Tokyo. To this list may be added some newcomers like Hong Kong, Singapore and Dubai, where the video industry is very much on the rise. The culture industry is comparable to any other industry, but the producers of culture demand absolute freedom for cultural penetration into every part of the globe. Paulo Freire (1968) describes cultural invasion as the last fundamental characteristic of anti-dialogical action, the other two being divisive tactics and manipulation, all three serving the end of conquest of the oppressed. The invaders impose their own world view upon the invaded by creating a sense of inferiority in the latter about their own culture. This is what Macaulay did in his 1835 Minute when it was said that all Sanskrit and Arabic knowledge was inferior to what a grade school in England would impart to its pupils. To quote Freire:

> In the last analysis, invasion is a form of economic and cultural domination. Invasion may be practised by a metropolitan society upon a dependent society . . . .
>
> Cultural conquest leads to the cultural inauthenticity of those who are invaded: they being to respond to the values, the standards, and the goals of the invaders.
>
> To this end, invaders are making increasing use of the social sciences and technology, and to some extent the physical sciences as well, to improve and refine their action.
>
> In cultural invasion, it is essential that those who are invaded come to see their reality with the outlook of the invaders rather than their own; for the more they mimic the invaders, the more stable the position of the latter becomes.
>
> For cultural invasion to succeed, it is essential that those invaded become convinced of their intrinsic inferiority . . . . The more invasion is accentuated and those invaded are alienated from the spirit of their own culture and from themselves, the

> more the latter want to be like the invaders; to walk like them, dress like them, talk like them . . .
>
> Cultural invasion, which serves the ends of conquest and the preservation of oppression, always involved a parochial view of reality, a static perception of the world, and the imposition of one world view upon another. It implies the 'superiority' of the invader and the 'inferiority' of those who are invaded, as well as the imposition of values by the former, who possess the latter and are afraid of losing them (pp. 150–152, 159).

Cultural synthesis can certainly occur in India, but not when cultural invasion goes on from within and without. Synthesis takes a long while to materialise and South Asia for a long time had seen a certain synthesis of religious cultures based on the Indic civilisation. But modern educational systems and the modern *media of communication* have not helped in strengthening that cultural base, unfortunately having weaned away the intellectuals in India to the commercialism which is the hallmark of market economies that introduced the modern systems of education and communication.

The way out is to go back to the basics of the Indic (including Hindu, Buddhist, Jain, Christian, Islamic and Sikh) civilisation which are at the root not only of Indian but other South Asian cultures. This trip back in history is religious in character (but not narrowly religious or ritualistic, not parochial or denominational). Returning to a religious base does not mean revival of fundamentalism, but reinforcing the neo-foundationalist original principles of ancient and modern religions. While doing this, one may find much in common among the various religions of the South Asian region. One may also find the same revolutionary core in all religions, a core that can motivate planners and leaders to think in terms of social justice and a more equitable distribution of opportunities and benefits of economic and social development. Instead of starting new projects, already launched projects have to be perfected so that the infrastructure of economic development can be strengthened. Uranga (1984) has observed:

> I do not deny the persuasive capacity of the media propaganda put out by the ruling transnational classes. My point is simply

> that its power is over-estimated and should be divested of its mythical irresistibleness, that according to some, would leave an invaded culture practically defenceless (p. 11).

There is no pure culture anywhere in the world. Interactions between various human groups lead to new cultures, but national cultures can present distorted pictures of their own society if dominated by elites who identify themselves with an artificial culture that is based on purely commercial considerations without any direct link to the large majority of their own populations. By so doing, the elite media suppress or distort the social realities to conform to some unwritten, unspecified but very alive international culture, which works against the interests of the poor. Whatever the poor need is ignored, whatever they plead for goes unheeded, whatever they say is misconstrued. A *psychic perestroika* is what the national elite and the international 'developers' need in today's world. Unless this mental and spiritual transformation occurs, inspired by the revolutionary teachings in major religions and motivated by the misery of fellow human beings, the same old world order will continue, privatisation or not.

The full implications of such a psychic perestroika and its need can only be well understood through an examination of the evolution of the dominant development paradigms and their connection with the media of communication.

References

Bagdikian, B. (1983). *Media monopoly*. Boston: Beacon Press.

Chatterji, P.C. (1991). *Broadcasting in India*. New Delhi: Sage.

Freire, Paulo (1968). *Pedagogy of the Oppressed*. New York: The Seaburry Press. Chapter IV of the book discusses cultural invasion in detail.

Gandhi, M.K. (1921). *Young India*. 1 June. See also *The Collected Works of Mahatma Gandhi-XX (April–August 1921)*. New Delhi: Publishing Division, Ministry of Information and Broadcasting, Government of India.

Hamelink, Cees (1983). *Cultural Autonomy in Global Communication*. London: Longman.

Joshi, P.C. (1987). *An Indian personality for television*. New Delhi: Publishing Division, Ministry of Information and Broadcasting, Government of India.

Rostow, W.W. (1960). *The stages of economic growth: A non-communist manifesto*. Cambridge: Cambridge University Press.

Uranga, Washington (1984). 'NWICO: New World Information and Communication Order'. In Lee, Philip (ed.). *Communication for all*. Indore: Satprakaashan Sanchaar Kendra.

5

Expansion of the Korean Television Industry and Transnational Capitalism[1]

Shin Dong Kim

Introduction

On 31 August 1993, after some five years of controversy and discussion, the Korean government concluded the debates on the introduction of a cable television system in Korea by selecting 20 programme providers. The following 11 fields of programming were allocated among the firms: news, movies, sports, culture, entertainment, education, music, children, women, transportation and tourism, and religion. Provider licences would be given to additional firms or organisations in the near future with plans to have 40 channels available within the next five years. Licensing of 116 cable stations over the country also followed by the end of October 1993.

Cable television has long been perceived as one of the most profitable and promising businesses in Korea. It is expedient for large corporations to be eager to take part in this industry. In fact, many large firms have anticipated and prepared for the inception of the cable television business for years. Among the 20 selected programme providers, most of the potentially profitable fields were allocated to the established 'chaebol' groups (massive conglomerates which have multiple subsidiary companies). Samsung, which already subsidises a large media conglomerate, took movies and culture; Daewoo took movies; Hyundai took entertainment; and the news field was taken by two media firms, Yonhap News Agency and Maeil kyongje sinmunsa (*Hankook Ilbo* [The Korea Chicago Times], 4 September 1993).

The introduction of cable television is not the only factor that loudly heralds a great transformation of the Korean mediasphere. Following cable television, the government also announced that it will licence regional private broadcasters in four large cities of the country: Pusan, Taegu, Kwanju, and Taejon. The competition among consortiums, which comprised of large companies, to apply for the licences was intense. Twenty-three consortiums competed for four licences and there were virtually 642 firms which took part through these consortiums (Yun and Ch'on, 1994).

The introduction of cable and regional privately-owned television means a full-scale return to commercial broadcasting after a decade of duopoly by two public broadcasting organisations, the Korean Broadcasting System (KBS) and the Munhwa Broadcasting Corporation (MBC). In 1991, licensing of the Seoul Broadcasting System (SBS), a privately-owned commercial network gave rise to much controversy. When SBS got its licence from the government, a decade's endeavour devoted to the stabilisation of the public system since its inception in 1981 suddenly seemed to be undermined. However, the introduction of SBS was just a minor change compared to the inception of mass-scale cable television.

The privatisation of the broadcasting system was based upon the rationale that it would increase diversity of content and viewers' choice, and supply adequate channel capacity for the rapidly increasing advertising demand. Unlike the SBS case, the question of ownership form was not even discussed in cable television and regional broadcasting. Controversies regarding cable television were largely centred around the appropriate time of inception of the business. Private ownership in cable and regional television was unquestionably assumed by all the participants in the debate (Han, 1993).

Why privatisation and commercialisation in network, cable, and regional television? Why now? Who needs it? Is this just a part of the current global trend of privatisation? If this was the case, how would it be different from the experiences of and conditions in other countries? Is this a desirable choice for encouraging cultural diversity and economic progress? And what is the future for the existing public networks?

In this paper, the analysis will focus on identifying those fundamental factors from which the revival of the commercial broadcasting system in Korea was derived. Changing conditions of global capitalism will be discussed as one of the major factors that influence the current transformation of the Korean television industry. Economic conditions, such as the growth of the advertising market as well as overall economic development, will be given particular consideration.

The argument will, in particular, focus on identifying the role of the state, and domestic and international economic forces (i.e. transnational firms) on the formation and privatisation of the Korean broadcasting industry. This paper will also demonstrate that the Korean public broadcasting system has actually never been a public system. On the contrary, despite continuing emphasis on the 'publicness' of the system, it has accumulated a huge amount of capital by exploiting the state-protected duopoly during the last 10 years. Finally, the paper argues that this unique expansion of the Korean broadcasting industry could possibly be attributed to the government's intention to control the media.

Privatisation

Privatisation of the public sector, including public broadcasting corporations, has increasingly attracted researchers' attention in recent years. BBC and other European broadcasting organisations have suffered difficulties in finding financial backing for their operational needs, as well as the huge investments required to keep up with fierce international competition. Since a public organisation does not have profit incentives, it finds it hard to compete with private sector organisations. According to Richeri (1986), for example, at least four crisis factors placed the European public broadcasting services under pressure: (*a*) the inflation spiral caused by the overall economic crisis which eroded the financial basis of public broadcasting; (*b*) the expansion of the audio-visual market and the eruption of new media which brought about challenges from both private industries and viewers; (*c*) the diversification of viewers' demand which overtaxed the capability of the public services; and (*d*) the once dominant political powers having lost control over broadcast information tending to favour private initiatives. Although this may not be an exhaustive nor representative study of the privatisation of European public broadcasting, the list of crises factors covers some important issues.

The fundamental rationale of privatisation of the public sector may be summarised as a response to the alleged inefficiency and inferiority of the public system to corporate capital in the production and distribution of electronic media products. Public systems of course are not usually expected to achieve economic efficiency as their prime objective. As one of the most fundamental organising principles for production and exchange, the public system acquires its own legitimacy in providing services which are not adequately provided for by the private sector. Market failure, for example, would be a good cause for government involvement in public service (Donahue, 1989).[2] In fact, broadcasting has been considered a public good (in most countries other than the United States), which therefore needs to be organised as a public system. The reason broadcasting was conceived as a public good is because its material resource, the electronic spectrum, has the characteristics of non-exclusivity (once a public good is provided, nobody can easily be prevented from benefiting from it) and non-rivalry (one person can enjoy a public good without diminishing the benefit to anyone else) (*ibid.*).

Whether a good is public or not, the way it is served can vary. For instance, in the US, the postal service is operated by a government corporation, whereas all other communication services including telephones, are run by private industries. The criteria for operational evaluation of the different systems can also vary. Two different questions may be formed about the form of a public good server: (*a*) should a public good be provided by private industry or by a public system? and (*b*) how competitive is a public system in comparison to a private corporation? These are questions at different levels and it is with the second one that this paper is concerned.

Transnational Capital and Global Competition

As Richeri (1986) points out, the crisis of public broadcasting in Europe mainly originated from the challenges of the private media industry. In other words, European broadcasting is experiencing a new market principle which has been dictated by competition. Two major factors are identified as the driving forces of this change in the media market structure: technology and transnational media corporations. British economist Strange (1992) argues that the accelerating rate and cost of technological change has speeded up the internationalisation of production and the dispersion of manufacturing. She also points out that the liberalisation of international finance has increased capital mobility. With the steady and cumulative lowering of the real cost of transborder transport and communication, she argues that these factors characterise a structural change of contemporary capitalism.

The development of new media technology by cable television and direct broadcasting satellite (DBS) among others, has increased the opportunities for private firms to enter the media market more easily. In addition to this, the ever growing potentiality of the information economy which called for massive amounts of capital investment in the field was hard for the public sector alone to sustain. The use of satellite technology in broadcasting made national borders pointless. In its initial stage of commercial use, the dispute concerning spill-over seemed to hinder the development and application of satellites in the realm of broadcasting; however, satellite broadcasting has finally succeeded in gaining a broader market during the last decade.

Technology also opened a wider opportunity for transnational corporate capital, which has most actively developed and utilised media technology, to serve its own profit motivation. Recent reports in trade magazines and newspapers list endless expansions of transnational media firms over the globe. The application of satellite technology in commercial broadcasting has been demonstrated by Rupert Murdoch's Star TV business in the Asian region. On 2 December 1993, the *Wall Street Journal* reported the beginning of a battle for Asia's television viewers when a group of seven international broadcasters signed an agreement to lease capacity on a satellite (Apstar-2) that could reach nearly two-thirds of the world's population from Europe to Japan and from North Asia to Australia (Goll, 1993).[3] In the same issue of the *Wall Street Journal*, it was also reported that western media products were gaining popularity in China as the country's television market expanded. According to the report, Shanghai had four television stations (two of which were added only 18 months earlier), including a cable network with 11 channels currently and 19 more planned. In this cable network, foreign programmes accounted for 30 per cent of the total. The reports also stated that Rupert Murdoch's Hong Kong based Star TV had been a catalyst for many of these changes in the Chinese media (Kahn, 1993).

DBS is in fact more than a catalyst for many Asian countries, including China. When Japan's NHK started its DBS broadcasting in 1990, the Korean government and broadcasting industry viewed this as a serious threat for both economic and cultural reasons. Industry people worried about the possible decrease in their ratings and the government was afraid of losing control over information. However, this kind of negative sentiment was soon diluted after finding that most of NHK's programmes were moderate in content and few people were actually active enough to buy and install receiving antennas. Although Star TV is attracting a small audience so far, it is adding more pressure on the Korean government to hasten its own DBS development. The potentiality of this commercial channel, which has massive transnational capital behind it, is certainly perceived as a caveat by many Koreans.[4] Full-scale application of satellite technology in the broadcasting business is, however, yet to come. Besides satellite, the increasing use of VCRs and cable has already created a vast market for American made films and television programmes.

The transnationalisation of contemporary corporate capital reveals some distinctive characteristics. According to Heilbronner (1985), high mobility of capital and dispersion of its accumulation have been achieved through a highly sophisticated global financial system. Harvey (1989) would call the latter a 'flexible accumulation' through temporal and spatial displacement (p. 194). First, as Heilbronner (*ibid.*) appropriately puts it, capital is now financed on a global scale: 'The label "Made in Hong Kong", stamped commodities, . . . becomes a symbol of the ability of capital to move wherever low labour costs or strategic sites for distribution offer competitive advantages' (p. 171). Indeed, capital goes wherever it has a better chance to accumulate surplus or profit. According to Jeffrey Ballinger (1992):

> In the 1980s, Oregon-based Nike closed its last US footwear factory, in Saco, Maine, while establishing most of its new factories in South Korea, where Sung Hwa Corp, is based. Sung Hwa is among many independent producers Nike has contracted, with. Nike's actions were part of the broader 'globalisation' trend that saw the United States lose 65,300 footwear jobs between 1982 and 1989 as shoe companies sought non-unionised Third World workers who didn't require the US rubber-shoe industry average of $6.94 an hour. But in the late 1980s, South Korean labourers gained the right to form independent unions and to strike. Higher wages ate into Nike's profit. The company

> shifted new factories to poorer countries such as Indonesia, here labour rights are generally ignored and wages are but one-seventh of South Korea's. [. . .] Today, to make 80 million pairs of shoes annually, Nike contracts seven dozen factories globally, including six in Indonesia. [. . .] By shifting factories to cheaper labour pools, Nike posted year after year growth. [. . .] The labour costs to manufacture a pair of Nike that sells for $80 in the United States is approximately 12 cents (pp. 46–47).

The capitalists' efforts to continuously seek cheap labour is not a new fact at all. What is new is that this ceaseless search for cheaper costs of production pushed companies to spread across borders in a more complex mode. The standardised production system which is built up under Fordism shifts to the periphery. The above mentioned Sung Hwa Corp. of Korea is just one of the companies from semi-peripheral countries, companies which are operating in the poorer peripheral countries on behalf of the most advanced countries' capital. A Korean economist severely criticised the inhuman labour practices of some Korean foreign investment companies such as Sung Hwa Corp. in Indonesia (Sin, 1993). In a sense, semi-peripheral countries such as Korea are taking on the role of proxy in the Third World countries to protect core countries' and/or transnational capital invested in these regions.

Another significant characteristic of transnational capital is found in its dispersion of accumulation in multiple countries. As management consultant Kenichi Ohmae (1990) puts it, the nationality of many giant corporations are becoming more and more obscure:

> Is IBM Japan an American or a Japanese company? Its work force of 20,000 is Japanese, but its equity holders are American. Even so, over the past decade IBM Japan has provided, on average, three times more tax revenue to the Japanese government than has Fujitsu. What is its nationality? Or what about Honda's operation in Ohio? Or Texas Instruments' memory-chip activities in Japan?
>
> The very idea of 'American' products made by 'American' firms is becoming obsolete. Lee Iacocca warns of the Japanese invasion of America, but American-made parts now constitute a smaller portion of the top models of the Big Three than they do of Honda's top-of-the-line cars (p. 8).[5]

For the movement of capital, national borders are no longer a constraint. On the contrary, according to Ohmae (1990), 'most companies have to move more deeply into the countries where they seek to neutralise the impact of currency as well as the possibilities of protectionism' (p. 7). The transnationals, in fact, form world powers with their massive amounts of capital power as well as their diversified investment. The annual sales of many transnational firms are far larger than the GNPs of developing countries, not to mention the underdeveloped countries. For example, in 1981, the annual sales of Exxon were 108.1 billion dollars, whereas the GNPs of Indonesia, Austria, Denmark, and Korea were less than that amount. Only 19 countries had a higher GNP (Morgan, 1986, pp. 299–304). Hamelink (1993) reminds us that the 'oligopolistically controlled communication flows did erode the decision-making capacity of national governments' (p. 371).

Globalisation (particularly economic) is also a direct outgrowth of the transnational corporation's (TNC) world marketing strategy. If on the one hand the motivation to reduce costs in the production stage makes the TNC pursue a global strategy, on the other hand, companies are now forced to develop broader global markets. Many items previously considered variable costs, such as technology and promotion, are now fixed costs for businesses. To ensure a competitive advantage, companies are now forced to seek markets outside. By boosting sales, they intend to minimise the fixed costs, and this logic drives them towards globalisation. Wider markets are especially important for the producers of cultural commodities, because the information and culture industries are vulnerable to economies of scale.

Transnational capital, therefore, emerges as the most powerful force pushing nation-states to do 'something' to compete with TNCs. Privatisation of public broadcasting is basically a response to this external pressure and needs to be understood in this context. One of the assumptions of current privatisation theories is found in the concept of competition between the public sector and private capital. If the entry of private capital could be blocked by a political device for the sake of public interest, then privatisation would be deterred on a domestic level. If a country preferred the public organisation (despite its economic inefficiency) to the private corporation in a certain domain, it might adopt that institution.

On the international level, where transnational capital is forever seeking markets to sell products, sticking to a public system is an inconceivable choice unless a certain country gives up international trade, which means a secession from the capitalist world system.[6] This is not to say that every motivation for privatisation comes from outside the borders. On the domestic level, the growth of the advertising market, which itself is encouraged by the growth of the domestic production of consumer products, creates a demand for more advertising channels. But the global trend of privatisation in the 1970s and 1980s is mainly driven by the competition among advanced capitalist countries and their transnational firms. In a sense, privatisation is an inherent element of capitalist development under global competition. As Strange (1992) rightly puts it, 'the name of the game, for governments just as for firms, is competition' (p. 10). Using Braman's 1990 study on the evolution of GATT, in which she argues that 'the commoditisation of information and cultural materials should be a major point of consideration for all countries within the negotiations at GATT', Hoover et al. (1993) propose a similar diagnosis: 'There is only one game in town, and it is defined by GATT' (p. 124).

Capitalist Development and Political Confrontation in Korea

Unlike the European cases, KBS and MBC have hardly suffered from problems of financing; instead, they have raised adequate revenues from advertising as well as licence fees (Kim, 1992). Since other private capital was prevented from entering the broadcasting market by law, these two companies' profit making has been almost guaranteed under state protection. This is not an unusual style of industrial growth in Korea when we consider the development of Korean corporate capital in the form of 'chaebols'.[7] Though contending development theories on the Korean economy provide us with different explanations, it is generally agreed that the state exercised a dominant role in the process of capital accumulation (Amsden, 1989; Barrett and Chin, 1987; Haggard, 1990; Kuznets, 1977). The export-led development policy of the government strongly supported monopolistic capital through privileged loans and taxation. Dependency on foreign capital and markets has been an unavoidable outcome of this export-led development. Even before the notion of globalisation emerged, the development of the Korean economy was inconceivable without thinking about its close relations with the international economy.

The notion of globalisation refers to the increasing impact of globalised corporate capital moving in and out of individual countries. On a domestic level, however, this transnational movement of capital has to be negotiated within each country's political arrangement. In Korea, the process of development of the media market had been interrupted by the new military coup group which wanted to secure strict political control over capital and the liberal press. This kind of direct state intervention shows a sharp contrast with the situation in an advanced capitalist state where civil societies have long been formed against state power. However, state intervention always imposes a certain limitation against the force of capital. To give some background information on Korean broadcasting and its recent changes, the following section will review some characteristics of the capitalist development of the Korean economy and its relationship with both domestic politics and the global structure of capitalism.

Capitalist Development of the Korean Economy

The development of capitalism in Korea can find its distinctive characteristics in the rise and evolution of the 'chaebol' groups. These massive corporations formed their bases of power during the 1960s and 1970s when state-initiated industrialisation was advanced. These corporations, however, were so vulnerable that they had to rely heavily upon government's financial subsidies and on foreign capital. During the 1960s and 1970s, these 'chaebol' groups achieved large accumulations of capital through ways which brought about many of the current economic, political, and social problems (i.e., frail structure of finance, partial distribution of wealth, political corruption, etc.). Despite the leading roles that the 'chaebol' groups performed in the course of the country's economic development, they are largely associated with negative images. According to a dissident Korean economist, the 'chaebol's' regime of capital accumulation during the 1960s and 1970s should largely be depicted as monopolistic, anti-democratic, and speculative (Hong, 1993).

First, 'chaebol' groups grew through monopolistic accumulation. The export-led development policy encouraged the monopolistic or oligopolistic formation of industries to realise economies of scale in order to compete with foreign companies. Unlike the monopoly capitals of the advanced capitalist countries which tend to monopolise markets through competition, the Korean 'chaebol' groups were monopolised since their inception through government support. They acquired massive profits from high prices in the monopolised domestic market. Second, 'chaebol' groups accumulated capital in an anti-democratic way, by excluding workers from participating in the processes of production and distribution. The family ownership structure of the 'chaebol' groups was utilised to prevent the workers from participating, which secured low labour costs. Third, 'chaebols' accumulated capital by exploiting foreign technology rather than their own research and development. The problem of this strategy emerged after they achieved a certain level of productivity by applying foreign technology in the mass Fordist production. The force of production dependent on imported technology, however, did not ensure endless development and accumulation. When they reached a limit of accumulation, the 'chaebol' groups extended their businesses to new arenas (so-called octopus-like expansion) which were easy to monopolise or speculative enterprises, instead of investing in research and development.

The media industry has not been an exception in terms of its ownership, management, and in its relations with political power. The so-called 'Big Four' central daily newspapers (*Chosun Ilbo, Dong-A Illbo, Jooangang Illbo, and Hankook Ilbo*) enjoyed special financial treatment from the government as a reward for sacrificing freedom of press. Television networks were more strictly controlled by the government. Whether it was state-owned or privately-owned, or reorganised in the form of a public system, broadcasting in Korea has always been on the top of the list of political control. Monopolised markets protected by the state offered vast opportunities for broadcasting organisations to accumulate their own capital in a relatively short time.

The 1980s saw the emergence of forces that struggled against this limping regime of accumulation from two sources: one, from inside the monopoly capital, and the second from outside. Since the regime of accumulation was so feeble, the 'chaebols' or monopoly capitals were forced to rely upon repressive political power, which supported them, to fully exploit internal (labour and loan) and external (foreign capital) resources. However, the happy marriage of repressive political dictatorship and monopoly capital has made the capitalists pay dearly. Since the preference of a dictator is the key in the rise and fall of a capitalist under an illegitimate regime, dictatorship is not always welcomed by established capitalists. In Korea, when the capitalists achieved a relatively stable economic foundation in the 1980s, they preferred their own initiation to that of government's guidance (Kim, 1993). Also, the people's resistance and struggle against political dictatorship and the biased economy brought about another more fundamental change to the regime of accumulation. In 1987 and 1992, the democratisation of Korean politics made great advances. Recent political and economic reforms under the Kim Young Sam administration have mainly been focused upon cleaning up political corruption and economic rearrangement. The new government has openly said that it will accomplish structural adjustment to renew the nation's economic competitiveness in a challenging global, political economy.

Re-configuration of Political Economy in Korea

Recent political and economic changes, however, should not be taken as a fundamental measure to overthrow the capitalistic contradictions. On the contrary, it is basically a rearrangement of the labour–capital relationship in an even more capitalistic way. Capitalism has stabilised its mechanism only through liberal democracy, in which the right of private property is ideally justified. As the most fundamental organising principle of production and distribution, capitalism has kept a market system in which individuals freely participate as the subject of economic activity. In securing the marketplace, establishment of democracy is the necessary condition.

When the capitalists in Korea attained a relative dominance over the political power based on their earlier accumulation, they began to realise the importance of a stable marketplace. Low labour cost has not been a reliable source for accumulation since the late 1980s when unionised labour began to claim higher wages. The government itself also recognised the need for rearrangement of the industrial structure to ensure a competitive edge in the global market. In an effort to increase the efficiency of industry, the government recently formulated a restructuring policy for the 'chaebol' groups. This policy is basically aimed at specialisation of the business type, liberalisation of 'chaebol' groups through the stock market, and separation of management from ownership. The ultimate purpose of this rearrangement is, however, focused on fostering more efficient monopoly capital which can effectively compete with massive transnational capitals.

Korean Economy in the World Capitalist System

The export-led development strategy provided the Korean economy with both positive and negative outgrowths. On the positive side, it enabled Korea to emerge from a poor post-war peripheral country to a moderately achieved semi-peripheral country. Despite the political repression and labour exploitation during the last three decades, it is now freed from the absolute poverty of which most of the older generation still hold vivid memories. It is in this respect that the 1960s and 1970s 'development dictatorship' or the Park Chung Hee regime could acquire a spontaneous consensus from the people to some degree. It is also the economic achievement attained from this development policy that empowered the people to fight against brutal military dictatorship. Without basic supply of food and education, no struggle can be organised in an effective way.

The other side of the export-led development has doomed the structure of the Korean economy to a catastrophic category. The devastating outcomes of this policy in the domestic arena have been described earlier. In the global context, the peripheral and semi-peripheral locations in the hierarchical order of the capitalist world system have forced the country to relentlessly seek pathways to the core. The shift from the periphery to the semi-periphery of the Korean economy is in a sense an outgrowth of the global rearrangement of the capitalist system for flexible accumulation of transnational monopoly capital.[8] On the one hand, Korean capitalists could accumulate their own capital through exports of labour-intensive products based on low labour costs, derived from surpluses by minimising the variable cost. On the other hand, the country is doomed to grow its own monopoly capital, which itself tends to become transnational, to secure a competitive advantage—economies of scale and scope—in the global market.

Economic Development and the Expansion of Broadcasting Industry

Commercialisation of the Public System under the New Military Regime (1981–1990)

One of the primary initiatives which the new military regime put into place shortly after its coup in 1980 was to reform the then current media system. By the end of 1980, the new military regime had made the 'Prime Press Law' by which it totally restructured the newspaper and broadcasting industries.

Commercial broadcasting firms were immediately transformed into public entities; however, the 'publicness' of this new system was nominal. The name of 'public' was applied only to provide the new military regime with an excuse for their control over the entire media system. The main source of revenue was from advertising rather than licence fees. Throughout the 1980s, the broadcasting industry in Korea developed as a massive monopoly capital. For instance, by the end of 1990, the KBS subsidised 25 local stations with 6,088 workers and had revenues of 440 billion Won, which is roughly about $550 million (Kim, 1992). According to a report of *Television Business International* (March 1994, pp. 21–24), both MBC and KBS ranked 51st and 56th among the world's 100 largest television companies as measured by television revenues only. Both companies were 11th and 12th when only public broadcasters were considered. Interestingly, MBC was the only public broadcaster which got no support from publicly generated funds (e.g., licence fee and government support). The entire revenue of MBC and more than half of KBS came from advertising.

When the first five year economic development plan was launched in 1961, the broadcasting industry of Korea was pretty meagre. As can be seen from Table 5.1, one state-owned radio station, KBS, and a religious station, CBS, basically accounted for all broadcasting. In the early 1960s, with the inception of television broadcasting,

Table 5.1: Forms of Broadcasting System in Korea

Period	*Major Networks*
Colonial (1926–1945)	Kyongsong pangsongguk
State (1945–1961)	kbs(S), cbs(R: 1954–)
State and Commercial (1961–1973)	KBS(S), MBC(C), TBC(C: 1964–) kbs(S), mbc(C), tbc(C)
Public and Commercial (1973–1980)	KBS(P), MBC(C), TBC(C) kbs(S), mbc(C), tbc(C), dbs(C)
Public (1981–1990)	KBS1, KBS2, KBS3, MBC kbs1, kbs2, kbs3, kbs–1FM, kbs–2FM, Radio Seoul, mbc, mbc–FM, cbs(R)
Public and Commercial (1991–)	KBS1(P), KBS3(P), MBC(P), SBS(C), EBS(S) kbs1, kbs2, kbs–1FM, kbs–2FM, Radio Seoul, mbc, mbc–FM, sbs(C), ebs(S), cbs(R), bbs(R), pbc(R), bbs(P), febc(S)

Small letters were used for radio networks.
P = public, S = State, C = private commercial, R = religious.
Source: Chong, Sun-il (1991). *Han'guk pansong ui oje wa onul* (The past and present of the Korean broadcasting).

Korea saw the beginning of the commercial era. Although KBS has been maintained under either state or public ownership from 1961 to 1980, this period saw the development of a broadcasting industry with government subsidies. Broadcasting in turn provided the repressive Park regime with a powerful channel and a monolithic ideological apparatus during his dictatorship.

During the period 1961–80, both MBC and Tongyang Broadcasting Company (TBC) became media conglomerates. TBC, owned by the Samsung 'chaebol',[9] was just one of the many companies which accumulated its capital through monopolistic market structures. MBC also owned one of the major daily newspapers, which added institutional power and stability to the broadcast partner. In the economic sense, there was no necessity for the media firms to reform the broadcasting structure. On the part of their audience, there were hundreds of reasons to reform the broadcasters, mainly due to their role as mouthpieces for the government. This atmosphere was fully exploited after a new military regime came to power in a most brutal coup in 1980.

The limitations of the broadcasting reform of 1980 initiated by this illegitimate government was evident from its initial stage; the distorted broadcasting structure that was put into place was the result of both the monopoly market structure and the illegitimacy of the regime. After the reform, the government had no viable alternative to finance the already massive broadcasting industry but to rely on the advertising market. This reform was thus just a change of the broadcasting market structure from oligopoly and duopoly, and it strengthened the market power of the two broadcasting companies. Table 5.2 shows the continuously increasing reliance of KBS on advertising revenues which had exclusive possession of the licence fee.

Table 5.2: Composition of Licence Fee in the Total Revenue of KBS

(Thousand Won)

Year	*Total Revenue*	*Growth*	*% in Total*
1981	60,301,081	–	56.2
1982	77,721,093	28.9	49.2
1983	98,881,684	27.2	46.6
1984	114,876,530	11.6	42.2
1985	107,967,428	−6.1	40.5
1986	96,632,282	−10.5	37.5
1987	91,882,923	−4.9	34.2
1988	79,003,373	−14.0	23.4
1989	103,995,780	31.6	26.8
1990	122,964,716	18.2	28.0

Source: Korean Broadcasting System (1991). *KBS Statistical Handbook*.

As soon as the military dictatorship relaxed its coercive reign in 1987, and with the assumption of power by a civilian government in 1992, the privatisation process accelerated its uninterrupted development at the formal level. One important thing that must be mentioned at this point is the surprising growth of advertising. The rapid growth of the Korean broadcasting industry in recent years is based on the growth of the advertising market, which itself is the outgrowth of overall economic development and the expansion of the consumer market in particular. During the 1980s broadcast advertising experienced considerable growth rates, averaging 20.13 per cent, which is even higher than Korea's notably high GNP growth rate (Table 5.3). The total sales amount of broadcast advertising, about 120 billion Won ($15 million) in 1981, increased to about 700 billion Won ($87.5 million) in 1990. Table 5.4 shows

Table 5.3: Growth Rate of Broadcasting Advertisement and GNP (Based on Constant Price)

	1981 (%)	*1982 (%)*	*1983 (%)*	*1984 (%)*	*1988 (%)*	*1989 (%)*	*1990 (%)*	*Average (%)*
Advertise-ment	8.24	33.07	36.31	29.78	24.00	18.56	17.75	19.97
GNP	23.89	14.62	18.28	13.55	19.06	11.75	17.71	16.33

Modified from the original table.
Source: Han'guk Pangsong kwanggo kongsa (Korean Broadcasting Advertising Corporation) (1991). *Pangsong kwanggo yongop paekso* (A sales white paper of broadcasting advertisement).

Table 5.4: Total Advertisement Revenues by Media, 1991 and 1992

Media	*Advertisement Revenues (US$)*		*Growth Rate (%)*		*Percentage*	
	1992	*1991*	*1992*	*1991*	*1992*	*1991*
TV	1,072	880	129.5	107.9	29.7	27.0
Radio	166	165	107.2	126.8	4.6	5.0
Newspaper	1,463	1,390	111.9	119.6	40.5	42.6
Magazine	156	171	96.8	107.2	4.3	5.2
Total	2,857	2,606	116.5	110.9	79.1	79.8

Source: Cheil Communications. *Business Korea*. July 1993, p. 104.

that the television advertising revenue was $1,072 million in 1992, out of a total of $2,857 million in revenues. Although the portion of television advertisement revenue was less than 30 per cent of the total amount in the same year, it is not difficult to foresee that the portion of advertising taken by the television industry will exceed that of newspapers in the near future with the beginning of cable and regional television. The broadcasting advertising market anticipates more rapid expansion after the liberalisation of the advertising market, in which foreign firms have taken part since 1992.

Growth of overall economic capacity is thought to be the main cause of increased private consumption. During the last five years, Korea doubled its per capita GNP from $3,218 in 1987 to $6,757 in 1991, and in 1993 it reached $7,466 (*Business Korea*, September

1994, p. 64; KEIA, 1993). With this enhanced material condition, there has emerged a vast consumer market since the mid-1980s. College students and young female workers have also rapidly developed consumer groups with their increased capacity to spend and have been added to the already swollen targets of advertising (Kang, 1993). The effect of economic development has been directly transferred to the broadcasting industry through this growing advertisement market. In addition to this, the broadcasting industry could enjoy a monopoly rent of channels thanks to the natural monopoly in the market. Entry into the market has been prohibited by the Prime Press Law throughout the greater part of the 1980s and this has resulted in even better conditions for the two broadcasting companies (Chang, 1989).

The decade of the 1980s displayed a unique form of monopolistic development in the Korean broadcasting industry. Nominally it took the form of a public corporation, but in practice it accumulated massive capital and strengthened its capacity in both human and material resources. As the broadcasting industry undergoes restructuring with the inception of the commercial system based on private ownership, this expanded resource base possibly will make the system more capable of dealing effectively with the problems that come up. Although the government justified commercialisation based on the argument for diversity and freedom of choice, and supplying channels for exploding advertising, none of these seem to be realisable in the near future.

Tentative Conclusion

This paper, has tried to identify both the external and internal factors which have greatly influenced the current privatisation and deregulation processes expanding the Korean television industry. Transnational capital in the form of various business strategies of TNCs represents the foremost and most important external driving force. With enhanced super mobility based on global communication technologies and sophisticated financial networks, transnational capital urges nations to play in the eternal competition game under the rule of GATT. Privatisation, whether it is welcomed or not by individual countries, seems to have become an imperative of the times. The rise of domestic industrialism has enabled a rapid growth of the advertising market in Korea during the last decades. In the age of consumer capitalism, television is too attractive a medium to be ignored by advertisers. Furthermore, in the information age, the fusion of telecommunications and broadcasting transforms the traditional notion of broadcasting as a public good into media business as just one of the many profitable industries (Hoover et al., 1993). In these circumstances, the domestic policies of each nation, including Korea, which tend to seek privatisation and deregulation as solutions seem not so strange.

The introduction of cable television and satellite broadcasting, and the construction of ISDN (Integrated Services Digital Network) will further expand and strengthen the private market structure of the Korean electronic mass media. This commercialisation of the media market has in fact been in progress since 1961 and had continued even under the public broadcasting period within its unique monopolised structure of accumulation. State intervention, caused by political motivations, to tighten the control over information flow in the 1980s was an important factor in the process of establishing this structure of accumulation of the broadcasting industry in Korea.

Recent developments in the theories of media privatisation seem to be stuck in a narrow perspective centred around the experiences of advanced capitalist countries, European countries in particular. A focus on the domestic economy alone is not enough to explain the current tide of privatisation and deregulation in the media industry. Too often, a pro-privatisation perspective is assumed because of the operation of the harmonious 'invisible hand' and therefore, competition in the market is expected to better serve the users. The question posed in this paper, however, was not how 'to serve' but 'to survive'. A public system may provide its audience with quality programmes and thus serve better, but it is not only possible after it survives the harsh competition against transnational media capital. The rapid and fundamental political and economic changes at the global level require broader theoretical formulations of questions, in which the global movement of capital should be fully considered. These aspects which have emerged at a global level can not be reduced to national level explanations.

Notes

1. An earlier draft of this paper was presented to the Speech Communication Association Annual Convention, New Orleans, Louisiana, November 1994. Special thanks are due to Michael Curtin and Christopher Anderson for their interest and comments on this paper.
2. Donahue (1989) argues that there are three organising principles for production and exchange: voluntarism, price system (market), and government (public sector). According to him, government involvement (spending) is made either on market failure or collective consensus for non-market goals or opportunities.
3. The consortium is made up of Turner Broadcasting System Inc., Time Warner Entertainment, ESPN Inc., Discovery Communications Inc., Viacom Inc., Home Box Office Asia, and Hong Kong's Television Broadcasts Ltd.
4. Debates and research on DBS have been proliferating during the last several years in Korea. A Korean broadcasting research journal, *Pangsong yon'gu* (Journal of Broadcasting Research), recently devoted one of its issues to the DBS research. Precautions sentiment against transnational broadcasting was commonly shared by the writers of this issue.
5. The original source of this paragraph is an article in *The New Republic* (1989); re-cited from Ohmae (1990).
6. Dependency perspective, in this respect, tends to result in self-reliance of an individual nation's economy through cutting off the relationship with the world capitalist system. This line of argument, however, overlooks the transnationality of accumulation and thus, fails to yield effective strategy on both political and economic levels. In the world capitalist system, the politics of self-reliance only brings isolationism (i.e.,North Korea) and does not appropriately respond to the labour–capital confrontation at the international level.
7. Most of the Korean large firms are generally referred to as chaebols. A chaebol can be defined as 'business group consisting of large companies which are owned and managed by family members or relatives in many diversified business areas' (Yoo and Lee, 1987, p. 97). According to Steers et al. (1989) a chaebol's distinctive features include family control and management, paternalistic leadership, centralised planning and co-ordination, an entrepreneurial orientation, close business–government relations, and strong school ties in hiring policies.
8. Bruce Cumings (1987) argues that the economies of Northeast Asian countries such as Korea and Taiwan were initially formed as peripheries of the hegemonic Japanese economy during the pre-war era, and continued to serve as peripheral zones after the war to boost the Japanese post-war economy; while Japan became a semi-periphery of the US dominated world capitalist system.
9. Samsung has been trying to merge with Orion Pictures since 1990 (Carveth et al., 1993).

References

Amsden, Alice H. (1989). *Asia's next giant: South Korea and late industrialization*. New York: Oxford University Press.

Ballinger, Jeffrey (1992). 'The new free trade heel'. *Harper's Magazine*, August, 46–47.

Barrett, Richard E. and **Chin, Soomi** (1987). 'Export-oriented industrializing states in the capitalist world system: Similarities and differences'. In Deyo, F.C. (ed.). *The political economy of the new Asian Industrialism*. Ithaca, NY: Cornell University Press.

Braman, Sandra (1990). 'Trade and information Policy'. *Media, Culture and Society*, 12(3), 361–85.

Carveth, Rod, Owers, James and **Alexander, Alison** (1993). 'The global integration of the media industries'. In Alexander, Alison et al. (eds.). *Media economics: Theory and practice*. Hillsdale, NJ: Lawrence Erlbaum Associates.

Chang, Yong-ho (1989). 'Han'guk pangsong inyom e taehan kyongjeronjok chopkun' (An economic approach to the ideology of Korean broadcasting). *Ollon Munhwa Yon'gu* (Sogang Journal of Media and Culture), 7, 21–54.

Cheil Communications. *Business Korea*, July 1993.

Chong, Sun-il (1991). *Hang'guk pansong ui oje wa omul* (The Past and Present of the Korean Broadcasting). Seoul: Nanam Publishing Co.

Cumings, Bruce (1987). 'The origins and development of Northeast Asian political economy: Industrial sectors, product cycles, and political consequences'. In Deyo, F.C. (ed.). *The Political economy of the new Asian industrialism*. Ithaca, NY: Cornell University Press.

Donahue, John D. (1989). *The privatization decision: Public ends, private means*. New York: Basic Books.

Goll, Sally D. (1993). 'Seven TV firms agree to lease satellite in Asia'. *Wall Street Journal*, 2 December, A12.

Haggard, Stephan (1990). *Pathways from periphery: The politics of growth in the newly industrializing countries*. Ithaca, NY: Cornell University Press.

Hamelink, Cees J. (1993). 'Globalism and national sovereignty'. In Nordenstreng, K. and Schiller, H.I. (eds.). *Beyond national sovereignty: International communication in the 1990s*. Norwood, NJ: Ablex.

Han, Tae-yol (1993). 'CA-TV yon'giron ui hogu rul panbakham' (A confutation on the delay of the CA-TV inception). *Sindonga*, 406 (July), 638–47.

Han'guk Pangsong Kwanggo Kongsa (Korean Broadcasting Advertising Corporation) (1991). *Pangsong kwanggo yongop paekso* (A sales white paper of broadcast advertisement). Seoul: KOBACO.

Harvey, David (1989). *The condition of postmodernity*. Cambridge: Blackwell.

Heilbronner, Robert (1985). *The nature and logic of capitalism*. New York: Norton.

Hong, Chang-pyo (1993). 'Han'guk chabonjuui wa tokjom chaebol' (Korean capitalism and monopolistic chaebol). *Sahoe pip'yong*, 9, 402–27.

Hoover, Stuart M., Singh Venturelli, Shalini and **Wagner, Douglas K.** (1993). 'Trends in global communication policy-making: Lessons from the Asian case'. *Asian Journal of Communication*, 3(1), 103–32.

Kahn, Joseph (1993). '"Dynasty" in Shanghai is aiming for profit'. *Wall Street Journal*, 2 December, A13.

Kang, Myung-Koo (1993). 'A critique of commodity aesthetics of postmodern advertising on Korean television'. *Korean Social Science Journal*, 19, 7–22.

KEIA (Korea Economic Institute of America) (1993). *Korea's Economy* 9.

Kim, Dong Gyu (Kim, Tong-gyu) (1992). '1980 nyondae han'guk pangsong sanop ui kyongjejok t'uksong e kwanhan yon'gu (Economic characteristics of the Korean broadcasting industry in the 1980s). *Ollon Munhwa Yon'gu* (Sogang Journal of Media and Culture), 10, 135–60.

Kim, Su-haeng (1993). 'Han'guk sahoe rul ottoke punsok hal kosinga?' (How to analyze the Korean society?) *Sahoe pip'yong*, 9, 386–401.

Korean Broadcasting System (1991). *KBS statistical handbook*. Seoul: KBS.

Kuznets, Paul W. (1977). *Economic growth and structure in the Republic of Korea*. New Haven: Yale University Press.

Morgan, Gareth (1986). *Images of organisation*. Newbury Park, CA: Sage.

Ohmae, Kenichi (1990). *The borderless world: Power and strategy in the interlinked economy*. New York: Harper Business.

Pangsong yon'gu (Journal of Broadcasting Research), 35 (Winter), 1994.

Richeri, Giuseppe (1986). 'Television from service to business: European tendencies and the Italian case'. In Drummond, P. and Patterson, R. (eds.). *Television in transition*. London: British Film Institute.

Sin, Yun-hwan (1993). 'Han'gugin ui che 3 segye t'uja' (Korean direct investment in the Third World countries). *Ch'angjak kwa pip'yong* (Creation and Criticism), 21(3), 303–23.

Steers, Richard M., **Shin, Yoo Keun** and **Ungson, Gerardo R.** (1989). *The chaebol: Korea's new industrial might*. New York: Harper Business.

Strange, Susan (1992). 'States, firms and diplomacy'. *International Affairs*, 68(1), 1–15.

Yoo, Sangjin and **Lee, Sang M.** (1986). 'Management style and practice of Korean chaebols'. *California Management Review*, 29(4), 95–110.

Yun, Ch'ang-bin and **Ch'on, Won-ju** (1994). '23 consortiums, 642 firms participated in spectrum scramble'. *Sinmun kwa pangsong* (Newspaper and Broadcasting), 284 (August), 49–61.

6

Television in Pakistan: An Overview

Seemi Naghmana Tahir

Structure and Background of Contemporary Television in Pakistan

On 29 October 1963, a governmental conference recommended that television should be set up in Pakistan with the objectives of informing, educating and entertaining the audience. As there was a dictatorial regime in Pakistan at that time, an additional purpose of television was to project the policies and personalities of the then rulers (Nasir, 1993).

The Nippon Electric Company (NEC) of Japan got the contract to establish two television stations (then called Pilot Stations), one at Lahore and the other at Dhaka. They were to run these stations entirely on their own and a representative of the Government of Pakistan was supposed to monitor their performance (Nasir, 1993).

The first TV studio was in the premises of the Radio Pakistan building, Lahore. It was a make-shift arrangement, there were no recording arrangements, everything was live and it had about three hours of transmission every day. The NEC employed Pakistanis from the private sector, especially those who had some experience in radio journalism. This continued for a month, and after that the second pilot station at Dhaka came into existence. On 25 December 1964, President Ayub Khan inaugurated the second pilot station, and on the very first day 40 commercials were screened (Zia, 1994).

The stations in Dhaka and Lahore continued to function and in March 1967 the government established a Television Training School at Chaklala, Rawalpindi, which, after a few months, became a full-fledged TV station. The fourth TV station was at Karachi, coming on air in November 1967. In 1974 two more stations were established at Peshawar and Quetta. In the same year the first satellite link was established, and the stations were linked to broadcast programmes simultaneously.

In 1964 the total area covered was only 1 per cent of the country, with only two stations at Lahore and Dhaka. This progressed by 1988 to five stations and 29 transmitters, covering 35.47 per cent of the total area of Pakistan. The population covered in 1964 was only 9.32 per cent, but by 1988 it had grown to 86.39 per cent. The number of viewers is, however, only about 12 million due to the limits of electrification and the high costs of sets. The total number of sets is estimated to be 1.5 million. Colour transmission started in Pakistan in 1976 and now all programmes are produced in colour. Pakistan entered the satellite age in 1972 by commissioning the earth station at Deha Mandro near Karachi.

Pakistan Television–1

Today there are five linked stations working in the country, four in the provincial capitals and one in the federal capital. The number of transmitters working at present in 32, and between them they cover 87 per cent of the population and about 36 per cent of the land area of the country (Nasir, 1993, p. 21).

The five Pakistan Television (PTV) Centres and the Rebroadcast Stations in the country average more than 82 hours of broadcasting each week, not taking into account live sports coverage, the coverage of festivals, etc. The total commercial time was 1,282 hours during 1993–94 (Orient/McCann, 1993, p. 59).

In the ensuing years satellite transmission was used sparingly to broadcast special live programmes like cricket and hockey matches. However, the scene changed drastically in 1991 when Shalimar Television Network (STN), a semi-private TV channel, began operating by telecasting CNN round the clock to viewers of Islamabad first, and then to viewers in Lahore and Karachi. Peshawar and Quetta, the other two provincial capitals, were to be added to the list later.

On 26 November 1992, another channel of official television, PTV2, started. Reserved largely for educational purposes, this third channel transmits for seven hours daily, offering mainly educational programmes along with repeats of PTV1's popular programmes. It covers about 56 per cent of the population and may also be seen in 36 other countries through satellite. Following this development, the private acquisition of dish antennas began, initially slowly, but soon increasing in pace. According to market research, about 225 dish antenna receivers were being sold every month by 1991. The prices ranged between 1,000 to 12,000 US dollars. Today the prices have gone down to 350 US dollars and, according to one estimate, there are 25,000 dish antenna receivers in Karachi alone. So, television in Pakistan has proved to be a viable and profitable medium, free from financial attachment to the government (Yousaf, 1990, p. 21). However, perhaps more significant than the development of stations are the achievements of outstanding individuals who are working within the limitations imposed by policies and technology. The performance of television cannot be assessed as a phenomenon isolated from the culture that nourishes it, for culture is the manifestation of the social, economic and political relations that exist within any society.

Television and radio mainly project the ruling party's views and opinions. News, talk shows, and national programmes are all in favour of the current government's policy, as is usual in Third World democracies. The introduction of the second channel, STN, however, brought a change, for STN shows mostly imported entertainment, sports, and locally-produced musical programmes.

As compared to many neighbouring South Asian nations, TV ownership in Pakistan is high. This is because Pakistan opted for television as a medium of mass information and entertainment over a quarter of a century ago, which was way ahead of its neighbours. This early start has given television in Pakistan a good start in terms of expertise, talent and technical competitiveness (Orient/McCann, 1993).

PTV–Information Front

Given the recent situation of five news broadcasting centres with bulletins in English, Urdu and regional languages, reporters and cameramen posted in many cities with outside broadcast facilities, plus a large staff and computerised equipment, PTV is a long way from the situation in 1964 when there was a single station in

Lahore with one newsman who produced two news broadcasts and three weekly programmes. There was no regular news service, no cameramen, not even a typist, and no question of a photo service or a picture library. The first few days of television news were radio news read in front of a camera (Samdani, 1984). But despite the technical and policy restrictions, TV in the 1960s remained a credible medium. In 1970 the decade of development ended in disaster. Television's role during the tragedy of 1971 left much to be desired, despite the fact that it tried to lift the nation's sagging spirits.

Political coverage began in 1970 with the election broadcasts by leaders of political parties. PTV's political coverage expanded in the next couple of years to show a trilogy of interviews by foreign journalists with Sheikh Mujib, Mr. Bhutto and Mrs. Indira Gandhi, followed later by a documentary on Lenin (Yousaf, 1990).

Technically, PTV took a giant step forward when it made its first live satellite transmission from Australia of a test match between Pakistan and Australia. The vitality that television showed in the 1970s can be attributed to two facts. First, it was the producer who ran the show and bureaucratic control was confined to administration. Second, the production staff were relatively young and free from the constraints that experience can produce. For instance, in 1974, the average age of relatively senior TV employees was 29 years.

Deterioration set in soon after General Zia's midnight coup on 5 July 1977. The first directive issued by the Ministry of Information implied that PTV would continue to enjoy full powers of freedom. But within a few months the military regime showed its true colours; with the result that television workers at all stations, except Karachi, went on strike on 16 February 1978 in support of their long standing demands. On 17 February, 28 workers were arrested and on 19 February, six of them were sentenced to one year's detention and 15 lashes by a summary military court. The message was loud and clear: 'instant justice'.

From then PTV 'walked on all fours' for a full decade. General Zia's regime marked a particularly dark chapter in the history of Pakistani media and was characterised by an almost total disregard for the concept of freedom of expression. The period was marked by the General's crude use of the electronic media for projecting himself and attacking his opponents. Objective analysis and opposing view points were completely forbidden (Yousaf, 1990).

A Wave of Relief

A remarkable change however took place in media policy after the 1985 non-party elections when Mohammed Khan Junejo's government was formed. The right of the media to criticise the government and the discontinuation of the press advice system were new departures. Similarly Ms Bhutto's election manifesto had promised a completely free media which entailed disbanding the National Press Trust, ending the press advice system, removing the controls on advertisements and newsprint quotas, and a free radio and television. After coming to power in 1988 it seemed that her government was serious about implementing its declared media policy and was slowly working towards its implementation. Even if sufficient coverage was not given to the opposition, at least their faces could be seen and their voices could be heard on the electronic media. But the situation reversed when the government changed once more.

PTV Coverage of Elections

A barometer of the changing times is the quality of coverage given to the few elections held in this country. Although PTV was only six years old then, the 1970 pre-election programmes and live transmission of results were handled more professionally than any other that followed. Presenters communicated a degree of tension and enthusiasm and the pre-election coverage devoted equal time to the leaders of all political parties.

However, in 1977, while covering the election campaigns of both the Pakistan People's Party (PPP) and the Pakistan National Alliance (PNA), PTV followed a strongly discriminatory policy: opposition leaders could be seen but not heard! That is, the speeches of PPP leaders were recorded with sound and those of PNA leaders without. After protests, other PPP leaders were also silenced. The next challenge came in the 1988 general elections.

PTV got off to a partisan start by keeping the medium out of bounds for the opposition, while continuing to show the contesting 'caretakers' (Yousaf, 1990).

Saeed (1988) examined the content of the 9 o'clock news over a period of 10 days during the 1988 general election. The total news time of main bulletins (excluding sports and commercial news) over that period was 195 minutes. The news was divided into four parts.

1. Government personalities
2. Domestic events
3. National Assembly
4. International news

The percentage of total news time coverage given to Government personalities came to 57, of which the Prime Minister got 21 per cent, the President received 10 per cent, parliamentarians, governors, diplomats and other officials also included in the list of government personalities received 3 per cent. One per cent of total coverage was devoted to diplomats and 2 per cent to other political personalities. The news did not include a single reference to opposition parties. The second component was domestic news. This part included local news, like bomb blasts, riots, accidents, etc., which covered only 1 per cent of the total coverage; while coverage of national events like seminars and conferences received 5 per cent of available time. The third part consisted of National Assembly news, the 'space' given to this subject was 16 per cent. International news was the last part and it grabbed a share of 20 per cent of the total news time. Thus, the study suggests that only a share of 6 per cent was given to hundreds of important 'local' economic and social events happening every day in Pakistan's large cities.

Democracy in PTV

In 30 years, PTV, though for brief periods, was democratised three times. The first time was during the regime of Yahyah Khan who had, at least prior to the 1970 elections, no stake in the political race. The second liberalisation came during the early days of the first PPP government. However, following the uproar over the screening of the film report on the surrender of the armed forces in Dhaka, PTV retreated to the safety of rhetoric in its news broadcasts. The third brief spell lasted from December 1988 to February 1989. Successive governments in Pakistan have liberalised the media, or left it alone in their early days of power, cracking down as soon as the first serious challenge to their authority came along. Heavy doses of propaganda, whether of party or ideology, have usually followed.

Freedom of Creative Expression

All governments, with the exception of General Zia's, were content to control news broadcasts alone. Entertainment programmes remained outside the purview of propaganda. Within this freedom of creative expression, excellent plays, cultural programmes and documentaries were produced in the 1960s and 1970s. In 1976, for the UN Decade of the Woman, a bold series of plays, *Haxxa Ke-Naam*, was broadcast; Naheed Siddiqui's classical demonstrations in *Payal* brought a delightful sense of rhythm to the medium; and the *Zia Mohiyuddin Show* set a new trend in entertainment (Yousaf, 1990).

Pakistan Television Academy

In order to keep abreast with the latest techniques and trends, PTV has established an academy (Ministry of Information, 1993–94). The Academy has been created to achieve the educational and developmental goals of PTV. It collaborates with training institutions abroad in the fields of broadcasting development, training, research, reference and feedback. The Academy also arranges basic courses for new entrants, refresher courses, seminars and workshops for in-service employees, and is now in a position to extend training to foreign students. It has plans for instructor exchange with international institutions, which will improve the standard of the instructional staff.

The PTV Academy also arranges regional courses in co-operation with the Asia Pacific Institute for Broadcasting Development

(AIBD), Kuala Lumpur, Malaysia and Sender Fries Berlin (SFB), Germany. In addition to its normal training activities, the PTV Academy has also been given the task of planning and setting up a computer network in PTV. It also offers training in this very important field of technology. It also produces model/experimental productions based on research and folklore history. Programmes like *Tansen*, a musical drama, and *Mehmil*, a musical serial depicting the folk-lore of Pakistan, have won acclaim in Pakistan and abroad.

Dramâ–A Success Story

When TV first came to Pakistan, plays used to be beamed from temporary studios set up hurriedly in Lahore. They lacked even the most basic facilities for quality productions. Now, five large stations with modern buildings and ultra-modern equipment are served by a powerful microwave link. In daily transmission schedules, plays are more popular than even musical or quiz shows. That is why PTV regularly broadcasts more than seven plays a week in Urdu, besides plays in regional languages. During the last 30 years, PTV has transmitted several thousand plays and the popularity of the teleplay in Pakistan lies in the fact that even when there is strict control and policy limitations ways have to be found for expression which is not possible in news, current affairs, or in talk shows; drama is perhaps a more flexible genre. In the words of Aslam Azhar (1984a):

> There are many facilities within the state controlled frontiers of tolerance to make social comment. The teleplay in particular is a form of art through which one can speak between the lines, and in the days of strong state control some years ago, we in television from every station, were able to say and do a great deal (p. 50).

Beyond the technical landmarks PTV achieved in the first few years, it did much more. It was successful in creating a powerful platform for cultural expression. While reflecting national tastes and taboos, it made a genuine attempt to develop them. PTV's *Khuda Ki Basti* was in fact an affirmation of the fact that TV drama could do more than entertain viewers. Shaukat Siddiqui's novel was a disturbing and starkly real account of ordinary people. This serial was also a reminder that television could be a powerful agent in terms of raising social awareness.

Television's first serial was *Taaley Thalley*, written by Ashfaq Ahmad and produced by Nisar Hussain. It helped television to build up consistent and loyal audiences despite a situation where inflation was rising quickly. People continued to demand luxury items like televisions because things were happening on the screen. Television was offering both entertaining and bold fare.

Humour and Satire

While Zia Mohyuddin brought style to the concept of entertainment on television through his immensely popular show, PTV's *Mantorama* was the first attempt to visually interpret one of the sub-continent's most vocal and controversial Urdu writers, Saadat Hassan Manto. But the first programme which really explored television's true entertainment potential was *Alif Noon*. Alif (Kamal Ahmad Rizvi) and Noon (Nanah) were television's first fully rounded characters. That was the time when TV was not shy of originality. The establishment was able to laugh at itself. Shoib Hashmi's *Gup Shows* and *Tall Matol* tested the limits of tolerance. The targets of his satire of the 1970s included federal ministers, but by the 1980s the level of tolerance had fallen and so, also, had the range of targets, to policemen and custom officials. It is an indication of the times that programmes lampooning them, such as *Fifty Fifty* and *Sho Sha*, were applauded for their courage.

Limitations on Creative Expression

The Zia regime's policy of Islamisation intruded into the area of programming. Policy imperatives were outlined by the newly appointed Minister of Information Maulan Mohammed Azam Farooqi. Ideological changes included 'proper dress' for women appearing on television, no singers and no film starlets. Seven out of the 15 programmes announced for the new quarter were religious floor shows. During 1987–88, religious programmes accounted for almost 8 per cent of total transmission time, compared to 7.7 per cent for dramas (Yousaf, 1990).

Thirty years is not a considerable amount of time in the life of any complex artistic audio-visual medium, and yet, despite some shortcomings, many fine productions have been produced which have introduced a large number of talented men and women of great promise.

Music Programmes

For the last 30 years PTV has been contributing substantially to musical programmes. These programmes have played a major role in the field of music by introducing and encouraging budding musical talent. In the beginning, the majority of singers who used to appear regularly in TV music programmes did not differ much from those on radio, except that the singers now faced TV cameras in addition to the microphones. The use of attractive sets and colourful backdrops came much later. These clearly added to the entertainment value of programmes and there was a change which was visible in all fields of musical expression–light, folk and classical (Hussain, 1984).

A major outcome of these technical innovations has been an increase in the range and size of the audience. It is to the credit of television that through its attractive and entertaining programmes of *ghazals* and *geets*, it opened new doors of sophisticated entertainment for ordinary music lovers. The entire pattern of music listening changed and spread from a small circle of admirers of ghazals and classical music to a large spectrum of society, almost revolutionising the taste of the ordinary music lover.

During this period PTV also experimented with musical programmes which instantly became popular with viewers. For example, the use of old film songs in the programme *Silver Jubilee* which were sung by young amateurs. Another experiment which turned out to be successful was in *Sur Ka Safar*. Tahira Sayyed, a young semi-classical singer, sang with her mother, Malika Pukhraj, allowing the producer to blend the old with the new. The popularity of the *ghazals* and *geets* sung by Mehdi Hassan, Ghulam Ali, Nayyera Noor and Abeda Perveen in the programme *Meri Passand* continues and their cassettes still have considerable sales. The rise to fame of many singers of today is mainly due to PTV; of the younger ones, many came into prominence either in Sohail Rana's series of musical programmes for children or in Anwar Maqsood's stage show *Silver Jubilee*. So far, although progress in the field of music on television remains slow, despite the restrictions which have been imposed on it, PTV has played a substantial role in patronising the art of music by encouraging new talent. PTV has contributed a great deal in bringing various cultural dimensions to the small screen.

PTV and Education

Television was introduced in Pakistan to promote awareness, to develop a consciousness about the cultural heritage, social and economic growth of the country, and to provide a direct linkage with the world around. Television was at last considered an imperative for social change, apart from its role as an effective medium of education, entertainment and information. Speaking on the objectives of PTV, Azhar (1984b) said:

> For the unskilled and the jobless there will be programmes to teach them a vocation. For the peasant and the farmer there will be instruction in the use of new and improved techniques; for the illiterate, television lessons on literacy. The use of television will be geared to the objectives of the country's education policy (p. 47).

Although PTV could not set new standards in news and information coverage due to policy limitations, it played a substantial role in promoting social awareness and fought against illiteracy. In a country like Pakistan, where most of the population is illiterate, the role of television as an educational institution is of real importance. Promotion of education has always been a priority. For many years adult education programmes were broadcast regularly, and adult education centres were established in rural areas equipped with television sets where adults were persuaded to and watch adult literacy programmes.

There are various types of educational programmes on PTV, including special programmes for children, quiz shows, debates, and stage shows for young people. Special documentary programmes are also produced on the history, tradition and role of different important educational institutions. Programmes on religious issues and teachings are a regular part of transmissions.

Pakistan has used television to safeguard its ideological boundaries. Television has played a very important and powerful role in strengthening national identity and in national integration; for example, through programmes on national history and national heroes which are frequently shown.

Its instructional programmes, which include physical education, calligraphy, fine art, legal consultation, and education about traffic rules, are transmitted regularly. It also includes various programmes to boost civic sense and lectures on the different courses taught at Allama Iqbal Open University have been a regular feature of educational programming.

More recently PTV has stepped up its policy of educational broadcasting by commissioning another channel, Educational Television (ETV) or PTV2, particularly for educational purposes.

In 1988, the Government of Pakistan requested the Government of Japan to set up an educational TV channel to reduce the literacy problem in Pakistan. ETV was a part of the government's Seventh five-year national development plan and was divided into two phases (Mustafa, 1993). The first phase for the education channel was completed in 1992 with a capital outlay of Rs. 627,000 million, including the Japanese grant-in-aid of Rs. 507,000 million. PTV2's first phase comprised an ETV centre at Islamabad and 16 rebroadcast stations, covering 56 per cent of the population and 24 per cent of the area of the country (Haque, 1992). PTV2 started functioning on 26 November 1992. Its basic aim is to help eradicate illiteracy by televising education programmes in basic science and medicine, the setting up of small business industries, computer working and applications, agricultural information, population welfare, quizzes, and the importance of pre-school education. It also provides facilities to meet the growing needs of the Allama Iqbal Open University and planning agencies such as the Population Planning Division and the Agriculture Division (Orient/McCann, 1993; see Ministry of Information, 1993–94 for further background).

As PTV operates on a terrestrial microwave network which can transmit only one channel, the satellite transmission system has been chosen for ETV. TV signals are beamed via a transponder leased from Asiasat, and thus programmes can be transmitted all over Pakistan regardless of terrain (Mustafa, 1993). In addition to the educational aspect of PTV it also broadcasts popular drama series/serials, music programmes and sports programmes. News is broadcast in Arabic, English and Urdu. PTV2 is hooked onto the main PTV national network, both during morning transmission and in the late evening, and thus carries PTV's main programmes over Asiasat to more than 30 countries of the Far East and the Middle East. Its regular transmission is over 11 hours per day.

Shalimar Television Network

A third channel, STN, has been operating for the last five years. It was started as the result of a government decision to have a channel in the private sector. In 1990 the first station was created in Islamabad. In future there are plans to open up stations in other major cities (Orient/McCann, 1993). Most audiences have access to three television channels: the wholly state-owned PTV, ETV (recently started), and the partly privately-owned STN. The latter shows mostly canned programmes which are of no particular attraction to the adult viewer. Children, however, are overwhelmingly attracted to colourful cartoons, and the adventure and detective films run by STN, while programmes on world politics and economics and local issues draw 'serious' audiences towards PTV. However, the regular 9.30 slot on STN is very popular amongst housewives attracted to the Urdu feature film run on alternate days on STN. As a result, STN has set a different prime time pattern to that of PTV and has been able to capture a sizable proportion of the television advertising budget, but it still has a long way to go before it becomes a real threat to PTV.

Network Television Marketing (NTM), the marketing agency for STN, carried out audience surveys and in a random survey 200 readers were asked which of the two television channels (PTV and STN) provided better entertainment. The results indicated that a staggering 48 per cent chose PTV, 19 per cent voted in favour of both the channels while the other 15 per cent rejected both on the entertainment scale (Orient/McCann, 1993). Another study conducted by final year students of the Institute of Business Administration, Karachi, in March 1991, had shown less disparity in the preference of PTV over STN. This suggests a substantial proportion of viewership for STN and lends weight to the argument that Pakistani viewers want to see more entertainment on television.

The 1991 survey also revealed which type of programme was preferred on each channel. Most viewers listed superior English and Urdu feature films as their main reason for watching STN, with the comedy hour as a popular second. There was also a general consensus that STN's programming was more in tune with what viewers wanted to watch. PTV's strength lay in its drama productions, which respondents felt gave the channel a stronger cultural significance. Although the news *Khabarnama* is the same on both the channels, more people watch it on PTV than on STN. The audience's view is that the *Khabarnama* broadcast quality is better on PTV, which may be due to the fact that STN relays this programme while it is aired directly by PTV.

Satellite Transmission–Another Challenge

The social and cultural impact of satellite transmission began to emerge in Pakistan in November 1991 when CNN was made available to Pakistani viewers. Prior to the availability of CNN, Pakistan's official television, PTV, was broadcasting a daily programme of only about seven hours. In comparison, STN offered CNN transmissions, which in the beginning were round the clock and uncensored. It introduced a sizable number of Pakistanis to international standards in television programming. Later on, due to the change of Government, STN was instructed to censor some of the programmes, especially entertainment and fashion news and features. Consequently, there began a wave of acquiring dish antenna receivers and to watch CNN uncensored. Before that dish antennas were rare in the country. Now a wider choice is available to Pakistani viewers through dish antennas, including ZEE TV, BBC, Star Plus, Prime Sports, Music Television, and CNN. The increasing viewership of international media has become a challenge for PTV.

To gain some indication of the impact of satellite transmission in the field of television a small pilot survey was conducted in Karachi during the first week of January 1993 by Professor Nisar Ahmad Zuberi of the Department of Mass Communication, University of Karachi.

Among these respondents, 40 per cent revealed that they were watching more TV today as compared to 1990 when satellite transmissions were not available. About 27 per cent said that the reason for their increased viewing was the quality of international programmes, more entertainment and more choice. Reviewing the quality of programmes beamed through satellites, 48 per cent rated it as 'good'. However, 32 per cent were of the view that such programmes were overly explicit and thus were bad morally. A clear majority of 70 per cent of the respondents agreed, however, that these programmes were much needed (Zuberi, 1993).

Contemporary World Television

In the world generally, international television has played an important role in the formation of public opinion in safeguarding particular political and economic interests. The US and allied European countries have often claimed that they owe their success in the cold war partly to television. This powerful medium has not only managed to establish new markets for products by means of advertising, it has also propagated and spread its culture to be incorporated into a new international culture.

The democratic system derived from a few capitalist states could not be implemented in developing countries. In that context, capitalist nations found an opportunity to dominate the weaker nations. The division between prosperous and non-prosperous cultures is widening. For example, the once modest expenditure required for the purchase of radio has now been replaced by the demand for television, but at a greater cost. In this way the capital growth of the underdeveloped countries is being exploited by the developed nations. This neo-capitalist mentality which has established powerful techniques of advertising for products increases frustration and a feeling of inferiority amongst the underdeveloped and undeveloped nations.

PTV in the International Scene

PTV's International Relations Department was created as a separate directorate in 1972. It encompasses a variety of functions of which the following are among the more important:

1. *Bilateral Agreements*: The Government of Pakistan signs various cultural, economic and scientific agreements with other countries from time to time. PTV, on its own part, undertakes to expand its bilateral professional co-operation with sister TV networks and enters into various kinds of understanding at official levels with selected countries. The main thrust, however, is the exchange of programmes and news, facilitating the exchange of professional teams, exploring co-production opportunities and training in professional disciplines.
2. *Activities of Broadcasting Unions*: PTV works in close collaboration with other national broadcasters to keep down its costs and to share experiences. 'Broadcasting unions, of which ABU [the Asian Broadcasting Union] is of principal concern to us, provide an umbrella for the broadcasting community of the Asian and Pacific regions' (Ministry of Information, 1993–94, p. 23). Collective bargaining for rights of international sporting events, news and programme exchange, co-productions and training, are some of the principal areas of ABU's activities.
3. *Marketing PTV Programmes*: In recent years, the demand for PTV programmes has been growing, although on the home video market front most of it is pirated and this poses problems. PTV is nevertheless engaged in a sales effort to various network and cable TV companies, with some degree of success. Despite the language barrier, PTV's programmes have been sold in the US, the UK, Saudi Arabia, China, Sharjah, Turkey, Nepal and Mauritius. Efforts are also afoot to syndicate PTV programmes in other countries where the ethnic population of the Indian sub-continent is present in sizable numbers. For example, in January 1995, BBC2 in the UK showed a popular, recently produced PTV drama series, *Marvi*, with English subtitles. It was the story of a young Sindhi girl, who after achieving a university degree becomes a victim to the age old feudal system of her village, and the way she and her family overcome the hurdles of tradition and stereotypes.
4. *Projection of Pakistan*: PTV programmes are a way of projecting Pakistan abroad, as documentaries and cultural programmes are regularly supplied to missions through the

External Publicity Wing of the Ministry of Information. For some years now, 'PTV has been an active contributor to the SAARC Programme for Audio Visual Exchange (SAVE) . . . and since 1987, 19 PTV programmes have been broadcast over the national networks of SAARC member countries' (Ministry of Information, 1993–94, p. 23).

5. *Procurement of Foreign and Canned Programmes*: About one-fifth of PTV programmes are sourced from abroad, 'comprising series, serials, documentaries, sports, specials, children's cartoons and animated programmes. These are procured through various American, European and Asian sources' (Ministry of Information, 1993–94, p. 23). Efforts are also being made to dub more documentaries, in particular, into Urdu to increase their viewership and some of these have already been televised.
6. *Participation in International Festivals and Competitions*: PTV's International Relations Division regularly selects relevant programmes from PTV productions and enters them in international competitions. PTV now has the distinction of having been awarded 26 different international awards, while some of its programmes have received more than one award on the same occasion. (Ministry of Information, 1993–94, p. 23.)
7. *Co-productions*: PTV has undertaken co-productions with various national and international institutions in the fields of drama and documentaries. A total of 13 international co-productions have been completed so far.

Television in Pakistan: A Review

The media of dominating states have always preferred political slogans to objective truths, enabling them to target the weaker nations. Now that the world's economy has been monopolised by developed countries, its television has come forward with new versions to use against the Third World countries, which tend to weaken the position of the underdeveloped and technologically backward. They are being labelled, amongst other things, as fundamentalists, terrorists, drug traffickers, and human rights violators. With this type of language, the developed countries are looking after their own economic interests, and in this process television is a powerful weapon. Within this global context, PTV has consistently had to address the problem of its own identity and role. Throughout its existence it has had to negotiate its position in conditions of considerable political and social turmoil and to reconcile pressures from a succession of governments with a concern for the needs of the subordinate groups in society. This task was particularly difficult when semi-literate, semi-tribal, semi-industrial and semi-agricultural values were in conflict. In addition, PTV has sought to achieve programme qualities consistent with international standards and its performance in this respect is demonstrated by its increasing international programme sales. PTV claims considerable success in achieving its aspirations, a view strongly endorsed by this author.

Notes

1. The editors acknowledge the valuable contribution of Naeema Farooqi in providing additional material for this chapter.

References

Azhar, A. (1984a). 'Frontiers of Tolerance'. *Star Special Report*. December.

———. (1984b). 'Television and social responsibility'. *PTV Time Traveller 1964–1984: Star Special Report*. December.

Hanif, M. (1990). 'Good times, bad times'. In Ahmed M. (ed.). *25 years of PTV*. Islamabad: Media Home.

Haque, I. (ed.). (1992). *Pakistan Television Corporation: Inauguration of PTV2*. Karachi: Pakistan Television Corporation Ltd (Central Sales Office).

Hussain, T. (1984). 'Comparing notes'. *PTV Time Traveller 1964–1984: Star Special Report*. December.

Ministry of Information (1993–94). Reference file on PTV. (Unpublished document).

Mustafa, H. (1993). 'Evolution of educational television'. *Daily News International*, Islamabad, 3 September.

Nasir, A. (1993). 'History of television broadcasting in Pakistan'. *Daily News International*, Islamabad, 3 September.

Orient/McCann (1993). *Pakistan Advertising Scene 93*. Karachi: Orient Advertising (Private) Ltd. (Market Research Department).

Saeed, S. (1988). 'Khabarnama'. In '40 years of mass media—A special report'. *Daily Dawn*, 24 January (Sunday).

Samdani, Z. (1984). 'This was the news'. *PTV Time Traveller: Star Special Report.* December.

Yousaf, Z. (1990). 'A jubilee of hits and misses'. In Munir, A. (ed.). *25 years of PTV*. Islamabad: Media Home.

Zia, R. (1994). *PTV ka safra: 1964 to 1969*. PTV (Original script of the programme broadcast on 26 November 1994 to mark the thirtieth anniversary of PTV).

Zuberi, A.N. (1993). *Social and cultural impact of satellite broadcasting in Pakistan*. AMIC Seminar, Singapore, 1–3 February.

7

Structures of Television in Singapore

Mark A. Hukill

Introduction

Broadcasting in Singapore can be characterised as having evolved through two major periods of operation since its inception in the early 1960s. These two periods correspond respectively with the structural arrangements of the strictly government-owned operations of Radio Television Singapore (RTS) in the 1960s and 1970s, and the Singapore Broadcasting Corporation (SBC) of the 1980s and early 1990s. As of October 1994, broadcasting in Singapore has entered what may be described as a third phase of structural arrangement and operating characteristics, through the creation of Singapore International Media (SIM) as the holding company for government and mixed-ownership broadcast operating companies. These structural changes, which are part of a nominal privatisation plan for government-owned broadcasting in Singapore, are in fact an attempt to adjust the staid monopolistic operations in order to become more competitive, not only for audiences in Singapore but also internationally. These changes are in direct response to significant changes world-wide for choice and delivery of programming on an international level, as well as in response to pressures locally to provide a greater choice of programming for viewers in Singapore.

Television broadcasting in Singapore, as in many other countries, remains a predominantly government-owned and operated affair. However, in Singapore, the former national monopoly television broadcaster SBC, with, until October 1994, its nine radio stations and three television channels, had evolved into a somewhat autonomous entity providing at least a semblance of viewer and listener choice. As a government monopoly for broadcasting within Singapore, SBC was facing new competitive challenges from outside the small geographic borders of Singapore in the form of both radio and television broadcasts which could be received from neighbouring Malaysia and Indonesia, as well as internationally via satellite. New commercial broadcast ventures in each of these countries have altered the pattern of programming, especially in terms of scheduling, formats and variety. Television does not face the same intense level of competition from outside Singapore as does radio, although this is increasing. The state-run television stations of Malaysia, RTM1 and RTM2, as well as the quasi-private station TV3, can be received in Singapore free-to-air. This competition forced SBC, in part, towards a strategic rethinking of its programme fare. The possible addition of a privately run television station on Batam Island, Indonesia, which will also be receivable in Singapore, will add to the competitive pressure, despite the free-to-air monopoly for broadcasting by the successor companies of SBC now held under SIM.

In addition, technological advances, broadening viewer demands, and international broadcasting, especially via satellite, have also forced broadcasters and the government towards an expansion of available services. This has been undertaken in the form of a three-channel, ultra high frequency (UHF) subscription service and advance planning for a cable television system to begin installation nationwide in mid-1995.

Changes in broadcasting structures in Singapore have been encapsulated in the Singapore Broadcasting Authority Act 1994, which has created a separate regulatory authority for overseeing broadcasting, and the licensing and regulation of broadcast activities within Singapore. This law also serves as an enabling legislation to nominally privatise the successor companies of SBC, most notably the Television Corporation of Singapore (TCS) which was established on 1 October 1994 to operate two of the three former SBC television channels.

Through the new legislation, which still requires a licence for all broadcast apparatus, Singapore continues to effectively enforce a ban on television receive-only (TVRO) satellite dishes as a commercial and social protectionist measure. While technological advances will see to it that such a ban is unenforceable in the future, Singapore is taking great care in the meantime to protect and strengthen its local broadcasters through an aggressive expansion programme, corporate reorganisation, and the addition of new services. A historical overview is provided first, which gives rise to an analysis of the new structural phase of television broadcasting in Singapore.

Development of Television Broadcasting in Singapore

Television broadcasting in Singapore began with a pilot monochrome service in February 1963, which led to the beginning of regular transmissions in April 1963. By November of the same year a second broadcast channel has also begun operating.

In August 1963, when Singapore became part of Malaysia, its broadcasting service was amalgamated with the Malaysian broadcasting service into one entity. But this merger was short-lived as Singapore separated from Malaysia in 1965. Subsequently, television broadcasting became a state-run operation under the Singapore Department of Broadcasting within the Ministry of Culture. The Department was more popularly known as Radio Television Singapore or RTS. With Singapore's Independence in August 1965, RTS, similar to the policies of many newly independent nations, was given the broad mandate to help in bringing about the nation's development.

Television broadcasting soon took on new dimensions with the completion of a TV Centre in 1966 which was furnished with modern production equipment. By 1967, an educational service for schoolchildren was added. Transmission time was also extended so that both broadcast channels were operating six hours on weekdays and 11 hours on weekends.

With advancing technology and the Republic's rapidly expanding economic base, RTS was in a position to continuously tap the latest modern communications technology to enhance the technical quality of its broadcasting service. Singapore installed its first satellite earth station (Intelsat A) on Sentosa Island in 1971. Reception of satellite broadcast signals, retransmitted through RTS, made its debut in 1974. In the same year, partial colour television transmission, using the 625–PAL colour system, was introduced. Full colour transmission on both broadcast channels began in 1976.

By 1980, Singapore was on its way to an economic expansion, which was rapidly transforming the island nation, led by government and multinational industrial and commercial enterprises. The government was investing heavily into its own corporate operations and soon large international scale operations in the form of a container port; airline, banking and finance organisations; telecommunications; and many others were growing rapidly. This economic transformation helped provide a catalyst to change the broadcasting authority, RTS, from a government department into a semi-autonomous corporate structure.

SBC in the 1980s and early 1990s

In 1980, RTS became SBC, a statutory board under the purview of the Ministry of Communication and Information. The aim of SBC was to improve the quality of its services through the use of the latest broadcast technology and the upgrading of the content and presentation of its own productions. These changes came about through the implementation of the Singapore Broadcasting Act of 1979, modified in 1985, which empowered SBC to:

1. provide television and sound broadcasting services for disseminating information, education and entertainment;
2. exercise licensing and regulatory functions in respect of the sale and use of television receivers and broadcasting receiving apparatus; and
3. act as the national representative of Singapore with respect to international matters related to broadcasting.

In line with SBC's stated aim of enhancing the quality of its services through the exploitation of modern technology, new developments in television broadcasting proceeded at a fast pace. In 1980, television enhanced its role as a national provider of news and information with the introduction of electronic news gathering. In the same year, voice dubbing and subtitling made its debut, bringing to viewers foreign programmes in English, Malay, Mandarin, and Tamil—the four official languages in Singapore.

Television continued to play an increasingly significant role as an information provider through the introduction of SBCText in

1983. This teletext service provided viewers with the latest information on financial news, share prices, flight information, shopping tips, as well as general information and sports news. By 1989, this service had a competitor when a videotex system, Teleview (provided by the telecommunications authority, Singapore Telecom, using UHF frequencies), was started. As a result, SBCText upgraded its services and changed names to INtv in 1992, with a system capable of delivering hundreds of screen pages of information to viewers through the vertical blanking interval on home TV sets.

In 1984, a third television broadcast channel was introduced by SBC. In addition to the two channels (Channels 5 and 8), the third channel (Channel 12) was specifically set up to help promote the arts and culture by providing entertainment programming in this area.

SBC also continued to air scholastic educational programmes directed at primary, secondary and pre-university students. Airing of educational television programmes began in 1967. The programmes were then produced by the Educational Television Service, an independent unit of the Ministry of Education, but the job was later taken over by the Curriculum Development Institute of Singapore (CDIS).

Initially, educational programmes catered to lower secondary school students, but was later extended to pre-university and primary school students. Subjects covered include science, mathematics, general studies, home economics, arts and crafts, phonics, and English literature. Subjects are conducted in four official languages, in accordance with the official multi-racial character of Singapore society. Educational programmes, until 1994, were broadcast on Mondays for about eight hours, from 8.00 AM to 4.00 PM, and repeated on Wednesday afternoons.

Selected live satellite feeds for broadcast retransmission have increased with the setting up of two TVRO satellite dishes at the broadcasting compound at Caldecott Hill. The TVROs, established in 1988 and 1990, automatically track satellites such as Intelsat, Asiasat, Palapa, and Gorizont over the Indian Ocean and Pacific Ocean regions. Selected news feeds sourced from a broad spectrum of the world's top television news agencies, including CNN, ITN, Visnews, Eurovision News and Trans World News, now form a selected part of the television news fare.

In continuing efforts to provide the best in broadcasting technical quality, SBC introduced stereo transmission on Channel 5 in 1990.

This was soon extended to the other two channels. The system adopted is the BBC-developed Near Instantaneously Companded Audio Multiplex system, or NICAM. About 10 per cent of programmes aired currently are available in stereo. The high cost of home reception equipment has, however, in part somewhat limited the viewing public's ability to receive broadcasts in stereo. Since only a small part of the programmes transmitted are in stereo, there is a perception among viewers that a NICAM-equipped television set may not be worthwhile.

As a monopoly broadcaster SBC had made substantial progress, reflected in the increase in its viewership and transmission hours (see Tables 7.1 and 7.2).

Daily viewership reached a record high of 2 million in 1992–93, as compared to 1.6 million in 1987–88. This is against a total

Table 7.1: Television Viewership

Audience Build–Average Daily Audience ('000)	
1987–88	1,556
1988–89	1,667
1989–90	1,745
1990–91	1,711
1991–92	2,070

Source: *SBC Annual Report*, 1992–93.

Table 7.2: TV Transmission (hours per week) 1981–1993

Year	*Hours per week*
1981	115
1982	115
1983	115
1984	132
1985	149.2
1986	155
1987	155
1988	156
1989	161
1990	172.4
1991–92	186.6
1992–93	198.8

Note: Channel 12 was introduced in 1984.

Sources: *Yearbook of Statistics*, 1992; *SBC Annual Report*, 1992–93.

population base of 2.8 million, as of 1992. Weekly transmission time jumped from an average of 115 hours in 1981, a year after SBC's establishment, to almost 200 hours in 1992. SBC has also succeeded in carving out an identity of its own by producing more local programmes, especially drama serials, in Mandarin as well as news, information and entertainment programmes in English. Locally-produced programmes have taken up an increasing share of transmission time, from 29 per cent in 1981–82 to nearly 36 per cent in 1992–93. Total air time for both entertainment and information programmes has increased steadily in the late 1980s and early 1990s (see Tables 7.3 and 7.4). Today, 99 per cent of all Singaporean households have at least one television.

Table 7.3: Television Entertainment Programmes (hours per year)

Year	*Hours*
1987–88	6,417
1988–89	6,630
1989–90	6,734
1990–91	7,607

Source: *SBC Annual Report*, 1990–91.

Table 7.4: Television Information Programmes (hours per year)

Year	*Hours*
1987–88	1,685
1988–89	1,836
1989–90	1,650
1990–91	2,075

Source: *SBC Annual Report*, 1990–91.

SBC was, until October 1994, a statutory board that ran its operations somewhat independently of day-to-day government affairs, similar in structure to the BBC of the United Kingdom. However, unlike the BBC which is largely autonomous of the government especially in areas of programme content, SBC's policies were determined directly by the Ministry of Information and the Arts, set up in 1990. The previous corporate structure of SBC (until October 1994) is provided in Figure 7.1. It was characterised by its corporate organisational lines but had remained largely bureaucratic in operation.

Figure 7.1: Organisation of the Singapore Broadcasting Corporation (prior to October 1994)

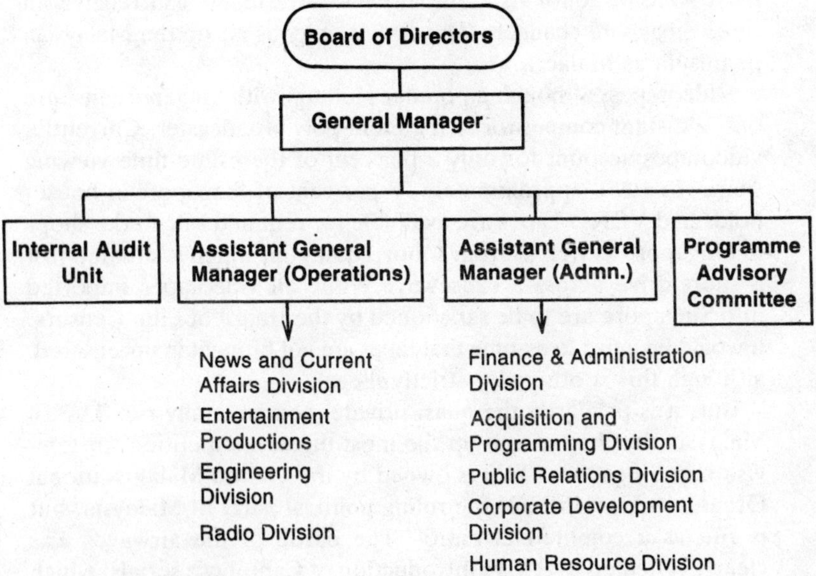

The government's plans to nominally privatise SBC came in the late 1980s as part of an overall economic restructuring plan of government-held enterprises. Singapore Telecom was the first to be privatised in late 1993, with 11 per cent of that company's equity sold in a public stock listing. This pattern is likely to be repeated when a percentage of the successor companies to SBC are also put to a public listing in 1995 or 1996. The government will, however, retain a controlling interest.

Challenges to the SBC Monopoly

Although television broadcasting origination in Singapore was a monopoly, SBC was not without its share of competitors. SBC faced increasing competition from three neighbouring channels, RTM1, RTM2, and quasi-private Malaysian station, TV3. In addition, one new free-to-air station (TV4) and a three-channel subscription news service are being developed in Malaysia. Singaporeans can receive all three current Malaysian channels free-to-air. SBC, in turn, has an appreciably large following in the southern most state of Johor in Malaysia, whose residents can receive all three Singapore channels. The signals carry as far up the Malaysian peninsula as Malacca.

Videotapes, although a popular medium with Singaporeans, are only a distant competitor to the monopoly broadcaster. Currently, videotapes account for only 2 per cent of the prime-time viewing share. In 1990, approximately 78 per cent of Singaporean households had VCRs. Tapes are available for rent and sale in the shops in Singapore as well as from Johor, Malaysia, which is situated just a short drive across a causeway. While all videotapes imported into Singapore are to be sanctioned by the Board of Film Censors, it would be naive to assume that tapes are not brought in uncensored, although this is otherwise strictly illegal.

But, it is primarily the quasi-private, commercially-run TV3 of Malaysia that has stirred up the most direct competition for television in Singapore. TV3 is owned by the United Malay National Organisation, (UMNO) the ruling political party of Malaysia, but is run as a commercial entity. The battle of the airwaves was clearly reflected by TV3's introduction of Cantonese serials, which seriously affected both RTM's and SBC's viewership. This compelled SBC to make some innovative changes in its programming. SBC introduced *One Plus One*, a Mandarin drama programme which started off as a combination of an SBC-produced drama and a Hong Kong drama, in the daily prime-time slot, five days a week. Overall, SBC has gradually increased its local drama programmes from two hours fortnightly in 1982 to 10 hours a week in 1992. Its efforts have paid off well and have enabled SBC to maintain its competitive edge above its neighbouring rivals. A majority of the audience share has since returned to the Singapore stations.

According to SBC, its two major channels, Channel 5 (broadcasting primarily in English) and Channel 8 (with predominantly Mandarin programmes) are ahead of their Malaysian competitors, with 50 per cent and 71 per cent of Singapore's population tuning in during some part of the broadcast day to each channel. Channel 12 has a 12 per cent share. RTM1 and RTM2 have 7 per cent and 3 per cent respectively, while viewership of TV3 has been reduced to only 1 per cent. TV3 disputes these figures, but there is no other independent audience share data available. It would, however, be wrong not to acknowledge the popularity of TV3 in Singapore, especially for foreign produced drama and comedy series not available on the Singapore channels.

A growing competitive threat to television in Singapore has come from direct satellite broadcasting which has whetted the appetite of Singapore's viewers for more instantaneous news and information, as well as a greater variety of entertainment programming. While direct satellite broadcasting to homes will not be allowed for Singaporeans in the near future, SBC first began to pander to audience's information needs with two hours of live CNN fare daily, one hour in the morning and the other hour in the evening, in 1991. The addition of CNN to the programming schedule was a direct result of the Gulf War in early 1991.

Singapore's financial institutions, as well as the general public, were without the instantaneous CNN feedback when the War broke out in January 1991. CNN was the first to announce the start of the international coalition operation world-wide. Singapore did not receive the news until nearly half a minute after most of the rest of the world. Its financial markets took a severe hit due to this delay. Soon, thereafter, the government allowed SBC to air CNN live for two hours per day. This was mainly for the benefit of Singapore's financial institutions, although the public was served as well. New regulations were quickly established that allowed certain organisations, primarily financial and banking institutions, to apply for a TVRO satellite dish licence in order to receive news more quickly. However, the ban on TVRO dishes for Singapore's citizens in general remains firmly intact as no licences can be procured for this equipment. The free-to-air retransmission of CNN was soon ended, however, when Singapore's subscription television service began in April 1992.

Besides the challenge arising from direct satellite broadcasting, increasingly affluent, better-educated and wider-travelled Singaporeans are driving the government to look at the possibility of relaxing the monopolistic control of broadcasting, as well as allowing the broadcasters themselves to exercise greater direct control of programming content. While no television broadcaster will be allowed to compete with the established free-to-air stations from within Singapore, several private operations are now using Singapore as a programme and satellite up-link hub to the region. These include Home Box Office (HBO) and Asian Business News (ABN). ESPN and MTV are also going to establish facilities in Singapore. This situation allows for Singapore to reach its stated goal of becoming a broadcasting hub for the region, without such programming and distribution falling outside the local broadcaster's control for the local market.

Audiences and Revenues of SBC till 1994

Pressures from international broadcasts which penetrate Singapore, new delivery technologies, as well as increasing viewer demands, are driving changes in the delivery and content of programming provided to the Singaporean audience. In the area of news, for example, daily satellite feeds from international sources are used selectively for the latest international news events. Round-the-clock news updates were provided for the first time during the Gulf War in 1991. This resulted in a record number of viewers for both the Chinese and English news. Daily viewership for the Chinese news soared to 773,000 while the English news audience rose dramatically to 225,000. These figures compare even more favourably with the annual averages of 472,000 and 96,000 respectively. The addition of computer generated three-dimensional animated graphics have enlivened the news bulletins, along with an attempt at less turgid presentation styles. The news programmes have been extended to two 30-minute programmes for the Mandarin and English news daily.

In the entertainment field, television broadcasting has acquired more foreign movies, dramas, comedy serials and game shows, while it has also continuously enhanced the quality of its own drama productions. Chinese drama serials have an average following of more than a million viewers, compared to 600,000 when they began in 1982.

Through the 1980s and early 1990s, serious attempts to enhance the quality of television services are reflected by the large investments in the latest broadcast technology (see Table 7.5).

SBC spent nearly S $100 million (US $60 million) in two years till 1993. These costs are, however, more than adequately offset by continued profitability.

Table 7.5: Broadcasting Capital Investment (Singapore dollars) and Per cent of Total Spending

Year	*Investment*	*% of Total Spending*
1987–88	20.0 million	15.9
1988–89	20.6 million	14.5
1989–90	48.7 million	25.1
1990–91	36.9 million	19.2
1991–92	42.0 million	18.5
1992–93	53.0 million	23.0

Source: *SBC Annual Reports* till 1992–93.

Commercial advertising on radio was introduced in January 1964. Today, advertisements form 55 per cent of broadcast revenue. This amounted to nearly S $166 million in 1992–93. Considerable opportunities were created for advertisements with the introduction of Channel 12 in 1984 (along with four additional radio stations since 1989), as well as the debut of INtv (teletext), KIDSText and commercial breaks during the English and Mandarin news. Live coverage of local and international events also contributed significantly to the increase in advertising revenue. Advertising air time rates have increased dramatically over the past several years, which reflect monopolistic charges for the increasing average daily viewership. In view of the increased competition from neighbouring countries, SBC has adopted more aggressive marketing approaches and has introduced new advertising packages that have successfully wooed advertisers.

Just over twenty per cent of broadcasting's annual revenue comes from television and radio sets licence fees, which are its second largest source of revenue at S $66.2 million (US $40 million) in 1992 as compared to S $20.4 million (US $12.2 million) in 1982. The annual licence fee for a monochrome TV set is S $36 (US $21.5) and S $100 (US $60) for a colour set, while it is S $24 (US $14) for a vehicle radio receiver. Household radio licences have been abolished (see Table 7.6).

The Government of Singapore also provides annual subsidies to SBC for public broadcasting purposes. This government grant is for the production, acquisition, and broadcasting of public service programmes such as minority language programmes, news, current affairs, and special interest programmes. SBC was provided

Table 7.6: Radio and Television Licences 1980–1990

End of Year	*Radio Licences Issued*	*Radio and Television Licences Issued*
1980	62,294	397,155
1981	66,897	414,535
1982	73,602	424,089
1983	104,735	464,269
1984	111,009	474,877
1985	108,735	481,907
1986	111,568	509,908
1987	109,453	531,215
1988	107,101	554,133
1989	105,120	533,021
1990	126,778	582,540

Source: *Yearbook of Statistics*, 1991.

S $28.2 million (US $17 million) in government grants in 1992, compared to S $21 million (US $12.5 million) the previous year. This government recovery amounts to just under 10 per cent of total group income.

The remaining 15 per cent of revenue is from non-operating and other sources, including subsidiary business ventures and sponsorships. Sponsorships have assumed increasing proportions as a means to fund programmes. From the long-established sponsorship of sports events, sponsors have made new inroads into other programmes such as variety shows, documentaries, and movies.

In 1993, the SBC Group retained nearly S $60 million (US $36 million) as surplus after taxes and contributions to the consolidated fund. As of 31 March 1993, SBC had a total retained surplus of nearly S $360 million (US $216 million), adding it to Singapore's impressive list of highly successful government-owned enterprises. With such financial success, the timing was right to move forward with plans to change government-held broadcasting as a statutory body, to a private company structure with the developing of regulatory powers from the operators to a new authority created for that purpose.

Corporatisation and Privatisation

The changing face of Singapore's television broadcasting has been further underscored by the Minister for Information and the Arts, George Yeo. He said in early 1993 that:

> . . . the ability of governments to control the flow of information is being weakened . . . with TV satellite receivers shrinking in size the floodgates will open regardless of what we do . . . . But we should go on the offensive and support our own values and way of life. There are two measures we must take. First we must ensure adequate funding of public service programmes . . . . The second is to facilitate the growth of Asian media companies who can take on the Western giants (Yeo, 1994, pp. 104–5).

As such, the government's objective has been to strengthen its national broadcasting in the wake of dynamic technological changes and new service challenges. This is being accomplished by the reorganisation of SBC to operate as a more efficient market-oriented set of companies.

In 1986, SBC hived off some of its commercial operations into a wholly-owned subsidiary, SBC Enterprises (SBC–E). SBC–E was responsible for all business ventures, which included the sale of air time and SBC-produced programmes. SBC-produced programmes, particularly Chinese dramas, are now being marketed aggressively abroad. Although SBC started selling its Chinese dramas as early as 1983, aggressive marketing was pursued only after 1988 when SBC–E had been well established. Sales increased from about 500 hours in 1984 to 1,000 hours in 1988 to more than 3,000 hours in 1990. SBC's Chinese dramas are broadcast in more than 30 countries, with leading markets in Malaysia, China, Taiwan, Macau, Thailand, and Brunei. Forays are being made into less established markets such as North America, Australia, New Zealand and Africa.

Revenue also comes from the sale of weekly entertainment magazines, *Radio and TV Times* (Chinese) and *8 days* (English). These self-promoting glossies, which include programme guides, have the highest circulations of any weekly publication in Singapore, with 60,000 copies for the English edition and 120,000 for the Chinese edition.

In 1990, Caldecott Productions was set up as an independent arm of SBC to produce commercials and video entertainment programming, both locally and in co-operation with outside ventures. Figure 7.2 shows the corporate structure of the SBC Group as a Statutory Board prior to its reorganisation in October 1994.

Figure 7.2: The SBC Group prior to October 1994

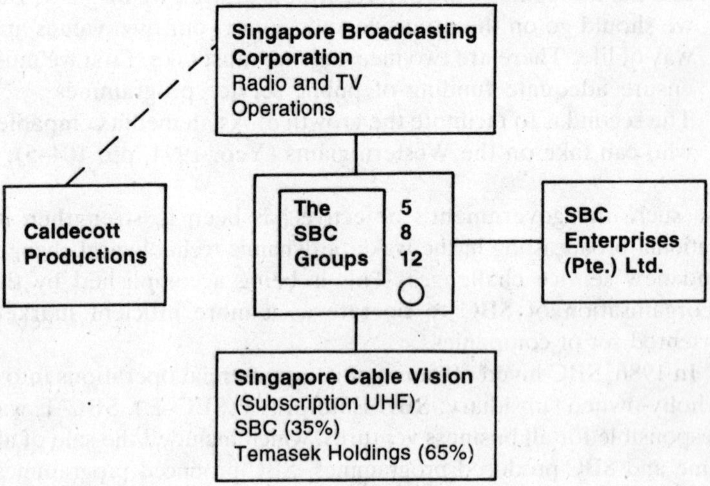

SBC also generated income from the production of video commercials and short films for advertisers. Since January 1983, SBC has extended its operations to include production of short documentaries, and promotional and instructional programmes for commercial and other organisations. In 1983–84, SBC captured 55 per cent of the market share of locally-produced video commercials, and increased it to 74 per cent in 1985–86, where it also stands today. By the early 1990s, SBC had entered into joint venture agreements in Hong Kong and Taiwan for the co-production of Chinese drama serials.

Recognising the twin trends of globalisation and segmentation in the international marketplace, the Ministry for Information and the Arts had pointed out the need for SBC to be privatised in order to compete more effectively in the international arena. The process, as expected, is being carried out gradually and systematically till 1994 and beyond. In reality, privatisation will mean a greater expansion of services, and in preparation for this a new broadcasting structure has been established in 1994.

Singapore Broadcasting Authority (SBA) and the Successor Companies to SBC

The Parliament of Singapore in August 1994 endorsed Singapore's latest broadcasting law—the Singapore Broadcasting Authority Act. This law replaces previous legislation known as the Broadcasting and Television Act (Chapter 28, 1985 revised edition) and the Singapore Broadcasting Corporation Act (Chapter 297, 1985 revised edition). With the new law, Singapore's evolution to a privatised structural arrangement for broadcasting has been established. This arrangement is notable for three important aspects as outlined by the new law. The first is the separation of the regulatory powers of broadcasting from the broadcast operator to a new authority established for this purpose, the Singapore Broadcasting Authority (SBA). The SBA is to promote and regulate the broadcasting industry and take over the regulatory and licensing functions previously exercised by the Ministry of Information and the Arts and SBC. Second, the operating entities of broadcasting have been reorganised into new companies under one holding company, SIM. The law allows the transfer of appropriate properties, rights and liabilities of SBC to SBC's successor companies and the SBA, which enables the government, in effect, to corporatise and privatise SBC. Third, the law also allows the government to offer for sale to the public, shares or debentures of the corporatised SBC successor companies at a later date.

Figure 7.3 represents Singapore's new structural arrangement, as well as showing the position of other broadcast operations, including the new cable system.

The new operating companies which replaced SBC on 1 October 1994, include TCS which is in control of both the English and Mandarin stations, Channels 5 and 8 respectively. TCS is unashamedly commercial in its outlook. As its first Chief Executive Officer, Lee Cheok Yew, has stated, TCS 'was going after the mass market . . . to appear to most people, most of the time' (TV interview, 4 October 1994).

Figure 7.3: Broadcast Media Structures of Singapore (from October 1994)

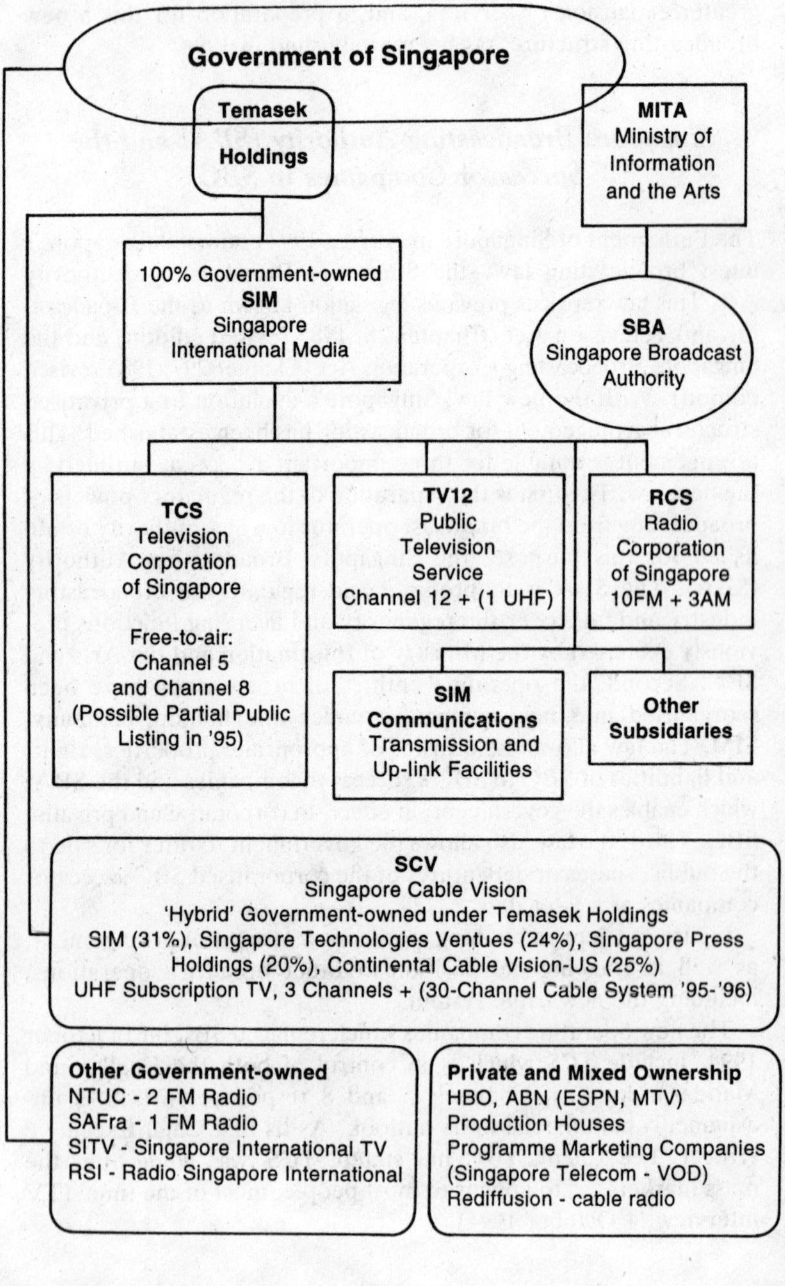

A separate company, TV12, has been set up for public service broadcasting and operates Channel 12, for what will be predominantly Malay and Tamil programming. TV12 will eventually operate a UHF channel as well for documentary, arts and other public service programmes of a largely non-commercial nature.

In addition to the two television broadcasting operating companies, the Radio Corporation of Singapore (RCS), with its now 10 FM stations, and SIM Communications have been set up.

This latter company is charged with the operation of all transmission facilities, including up-link systems to satellites. It is the only organisation operating these types of facilities, apart from Singapore Telecom, although international broadcasters who use Singapore as a regional hub may be allowed to operate their own link-up facilities in the future.

The four main operating companies of SIM may eventually be sold, in part, through public share offerings or other placements, but remain 100 per cent government-owned at the end of 1994. The most likely candidate to be sold first in a partial equity offering will be TCS, which operates Channels 5 and 8.

Subscription Television

The transformation of television broadcasting in Singapore, beyond its three free-to-air channels, began with a subscription television service on 2 April 1992. The service is being offered through a separate corporation set up for this purpose called Singapore CableVision (SCV), which is also the company that will eventually operate Singapore's cable television system. The company was originally owned by one of the government's largest holding companies, Temasek Holdings (65 per cent), and SBC (35 per cent), shown previously in Figure 7.2. SCV, as of late 1994, is under a mixed ownership scheme with four partners. They are, Continental CableVision of the United States (25 per cent), Singapore Technologies Ventures (24 per cent), Singapore Press Holdings (20 per cent), and Singapore International Media (31 per cent).

SCV first offered a channel called NewsVision, a 24-hour news service featuring primarily live CNN news on a scrambled UHF channel. Subscription television is only available in limited areas in Singapore and the corporation is looking towards an eventual 20 per cent market penetration for profitability.

Singaporeans can subscribe to the service by paying a start-up fee and monthly subscription fee. They are then provided with a descrambler for the UHF channels. Two entertainment channels, a 12-hour English Movie-Vision and an 18-hour Chinese Variety-Vision (24 hours on Saturdays) were added in May 1992.

In anticipation of adding a fourth subscription channel to air, the American MTV, SBC began broadcasting MTV free-to-air on Channel 5 for two hours on Friday and Saturday nights in July 1992. These broadcasts are in effect sales promotions not dissimilar to the original airing of CNN live for two hours per day. Just as CNN is now available only through the subscription service, so MTV is no longer broadcast free-to-air. MTV itself is planning to set up a broadcast hub service in Singapore.

SCV originally had plans to establish upto 12 subscription channels to be distributed via Multi-channel Multi-point Distribution Service (MMDS) technologies. The over-the-air subscription service is, however, likely to be discontinued when the company establishes full cable service.

Cable Television

Singapore now has ambitious plans to build a nationwide 30-channel cable television network. Singapore Telecom and SBC originally combined to conduct a feasibility study for a cable television system.

The merger of technologies, which is gradually making the telephone, broadcasting and information systems industries overlap, is having effects in Singapore. While the Federal Communication Commission (FCC) in the United States is making rules allowing for telephone companies to provide television programming, a similar comparison can be seen in Singapore, with the telecommunications operator, Singapore Telecom, claiming initially some jurisdiction of a cable television system along with the then SBC. Singapore Telecom already has a fibre-optic trunking system throughout the country which can be adapted for cable television services. It also could eventually provide direct-to-home fibre-optic cable links. SBC claimed a content jurisdiction for any broadcast or publicly distributed narrowcast television service, from its interpretation of the Broadcasting Act of 1985 giving SBC monopoly broadcast rights. However, with the new broadcasting law of 1994 and the devolving of SBC into successor companies, neither the television broadcasting companies nor Singapore Telecom have an equity interest in the cable system. SCV, under its new ownership structure, is now moving ahead as a separate entity to establish the cable service. It will probably lease line capacity from Singapore Telecom as needed through the latter's fibre-optic network. Singapore Telecom, like many other telecom operators world-wide, is beginning trials of its own services for video-on-demand (VOD). Telecom could eventually become a video service competitor or even operate one or more of the SCV channels.

However, most Singaporeans will only be able to receive this alternative television delivery service and its potentially wider programming choices in 1997 or later, as it will take this long to complete the island-wide fibre-optic cable system to all homes and public housing estates and to build out the cable television system. This, despite the fact that Singapore already has the highest optical fibre density in the world—over 16,000 km of fibre-optic cables linking all 26 telephone exchanges. Nonetheless, SCV plans to begin linking homes to a television cable service, initially with approximately 20,000 subscribers, by mid-1995.

The original Singapore Telecom/SBC joint feasibility study was conducted by Malarkey–Taylor Associates of the United States, along with US cable operator Continental CableVision (now an equity partner and manager of SCV) and Survey Research Singapore (Pte) Ltd. The results of the study came in early 1993. Among important issues studied for the cable system, along with its potential demand and economic viability, was the kind of regulatory framework that would best suit Singapore for such a system. As a result, an exclusive franchise has been given to SCV consisting now of both government and foreign private participants. While no longer holding an equity position in SCV, TCS and TV12 will be given prominent positions on the cable system.

Censorship

In all of these changes, one can note the very gradual relaxation of programming content constraints in Singapore as the changing economic imperatives of television and audience demands begin to take precedence. Political, social and cultural considerations of the government are of course still important for broadcasting in this multi-cultural, multi-ethnic and multi-lingual society.

General guidelines for entertainment programming are provided by the government through the SBA with the stipulation that programmes should not contain nudity and undue violence or vulgar language. A 'least common denominator' programme philosophy to garner audience share tends to guide entertainment programme acquisition. There is also an attempt to acquire programmes from foreign sources which best reflect the Singapore government's perceived and encouraged moral values.

General guidelines of censorship for local news and government affairs are implemented on a conservative tone. Singaporean journalists practise self-censorship under the vague and perceived restrictive guidelines of the government. This self-censorship is borne of interpretations of two laws in Singapore which provide the government with strong powers to sanction what it may regard as anything running counter to its desires. These are the Internal Securities Act and the Official Secrets Act, which the government does not hesitate to enforce to the fullest extent provided by the law. In fact, it can be argued that the Official Secrets Act in particular has a pervasive effect in Singapore with regard to perceptions for the need to protect the confidentiality of almost all information to an extremely high degree. This is in spite of frequent musings on the relative merits of providing for a more open information environment. The relative inaccessibility of information itself, especially regarding government affairs, renders the journalist's task all the more difficult. Various cases, from time-to-time, where to Government believes journalists to have breached these laws, effectively provides the rationale for most to practise self-censorship and to 'err on the side of caution'.

An argument given for censorship, which rationalises journalists' behaviour in general support of the government, is that it is their national duty and responsibility. Opposing opinions and suggestions for change, especially from non-ruling party politicians, are not strictly disallowed and are not infrequent in the print media. They are, however, notably absent from television and radio broadcast news.

Local television broadcast news content is monitored by government officials. Journalistic self-censorship, therefore, creates a credibility problem as a result of direct and largely unchallenged (and rarely publicly debated) dissemination of government pronouncements. News readers, rather than broadcast journalists, are the mainstay of local television news. As a result, they represent little more than confirmation for viewers of official government policy. While the government in Singapore is of the view that the broadcasters should work in support of the government, local television broadcast news, in particular, is nearly completely devoid of any story which may reflect negatively on the ruling People's Action Party (PAP) or the government's activities and policies. Efforts are under way to revamp the local news, but most changes so far are cosmetic, as the government insists that television news remain the government's 'strategic partner'. This carries into current affairs programming as well, for which topics are largely 'suggested' by various government ministries and agencies.

There is, on the other hand, almost no censorship of international news as long as the content is not perceived to be interfering in Singapore's domestic political affairs. In such cases, the item is simply not retransmitted. This has been more a concern in the print media than in broadcasting. What is retransmitted from internationally available television news is of course highly selective. But, it is argued, selection also tends to be influenced by the same time constraints and newsworthiness needs as in other countries and CNN television news is redistributed on the subscription channel with no censorship.

Conclusion

While television broadcasting within Singapore remains the domain of predominantly government-owned and controlled systems, new pressures have brought structural changes. Television is now evolving from two previous periods which saw broadcasting as a government department in the 1960s and 1970s, and then as a national broadcast statutory board in the 1980s and early 1990s. Singapore has now moved into its third structural phase with television organised as separate companies under a government-owned holding company and the establishment of a separate regulatory authority. The holding company, SIM, will be expanding aggressively, taking advantage of huge cash surpluses to develop new programming and production interests. The government's strategy is to continue to strengthen the position of national broadcasters, as changes in technology, increasing audience demands, and competitive forces come to the fore, by developing systems which will continue to provide the largest audience share to government-controlled sources in the wake of changing technologies which may eventually by-pass such systems. Audience demands and competition from broadcasters in neighbouring Malaysia and Indonesia are also forcing local television broadcasters to increase the variety and quality of programming. The eventual move to partially sell, in a public listing, the shares of the new TCS is seen as necessary in order for the company to more effectively take advantage of strategic international interests and strengthen operations at home as the dominant free-to-air terrestrial broadcaster.

The expansion of partial government-owned television services, including the subscription services and eventually a cable television system, are attempts to maintain as much of an exclusive control of broadcasting within Singapore as possible while adapting to the inevitable changes.

A separate private broadcaster competing directly with government-led services is unlikely in Singapore. Instead, private programme producers, especially foreign, may be able to participate via acquisition of their material for retransmission on the dominantly government-owned systems.

Perhaps one factor which might eventually change the exclusivity of government-controlled television systems in Singapore will be the need to act reciprocally as it expands internationally. For example, Singapore Telecom holds a 9 per cent stake in the Shinawatra group of Thailand. With changes in policy in Thailand on the establishment of private television stations, a largely government-owned Singaporean company now finds itself linked to a company with a stake in private television concerns in Thailand. Singapore Telecom also has an agreement which allowed it to set up a commercial television station in Colombo, Sri Lanka. Under the agreement, Singapore Telecom International (STI) manages the channel as well.

More significantly SIM, as its name implies, is also looking to expand internationally, which means it will also eventually face the increasingly important international issues of reciprocity and trade in services. The question remains as to whether pressure may eventually be brought to bear to reciprocate with private systems in Singapore. In the short run, it may be more likely that partial foreign ownership, alliance and joint venture participation in the government-led Singapore television systems will be possible. The government wants to tap foreign technical expertise along with its global market network connections in order to establish Singapore's competitive edge in television broadcasting and as a regional broadcasting hub. All of these efforts are aimed at maintaining, for now, the strengths of national broadcasting while adapting to the ever changing international environment. Will this 'third phase' of television's structural arrangements in Singapore serve it well? Looming on the horizon are computer network broadcast systems and technological changes to existing systems which may render useless even enlightened national broadcast protectionist efforts. For better or worse, Singapore is meeting the challenge head-on and has staked its claim.

References

Goonasekera, A. and **Holaday, D.** (eds.). (1993). *Asian communication handbook*. Singapore: Asian Mass Communication Research and Information Centre (AMIC).

Hukill, M. (1991). 'Film/TV education and culture in Singapore'. Paper presented at the Asia–Pacific Film and Television Conference, Beijing, China, June.

———. (1994). 'Communication education in Singapore: Responding to media needs'. Paper presented at the seminar Communication, Education and the Needs of the Media, Kuala Lumpur, Malaysia, September.

Leonard, H. (1991). 'Broadcasting developments in SouthEast Asia'. Paper presented at the Annual Conference of the International Institute of Communication (IIC), Singapore, September.

Lent, J. (1978). *Broadcasting in Asia and the Pacific*. Hong Kong: Heinemann Asia.

Moses, C and **Maslog, C.** (1978). *Mass communication in Asia: A brief history*. Asian Mass Communication Research and Information Centre (AMIC): Singapore.

Singapore Broadcasting Corporation (SBC) *Act* (Revised), 1985.

Singapore Broadcasting Authority (SBA) *Act*, 1994.

SBC Annual Reports (till 1992–93). Singapore: Singapore Broadcasting Corporation.

Tan, Y.S. and **Soh, Y.** (1994). *The development of Singapore's modern media industry*. Singapore: Times Academic Press.

Yeap, S.B. (1994). 'The emergence of an Asian-centered perspective: Singapore's media regionalization strategies'. *Media Asia*, 21(2), 63–72.

Yearbook of Statistics (1991). Singapore: Department of Statistics, Ministry of Trade and Industries.

——— (1992). Singapore: Department of Statistics, Ministry of Trade and Industries.

Yeo, G. (1994). 'The technological revolution poses threats or opportunities?' (Speech to conference of ASEAN Ministers of Information, Manila, December 1993). *Media Asia*, 21(2), 104–6.

8

The Impact of the International Marketplace on the Organisation of Malaysian Television*

Zaharom Nain

> The expected and actual role sets and performances of mass media, their autonomy, their entrepreneurial structure, and the control over news management and editorial policies are, to a large extent, a function of the political, economic, and socio-cultural institutions of a given country. (Raju, et al., 1984, p. 101).

Introduction

Ever since Malaysia[1] formally attained political independence from Britain in 1957, successive Malaysian governments, like many others in the developing world, have been grappling with the task of creating an elusive 'national identity'. Numerous policies, such as the National Culture Policy (NCP) and the New Economic Policy (NEP), have been implemented with varying degrees of success, despite their inherent weaknesses and the controversies they raised when they were initially implemented in the early 1970s. Central to this forging of a national identity has been—and continues to be—the role that the media (especially television) have to play, as perceived by those in power.

The organisation of contemporary Malaysian television, thus, has to be seen in this context and in relation to two other inter-related and equally important factors—the complex socio-political

* I wish to thank Jacqueline Chue for her substantial comments on an earlier draft and for helping to tabulate the figures.

make up of the country and the way the Malaysian economy has been structured, especially since the early 1980s when Malaysia opened up its economy to world markets. These factors, it is argued here, have not only helped to shape the type of television that Malaysia has, but also, in varying degrees, have impinged upon the development of possible alternatives.

In short, what this chapter attempts to do is to indicate that the impact of the international marketplace on the organisation of Malaysian television needs to be assessed based on an initial understanding of, first, internal tensions and contradictions that presently exist in contemporary Malaysian society; and second, how these tensions, in turn, have contributed to greater dependence on the international (television) market.

Malaysia: The Socio-cultural Dimension

In terms of land mass, Malaysia covers 130,000 square miles. Peninsular or West Malaysia, which is made up of 11 states, covers 52,000 square miles while East Malaysia, which consists of two states, has an area of 78,000 square miles. The population is multi-ethnic and multi-religious, with three major ethnic groups—Malays, Chinese and Indians—and numerous other ethnic minorities (including Ibans, Kadazans, Bajaus and Muruts), particularly in East Malaysia. According to the 1980 Census, out of a total population then of 13.07 million, 6.9 million Malaysians were Muslims. The rest were made up of Buddhists, Hindus, Sikhs, Christians and followers of traditional Chinese religions such as Taoism.[2] Islam has been the official state religion since Independence, although Malaysia is not an Islamic state.

Given its multi-ethnic nature, not surprisingly, Malaysia's history has been dominated by ethnic-based parties and ethnic politics since it attained Independence. The three major political parties that form the basis of the 'Barisan Nasional' (EN) coalition government, for instance, are ethnic-based.[3]. Indeed, it would not be an exaggeration to suggest that ethnic preoccupations continue to dominate Malaysian society and culture as a whole. There is a deep sense of being part of specific ethnic and cultural communities. And this has always been nurtured, cultivated, even reinforced, by these ethnic-based political parties. As rightly pointed out by Jomo (1990, p. 229),

> Political issues are invariably blatantly ethnic, or have ethnic overtones, while career advancement in politics is generally contingent on effective identification with or advocacy of such issues. Major social organisations with significant followings besides cultural and religious groups are also ethnically based, including business associations, youth movements, women's associations and other societies.

What is abundantly clear is that after nearly four decades of political independence, genuine national unity in Malaysia remains elusive. And the very policies created to purportedly achieve this goal, such as the NEP and the NCP, ironically appear to be working against realising this goal. The causes for this state of affairs are both historical and structural.[4] Brennan (1985, p. 93), for instance, pertinently argued that

> The Malaysian social formation . . .came into existence as a direct result of imperialism and colonialism . . . The composition of the population was changed radically in a short space of time as imperialism ensured that labour was shifted from India and China to create surplus value on the basis of British capital. Thus, by the Second World War a society had been created which appeared to be a vast medley of peoples which on the one hand 'mixed but did not combine', while on the other hand was divided into discrete ethnic blocs composed on Malays, Chinese and Indians.

And what originated in colonial Malaya evidently has been extended and reinforced in post-colonial Malaysia to this present day. It is widely believed in Malaysia, for instance, that the riots following the general elections in 1969 were ethnically inspired. Ethnicity has become an emotive issue, exploited by politicians both in government and in the disparate opposition. As Jomo (1990, pp. 143–44) puts it,

> After successful repression of the legal left in the mid and later 1960s, essentially racialist ideologies had little competition for political influence. Consequently, the deteriorating socio-economic and political situation in the 1960s came to be interpreted and seen primarily in ethnic terms.

Indeed, when the Mahathir administration launched 'Operation Lallang' in October 1987, detaining (without trial) over 100 politicians, opposition leaders, academics, environmentalists, social activists and members of religious groups, the spectre of the 1969 riots was raised by the administration to justify the detentions.[5] And a similar strategy was employed during the 1990 Malaysian general election, a strategy which the mainstream media also latched on to.[6] These events aside, the major economic and cultural policies, such as the NEP and the NCP, have a decidedly racist ring about them.

Formulated soon after the riots of 1969, the NEP has become the key reference point for Malaysia's economic development policies. Its objective is nicely summed up in the *Third Malaysia Plan 1976–1980* (Government of Malaysia, 1976, p. 7):

> The NEP seeks to eradicate poverty among all Malaysians and to restructure Malaysian society so that the identification of race with economic function and geographical location is reduced and eventually eliminated, both objectives being realised through rapid expansion of the economy over time . . .the present compartmentalisation of racial groups by economic function, with the Malays and other indigenous people concentrated in the traditional sectors of the economy, is the core of the problem.

The dichotomy between the 'Bumiputera' (literally 'prince of the soil', meaning the Malays and other indigenous groups) and the 'non-Bumiputera' (meaning the Chinese, Indians and similar 'migrant' groups) which the NEP highlights, continues to concern many Malaysians, particularly those who belong to the latter group. It has resulted in ethnicity being institutionalised further.

The controversial NCP was formulated after a Congress on National Culture held in 1971. From the proceedings of the Congress, three principles have been taken to be the basis of the Malaysian National Culture. First, it must be based on the indigenous culture of this region. Second, suitable elements from other cultures could be accepted as part of the National Culture. And third, the Islamic religion needs to be an important component in the moulding of the National Culture. More than that, it is also clearly stated that acceptance of the second principle would only be in the context of the first and the third.[7]

As can be expected, the NCP has met with substantial opposition for its rigid and static view of 'culture', and equally, its overtly ethnic character. Controversial though it may be, thus far it has not been amended, further reflecting the emphasis on ethnicity in Malaysian society. It could be argued that the NCP was formulated as a powerful channel for asserting ethnic identity, just as religion has been utilised in contemporary Malaysia.

Indeed, since the early 1970s, signs of Islamic resurgence have become more pronounced—in form if not totally in substance. The causes of this resurgence cannot be delved into in any great detail here.[8] For our purpose, the fact that there has been such a resurgence is what is important, plus the fact that the state is also involved. As Chandra (1987, pp. 9–10) succinctly put it:

> with the advent of Islamic resurgence, the State has gone beyond mere public projection of religious rituals and practices. It is now concerned . . .with the role of Islamic values and institutions in the larger spheres of public life. Its Islamisation programme has therefore given a more national character to the religion in relation to Malaysian society as a whole. Islam is no longer a Muslim affair; it is as much the concern of non-Muslims. Islam becoming more national, more pervasive, more ubiquitous, is part of the transformation that has taken place under Islamic resurgence.

Given this resurgence and its distinctively ethnic composition—all Malays are, by law, Muslims; it is virtually impossible for a Malay Muslim to convert to another religion—together with present official attitudes, policies, and practices, it would, therefore, be pertinent to characterise contemporary Malaysian society as one that is ethnically dichotomised. And increasingly so. Hence, it is argued here that any analysis of the organisation and perceived roles of Malaysian television needs to, at least initially, appreciate this wider Malaysian social canvas which provides the backdrop that invariably affects and influences such organisations and their roles. Indeed, ethno-religious sentiments continue to penetrate media institutions, including television, in Malaysian society, aided and abetted by the state which, invariably, has vested interests in what is depicted by television and the manner of such depiction.

Malaysian Television and the State: Early Links

Television was first introduced in Malaysia in December 1963 with the help of technical consultants from Canada. The initial set-up comprised a single channel national network under the control of the Department of Broadcasting (RTM), which in turn was one of three departments under the control of the Malaysian Ministry of Information (see Lowe and Kamin, 1982; and Karthigesu, 1991). Hence, right from its inception, Malaysian television essentially has been under the direct control of the government of the day. Indeed, as one media academic (Karthigesu, 1991, p. 422) observed:

> establishing the television service as a full government department was tantamount to appropriating the principal mass medium of the country for the exclusive service of a segment of a democratic society. It was being cast so concretely that liberalisation even at a gradual pace for later changes was rendered impossible.

Surprisingly, the Malaysian Parliament then seemed oblivious to and unconcerned with the planning stages and details of the pioneer television station. It has been observed (Karthigesu, 1991, p. 92), for example, that 'Members, including the Opposition, had allowed the government to develop the service according to its own mould and pattern, almost as if they had nothing to do with it'.

In October 1969, a second channel was launched, also under the direct control of the Ministry of Information and guided by the same directives as that which governed the operations of the first channel. These directives, which have remained virtually unchanged, are:

1. to explain in-depth and with the widest possible coverage the policies and programmes of the government in order to ensure maximum understanding by the public;
2. to stimulate public interest and opinion in order to achieve changes in line with the requirement of the government;
3. to assist in promoting civic consciousness and fostering the development of Malaysian arts and culture; and
4. to provide suitable elements of popular education, general information and entertainment.[9]

What is, therefore, apparent is the fact that television—and more generally broadcasting—in Malaysia has always been closely aligned to the government. Both the early channels—now called TV1 and TV2 respectively—were set up not through an Act of Parliament or by a Royal Charter, but via decisions made by the Malaysian government which, in turn, formulated the policies that would determine the role television would play. It would be pertinent to state that notions of *public service*—as they are conceived of in Britain, for example—have never been seriously entertained, let alone debated. Instead, television in Malaysia can more appropriately be seen as a *government service*, being as it is the mouthpiece of the government of the day.

In this connection, the findings of two studies done on Malaysian television are illustrative. Glattback and Balakrishnan (1978, p. 154) observed that:

> Broadcasting has to toe the line, probably having even less freedom than the printed media. Any political discussion is heavily authoritarian, and there is little live debate on serious issues. The audience is lectured rather than involved. An independent approach is inhibited and the better organised pressure groups—particularly Islamic religious leaders and the Women's Section of United Malays National Organisation—are able to make their voices forcefully heard.

Lowe and Kamin (1982, p. 31, emphasis added) argued in a similar vein that:

> Most of the decisions on local media content come from sources outside of the professional structure of the department. *The main influence on these decisions are therefore external and they emanate from the delicate political position of the country resulting in delicate racial balances as shown by compromises and different emphasis on questions of religion, language and culture* . . . . News items which are likely to be controversial and which do not provide enough time to be ruled on by people 'upstairs' are underplayed . . . . All forms of communication, including entertainment and advertising, are seen as having political effects . . . . Audiences are assumed not to be able to suspend

their literal interpretations even in the case of fiction for as long as these programmes are produced locally.

Although these studies were conducted more than a decade ago, the contemporary picture is no different in spite of the so-called 'liberalisation'—or more accurately 'privatisation'—policies of the current regime, which came to power in 1981.[10] These policies, particularly the Look East, Malaysia Incorporated and Privatisation policies, were introduced by the Mahathir government in 1983 and are all geared towards the 'corporatisation' of the Malaysian economy. The official line as asserted in the *Mid-Term Review Of The Fourth Malaysia Plan 1981–1985* (Government of Malaysia, 1984, pp. 22–25) is:

> The ultimate objective of privatization is the reduction of the size and presence of the Government and, conversely, the need to expand the role of private enterprise in the economy . . .
>
> Malaysia Inc. emphasizes cooperation between the Government and the private sector for the mutual benefit of both and ultimately the nation. The private sector will form the commercial arm of the national enterprise while the Government provides the major policy framework, direction and the necessary back-up services. The concept . . .inculcates the viewpoint of the country as a corporate entity . . .
>
> Malaysia's Look East Policy is the framework for learning and adapting to our own needs the experiences of successful eastern nations. The major objective of the Look East Policy is to inculcate among Malaysians values, work ethics and management practices which stress hard work, loyalty to the enterprise, dedication and the need to be self-reliant through the individual's own hard work, determination and initiative . . .

Following the introduction of these policies, not surprisingly, the potentially lucrative television industry invariably was earmarked for a dose of privatisation.

Television in Malaysia: The Contemporary Scenario

Throughout the fourteen-year period that the present Malaysian Prime Minister, Mahathir Mohamad, has been in office, legal and political controls on the mass media industry have been tightened considerably.[11] Ironically, this has happened along with a greater expansion of the mass media, especially television.

Indeed, in June 1984, a supposedly 'alternative' television station (TV3) was set up, initially serving the country's capital Kuala Lumpur and nearby areas, but later expanding nationwide. The media hype that preceded its formation was quite sensational. Certainly, in an atmosphere of virtually unbridled privatisation, the arrival of a commercial television station was welcomed with open arms by the policy-makers and by the mainstream Malaysian media. It was, after all, a development that subscribed to everything that the Mahathir administration believed in. As Mahathir (1983, p. 207, emphasis added) himself announced,

> The government may be able to obtain substantial revenue from telecommunications, ports, radio and television, railways, etc. However, the government would still be able to collect taxes if these services are run by the private sector instead. *And if these services can be better run on a commercial basis, there is a possibility of higher government income than when the government owned these services. In view of this possibility, there is a need to transfer several public services and government owned business to the private sector.*

Not surprisingly, there was the general expectation or belief '. . .that a commercial television station will provide newer, better quality and better choice of programmes' (*Malaysian Business*, 1 June 1984, p. 23). And after TV3 was established, an air of misplaced optimism prevailed—a misguided belief that the commercialisation of television would simply lead to the production of a greater variety of media artefacts, particularly local ones. More than that, the increasing commercialisation of Malaysian television created an illusion of greater freedom. (Even the previously staid RTM stations, TV1 and TV2, were pressured to brush up their act and to compete with TV3 for the advertising dollar, and introduce new programme schedules that even now appear to reflect nothing more than the best soap operas, situation comedies, musicals and sports programmes that transnational media companies have to offer.) However, despite the optimism, the reality is quite different. Increasing commercialisation has, in fact, resulted in two worrying developments.

First, it has resulted in greater state intervention in and domination of the mass media industry. Indeed, in the midst of all that privatisation and deregulation, the Broadcasting Act was passed by Parliament[12] in 1988, giving the Minister of Information extremely wide-ranging powers. In the first place, under this Act, any potential broadcaster would need to apply for a licence from the Minister. In Part III, Section 10, Subsection (1) of the Act (Broadcasting Act, 1988, p. 8, emphasis added), it is stated that

> It shall be the duty of the licensee to ensure that the broadcasting of the broadcast matter by him *complies with the direction given, from time to time, by the Minister.*

Also, direct political party ownership of television and the other mass media has increased tremendously during this period, with parties in the ruling BN coalition virtually having a stranglehold on media ownership.

Second, because the commercialisation of television has not been accompanied by any liberalisation of policies and broadcasting practices, a trend has developed where there is greater emphasis on the production and importation of particular television genres; those, it has been argued elsewhere, '. . . which do not address, let alone question, the existing order' (Zaharom, 1991, pp. 40–41).

To expand on the first development, a disturbing feature of the privatisation exercise conducted by the Mahathir regime since the early 1980s is the fact that what were previously state monopolies—such as the National Electricity Board (now Tenaga Nasional) and Telecoms (now Telekom Malaysia)—have been transformed into private monopolies, with groups and individuals closely, if not directly, aligned to the ruling coalition heading them. As far as television is concerned, such is certainly the case with TV3. Until January 1993, via its investment arm Renong Holdings, the United Malays National Organisation (UMNO) (the largest component part in the BN coalition government) held controlling interests in TV3; and the local media giant New Straits Times Press (NSTP), which publishes English national dailies such as *The New Straits Times* and *The Malay Mail*, Malay dailies such as *Berita Harian*, their Sunday editions, and the Chinese daily *Shin Min Daily News* (see Gomez, 1994). In January 1993, through what has been described as 'the biggest management buy-out in the local corporate sector' (*Corporate World*, 1993), this local media empire came under the control of Realmild Sdn. Bhd., a private limited company. Realmild is in turn fully owned by a publicly listed company Malaysian Resources Corporation Bhd. (MRCB), which is effectively controlled by four individuals widely acknowledged as close associates of Anwar Ibrahim, Malaysia's Deputy Prime Minister (see Cheong, 1993; and Gomez, 1990, 1991, 1993, and 1994).

More recent developments further illustrate the continuing concentration of media ownership. In early 1994, another local media giant closely aligned to UMNO, the Utusan Group, became part of a consortium of four companies that was awarded a tender by the government to operate Malaysia's second commercial television station, TV Metro (see Zaharom, 1994). Yet another company in the consortium is Melewar Corporation, controlled by Tunku Abdullah of the Negeri Sembilan royal house and a longtime close associate of Prime Minister Mahathir.

Malaysia's first pay-TV network, scheduled to begin operating in the third quarter of 1995, is also run by a consortium using the company name Cableview Services Sdn. Bhd. The largest shareholder in this consortium, with a 40 per cent stake, is Sistem Television Malaysia Berhad or TV3. The Malaysian Ministry of Finance has a 30 per cent stake, while Sri Utara Sdn. Bhd., a wholly-owned subsidiary of Maika Holdings Bhd. (the investment arm of the Malaysian Indian Congress [MIC], another component of the BN coalition) has a 5 per cent stake (*The New Straits Times*, 16 December 1994).

Hence, as far as the media, particularly television, is concerned, what we have is a situation where the selective privatisation exercise continues to widely spread the tentacles of the ruling coalition and its allies across the Malaysian economy, adding economic and cultural domination to what is already virtual political domination.

As far as the second development is concerned, the increasing emphasis on the production and importation of 'safe' television artefacts has further opened up Malaysian television to the international marketplace. As discussed in the following section, this, in turn, has resulted in a shifting of declared priorities within the television organisations, especially those of RTM.

Malaysian Television and the International Marketplace

The international presence, to be sure, has always been felt on Malaysian television—in terms of organisation and, more visually, in terms of content. Indeed, the lack of any local expertise in television organisation, management, and production prior to the setting up of TV1 in 1963 forced the Malaysian government to consider foreign experts. Two Canadian consultants—an engineer and a programme expert—were engaged for two main reasons. First, it was felt that Canada's experience with multi-lingual broadcasting would prove useful in a multi-ethnic, multi-lingual country like Malaysia. Second, it was a question of logistics, because Malaysia was offered the services of the Canadians through the Colombo Plan (Karthigesu, 1991).

Be that as it may, what is more important is that these consultants, more so the programme expert G.F. Brickenden, were instrumental in laying the base for the overall organisation of television in Malaysia. Indeed, Brickenden had a big say in terms of training, staff build-up, programming, programme distribution among languages, and even the system of advertising that was to be implemented in TV1 (Karthigesu, 1991). In other words, even in terms of initial organisation, Malaysian television was never, as it were, hand sown and home grown. At best, as with the organisation of television in most other developing countries, the early organisation of Malaysian television was a compromise between foreign expertise, norms, practices and values, and local ones.

This is certainly still being reflected in the programme content of Malaysian television. Back in 1963, when TV1 was first established, one of the first problems that came up was how to provide sufficient programmes to fill the time slots. It has been observed (Karthigesu, 1991, p. 135, emphasis added), for example, that

> Right at the outset of launching TV Malaysia, the problem of finding enough local material to fill even the short stretches of airtime surfaces. *But there was, of course, the ready-made solution of using syndicated films from the West. Malaysia succumbed to this easy solution.*

This practice, as we shall see, has continued to the present day.

A study[13] conducted on a weeks' output of programmes by the three Malaysian television channels (Table 8.1) reveals that almost

Table 8.1: Number of Broadcasting Hours for Local and Foreign Programmes on Malaysian Television in a Week (hours)

Day/Channel	*TV1*	*TV2*	*TV3*	*Total*
Sunday				
Local	13 hrs 50 mins (78.8)	4 hrs (25)	11 hrs 50 mins (64.3)	29 hrs 40 mins (56.1)
Foreign	4 hrs 40 mins (25.2)	12 hrs (75)	6 hrs 35 mins (35.7)	23 hrs 15 mins (43.9)
Monday				
Local	11 hrs 24 mins (63.3)	3 hrs (42.8)	9 hrs 25 mins (51.1)	23 hrs 49 mins (54.9)
Foreign	6 hrs 36 mins (36.7)	4 hrs (57.2)	9 hrs (48.9)	19 hrs 36 mins (45.1)
Tuesday				
Local	11 hrs 28 mins (63.7)	2 hrs 30 mins (35.7)	9 hrs 25 mins (51.1)	23 hrs 23 mins (53.9)
Foreign	6 hrs 32 mins (36.3)	4 hrs 30 mins (64.3)	9 hrs (48.9)	20 hrs 02 mins (46.1)
Wednesday				
Local	11 hrs 55 mins (66.2)	2 hrs (28.6)	12 hrs 57 mins (66.7)	26 hrs 52 mins (60.5)
Foreign	6 hrs 05 mins (33.8)	5 hrs (71.4)	6 hrs 28 mins (33.3)	17 hrs 33 mins (39.5)
Thursday				
Local	12 hrs 50 mins (71.3)	2 hrs (28.6)	12 hrs 57 mins (66.7)	27 hrs 47 mins (62.6)
Foreign	5 hrs 10 mins (28.7)	5 hrs (71.4)	6 hrs 28 mins (33.3)	16 hrs 38 mins (37.4)
Friday				
Local	12 hrs 40 mins (70.4)	3 hrs (18.8)	9 hrs 27 mins (51.3)	25 hrs 07 mins (47.9)
Foreign	5 hrs 20 mins (29.6)	13 hrs (81.2)	8 hrs 58 mins (48.7)	27 hrs 18 mins (52.1)
Saturday				
Local	13 hrs 10 mins (71.2)	3 hrs 10 mins (19.2)	14 hrs 29 mins (74.9)	30 hrs 49 mins (56.7)
Foreign	5 hrs 20 mins (28.8)	13 hrs 20 mins (80.8)	4 hrs 51 mins (25.1)	23 hrs 31 mins (43.3)
Total				
Local	87 hrs 17 mins (68.7)	19 hrs 40 mins (25.7)	80 hrs 30 mins (61.1)	187 hrs 27 mins (55.9)
Foreign	39 hrs 43 mins (31.3)	56 hrs 50 mins (74.3)	51 hrs 20 mins (38.9)	147 hrs 53 mins (44.1)

Figures in brackets indicate percentages.

half (44.1 per cent) of the total number of programmes are imported ones. Broken down into channels, TV1 has a 69:31 ratio of local to imported programmes, TV2 has a 26:74 ratio, and TV3's ratio is 61:39.

When we break the programmes down to specific types, the figures become even more interesting. As indicated in Table 8.2, the bulk (80.4 per cent) of the imported programmes are made up of just four types—feature films (30.6 per cent), television dramas (18.4 per cent), animated cartoons (12 per cent) and documentaries (9.4 per cent). A large proportion of these, particularly the feature films, are broadcast at peak viewing times (between 8:30 PM and 11 PM). The documentaries broadcast are predominantly innocuous wildlife specials, such as *National Geographic Special*, and what are essentially travelogues, such as *Profile of Japan*, *French Focus*, and *USA: TV Satellite File*.

In a very real sense, therefore, while the number of imported television programmes may be on the decrease, these programmes are nonetheless scheduled to enable them to dominate Malaysian television. More importantly, the bulk of these imports is made up of specific genres which invariably are non-contentious, easily marketable, and certainly will not question or challenge the status quo. Indeed, when it has become the norm for transnational cigarette companies like Marlboro (which regularly 'sponsors' sports programmes), Perilly's (which specialises in sponsoring war movies), Dunhill (which has a regular twice-weekly *Dunhill Double* prime time film slot) and Benson and Hedges (whose gimmick is to buy-up whole prime time slots for films uninterrupted by advertising breaks) to dominate programming content on Malaysian television—with the prior approval of the television policy-makers of course— it is quite unlikely that these companies will sponsor anything but programmes that are commercially successful. And they are even less likely to do so otherwise under the prevailing social, cultural and political Malaysian climate.

Local programmes on offer also reveal specific tendencies. Not surprisingly, as indicated in Table 8.3, local news and current affairs programmes make up the bulk (41.6 per cent) of local productions. This is primarily because the news programmes have to cater to a multi-lingual Malaysian community, hence there are separate news productions in English, Malay, Tamil and Mandarin. Also, as of 1 March 1994, both TV1 and TV3 have increased their

Table 8.2: Foreign Programmes Broadcast in a Week on Malaysian Television 1994 (hours)

Programme/Channel	*TV1*	*TV2*	*TV3*	*Total*
Feature film	8 hrs 16 mins (20.8)	21 hrs (37.0)	16 hrs (31.2)	45 hrs 16 mins (30.6)
TV Drama	4 hrs 20 mins (10.9)	13 hrs 30 mins (23.8)	9 hrs 26 mins (18.4)	27 hrs 16 mins (18.4)
Animated Cartoon	7 hrs 15 mins (18.3)	5 hrs (8.8)	5 hrs 30 mins (10.7)	17 hrs 45 mins (12.0)
Documentary	3 hrs (7.6)	2 hrs (3.5)	8 hrs 58 mins (17.5)	13 hrs 58 mins (9.4)
Sports	3 hrs 50 mins (9.6)	30 mins (0.8)	3 hrs 30 mins (6.8)	7 hrs 50 mins (5.3)
Children and Youth	1 hr 45 mins (4.4)	3 hrs (5.2)	2 hrs (3.9)	6 hrs 45 mins (4.6)
Business	4 hrs 57 mins (12.5)	1 hr (1.8)	0 (0)	5 hrs 57 mins (4.0)
Comedy	0 (0)	2 hrs (3.5)	3 hrs (5.8)	5 hrs (3.4)
Game Show	0 (0)	4 hrs 30 mins (8.0)	0 (0)	4 hrs 30 mins (3.0)
Entertainment Variety	0 (0)	2 hrs (3.5)	2 hrs (3.9)	4 hrs (2.7)
News	3 hrs 35 mins (9.0)	0 (0)	0 (0)	3 hrs 35 mins (2.4)
Religious	1 hr 45 mins (4.4)	30 mins (0.8)	0 (0)	2 hrs 15 mins (1.5)
Fashion/Cooking/ Travel	0 (0)	1 hr (1.8)	0 (0)	1 hr (0.7)
Magazine	1 hr (2.5)	0 (0)	0 (0)	1 hr (0.7)
Talk Show	0 (0)	50 mins (1.4)	0 (0)	50 mins (0.6)
Other	0 (0)	0 (0)	56 mins (1.8)	56 mins (0.6)
Total	39 hrs 43 mins (100)	56 hrs 50 mins (100)	51 hrs 20 mins (100)	147 hrs 53 mins (100)

Figures in brackets indicate percentages.

daily broadcast hours significantly to 18 hours—an increase of about 6 hours daily for each channel. There have been two general consequences of this increase. In the first place, the extra time slots, particularly those in the morning, have been conveniently filled with a potpourri of light local current affairs items and

Table 8.3: Local Programmes Broadcast in a Week on Malaysian Television 1994 (hours)

Programme/Channel	*TV1*	*TV2*	*TV3*	*Total*
News and Current Affairs	26 hrs 35 mins (30.5)	13 hrs 55 mins (70.8)	37 hrs 25 mins (46.5)	77 hrs 55 mins (41.6)
Feature Film	10 hrs (11.5)	0 (0)	8 hrs (9.9)	18 hrs (9.6)
Entertainment Variety	10 hrs 25 mins (11.9)	1 hr (5.1)	5 hrs (6.2)	16 hrs 25 mins (8.8)
Teleshopping	9 hrs (10.3)	0 (0)	5 hrs 32 mins (6.9)	14 hrs 32 mins (7.8)
TV Drama	6 hrs (6.9)	3 hrs (15.3)	4 hrs 02 mins (5.0)	13 hrs 02 mins (7.0)
Sports	2 hrs 20 mins (2.7)	0 (0)	6 hrs 45 mins (8.5)	9 hrs 05 mins (4.8)
Religious	5 hrs 34 mins (6.4)	30 mins (2.5)	1 hr (1.2)	7 hrs 04 mins (3.8)
Business	1 hr 33 mins (1.8)	30 mins (2.5)	3 hrs 42 mins (4.6)	5 hrs 45 mins (3.1)
Health/Exercise	3 hrs 30 mins (4.0)	0 (0)	2 hrs 04 mins (2.6)	5 hrs 34 mins (2.9)
Magazine	2 hrs 20 mins (2.7)	0 (0)	1 hr 58 mins (2.4)	4 hrs 18 mins (2.3)
Cooking/Fashion/ Travel	1 hr 30 mins (1.7)	20 mins (1.7)	2 hrs 02 mins (2.5)	3 hrs 52 mins (2.0)
Comdey	2 hrs 30 mins (2.8)	0 (0)	1 hr (1.2)	3 hrs 30 mins (1.9)
Children and Youth	1 hr 15 mins (1.4)	0 (0)	1 hr (1.2)	2 hrs 15 mins (1.2)
Talk Show	45 mins (0.9)	0 (0)	1 hr (1.2)	1 hr 45 mins (0.9)
Documentary	1 hr (1.1)	0 (0)	0 (0)	1 hr (0.5)
Consumer Affairs	30 mins (0.6)	0 (0)	0 (0)	30 mins (0.3)
Other	2 hrs 30 mins (2.8)	25 mins (2.1)	0 (0)	2 hrs 55 mins (1.5)
Total	87 hrs 17 mins (100)	19 hrs 40 mins (100)	80 hrs 30 mins (100)	187 hrs 27 mins (100)

Figures in brackets indicate percentages.

repetitious news reports and summaries. Second, the extra time slots have paved the way for the introduction of a thinly disguised form of advertising called teleshopping. Having quickly increased in terms of allocated air time, teleshopping not only brings products into the audiences' living rooms but also provides the telephone numbers of the retailers for the 'benefit' of audiences. Needless to say, payment for the products is generally made using major credit cards. This increasing use of local television as a relay for the ever-expanding consumer society in Malaysia is further evidenced by the almost-overnight emergence of business-oriented programmes such as *Money Matters*, *Asian Business News* and *Dari BSKL* ('From The Kuala Lumpur Stock Exchange'). Local feature films (9.6 per cent) and television dramas (7 per cent) also continue to pepper the television schedules. And, as one television critic has pertinently pointed out, 'Tired themes about only the Malay community are constantly rehashed in these productions, as if the remaining 50 per cent of the Malaysian population didn't exist and didn't matter. And even when other ethnic communities are included in the storylines, their roles are more often than not peripheral ones' (*The New Straits Times*, 25 January 1992).

Indeed, what is evident is that the locally-produced television dramas, situation comedies, musicals, sports programmes, and even current affairs magazines, such as *Majalah 3*, are essentially pale copies of Western genres. To borrow a phrase from Mattelart et al. (1984, p. 18), each of these programmes appears to have 'a national label stuck on to what is essentially a transnational copy'.

It is, thus, argued here that as far as the links between the international market and Malaysian television are concerned, what may have initially been a convenient and, perhaps, necessary compromise is fast becoming an unholy alliance between transnational media companies and the local ruling elites. It would appear that in their seemingly relentless drive to get as much revenue as is feasible from television, the Malaysian policy-makers, consciously or otherwise, have aligned themselves with the transnational actors, leading Malaysian television even further into the international marketplace and its attendant pressures. At the same time, it would appear that any earlier notions, presumably sincere, about creating a national identity have been pushed further down the list of priorities. Indeed, the RTM Director General himself has declared: 'We want more sponsors for our programmes. Only by making our programmes more effective in terms of viewership can we hope to have any response. We cannot afford to screen ineffective programmes anymore with RTM on the road to corporatisation' (*The New Sunday Times*, 1 January 1989). From the bulk of feature films and soap operas, both local and foreign, currently dominating Malaysian television programming and the emergence of new business-oriented programmes, it would be fair to surmise that what the Director General essentially meant by 'effective' programmes were programmes that are commercially viable and hence attractive to potential sponsors.

Thus, what is being mooted here is that in considering the impact of international forces on Malaysian television, simple and simplistic notions that the West (or North) is Bad and the East (or South) is Good (and innocent) need to be discarded. Instead, the relationship needs to be assessed based on the more realistic premise that '. . .cultural, like economic imperialism, works through the specificities of the local power structure' (Garnham, 1984, p. 5). And this, as we have tried to indicate, certainly holds true for television in Malaysia.

The fact of the matter is that there is a lack of any clear production policy as far as Malaysian television is concerned. Given the immense powers which have been vested in the hands of the Ministry of Information and, more specifically, the Minister of Information, especially through the Broadcasting Act, such a policy, if it were to have any currency and legitimacy, would certainly need to be determined, introduced and implemented via this Ministry. Unfortunately, this has not happened. Instead, what is evident from not only the contents of the Broadcasting Act but also from ministerial declarations is that the emphasis of this government is almost exclusively on restrictions—those which are imposed on the types of material imported and also on programmes produced locally. In the mid-1980s, the declared aim was to impose a quota on imported programmes. Needless to say, because it was not backed with a viable production policy, that idea has been all but forgotten. As Mattelart et al. (1984, pp. 17–18) succinctly put it,

> While it [the quota system] limits foreign influence, it proposes no other alternative than the limit itself. For the quota system to be effective, it must at least be accompanied by the necessary complement of a production policy. A government that adopts the quota solution seems to be doing a lot when it had done virtually nothing.

In the Malaysian context, the reluctance to plan out a long-term television production strategy is, more than likely, due to the short-term material interests of dominant sections in Malaysian society. As has been rightly pointed out (Awang Rosli, 1991), the current cost of producing a local television drama ranges between M $200,000 to M $350,000. The cost of a syndicated movie, on the other hand, is currently around M $100,000. Add to this Malaysian television's drive towards privatisation and the sponsorship of programmes, the advertisers' desire to attract audiences to their products, and their desire to associate their products with certain types of programmes, then, not surprisingly, the syndicated movie would win sponsorship hands down—a fact borne out by the figures on Malaysian television output. It may be glibly asserted that these short-term (and short-sighted) interests are economically logical. However, it is our contention that these interests, coupled with the apparent lack of political will on the part of the Malaysian government, have wide-ranging negative implications, not only for Malaysian television, but also, more importantly, for the development of democracy.

Implications for the Present and Future

This modest preliminary attempt at assessing the implications of the developments discussed so far starts from the assumption that television in Malaysia, as with other mass media, is a site for contestation among different groups in Malaysian society. The major and dominant actors in this dispute would invariably include politicians, especially those in the government, religious bodies and big businesses, including the transnationals. Like many other struggles for overall control, bargains are struck and compromises made, as we have tried to show. But the way in which these compromises have been made thus far appears to indicate that only certain specific interests are being considered and catered to, while the wider interests of Malaysian society are being given short shrift.

The impending introduction of the pay-TV network in late 1995—initially in the lucrative Klang Valley area where the country's capital Kuala Lumpur is located—is a clear illustration of this state of affairs. When the setting-up of such a service was first announced in 1991, the Information Minister, Mohamad Rahmat, asserted that 'the new service will expose Malaysians to the most up-to-date information which they can use to improve their lives' and that the programmes would include 'balanced [*sic*] reporting with regard to American, European and Malaysian news' and 'foreign entertainment items' (*The New Straits Times*, 4 October 1991). At the same time, it was also pointed out that the service would invariably be aimed primarily at the tourist market (since the main intended clients would be the top hotels in the capital) and the business sector.

The argument this paper makes is that such developments, with the full approval of the policy-makers no less, are retrogressive. In the first place, these developments will invariably retard the growth of local television, turning local television productions even more into the poorer cousin, without much chance to improve due to the lack of facilities and incentives provided by a government that fails to see the need for a progressive production policy. Second, and more importantly for democracy, these developments will more than likely widen the already big gap that exists between the information-rich and the information-poor, whereby those who can pay will increasingly have greater access to the broadcast medium. Third, and equally important for democracy, such developments, including the increasing drift into the international marketplace, will all too likely further marginalise alternative explanations, forms of television content, and forms of expression which are not deemed to be commercially viable. In other words, as can be seen with the pale local imitations of Western genres that are currently available on Malaysian television, future developments of this nature will invariably pressure local programme makers to further conform to the dictates and logic of the market, leading to cultural conformity rather than cultural diversity.

Indubitably, such developments within the context of a society that is dominated by an authoritarian state[14] will reduce further the space for struggle and resistance. Hence, in attempting to further legitimise the present social order and to maintain its hegemony over the different groups in Malaysian society, the state will most certainly welcome and encourage these developments, as is already evident. While it is realised that, to paraphrase Garnham (1984), the state is actively collaborating in transferring its functions to the market, the view taken here as to the possible outcome of this transfer is a less optimistic one than that expressed by Garnham.

For Garnham (1984), a likely outcome of this drift into the international economy is that it 'can give rise to a situation in which multinational producers of culture can actually engage in battle with the State for the allegiance of its citizens' (pp. 5–6). The position taken in this paper, however, is that while it 'can', in all probability, lead to that (thus possibly opening up further the space for struggle, contradiction, and resistance leading to genuine liberation perhaps?), unfortunately the reverse is taking place in the context of Malaysia. Rather than engaging in battle with the state, these multinationals so far appear to have been given the red carpet treatment and have become firm allies of a reactionary regime; a regime which is in a position to bargain favourably (for its own interest that is), hence maintaining its own hegemony while, at the same time, helping the multinationals to maintain theirs internationally. And trampled underfoot—for the moment at least—in the wake of these developments, are the hopes for an alternative perspective.

Notes

1. When the country attained political independence on 31 August 1957, it was then called 'Malaya'. In 1963, 'Malaysia' was formed, comprising Malaya (now West Malaysia), Sabah and Sarawak (formerly British Borneo, now East Malaysia) and Singapore. Two years later, Singapore left Malaysia to form an independent state of its own.
2. See *Population And Housing Census Of Malaysia 1980*, Report of the Population Census, Vol. 2.
3. The largest component party is the United Malays National Organisation (UMNO Baru), followed by the Malaysian Chinese Association (MCA), and the Malaysian Indian Congress (MIC). The names of the parties themselves reflect their ethnic bias.
4. For extended discussions and analyses of ethnicity and class in Malaysia see Jomo, 1988a, 1990; Lim 1980; and Hua, 1983.
5. The official White Paper by the Ministry of Home Affairs regarding Operation Lallang was released five months later on 24 March 1988. Among the reasons given for the crackdown, the White Paper noted '. . .religious threats, including "Muslim groups which attempt to cause dissent among the Muslims themselves, and at the same time ferment hostility between followers of different faiths" and "those attempting to spread the Christian faith among Muslims"' (quoted in Jomo, 1988b, pp. 37–38).
6. See Mustafa, 1990, especially pp. 88–89.
7. See Kua (ed.), 1987 for a critique and a variety of alternatives.

8. See Chandra, 1987 for an exhaustive and lucid analysis of the resurgence in Malaysia.
9. See Malaysian Ministry of Information, 1983.
10. The current Malaysian government is essentially a continuation of previous governments—in so far as the main political parties in the ruling Barisan Nasional coalition are the same as those in previous governments. However, the policies enacted by the Mahathir administration, which has been in power for eleven years, especially with regard to deregulation or privatisation, are qualitatively different from those of previous administrations.
11. Four Acts crucial to the operation of the media have either been introduced or brought into operation since Mahathir took office in 1981. These are the Official Secrets Act, 1972 (OSA); the Internal Security Act, 1960 (ISA); the Printing Presses and Publications Act, 1984 and the Broadcasting Act, 1988. For an extended discussion of the utilisation of these Acts with regard to the media see Zaharom, 1991.
12. It is virtually a matter of course for a government-proposed Bill to become an Act since the ruling BN coalition has more than a two-thirds majority in Parliament.
13. The one-week period studied was constructed from the month of November 1994.
14. This notion of an authoritarian state is derived from Poulantzas's scheme of authoritarianism. As Jessop (1982, p. 170) put it, for Poulantzas the basic elements of authoritarianism comprise:

> Firstly, a transfer of power from the legislature to the executive and a concentration of power within the latter; secondly, an accelerated fusion between the three branches of the state—the legislature, executive and judiciary—accompanied by a decline in the rule of law; thirdly, the functional decline of political parties as the privileged interlocutors of the administration and the leading forces in organising hegemony; and, finally, the growth of parallel power networks cross-cutting the formal organisation of the state and exercising a decisive share in its activities.

References

Awang Rosli, A.J. (1991). 'Media import ancam budaya kita' (Imported media threaten our culture). *Dewan Budaya*, 13(2), 30–33.

Brennan, M. (1985). 'Class, politics and race in modern Malaysia'. In Higgott, R. and Robison, R. (eds.). *Southeast Asia: Essays in the political economy of structural change*. London: Routledge and Kegan Paul.

Broadcasting Act (1988). Kuala Lumpur: Government Printers.

Chandra, Muzaffar (1987). *Islamic resurgence In Malaysia*. Petaling Jaya: Fajar Bakti.

Cheong, S. (1993). *Bumiputera Companies in the KLSE*. Petaling Jaya: Corporate Research Services.

Corporate World (1993). 'Malaysia's biggest MBO'. February, 13–16.

Garnham, N. (1984). 'Introduction'. In Mattelart, A. et al. *International image markets: In search of an alternative perspective*. London: Comedia.

Glattback, J. and **Balakrishnan, R.** (1978). 'Malaysia'. In Lent, J. (ed.). *Broadcasting in Asia and the Pacific*. Hong Kong: Heinemann.

Gomez, E.T. (1990). *Politics in business: UMNO's corporate investments*. Kuala Lumpur: Forum.

———. (1991). *Money politics in the Barisan Nasional*. Kuala Lumpur: Forum.

———. (1993). 'Anwar's men gain media control: The management buy-out of NSTP and TV3'. *Aliran Monthly*, 13(2), 2–6.

———. (1994). *Political business: Corporate involvement of Malaysian political parties*. University of New Queensland, Australia: James Cook.

Government of Malaysia (1976). *Third Malaysia Plan 1976–1980*. Kuala Lumpur: Government of Malaysia.

——— (1984). *Mid-term review of the fourth Malaysia Plan 1981–1985*. Kuala Lumpur: Government of Malaysia.

Hua, Wu Yin (1983). *Class and communalism in Malaysia*. London: Zed Books.

Jessop, B. (1982). *The capitalist state*. London: Martin Robertson.

Jomo, K.S. (1988a). *A question of class*. New York: Monthly Review Press.

———. (1988b). 'White paper whitewash'. In *Tangled Web*. New South Wales, Australia: Committee Against Repression in the Pacific and Asia.

———. (1990). *Growth and structural change in the Malaysian economy*. Hampshire: MacMillan.

Karthigesu, R. (1991). 'Two decades of growth and development of Television Malaysia and an assessment of its role in nation building'. (Unpublished Ph.D. thesis, University of Leicester).

Kua, Kia Soong (ed.). (1987). *Defining Malaysian culture*. Petaling Jaya: K. Das Ink.

Lim, Mah Hui (1980). 'Ethnic and class relations in Malaysia'. *Journal of Contemporary Asia*, 10(1–2), 130–54.

Lowe, V. and **Kamin, J.** (1982). *TV programme management in a plural society*. Singapore: AMIC.

Mahathir, Mohamad (1983). 'New government policies'. In Jomo, K.S. (ed.). *The sun also sets: Lessons in looking East*. Kuala Lumpur: Insan.

Malaysian Ministry of Information (1983). *Radio and television Malaysia handbook*. Kuala Lumpur: Ministry of Information.

Mattelart, A. et al. (1984). *International image markets: In search of an alternative perspective*. London: Comedia.

Mustafa, K. Anuar (1990). 'The Malaysian 1990 General Election: The role of the BN media'. *Kajian Malaysia*, VIII (2), 82–102.

Population and Housing Census of Malaysia 1980. *Report of the Population Census, Vol. 2.* Kuala Lumpur: Department of Statistics.

Raju, S.K.S. et al. (1984). 'Treating the Indo-Pakistan conflict: The role of Indian newspapers and magazines'. In Arno, A. and Dissanayake, W. (eds.). *The news media in national and international conflict*. Boulder: Westview Press.

Zaharom, Nain (1991). 'Politics, economics and the media in Malaysia'. *Media Development*, 38(3), 39–42.

——— (1994). 'Commercialization and control in a "caring society": Malaysian media "towards 2020"'. *Journal of Social Issues in Southeast Asia*, 9(2), 178–99.

9

Television and the Emergence of 'Civil Society' in Thailand

Ubonrat Siriyuvasak

Channel 4 of the Thai Television Company, a state enterprise, started its first broadcast in 1955. There are now five national stations, eight regional stations and two cable stations serving 56 million Thais. Conceived during the rule of Prime Minister Phibunsongkram, who had a deep interest in using the mass media for his political and cultural legitimation, television came under state patronage. The seminal medium was thus rooted in the concept of state monopoly similar to radio, post and telegraph services and other types of public goods. However, the state, under the military regime of Field Marshal Sarit Thanarat, began to give privileged franchises to the private sector in 1967 and 1970. This practice continued into the early 1990s when International Broadcasting Ltd. (IBC) and Thai Sky Broadcasting were given their cable franchise by the Mass Communication Organisation of Thailand (MCOT).

During the political crisis in 1992 television was the main propaganda tool of the government, presenting lies and distorted information to its audiences. Newspapers, on the other hand, reported the event independently despite threats of censorship and internal editorial conflicts. In the aftermath of the May 1992 political crackdown the role of television was seriously questioned. It was charged that the state system, coupled with the privileged franchises, were the primary constraints to television's freedom of expression and the public's right to know. Hence, the call to reform the existing television system came along with demands to reform the political system. For a genuine participatory democracy to evolve, the democracy movement saw an open socio-political system, including the communication media, as central.

In this chapter an outline of the development of television broadcasting in Thailand is presented. The first part provides the ground for an analysis of television and freedom of expression and the right to know. The argument is that television must be a medium for public communication and not merely a political instrument of the state or a tool to propagate consumerism for the capitalist system. The two democratic movements, in 1973 and 1992, have started the major groundwork of shifting the power from the hands of the bureaucratic state. But the shift is neither easy nor will it automatically strengthen a participatory democracy. Although the emerging middle classes in the urban areas have spearheaded the transformation, the rural masses must be incorporated into the new civil society in this changing process.

Television and Political Legitimation

As Sinit Sithirak (1992) documented extensively in her *Kamnerd Toratat Thai, 2493–2500* (Inception of Thai television, 1950–1957), television in Thailand was conceived with a definite political objective. The Prime Minister, Field Marshal Phibunsongkram, initiated the idea of instituting television broadcasting expressly to shore up his political power.

During the late 1940s those who worked in radio had already shown serious interest in television as a new medium. It was seen as having 'magic eyes' which would open the minds of the people. Economic expansion of the West and the radio and television corporations, in particular, was another significant force that triggered interest in professionals and the government. The American company RCA, for instance, send detailed information and photos to the Department of Propaganda. It also offered to demonstrate how the new technology operated. At any rate, the interest in technological development and economic pressures were the pretext for establishing the first television network in Thailand. The decisive factor lay largely with Field Marshal Phibunsongkram's political impetus.

As a young army officer, Plack Phibunsongkram was one of the 1932 coup organisers which brought an end to absolute monarchy and introduced a parliamentary regime to replace it, but in 1938 he wrested power from the civilian leader, Pridi Phanomyong, of the Kana Rasadorn or People's Party. He was later ousted after World War II when he sided with the Japanese forces that occupied Thailand. The return of the civilian government, however, was fraught with power struggles. The civilian bureaucrats and politicians who supported a democratic state were on one side against the military, led by the Army, who cherished the idea of an authoritarian regime similar to Germany, Italy and Japan on the other side. It resulted in Field Marshal Phibunsongkram's rise to power for the second time. His second tenure from 1948, via a military coup, set the stage for extensive political suppression, which included the press. In order to legitimise his power he used both military and police force, or what Gramsci called the coercive forces, along with his socio-cultural modernisation project to hegemonise the political opposition and the masses in general.

During this period (1948–55) there were three major policies related to the political–cultural struggle in Thai society. First, the press, the majority of which was critical of the authoritarian regime and supportive of a parliamentary democracy, was censored and widely suppressed. Second, the government created a countrywide radio network in an effort to launch its 'ideological state apparatus' to counter press criticism and political opposition. Central to this project was the introduction of the new medium, television, which was thought to be highly effective in relaying government messages and suitable to fight back the press and its urban readers. The final policy on anti-Communism was the bedrock to wipe out any and all opposition. The Anti-Communist Act was passed in 1952 and the government joined with the US in sending its armed forces to fight in the Korean War. Sithirak (1992) argues that these were the crucial socio-political contexts at the time of the introduction of television broadcasting in 1955.

Since television was among one of Field Marshal Phibunsongkram's main instruments for political propagation, he made a systematic attempt to establish the first station. Two persons from his entourage, led by the Director of the Department of Propaganda, were sent to RCA in the US in 1951. The study tours were undertaken to gather vital information on television transmission and to prepare for the purchase of the technology (Sithirak, 1992). Although the Prime Minister personally supervised the matter it took four years to materialise.

The House of Representatives strongly opposed the idea and the press criticised the project without reservation. The editorial of *Kiatisak*, a newspaper of that time, said that it would have been better to have spent the 24 million baht budget on school buildings for rural students and on housing projects for the homeless. More importantly, this entertainment medium was to serve only a handful of Bangkok residents, perhaps no more than 500, as contrasted with 10 million in the Northeast, which faced severe drought but received only 5 million baht per annum for its relief fund (Sithirak, 1992).

Having encountered strong opposition from within the political and social spheres, the government withdrew the proposal to set up a state television wholly supported by a state budget. It turned to the form of state enterprise which allowed government involvement in certain industries such as logging, rubber, and postal delivery. To make the idea viable, the government hastily repealed the 1935 Radio Communications Act and was able to pass two new Bills—the 1955 Radio Communications Act and the 1955 Radio and Television Broadcasting Act—in Parliament within one day (Sithirak 1992). Although the project was legalised, the question of raising the capital remained unsolved. Four state enterprises and the Navy together contributed 5 million baht to the founding fund of the first meeting of shareholders in 1953. But the government was unable to allocate its share of 15 million baht committed to the Thai Television Company investment capital. Although inundated with numerous problems the Public Relations Department, previously the Department of Propaganda, which had been designated the legal, major shareholder of the government was, nonetheless, able to carry out its assignment. Thai Television Channel 4 was inaugurated on 24 June 1955, Thailand's National Day, to mark the significance of the critical political turn in 1932. Thus, the role of television to legitimise the political power of Field Marshal Phibunsongkram began.

Channel 4 was under tight government control. It was said that the Prime Minister himself was the real boss of the new television station. News and current affairs were the two major areas closely supervised and scrutinised by Prime Minister Phibunsongkram and the Director of the Public Relations Department. Obviously, the medium was part of a wider media campaign to orchestrate political support for the Prime Minister. Programmes and news that promoted the positive image of the Prime Minister and his government were created. These included daily news on the Prime Minister, live broadcasts of state events such as the celebration of the twenty-fifth century of Buddhism, programmes on Thai cultural heritage and the emphasis on proper manners and 'Thainess' in all forms of entertainment programmes. Lastly, Channel 4 broadcast the Seri Manangkasila Party's political campaign, led by the Prime Minister himself, prior to the general election in 1957. Other rival parties, especially the Democrat Party, were not allowed access to air space. The press openly criticised the government and Channel 4's deliberate attempt to prohibit freedom of political expression.

Despite an all out effort to legitimise his political platform, Prime Minister Phibunsongkram failed to hegemonise the military power bloc. His arch rival, General Sarit Thanarat, the Army Commander-in-Chief, was already vying for power against the Prime Minister's close aide, Police Commander General Pao Sriyanond. It was during the 1957 general election that General Sarit Thanarat decided to set up his own station, the Army television. But before Channel 7 was to start its broadcasts, General Sarit staged a coup in September 1957 and took over the Premiership from Field Marshal Phibunsongkram. On 25 January 1958, Army Day, Channel 7 was inaugurated. The new Prime Minister was legitimately in charge of two television stations as well as a whole range of radio networks under the Public Relations Department and the Army. These, among other things, provided for the consolidation of his military power for well over half a decade.

The historical details outlined here demonstrate how the political patronage of television broadcasting in Thai society was formed. The state hegemony deepened as it extended the network to the regions in the 1960s and 1970s (Panpipat and Thanasatit, 1983). In addition to the state networks it gave privileged franchises to two private enterprises, Krungthep Witayu lae Thoratat Ltd. and Bangkok Entertainment Ltd., to operate Channel 7 and Channel 3 respectively. The 'dual system' within this structure has become the primary constraint to freedom of expression and the public's right to know. In practice, the state remains the sole and legal owner of all stations according to the 1955 Radio and Television Broadcasting Act, and can exercise its power of control basically through its 'legal ownership right'.

During the military rule from 1950 to 1973, television was part of the 'state ideological apparatus' as opposed to the newspapers, which acquired a certain degree of freedom because of their structural autonomy. The press could operate independently from the state. Moreover, it did not yield easily to government censorship. But in the case of radio and television, after the 1973 student uprising which brought down the military regime, the civilian government neither restructured the dual system of broadcasting nor relaxed its measure of censorship. It, instead, set up the National Broadcasting Executive Board (NBEB) as a pre-censorship organ. Television and radio, therefore, continued their legitimisation role for the state on the one hand and on the other hand, fostered consumerism through advertisements and a variety of commercial programmes.

Stages of Television Expansion in Thailand 1955–1993

1. State Monopoly	
	State enterprise/State
1955 Channel 4*	Thai Television Ltd.
1958 Channel 7**	The Army, Ministry of Defence
1962–1986 Regional stations	The Public Relations Department
2. Privileged Private Franchise	
	Business enterprise
1967 Army Channel 7	Krungthep Witayu Thoratat Ltd.
1970 MCOT Channel 3	Bangkok Entertainment Ltd.
3. State and Privileged Private Franchise	
	State/Business enterprise
1987 Channel 11	The Public Relations Department
1990 IBC Cable	International Broadcasting Ltd.
1991 Thai Sky Cable	Thai Sky Cable Television Ltd.

In 1994 the government started a UHF channel and the franchise was given to a consortium of business enterprises via an open bidding—which is the first of its kind.

* Presently Channel 9 of MCOT

** Presently Channel 5 of the Army

The Hegemony of Commercial Television

The dual structure of the Thai broadcasting media, as outlined in the previous section, limits access only to two main power groups, i.e., the state and the media industry. After the downfall of the military regime in 1973, the state intensified the allocation of its 'economic right' to the private sector whilst continuing to keep its 'legal ownership'. Equally significant is the state censorship right, which was systematically broadened, rather than narrowed, during the short-lived 'democratic period' (1973–76). Since there was no arena for public programming on television, audiences had to choose between state propaganda or market discourse (see Tables 9.1 and 9.2).

Table 9.1: The Structure of Television Ownership in Thailand 1993

State Agencies	*No. of TV Stations*		
	National	*Regional*	*Cable*
1. The Public Relations Department (PRD)	1 (20%)	8 (100%)	– –
2. The Mass Communication Organisation of Thailand (MCOT)	2 (40%)	– –	2 (100%)
3. Ministry of Defence	2 (40%)	– –	– –
Total	5 (100%)	8 (100%)	2 (100%)

Table 9.2: The Structure of Television Operation in Thailand 1993

Type of Station	*No. of TV Stations*			
	National	*Regional*	*Cable*	*Total*
1. Commercial	4	8	2	14 (93.3%)
2. Non-commercial	1	–	–	1 (6.7%)
Total	5	8	2	15 (100.0%)

Between 1975 to 1987 the Thai economy grew at an average rate of 7.53 per cent per annum. But in 1988 and 1989 the GDP shot up by 13.22 per cent and 12.21 per cent respectively (TDRI, 1991). By comparison, however, the average growth rate of advertising expenditure was considerably higher. It grew at an average rate of

18 per cent during the same period. Consequently, the total spending reached 20,000 million baht (£570 million) in 1993. Over the past decade advertising expenditure on television has accounted for over 50 per cent of the expenditure for the entire media industry (Media Data Resources, 1986–1987; Leo Burnett, 1993)

As advertising expenditure becomes the main source of financial support for television, its hegemony increases. It dictates what *kinds* of programmes should be produced as well as the broadcast time of these programmes. From an analysis of the programme schedules of four commercial television stations in 1981, Supadilok (1984) showed that among the major programme types—news, information, entertainment, and advertisements—on average 60 per cent of the stations'outputs was entertainment. On Channels 7 and 3, the two popular channels, entertainment programmes accounted for 67.19 per cent and 70.12 per cent, and advertisements accounted for 16.67 per cent, which is more than news and information combined (see Table 9.3).

Table 9.3: Percentage of Four Programme Types on Commercial Television 1981

Programme Type	*Channel 3 (%)*	*Channel 7 (%)*	*Channel 5 (%)*	*Channel 9 (%)*
1. Entertainment*	70.12	67.19	60.99	58.48
2. Advertisement	16.67	16.67	16.67	15.38
3. News	6.32	6.65	8.49	14.78
4. Information	6.89	9.49	13.85	11.36

Source: NBEB, Dept of Public Relations, 1981, quoted in Supadilok, 1984. The percentage is calculated on a monthly average figure.

* Entertainment programmes include drama, music, game shows and variety shows.

Media research in the 1990s shows that news programmes now rank among the top three popular programmes (Leo Burnett, 1993). This is due mainly to the changing socio-political context and the initiatives of Pacific Intercommunications, which overhauled its news format on Channel 9 in 1987. The half-hour news programme was expanded to one-and-a-half to two hours and it led to the extension of the evening news bulletin on all channels (Prakobpol, 1991). There is also news in brief every two to three hours. Together, they have increased the time given to news as compared to the early 1980s (see Tables 9.3, 9.4 and 9.5).

Table 9.4: Percentage of Five Programme Types on Four Commercial Television and One Non-commercial Station 1994 (Weekday Programme)

Programme Type	*Channel 3 (%)*	*Channel 7 (%)*	*Channel 5 (%)*	*Channel 9 (%)*	*Channel 11 (%)*
1. Entertainment*	71.38	59.26	72.42	50.92	15.90
2. Advertisement	14.63	16.26	14.81	13.88	–
3. News	12.19	17.31	11.93	11.11	20.45
4. Information**	1.78	7.15	0.82	24.07	27.27
5. Education***	–	–	–	–	36.36

Source: Station programme logs, January 1994. The percentage is calculated on a weekly average figure. Broadcast hours start from 5.30 AM to 2.00 AM, except for Channels 9 and 11.

* Entertainment programmes include drama, music, talk shows, game shows and variety shows.

** Information programmes include documentaries, two to three minute information features and discussion programmes.

*** Education programmes include programmes from the Open Universities and the Ministry of Education.

Table 9.5: Percentage of Five Programme Types on Four Commercial Television and One Non-commercial Station 1994 (Weekend Programme)

Programme Type	*Channel 3 (%)*	*Channel 7 (%)*	*Channel 5 (%)*	*Channel 9 (%)*	*Channel 11 (%)*
1. Entertainment*	72.03	66.66	67.24	69.11	5.71
2. Advertisement	16.26	16.26	16.46	14.70	–
3. News	6.74	13.82	10.69	8.82	11.42
4. Information**	5.69	3.25	5.59	7.35	46.66
5. Education***	–	–	–	–	36.19

Source: Station programme logs, January 1994. The percentage is calculated on a weekly average figure. Broadcast hours start from 5.30 AM to 2.00 AM, except for Channels 9 and 11.

* Entertainment programmes include drama, music, talk shows, game shows and variety shows.

** Information programmes include documentaries, two to three minute information features and discussion programmes.

*** Education programmes include programmes from the Open Universities and the Ministry of Education.

Despite the growing popularity of the news programmes broadcast, journalists focus more or less on presentation rather than on the quality of news. As a measure of self-censorship there was no in-depth reporting or news analysis. The intense competition has also resulted in less diversity of news items and content. An added strategy which closes off audience choice is that all the evening news programmes are scheduled for 7.00 PM, except for Channel 11.

A closer investigation of prime-time programming reveals that there is no serious information programme scheduled on a weekday, except for Channel 9. Consequently, the evening hours of television viewing comprise news as a starter followed by hit serial dramas, game and talk shows, and late night movies and music. Throughout the seven hours, audiences are overwhelmed by a large number of entertainment programmes from three of the four commercial channels.

Since television must rely on advertising revenue as its major source of income, policies on production and programming are skewed towards advertisers targeting the consumer market and not audiences' communication needs. At present, the majority of the programmes are aimed at teenagers, women—both housewives and working women—men and children from upper-middle to upper-lower economic groups. There is no programme for minorities or underprivileged people such as hill tribes, the homeless, or single parents. Advertisers want to reach the largest audience in a cost-effective manner and television programmes are seen as the means to capture audiences for advertisers. Hence, they search for the lowest common denominator in order to achieve their prime objective (Curran, 1986; Leiss et al., 1986; Murdock and Janus, 1985).

On the commercial channels, entertainment programmes are narrowed down to three or four main types to serve market objectives and the quality of the programmes is low in order to save costs. These are game shows, talk shows, and variety shows that help to promote consumerism and the culture industry. Game shows, for example, are devised to sell products and to promote actors, actresses and celebrities. The format, which in theory is open to audience participation, is turned into real show biz since participants in the programmes are usually drawn from the entertainment industry and are not outside applicants or volunteers from the audiences at home or in the studio.

But as news and information programmes become popular with audiences, advertisers are concerned that dramas, and game and talk shows are losing ground. Recently, more light entertainment programmes, such as situation comedies and talk shows, have been devised to appeal to younger audiences. New production techniques and a variety of advertising tactics are also used to capture larger audiences as well as to promote consumerism. For example, the glamorous signs and products which appear in a large number of programmes are part of the whole advertising package. Critics argue that these kinds of tactics may produce subliminal effects on audiences, particularly on young children (Ewen, 1976). But the NBEB did not penalise producers who extended commercials into their programmes. The Board was more interested in censoring inflated claims and false information in the commercials. The 10 minutes per hour limit set by the NBEB was, in fact, nullified. This means that advertising could control the structure of television programming and could, at the same time, penetrate into a wide range of television programmes. It is quite obvious that market discourse now cuts deeper into the public arena as presented on the small screen.

Public Space and Television Programme

> Communication media, it is argued, should aim to empower a plurality of citizens who are governed neither by undemocratic states nor by undemocratic market forces. The media should be for the public use and enjoyment of all citizens and not for the private gain or profit of political rulers or businesses (Kean, 1991, pp. xi–xii).

Public space for Thai citizens to express themselves was still lacking in the 1980s, despite continual economic and social change and a growing middle class. The patron–client relationship between the state and the television industry exacerbated the duopoly structure, although their conflicting interests often brought tension to the industry. Whilst the fast growing television industry hindered access of new entrants to station ownership, the structure was unable to cope with rising demands from both advertisers and audiences. It was neither a free market system nor was there freedom of expression.

Revolutionary Order 17, issued after the student massacre in 1976, stipulates that all programmes should promote the official discourse on Nation, Religion and King and refrain from supporting the counter-ideology of Communism. Furthermore, political interviews, discussions, lectures, or entertainment programmes related to politics must be pre-recorded. This means a total blackout on public political discourse. The industry, therefore, practised self-censorship as a matter of routine until it was seriously questioned during the May 1992 political crisis.[1]

During the political confrontation in May 1992, one of the key issues was freedom of expression and the public's right to know. The state media, radio and television, were used to legitimise the official discourse. Hence, all oppositional discourses were censored, leaving the public furious and confused ('Angry viewers revolt against television', *The Nation*, 8 May 1992). The press, as the only open space, cried out against state manipulation of information ('TV propaganda distorts the issues and hides truth', Editorial, *The Nation*, 10 May 1992). When the government and the state media failed to convince the public and the demonstrators, they turned to violence to silence public expressions, but the Suchinda government was forced to step down as the King intervened to put an end to the conflict.

The demand for freedom of expression was overwhelming in the aftermath of the crackdown in May 1992. Two public discussions were organised on May 28 and 29 at Chulalongkorn University and Thammasart University calling for the liberalisation of television and state media as a whole. More than 6,000 people attended the events. For the first time in the history of broadcasting in Thailand, freedom of expression on radio and television was viewed as a 'natural right' equal to other basic human rights (Wasi, 1992). In order to acquire this 'natural right' it was suggested that the state media system should be liberalised and that state ownership should be diversified. This would enable the private sector to genuinely have access to the broadcasting system (Institute of Mass Communication Education, 1992).

This political juncture, Thirayut Boonmi (1992), a leading social critic pointed out, was the moment when social consciousness on democracy began to grow. Such is the time to liberate the broadcasting media from the state, as he demands.

> Press freedom is essential and is very important for the social and political development of the Thai society . . . but let's not rely on the military nor political parties to sustain this development. It is the society as a whole that would make it a reality,

> every part of the society must be strengthened . . . the mass media, the press and television, academia, doctors, lawyers, business people,etc., . . . past events showed that the middle classes have been strengthened, they have the courage to fight the authoritarian regimes, they have democratic spirit within their hearts . . . so we must rely on the people, on all groups and all professions in the society . . . and this is the moment to liberate television from state dominance . . . (Institute of Mass Communication Education, 1992, pp. 42–43).

Although May 1992 was a political watershed for Thai society, the emergence of the middle classes in the late 1980s, with their economic and political interests, was seen as the key context which circumscribed it. As Charoenlert (1993) suggests, the middle classes have broadened during the past two decades. They now include business entrepreneurs, small industrialists, professionals, intellectuals such as journalists, media practitioners, independent writers, and students, and blue and white collar workers, as well as bureaucrats. However, the strength of the democracy movement in the 1990s did not involve not only the middle classes in the urban areas. Manarungsan (1993), Ondam (1993) and Piriyarangsan (1993) argue that the urban poor and their grass roots organisations, blue collar workers, workers of non-governmental organisations, and peasant organisations are the real political catalysts in Thai society. Compared to the 1970s, when social movements were limited to a small circle of intellectuals, journalists, students and labour leaders, the formation of the civil society in the 1990s has been extensively expanded.

These new social blocks were discontented with the status quo and sought a liberal democracy instead of the old authoritarian regime. It is an era in which military intervention in the political sphere is rejected. The protests against the draft constitution in November 1991 that led in 1992 to the demonstrations opposing the non-elected Prime Minister, General Suchinda Kraprayoon, were an obvious indicator of this changing social formation (Charoenlert, 1993; Laothamatas, 1993).[2]

Laothamatas (1993) points out that the involvement of the urban middle classes or the so-called 'mobile phone mob' during the May 1992 demonstration shows how they have awakened to defend their economic and political interests. The Confederation for

Democracy and the Campaign for Popular Democracy which represents academics, students, politicians, labour leaders, women and non-governmental organisations command much broader support from the middle classes and business people than the two previous democracy movements in 1973 and 1976. Furthermore, they were able to gain access to the broadcast media to express their political concerns. The highlights were the political campaigns during the general elections in March and September 1993. Party leaders were invited to present party policies and debate current issues on television. At the same time, 'democracy fora' were organised in major cities throughout the country together with the Poll Watch campaign. These critical moments caught the spirit of the middle class.

With this new sense of political involvement there was a serious need to widen the public space which was previously closed off. After May 1992, leading journalists and academics from several universities enthusiastically seized the opportunity to push for new public spaces on radio and television. Although no new law has been enacted to guarantee their freedom of expression, they are able to broadcast programmes which discuss and criticise current political and social affairs with open line commentaries from audiences. This is totally in opposition to the customary 'culture of silence' in the radio and television industry.

The most popular format since 1992 has been the panel discussion format which invites experts or key figures from public and private sectors to debate particular issues.[3] The format is open to public participation in two ways. There may be a studio audience, such as on *Mong Tang Moom* on Channel 11 (similar to BBC's *Question Time*), or phone-in commentaries from home audiences, such as on *Trong Praden* (Right to the point) on Channel 9. In addition, there are three programmes which focus on information and commentaries from experts and well-known personalities. These are: *Nation News Talk* on Channel 9, *Jang Si Bia* (Open explanation) on Channel 3, and *Kor Wela Nok* (Time off) on Channel 7. The two most popular programmes, *Mong Tang Moom* and *Nation News Talk*, take the middle classes' *positions* in criticising the state on the one hand and the private sector on the other. Whilst *Mong Tang Moom* is well-known for bringing out different view points on conflicting issues in reaction to audiences' questions, *Nation News Talk* is popular because of the outspoken style of presentation of Suthichai Yoon, editor of *The Nation*. The programme is oriented towards the audiences' right to information, whereas *Mong Tang Moom* emphasises audience participation and freedom of expression. At the same time programmes such as *Kor Wela Nok* adhere to the tradition of airing official discourse, whilst *Jang Si Bia* leans towards corporate discourse.

The new trend in current affairs programmes on television is a structural break from the old pattern of censorship and control. The strength of the civil society is demonstrated by its active engagement in these programmes. In 1991, prior to the May crackdown, *Mong Tang Moom* was suspended because the programme criticised the National Peace Keeping Council (NPKC) for plotting to legitimise its power through the new constitution. But strong protests from the audience were able to prevent the state from axing *Mong Tang Moom* outright. Despite stringent efforts to control this kind of public discourse, the state is now faced with resistance from audiences whose appreciation of freedom and truth has become a new cornerstone for the democratisation of Thai society (Pinthong, 1993).

The programmes discussed earlier, although signifying more freedom of expression, account for a tiny portion of the total broadcasting hours on television. All of these programmes are 60-minute programmes broadcast weekly, except for *Kor Wela Nok* which is a 30-minute programme. On the entertainment side there is little qualitative change in programming. Advertisers continue to support corporate discourse and consumerism in the majority of the programmes. As demonstrated in the previous section, commercial programmes get priority and their main interest lies in capturing potential consumers for advertisers. They are concerned with transmitting the normative values and ideology of a patriarchal society. But at the same time, they promote individualism and sexual liberalism as exemplified by presenters, actors and actresses in middle-class life styles.

If the civil society is to be strengthened there must be sufficient public space for all groups to articulate their interests and concerns. The Anand government was in favour of liberalising the television industry as a means to extend freedom of expression for the middle-classes. It announced the launch of five new UHF channels in July 1992. They were to be equally divided between the government and the private sector and one channel would be reserved for emergency purposes (*Siam Rath Weekly*, 30 August–5 September 1992).[4] The television industry and the government believed that in liberalising the system the right to information and freedom of expression of audiences would be guaranteed. From the industry's point of view more channels and open competition would naturally lead to improvement in the overall quality of television programmes (Onwimon, 1993).

Academics and non-governmental organisations, however, argue that liberalism is an insufficient policy and that reforming the entire television system at this stage needs a democratising process. They propose a draft bill on radio and television which would guarantee freedom of expression and the right to information of Thai citizens (Creative Media Foundation, June 1992). In order to achieve such a goal, ownership rights must be shared between the state, the private sector, and non-governmental and public organisations. This will open the way for the public to have direct access to the television industry and to enable political and cultural diversity in programming. The draft bill also emphasises freedom of expression without state censorship (Waranyu et al.,1993).[5]

The rapid growth of new social groups and classes has been an essential force in bringing about political changes. As a result, more public space is made available on television for critical discussion of political and social issues. However, the public's right to freedom of expression and information has not been fully achieved. Indirect censorship often prevails when the government is openly criticised on political or social controversies (Pinthong, 1993). To democratise the television system, the civil society and the state must go beyond the free market idea. The notion of audiences as citizens, and not merely consumers of products, must be genuinely embraced in order to provide for active participation in the democratisation of Thai society as a whole.

Notes

1. For a summary of the May 1992 political crisis and military crackdown of demonstrators at Radjadamnern Ave., see, for example, *The Nation* special issue on 'Record of the May tragedy', May 1992 and The News Reporter Association of Thailand, 1993.
2. For a more detailed analysis of the role of the middle-classes see, for example, Piriyarangsan and Pongpaichit (eds.), 1993.

3. The Creative Media and Dr. Jermsak Pinthong were the catalysts spearheading the *Mong Tang Moom* programme in 1991. It received financial support from the Bangjak Petroleum Refinery, one of the state enterprises. Participants on the programme include politicians, academicians, journalists, non-governmental organisations, business people and government officials. The group also produces *Weti Chaobaan* (People's forum) which is a discussion programme for peasants and rural audiences. Participants are local community leaders and local intellectuals. In 1994, Dr. Jermsak started his own production company, Watchdog, and produced the programme *Kor Kid Duay Kon* (Let me express my idea) on Channel 9. The programme is aimed at the elite and urban audiences.)

   On Channel 5, the Army's programme *Sontana Panha Banmuang* (Forum on national problems) is revamping its presentation in order to compete with other discussion programmes. *Sontana Panha Banmuang* was started in 1981 as a platform for military discourse. All television stations were required to transmit this programme on Sunday evening, but the relay was reduced to two channels, Army Channel 5 and 7, in 1989. At present (1994), the programme is broadcast on Channel 5 only.
4. Anand's policy on providing new television stations is carried forward by the present government, but only one channel will be opened for bidding in May 1994. In this plan, there is no specific allocation for public programming.
5. Both the government and the opposition parties are reviewing the draft bill on radio and television before submitting it, albeit separately, to Parliament.

References

Boonmi, T. (1992). Discussion in Institute of Communication Education et al. *Wikrit Suemuanchon Thai* (The Thai mass media in crisis). Bangkok: Kledthai Press.

Charoenlert, V. (1993). 'Chon Chan Klang kab Hetkarn Prusapakom' (The middle class and May 1992). In Piriyarangsan, S. and Pongpaichit, P. (eds.). *Chon Chan Klang bon Krasae Prachathippatai.* (The middle class and Thai democracy). Bangkok: The Political Economy Centre, Faculty of Economics, Chulalongkorn University and Friedrich Ebert Stiftung.

Creative Media Foundation (1992). Seminar on Media Law Reform. 9 June. The House of Parliament.

Curran, J. (1986). 'The impact of advertising on the British mass media'. In Collins, R., et al. (eds.). Media, culture and society: A critical Reader. London: Sage.

Ewen, S. (1976). *Captains of consciousness:Advertising and social roots of the consumer culture.* New York: McGraw–Hill.

Institute of Mass Communication Education et al. (1992). *Wikrit Suemuanchon Thai* (The Thai mass media in crisis). Bangkok: Kledthai Press.

Kean, J. (1991). The media and democracy. Cambridge: Polity Press.

Laothamatas, A. (1993). *Mob Mue Tue: Chon Chan Klang lae Nak Thurakit Kab Pattanakarn Prachathippatai* (Mobile phone mob: The middle class and business people on the development of democracy). Bangkok: Matichon Printing Press.

Leiss, W., **Kline, S.** and **Jhally, S.** (1986). *Social communication in advertising: Persons, products & images of well-being*. London: Methuen.

Leo Burnett Ltd. (1993). *Media Pocket Guide*. Bangkok: Leo Burnett Ltd.

Manarungsan, S. (1993). 'Chon Chan Klang Kab Polawat nai Pak Kaset Thai' (The middle class and Thai agriculture). In Piriyarangsan, S. and Pongpaichit, P. (eds.). *Chon Chan Klang bon Krasae Prachathippatai* (The middle class and Thai democracy). Bangkok: The Political Economy Centre, Faculty of Economics, Chulalongkorn University and Friedrich Ebert Stiftung.

Media Data Resources Co. Ltd. (1987). *The Thai Advertising Industry Guide, 1986–1987*. Bangkok: Media Data Resources Co. Ltd.

Murdock, G. and **Janus, N.** (1985). 'Mass communication and the advertising industry'. *Reports and papers on mass communication No. 97*. Paris: UNESCO.

Ondam, B. (1993). 'Ongkarn Pattana Ekachon kab Prachathippatai Thai' (The NGOs and Thai democracy). In Piriyarangsan, S. and Pongpaichit, P. (eds.). *Chon Chan Klang bon Krasae Prachathippatai* (The middle class and Thai democracy). Bangkok: The Political Economy Centre, Faculty of Economics, Chulalongkorn University and Friedrich Ebert Stiftung.

Onwimon, S. (1993). Interview in *Siam Rath Weekly* (Special issue), 40(17), 26 Sept–2 Oct, 67–68.

Panpipat, K. and **Thanasatit, P.** (1983). 'Toratat Thai: Jak Bangkunprom tung Rabob Daotiem' (Thai television: From bangkunprom to satellite). In *Wiwatanakarn Suemuanchon Thai* (The development of the Thai mass media). Bangkok: The Faculty of Communication Arts, Chulalongkorn University.

Pinthong, J. (1993). Interview in *Siam Rath Weekly* (Special issue), 40(17), 26 Sept–2 Oct, 62–64.

Piriyarangsan, S. (1993). 'Lukchang, Kon Chon Muang kab Hetkarn Duan Prusapakom' (The workers, the urban poor and the May 1992). In Piriyarangsan, S. and Pongpaichit, P. (eds.). *Chon Chan Klang bon Krasae Prachathippatai* (The middle class and Thai democracy). Bangkok: The Political Economy Centre, Faculty of Economics, Chulalongkorn University and Friedrich Ebert Stiftung.

Piriyarangsan, S. and **Pongpaichit, P. (eds.).** (1993). *Chon Chan Klang bon Krasae Prachathippatai* (The middle class and Thai democracy). Bangkok: The Political Economy Centre, Faculty of Economics, Chulalongkorn University and Friedrich Ebert Stiftung.

Prakobpol, R. (1991). 'Kuam Kadyang Tang Karnmuang lae Setakit Nai Karn Plit Khao Toratat' (Political and economic conflict in the production of television news). *Journal of Communication Arts*, 12(1), 30–36.

Siam Rath Weekly (1992). 'Anand's policy on free TV'. 39(14), 30 Aug–5 Sept, 14–16.

Sithirak, S. (1992). *Kamnerd Toratat Thai, 2493–2500* (The inception of Thai television, 1950–1957). Bangkok: The 60th Anniversary of Democracy Project.

Supadilok, B. (1984). *Sidhi Karn Suesarn nai Prates Thai* (The right to communicate in Thailand). Bangkok: Thai Kadi Suksa Institute, Thammasat University and the Social Science and Humanity Textbook Project Foundation.

The News Reporter Association of Thailand (1993). *Record of news correspondents at Radjadamnern Battle Ground, May 1992*. Bangkok: The News Reporter Association of Thailand.

The Thailand Development Research Institute Foundation (TDRI) (1991). *Thailand Economic Information Kit.* Bangkok: TDRI.

Waranyu, W., Wisarupit, W. and Siriyuvasak, U. (1993). Draft Bill on Radio and Television Broadcasting. Bangkok: Creative Media Foundation.

Wasi, P. (1992). *Prachathippatai 2535* (Democracy 1992). Bangkok: Moh Chaobaan Press.

10

The Evolution of Prime-time Television Scheduling in Hong Kong

Terence Lo and Chung-bong Ng

Commercial broadcast television in Hong Kong, as elsewhere, depends on advertising revenues for profit. Television viewers are significant to the extent that they can be delivered as audience figures to advertisers. Development of commercial broadcast television is, therefore, closely related to the overall development of the economy. Rapid economic growth in a society increases its affluence and raises the purchasing power of consumers. With increased potential purchasing power available in society, more financial resources are invested in product advertising to tap this potential.

Commercial television as a medium of advertising has to compete against other media of communication for the advertising dollar. Thus, it will not hesitate to put pressure on television producers to adjust their programming and scheduling strategies to pull in as many viewers of the right type as possible, who can then be packaged as audience figures to attract advertisers.

As a mass-oriented medium, broadcast television in Hong Kong has tended to benefit economically when there has been a strong demand for advertising slots to promote standard products that are closely associated with the daily life of a large section of the population. With only a limited amount of air time for advertising, broadcast television has adapted its scheduling strategies to accommodate as much advertising as possible in order to boost its advertising revenues. This has been done by lengthening the prime-time period as a whole, especially when television audience figures show a steady growth in both quantitative and qualitative terms. On the other hand, during the years when fewer people with the adequate purchasing power have stayed in front of the television screen during prime-time, resources have been directed towards strengthening the programmes in certain parts of the prime-time schedule to boost audience figures strategically.

This paper will trace the evolution of Hong Kong Television Broadcasts Limited–Jade's (TVB–Jade) prime-time programme schedule since it started operation in 1967, and relate the changes in its scheduling strategies to some broad trends in Hong Kong's economic growth and socio-demographic changes in the last two-and-a-half decades.

Broadcast TV in Hong Kong

Broadcast television in Hong Kong started in 1967 when Television Broadcasts Limited (TVB) obtained governmental franchise to run a Cantonese channel and an English channel. Competition emerged when Rediffusion Television Limited (RTV), previously operating a wired television service, started its Cantonese channel in 1973, and its English channel in 1974. RTV changed its name to Asia Television Limited (ATV) in 1982.

For a time, competition further intensified when Commercial Television Limited (CTV) started a third Cantonese channel in 1975. The emergence of CTV provided an imaginary enemy for the other two Cantonese channels, and helped to boost competitive dynamism within the TV industry. CTV suffered serious financial losses and ceased operation in 1978. This happened at a time when both Hong Kong's economy and its television industry as a whole were enjoying very healthy growth.

Television viewership in Hong Kong increased from just over 6,000 people in 1957, when RTV started its wired television service, to over two million people by the end of 1970 (Hong Kong Government Press, 1971). Seventy-two per cent of all households in Hong Kong owned televisions in 1971. The proportion increased to 89 per cent in 1975 (Hong Kong Government Press, 1977), and further increased to over 98 per cent in 1987 (Hong Kong Government Press, 1989). As one of Hong Kong's principal leisure activities, television has been accepted as a major means which advertisers use to reach the local population.

Up to the mid-1980s, TVB–Jade constantly maintained an average of 80 per cent share of the prime-time audience viewing the two Cantonese channels (The Broadcasting Review Board, 1985), often achieving over 90 per cent share during weekday prime-time (TVB–Jade, 1987). The channel has established itself as a household name in Hong Kong, and is still commonly known as 'mo-sin' (wireless). Nevertheless, from the late 1980s onwards, the total TV audience size has been on the decline. Between 1987 and 1988, total television viewership fell by 14 per cent (*Media and Marketing*, 29 April 1988). TVB–Jade has also been losing its average audience share, which fell to 74 per cent in the second quarter of 1991 (TVB–Jade, 1991a) and 66 per cent in October 1991 (TVB–Jade, 1991b). Throughout 1994, reports in the printed press showed concern about whether TVB–Jade was able to stabilise its audience share at 60 to 70 per cent, while taking for granted that fewer people in Hong Kong are now likely to rush home to watch prime-time TV.

Still, with TVB–Jade remaining the stronger Cantonese television channel in Hong Kong, this study will limit its focus to the changes in the channel's programme schedule. This is also partly because TVB–Jade's direct competitor, ATV-Home, being the weaker competitor, has been much more flexible in its programme scheduling strategies. This makes it less suitable for a study focusing on broader trends.

News and the Definition of Prime-time

Television prime-time is known locally as 'gold time', a term that presumably originated in advertising sales sectors and later became popular among television viewers as well. The early evening news and weather reports have often been used as a signpost to indicate the start of prime-time television. In 1967, when TVB–Jade started operating, the early evening news and weather reports were scheduled at 7:30–7:59 PM. In 1976, the year which many veteran television producers identify as marking the beginning of the 'golden era' of Hong Kong television, the early evening news and weather reports were moved to the 6:30–6:59 PM slot, i.e., an hour earlier.

Weekday prime-time for TVB has been loosely understood by its production staff as extending from 7:00 PM, i.e., when the 6:30 evening news programme ends, to the time when *Enjoy Yourself*

Tonight (EYT)—a longstanding family-oriented variety show—ends, leading up to late news. In 1986, for example, TVB–Jade's market development researchers introduced, for internal discussion, the concept of 'non-Jade watchers' (TVB–Jade, 1986) to categorise people who did not normally watch the station's prime-time programmes but were nevertheless consistent watchers of its news reports.

This commonsense definition of prime-time accepted among television production staff reflects the importance of advertising as a source of revenue, and the traditional prohibition in Hong Kong of advertising breaks during news programmes. Still, this can be contrasted with the inclusion of the early evening news and late news reports as part of prime-time in RTV's public promotion campaign in 1980. It appears that while prime-time has been understood by television producers as starting from the end of early evening news, television viewers have been encouraged to start evening television watching when the early evening news begins. Many viewers have also taken the end of the late evening news as an indication of the end of interesting television programmes for the day.

It seems clear, therefore, that the early evening news and late news have been accepted as the common daily signposts of the start and end of prime-time television. The local Broadcasting Authority recently lifted the rule prohibiting advertising breaks during news programmes on the grounds that this would provide more incentive for extending the length of news programmes and improving their quality. In time, this development is likely to reinforce among television producers the conception of news as part of prime-time television. Financial reports, traditionally immediately following the news report, have also become more important, as an increasing number of local people get involved in various financial investment pursuits as part of everyday life. There have indeed been recent attempts to slot in financial reports before the early evening news as a way to shift, somewhat, the signposts of prime-time television.

Prime-time Programme Schedule Changes: 1967 to 1994[1]

In the course of the 1960s and the 1970s, TVB and RTV introduced various changes in their prime-time scheduling patterns, apparently in response to increasing demand for advertising slots. Prime-time was experimentally extended during various phases from 10:30 PM to after 11:00 PM, and even after 12 midnight, at which times late news was scheduled. These changes consistently occurred when the Hong Kong economy showed significant upturns.

Prime-time can also be lengthened by scheduling early evening news in an earlier slot. This is what happened in 1976, when TVB–Jade's early evening news was moved permanently from 7:30 PM to 6:30 PM, which effectively extended prime-time by one hour. The year also marked the start of what later became known, rather nostalgically, as the 'golden era' of television in Hong Kong. It was also a year when the Hong Kong community experienced unprecedented economic prosperity.

This section will trace, in more detail, the relationship between prime-time TV scheduling changes and economic developments in Hong Kong. It will look at TVB–Jade's prime-time scheduling in terms of four periods of development:

1. Early Development: 1967–72
2. Rapid Growth: 1973–81
3. Consolidation: 1982–88
4. Focus on Infotainment: 1989 onwards

Early Development: 1967–72

1967–68: Launching of Broadcast Television

In November 1967, when TVB–Jade started operating, its weekday prime-time programme schedule was simple and straightforward. Prime-time typically started with early evening news at 7:30 PM. Next came a Chinese feature film in the 8:00–9:29 PM slot. This was followed by *EYT*—a channel-produced variety show—in the 9:30–10:29 PM slot. Prime-time ended with late news in the 10:30–10:59 PM slot. There was a late-night viewing slot at 11:00–11:30 PM before the channel closed.

The Chinese feature films in the 8:00–9:29 PM slot were mostly in Cantonese, the most widely spoken Chinese language in Hong Kong. Some were in Mandarin and some in Swatow. The late-night viewing slot at 11:00–11:29 PM was normally filled with a 30-minute episode of imported drama series. For example, for several months in 1967 and early 1968, the slot was filled with *Addams Family*—a macabre comedy—on all seven nights.

1969–72: Emergence of Local Television

In this period, TVB–Jade gradually moved away from readymade television programmes and films purchased for broadcast on the channel to programmes produced by the channel itself. It also progressively introduced greater programming variety. Rather than relying on Cantonese feature films alone, the early part of prime-time was filled with a variety of imported drama series, and channel-produced game shows and music programmes. This was the period of gradual emergence of local television.

Start/End of Prime Time on One/Two Weekday Evenings a Week

	1967	1969	
7:30		*News & Weather*	7:30
8:00	Feature film (Chinese)	Games/Music Shows	8:00
		Drama series (imported)	8:30
		(Music shows/Drama series [imported]/Game)	8:30/ 9:00
9:30		EYT	9:30
10:30	*News & Weather*		
11:00	Drama series (imported)		
		News & Weather	11:15
		Late-night programmes	11:15
11:30	Close		

It should be noted that this was also a period when the popularity of broadcast television was growing phenomenally. Over 70 per cent of local households were television owning, and many people in non-television owning households did watch television regularly with neighbours. Advertisers rapidly recognised broadcast television as a highly efficient advertising medium.

In 1969, the Hong Kong economy experienced a substantial jump in its gross domestic product (GDP), with an annual growth rate of 18.2 per cent. In real terms, it was a 14.0 per cent increase and the per capita GDP increase was 12.2 per cent. During 1969, TVB raised its prime-time advertising rates twice, the first time by 80.0 per cent and the second time by 50.0 per cent (*Media and Marketing*, 29 April 1986), representing a composite 270.0 per cent increase. There was another increase of 30.1 per cent in 1970.

Table 10.1: Gross Domestic Product and Population: Annual Growth Rates

Year	Annual Growth Rates (%)			
	Gross GDP (at current prices)	*Gross GDP (at constant prices)*	*Per Capita GDP (at constant prices)*	*Population*
1972	15.2	7.2	5.4	1.7
1973	27.2	14.2	11.6	2.4
1974	15.3	1.8	−0.7	2.5
1975	3.9	2.2	0.5	1.8
1976	28.2	18.8	17.5	1.1
1977	14.5	10.2	8.6	1.5
1978	16.3	10.3	8.2	1.9
1979	31.9	11.7	6.8	6.1
1980	27.2	10.4	7.5	2.7
1981	20.3	9.4	7.1	2.4
1982	12.9	3.0	1.4	1.6
1983	11.4	6.5	4.9	1.5
1984	19.8	9.5	8.4	1.0
1985	5.3	0.2	−0.9	1.1
1986	14.3	11.1	9.7	1.3
1987	23.1	14.5	13.4	1.0
1988	18.0	8.3	7.4	0.8
1989	15.1	2.7	1.7	1.0
1990	12.0	2.8	2.4	0.3
1991	14.1	4.1	3.2	0.9
1992	15.0	5.3	4.2	1.0

Sources: *Hong Kong Social and Economic Trends, 1967–77.*
Hong Kong Social and Economic Trends, 1976–86.
Hong Kong Social and Economic Trends, 1980–90.
Hong Kong Annual Digest of Statistics, 1993 edition.

Hong Kong was definitely going through rapid economic growth. This encouraged investments in developing locally-produced television programmes, which proved to have higher mass appeal than imported programmes, which in turn justified higher advertising rates.

Rapid Growth: 1973–88

1973–75: Attempted Take-off

The station's prime-time programme scheduling format developed after a series of relatively cautious adjustments in the late 1960s and early 1970s, and remained virtually unchanged up to late 1973. A number of developments became noticeable round 1973. First, there was much more frequent use of channel-produced programmes, especially local drama series, to fill the early part of prime-time; second, there was substantial increase in programming variety in this part of prime-time over the week; third, prime-time was significantly extended, with late news scheduled shortly after midnight.

	1969	1973	
7:30		*News & Weather*	7:30
8:00	Games/Music Shows	Drama series (local) /Music shows	8:00
8:30	Drama series (imported)	Games	8:30
(8:30	Music shows/games	(Drama series [local/	
9:00	Drama series [imported])	imported] 8:30–9:30)	
		Drama series (local/ imported)/Current Affairs	9:00
9:30	EYT	News	9:30
		EYT	9:38
		Feature film/Sports/Drama series (imported)	10:38
11:15	*News & Weather*		
11:25	Late-night programmes		
		News	12:08

Thus, prime-time was significantly adjusted to bring in more advertising dollars, both by improving the quality of programming and by lengthening the prime-time period. It seems obvious that these changes were responses to the rapid economic growth in 1973, and were it not for the sudden economic slowdown later that year, local television would have entered its 'golden era' then.

In 1973, there was a substantial jump in Hong Kong's GDP, with an annual growth rate of 27.2 per cent. In real terms, it was a 14.2 per cent increase and the per capita GDP increase was 11.6 per cent. Nevertheless, such prosperity was shortlived. Following the Hong Kong stock market catastrophe in 1973, the GDP growth rate and the per capita GDP growth rate in real terms in 1974 fell to 1.8 per cent and −0.7 per cent respectively, even though the GDP growth rate at current prices was a seemingly healthy 15.3 per cent (see Table 10.1). Also, economic growth clearly slowed down in 1975. In 1973, TVB–Jade raised its prime-time advertising rates by a modest 13.9 per cent. There was no more substantial increase until 1976 (*Media and Marketing*, 29 April 1986).

1976–81: 'Golden Era'

In the course of 1975 and 1976, late news was repeatedly pushed to progressively later time slots, apparently to experiment with ways to lengthen the prime-time period. Then in late 1976, the prime-time programme schedule was changed radically. Early evening news at 7:30 PM was moved to 6:30 PM. Late news was scheduled after midnight at 12:30 AM. This represented a very significant extension of the prime-time period.

	1973	1976	
		News & Weather	6:30
		Drama serial (local)	7:00
7:30	*News & Weather*		
		Sitcom/Games/Drama Series (local)/ Documentaries (Drama II 7:55–8:54)	7:55/ 8:25
8:00	Drama series (local)/Music shows		
8:30	Games (8:30–9:30 Drama series [local/imported])		
		News	8:55
9:00	Drama series (local/imported)/ Current affairs	EYT	9:00
9:30	News		
9:38	EYT		
		Drama serial (imported)	10:30
10:38	Feature film/Sports/ Drama series (imported)		
12:08	*News*		
12:15	Close		
		News	12:30
		Late-night programmes	12:40

In 1977, late news was radically rescheduled from 12:30 AM to 10:30 PM, with programmes after late news categorised as late viewing. This was apparently a strategy to focus resources in channel-produced programmes. By 1980, TVB–Jade's prime-time schedule consisted simply of two tiers of local drama serials, followed by the variety show *EYT*. Such a programming strategy proved immensely successful. Those years are still known among veteran television practitioners as representing the 'golden era' of local television. This is apparently a reflection of their personal participation in the dynamic development of channel-produced programmes in the 7:00–10:30 PM time slot of prime-time, a slot that was responsible for bringing in a major portion of the prime-time advertising revenue.

	1976	1980	
6:30		*News & Weather*	6:30
7:00	Drama serial (local) I		
		Drama serial (local)I	7:05
7:55/	Sitcom/Games/Drama		
8:25	Series (local/Documentaries	Drama serial (local) II	8:00
(7:55	Drama serial [local] III)		
8:55	News		
9:00		EYT	9:00
10:30	Drama serial (imported)	*News*	10:30
		Drama serial (imported)	10:40
		& other late-night programmes	→
11:30	Drama series (imported)		
11:45	*News*		
11:55	Late-night programmes		

Vastly improved programmes between 7:00 PM and 10:30 PM on TVB–Jade ensured audience loyalty and advertisers' confidence, fended off any likely threat from the channel's long-term competitor RTV, and contributed to the demise of its new competitor CTV. The successful programme schedule adopted in early 1977 remained virtually unchanged throughout 1977–80, except that in 1981, a 30-minute situation comedy slot was inserted between the two tiers of 60-minute local drama serials, and late news was correspondingly rescheduled from 10:30 PM to 11:15 PM. This was apparently a move to lengthen the prime-time period using the channel's own successful drama production experience.

The 30-minute situation comedy series was called *Hong Kong 81* when it was introduced, and focused on the everyday life of several local household characters in fast-changing Hong Kong. The name of the series was changed in 1982 to *Hong Kong 1982*, and this went on until late 1986 when its popularity dwindled noticeably, and it was replaced by a new series called *City Japes* that followed a similar theme but focused on a slightly younger generation.

	1980	1981	
6:30		*News & Weather*	6:30
7:05		Drama serial I	7:05
8:00	Drama serial II	Sitcom	8.00
		Drama serial II	8:30
9:00	EYT	News	9:30
		EYT	9:35
10:30	*News*		
10:45	Drama series (imported) & other late-night programmes		
		News	11:15
		Financial report	11:30
		Late-night programmes	11:35

In 1976, the GDP showed a phenomenal jump of 28.2 per cent. In real terms, it was 18.8 per cent and the per capita GDP was 17.5 per cent. In the same year, TVB–Jade raised its advertising rates by 19.9 per cent in May and by another 20.5 per cent in October, which represented a 44.5 per cent composite increase in 1976. Hong Kong's economy sustained quite healthy GDP growth rates in the following two years, at 14.5 per cent in 1977 and 16.3 per cent in 1978. In real terms, the GDP growth rates in 1977 and 1978 were respectively 10.2 per cent and 10.3 per cent and the per capita GDP growth rates were respectively 8.6 per cent and 8.2 per cent (see Table 10.1).

With sustained growth in the economy and vast resources allocated for improving prime-time programmes, it was only logical that TVB–Jade should increase its advertising rates by 32.5 per cent in 1977 and again by 32.3 per cent in 1978 (*Media and Marketing*, 29 April 1986), even after the staggering increases in 1976 and the presence of two other Cantonese channels competing for the advertising dollar.

The figures in a survey on Hong Kong's television audience carried out by a local commercial survey company in 1974 show that the most enthusiastic prime-time television audience tended to consist of a higher proportion of housewives, and the under-20 and over-35 age groups (Survey Research Hong Kong Ltd., 1974).

In 1976, 52.4 per cent of the population was 24 years of age or under and 34.4 per cent was 35 years or over, representing a total of 87 per cent (see Table 10.2). The labour force participation rate among females was 43.6 per cent, indicating the presence of a high

Table 10.2: Population by Age

Year / *Age Group*	*1976* (%)	*1981* (%)	*1986* (%)	*1991* (%)
Under 15	30.4	24.8	23.1	20.9
15–24	22.0	23.0	18.8	15.2
25–34	13.0	17.7	20.3	21.4
35–44	10.8	9.7	12.0	16.1
45–54	10.6	10.3	9.7	8.8
55–64	7.6	7.9	8.5	8.9
65 and Over	5.4	6.6	7.6	8.7
Total	100.0	100.0	100.0	100.0

Sources: *Hong Kong Annual Digest of Statistics, 1978.*
Hong Kong 1991 Population Census Summary Results.

proportion of housewives in the female population. The fact that these people formed the bulk of the population provided substantial potential for development in television viewership. Coupled with rapid economic growth in Hong Kong, there was great potential for development in the mass consumption market, especially in youth-oriented and household-based consumption sectors.

CTV ceased operation in August 1978. TVB–Jade and RTV engaged in fierce competition for audience share in the following years. Immense resources were poured into programme production and promotion activities. Programming changes since 1976 had been mainly in the form of strengthening channel-produced programmes to suit local tastes. Channel-produced drama serials were particularly popular, and the two Cantonese channels invested immense resources in drama production to compete for audience share. By late 1980, TVB–Jade's weekday prime-time programmes were almost simply drama serials, *EYT* and news, which were all channel-produced.

Hong Kong enjoyed phenomenal economic growth in 1979 and 1980, with GDP growth rates at 31.9 per cent and 27.2 per cent respectively. In real terms, the GDP growth rates were 11.7 per cent and 10.4 per cent respectively. The per capita GDP growth rates in real terms, at 6.8 per cent in 1979 and 7.5 per cent in 1980 (see Table 10.1), were pulled down by the population boost due to a large inflow of immigrants from mainland China. However, with a much larger number of potential consumers and much higher total purchasing power available in the Hong Kong economy, TVB–Jade raised its advertising rates twice in 1980, the first time by 20.0 per cent in April and the second by 25.0 per cent in October (*Media and Marketing*, 29 April 1986), representing a composite increase of 50.0 per cent.

Some television producers attributed what they experienced as the 'golden era' of television to the opening in 1979 of the Mass Transit Railway (MTR)—a very efficient underground train system. They believed that the MTR made it possible for people to reach home faster after work and also to stay up longer at night without having to worry about getting up early to go to work the next morning, and that this made more people stay in front of the television screen.

Nevertheless, a media index produced in 1981 (TVB–Jade, 1981) shows that the heaviest viewers of Chinese television were within the 9–14 age group, the medium viewers within the 15–24 and the over-35 age groups, whereas the lightest viewers were within the 25–35 age group. Also, the heaviest viewers tended to be people with primary, and some secondary, education, and were mostly students and housewives; whereas the lightest viewers tended to be people with post-secondary/university education, and were within the professional/manager/executive occupational group.

In 1981, only 17.7 per cent of the population was in the 25–34 age group and only 44.6 per cent had completed secondary education or above. Also, only 8.5 per cent of the working population was in the professional/administrative/managerial occupational group. These figures together indicate that television still had a fairly strong audience base.

Consolidation: 1982–88

The period 1982–88 seems, in retrospect, a relatively less dynamic period in television programming. There were various attempts to identify the supposedly magical elements in the local drama serials that drew the masses of viewers. There were also attempts to increase variety in the prime-time schedule by slotting in mini-programmes. The introduction of mini-programmes was also a way to create additional advertising breaks, with the length of each advertisement regulated by the Broadcasting Authority. Otherwise, the prime-time schedule remained virtually unchanged.

	1981	1987	
6:30		*News & Weather*	6:30
7:05	Drama serial I		
		Drama serial I	7:10
8:00	Sitcom		
		Mini-programmes	8:10
		Sitcom	8:15
		Mini-programmes (incl. news)	8:45
8:30	Drama serial II		
		Drama serial II	8:50
9:30	News		
9:35	EYT		
		EYT	9:50
11:15	News		
11:30	*Financial report*	*News & Financial report*	11:30
11:35	Late-night programmes		
		Late-night programmes	11:50

The Hong Kong economy continued to sustain a high GDP growth rate in 1981 at 20.3 per cent, slowing down in 1982 to 12.9 per cent. In real terms, the GDP growth rates were 9.4 per cent in 1981 and 3.0 per cent in 1982 and the per capita GDP growth rates were 7.1 per cent in 1981 and 1.4 per cent in 1982 (see Table 10.1). In 1981, TVB–Jade's advertising rates were increased by 25.0 per cent. In 1982, they were increased by 20.0 per cent in June and by another 20.0 per cent in October (*Media and Marketing*, 29 April 1988), representing a composite increase of 44.0 per cent. However, starting from this period, advertisers were offered 12-month protection packages on current rates, clearly a response to slower economic growth trends.

Indeed, the growth of the economy slowed down from 1982 onwards, with real wages showing negative growth rates in the second-half of 1982 and in 1983. The economy did not pick up until 1986 and 1987, with GDP growth rates at 14.3 per cent and 23.1 per cent, GDP growth rates in real terms at 11.1 per cent and 14.5 per cent, and per capita GDP growth rates in real terms at 9.7 per cent and 13.4 per cent respectively. However, improved economic growth in 1986 and 1987 seemed to have only encouraged the less enthusiastic television viewers, who had been growing in proportion over the years, to develop other leisure and consumption habits rather than watching more television.

A study on TVB–Jade's prime-time audience carried out by the channel itself in 1986 revealed that the heaviest prime-time viewers tended to be in the student, housewife, or unskilled blue-collar occupational groups (TVB–Jade, 1986). They also tended to be in the 15–24 age group. The lightest viewers tended to include higher percentages of people in the professional/executive/managerial and the white-collar occupational groups. They also tended to be males within the 35–49 age group and females within the 25–34 age group.

The proportion of people in the working population in the production/transport occupational group had fallen from 52.2 per cent in 1976 to 43.4 per cent in 1986, whereas that in the professional/administrative/managerial group had risen from 7.5 per cent in 1976 to 12.5 per cent in 1991. Also, the proportion of the people in the 24 or under age group had fallen from 52.4 per cent in 1976 to 36.1 per cent in 1991, whereas that in the 25–44 age group had risen from 23.8 per cent in 1976 to 37.5 per cent in 1991.

The television audience base was therefore dwindling gradually. Programming changes around the mid-1980s began to be oriented towards improved development of news and enrichment programmes aimed at the increasingly affluent and educated sections of the population of Hong Kong, which were steadily growing in size.

Focus on Infotainment: 1989 onwards

In April 1989, TVB–Jade's weekday prime-time programme schedule was adjusted to accommodate the 30-minute productions by Hong Kong's public broadcaster, Radio Television Hong Kong (RTHK). The allocation of prime-time slots for these productions, which focus on current affairs and are presented in a variety of traditional and more dramatic formats, and which are intended to both inform and entertain, became accepted as one of broadcast television stations' licencing conditions. Such an allocation of prime-time slots for RTHK productions also reflected the falling popularity of television programmes intended purely for relaxed entertainment or drama serials designed to keep people in front of the television screen at regular hours during weekdays, and the rising popularity of various forms of infotainment programmes.

The adjustment on the programme schedule was made by putting the RTHK production in the 7:00–7:30 PM slot, i.e., immediately following the early evening news, pushing everything else to later time slots. A variety of more light-hearted infotainment programmes, ranging from filler programmes on popular music and showbiz gossip lasting a few minutes to 'cultural enrichment' programmes such as travelogues, were also introduced into the regular prime-time schedule.

	1987	1989	
6:30		*News & Weather*	6:30
		RTHK programme	7:05
7:10	Drama serial I		
		Drama serial I	7:35
8:10	Mini-programmes		
8:15	Sitcom		
		Pop music	8:35
		Sitcom	8:40
8:45	Mini-programmes (incl.news)		
8:50	Drama serial II		
		News	9:15
		Showbiz gossip	9:20
9:30	News		
		Drama serial II	9:35
9:50	EYT		
		EYT	10:35
		News & Financial report	11:20
11:30	*News & Financial report*		
11:35	Late-night programmes		
		Late-night programmes	11:40 →

A series of minor modifications were made in the programme schedule from mid-1989 onwards in response to the addition of a time slot for RTHK programmes in early prime-time. Then in late 1990, both the financial report and the government information bulletin, previously put after the 6:30 PM *News & Weather* slot, were moved respectively to 6:15 PM and 6:20 PM, i.e., before the news. They appeared in independent slots and their durations were somewhat extended. Considering the growing importance of information on the financial market to the average citizen of Hong Kong, including housewives, who have been among the heaviest viewers of television, these scheduling changes can be regarded as indicating a further extension of prime-time.

Changes in programming and scheduling were relatively more frequent during this period, apparently in response to the fall in total television viewership and audience share. Most of the changes have been relatively minor but erratic, with even the heaviest television viewers complaining that they are no longer able to memorise the prime-time programme schedule.

A significant change in late 1990 was the reduction of *EYT*, TVB–Jade's emblematic show, from five evenings a week to three, with Tuesdays and Thursdays allocated for various infotainment programmes and documentaries. In late 1994, *EYT*, which had for some time almost existed in name only, disappeared altogether, and this later part of prime-time, following the second tier of local drama serials, was mainly filled with a very popular infotainment programme *Focus on Focus*, and a variety of talk shows, travelogues, and documentaries.

	1989	**1994**	
		Financial report	6:15
		Govt info bulletin	6:20
6:30	*News & Weather*	News & Weather	6:30
		RTHK programme	7:00
7:05	RTHK programme		
		Drama serial I	7:30
7:35	Drama serial I		
8:35	Pop music		
		Sitcom	8:40
8:45	Sitcom		
9:15		News	9:15
9:20	Showbiz gossip	Drama serial II	9:20
9:35	Drama serial II		
		Focus on Focus	9:45
		Talk shows/travelogues/ documentaries	10:30
10:35	EYT		
11:20	*News & Financial report*		
		News & Financial report	11:35
11:40	Late-night programmes		
		Late-night programmes	12:10

A survey carried out by the Broadcasting Authority in 1990 (Broadcasting Authority, 1991) revealed that the 12–17 age group was the heaviest television viewers, whereas the 18–44 age group was the lightest viewers. Yet, the proportion of the 25–44 age group in the population had risen from 23.8 per cent in 1976 to 37.5 per cent in 1991. A study on audience lifestyle and television viewing behaviour carried out in 1991 (TVB–Jade, 1991c) observed that viewers had become much more selective. Another study in the same year on the profile of prime-time television viewers

(TVB–Jade, 1991b) also observed that the station had become less efficient in reaching the 'upscale audience'.

Socio-economic Changes and Prime-time Schedule Changes

It has thus been observed that TVB–Jade's prime-time programme schedules changed significantly in certain years. The changes in 1969 and 1973 mainly extended the duration of prime-time and increased programming variety, particularly in terms of including more channel-produced programmes targetted at local viewers. Scheduling changes in 1974 seemed hesitant, stabilising in 1975. Then in 1976, the schedule was radically changed, with prime-time starting an hour earlier. Further modifications occurred in 1980, 1981 and then 1987, all apparently related to efforts to attract viewers as well as advertisers to the station's prime-time.

In each of these years and/or the one before, Hong Kong's economy experienced somewhat higher than usual growth. Furthermore, during these years and/or shortly after, TVB–Jade raised its advertising rates quite drastically, obviously to take advantage of the increase in the advertising dollar available in the market.

The audience survey figures referred to in this study, while obtained in context that are not entirely comparable, do indicate that the more enthusiastic television viewers tend to have had primary or some secondary education, and tend to be students, housewives, and young male workers in blue-collar occupational groups. Changes in demographics and the structure of the Hong Kong economy have resulted in sharp falls in the proportion of such people in the population.

The proportion of the under-25 age group has been falling since 1976, whereas that in the 25–44 age group has been rising (see Table 10.2). Moreover, in 1976 only 24.4 per cent of the population had completed secondary education or above (Hong Kong Government Printer, 1987), in 1991 the figure rose to 62.0 per cent (Hong Kong Government Printer, 1991). The female labour force participation rate rose from 43.6 per cent in 1976 to 51.2 per cent in 1986 (Census and Statistics Department, 1986), indicating a reduction in the proportion of housewives in the population.

In 1976, the proportion of workers in the professional/administrative/managerial and the clerical occupational groups was 17.1 per cent of the working population; in 1991, it had risen to 33.0 per cent. In 1976, the proportion of those in the production and transport occupational groups was 52.2 per cent; in 1991, it was 35.1 per cent (see Table 10.3). The proportion of the working population in manufacturing industries fell from 44.6 per cent in 1976 to 28.2 per cent in 1991; and that in the finance, insurance, real estate, business services, and other service industries rose from 18.5 per cent in 1976 to 30.5 per cent in 1991 (see Table 10.4). Overall, the trend shows a proportional reduction in blue-collar workers and increase in white-collar occupational positions.

Table 10.3: Occupational Distribution of Working Population

Occupation	*1976 (%)*	*1981 (%)*	*1986 (%)*	*1991 (%)*
Professional, administrative and managerial workers	7.5	8.5	11.7	13.4
Clerical and related workers	9.6	12.0	14.5	19.6
Sales workers	11.4	10.3	11.7	12.5
Service workers	14.8	15.6	16.4	18.3
Production and related workers, transport equipment operators and labourers	52.2	50.7	43.4	35.1
Others	4.5	2.9	2.3	1.1
Total	100.0	100.0	100.0	100.0

Sources: *Hong Kong 1986 By-Census Summary Results.*
Hong Kong Annual Digest of Statistics, 1992 edition.

Advertisers have responded by diverting the advertising dollar away from television to other media of communication. In particular, as they increasingly realise that it is more efficient to use these other media of communication to reach the more affluent consumers, they start to find media survey figures indicating only 'programme audience' irrelevant and prefer to look for the 'commercial audience' (*Media and Marketing*, 2 November 1990). The proportion of advertising expenditure on Chinese television in Hong Kong was 43.0 per cent of total media advertising expenditure in 1977. It rose to 72.5 per cent in 1983, but fell back to 50.0 per cent in 1990 (*Media and Marketing*, 7 February 1992).

Table 10.4: Industrial Distribution of Working Population

Industry	*1976 (%)*	*1981 (%)*	*1986 (%)*	*1991 (%)*
Manufacturing	44.6	41.3	35.8	28.2
Construction	5.8	7.9	6.3	6.9
Wholesale and retail trade, restaurants and hotels	19.3	19.1	22.5	22.5
Transport, storage and communication	7.4	7.6	8.0	9.8
Financing and insurance, real estate and business services	3.3	4.7	6.4	10.6
Services	15.2	15.4	18.1	19.9
Others	4.4	4.0	2.9	2.1
Total	100.0	100.0	100.0	100.0

Sources: *Hong Kong 1986 By-Census Summary Results.*
Hong Kong 1991 Population Census Summary Results.

Television stations have responded by tightening their budgets, which is reflected in the sharp reduction in production personnel and a fall in production standards in recent years. To echo one of the theories of the globalisation debate, it is clear that the future of television in Hong Kong is, to a considerable extent, being shaped, not by the consumers of television as such but by the needs of advertisers in the commercial marketplace generally.

Notes

1. The information on the programme schedules is based on those published by Hong Kong Television Broadcasts Limited.

References

Broadcasting Authority (1991). *Television broadcasting survey 1990: Executive summary*. Hong Kong: Broadcasting Authority.

Census and Statistics Department (1986). *Hong Kong 1986 by-census. Summary results*. Hong Kong: Census and Statistics Department.

Hong Kong Government Press (1971). *Hong Kong: Report for the year 1970*. Hong Kong: Government Press.

——— (1977). *Hong Kong: Report for the year 1976*. Hong Kong: Government Press.

Hong Kong Government Press (1989). *Hong Kong: Report for the year 1988*. Hong Kong: Government Press.

Hong Kong Government Printer (1987). *Hong Kong social and economic trends 1976–86*. Hong Kong: Government Printer.

——— (1991). *Hong Kong 1991 Population Census: Summary results*. Hong Kong: Government Printer.

Survey Research Hong Kong Ltd. (1974). *The Hong Kong television audience July 1974*. Hong Kong: Survey Research Hong Kong Ltd.

The Broadcasting Review Board (1985). *Report of the Broadcasting Review Board*. Hong Kong: The Broadcasting Review Board.

TVB–Jade (1981). *Summary for SRH media index 1981 general report* (October). Hong Kong: Marketing Research Department, TVB–Jade.

——— (1986). 'Jade's prime-time audience profile'. Internal document produced by the Marketing Research Department (March). Hong Kong: TVB–Jade.

——— (1987). 'TV audience and ratings'. Internal document produced by the Marketing Research Department (April). Hong Kong: TVB–Jade.

——— (1991a). 'A study on TVB–Jade prime-time ratings'. Internal document produced by the Marketing Research Department (August). Hong Kong: TVB–Jade.

——— (1991b). 'Performance review of TVBJ and ATVH in early October'. Internal document produced by the Marketing Research Department (October). Hong Kong: TVB–Jade.

——— (1991c). 'A study on audience lifestyle and TV viewing behaviour'. Internal document produced by the Marketing Research Department (November). Hong Kong: TVB–Jade.

11

A Note on Television in Sri Lanka[1]

Sunanda Mahendra

Introduction

Television broadcasting was introduced in Sri Lanka in 1979 by a private organisation named the Independent Television Network (ITN). Regular transmission by this organisation covered only an area of approximately a 20 mile radius around Colombo, but discussions and plans were soon under way for the establishment of a state television network. This culminated in the formation of Sri Lanka Rupavahini Corporation (SLRC) on 15 February 1982, which was able to cover the whole island of Sri Lanka. SLRC, or 'Rupavahini' as it is widely known, is a statutory body established in 1982 under Act No. 68 of Parliament.

In the formative stages of ITN and SLRC, programme output was carefully controlled and reached reasonably acceptable professional levels. But as time passed, and as commercial interests began to dominate, the quality of output declined.

Broadcasting policy in Sri Lanka can best be described as authoritarian. Both radio and television remain state monopolies and from its inception the Sri Lankan Broadcasting Corporation (SLBC) has been a state institute, which was at first known as 'Radio Ceylon' and later changed to its present state.

In 1993 there were 3.1 million radios and 520,000 TV sets in the country.[2] The *Minister* of State for Broadcasting and Information controls the programme content of both radio and television,[3] ostensibly with the assistance of a number of advisory boards, whose agenda is, however, dictated by their own political interests.

Licensing and Audience

Towards the end of the licensing period in 1991, it was evident that SLRC revenue from the sale of licences was rapidly declining. In Sri Lanka, licences have to be purchased annually during a four month period in that year. If, however, a television owner buys his licence after this period, an additional premium of 10 per cent of the licence fee has to be paid, under the SLRC Amendment Act No. 43 of 1988, to the licensing authority of SLRC and the Post Master General (PMG), who has been appointed as the agent of SLRC for the issue of licences and the collection of licence fees through the network of post offices in the country. However, licence dodging has developed quite considerably, especially in the urban areas of the country.

Some Issues in Sri Lankan Television

Television is the youngest of the mass media systems operating in Sri Lanka. Questions as to whether television was viable in the country were first raised as far back as the early 1960s.[4] Similar to many other countries in the developing world, it was first visualised as a medium for educational purposes, to be used initially on a closed circuit basis and confined to colleges and universities. However, it took more than a decade to fully implement this. When ITN as a private group interested in developing a television service came on the scene in 1979, it experienced financial difficulties and was taken under the wing of the state to supposedly guarantee its financial viability. Thus, the very first television service, which is still known by the same name (ITN), is neither independent, in the strict sense of the word, nor fully state-owned. The unsuitability of the location of the transmitting antenna, constant power fluctuations in the area where it was situated, the low power of the transmitter (1 KW) which limited its service area to about a 15 mile radius, and the lack of funds are some of the factors which impeded its progress. In order to cater satisfactorily to the demand which had been created, the television facilities were moved to Battaramulla, a more suitable geographical location.

Programme Output

It should be noted that most programmes were imported and included *Voyages of Charles Darwin, Tarzan, The Incredible Hulk, Bionic Woman, The Long Search, Superman, Mysterious World*, etc. At times several Shakespearian classics too were introduced as an alternative for the more sophisticated viewers.

Following the wide popularity of these imported programmes, several local television play producers came on the scene. As a beginning, several radio serials were converted into television plays.[5] Similarly, those artists who produced comic strips for local newspapers also entered the teleplay scene. In fact, today this genre has become the most popular, as well as most controversial, in the local mass media scene. There are seven half-hour teleplay serials per week broadcast by SLRC, which are sponsored by multinational companies, such as the Singer Machine Company, as well as local banks and other successful business firms.

It has been said that with the inauguration of the Rupavahini network, a new world has been brought to our villages and changes have appeared in the lifestyles of our people, and that we have become part of a global audience receiving the same television fare as millions of others in both the East and West. One feature of this 'globalisation' is the growth in television advertising.

As elsewhere in Asia, studies on audience viewing habits in Sri Lanka have shown that advertisements shown on the television may have brought about adverse effects on the value patterns of poor rural families. Children, it is reported, often pester their parents to buy various food products advertised on television.[6] This has developed to such an extent that several parents have written to the television authorities asking them to put a total stop to food and beverage commercials. Religious bodies too believe that advertisements glorifying the eating of meat and sausages should be stopped. But commercial advertising brings a substantial amount of money, which of course helps to sustain programming.

Educational TV

As in many other Third World countries, television was established with a strong developmental mission. It was believed that educational levels in the country could be raised by educational broadcasting, initially to schools. But Mahendra (1983) has shown that although educational programmes were specifically designed and broadcast to schools during the morning hours, when the schools are in session, only a few schools in urban and semi-urban areas made any use of this opportunity. As such, educational television was, and still is, the subject of much criticism. Though money is spent on educational television, local schools either do not have the time to use its output or are not interested in linking the material to their curriculum. Though TV sets are freely issued, video cassette recorders are not supplied, so time switching is not possible.

Some Research Findings

From the very early stages of television in Sri Lanka, the most active research organisation has been the Audience Survey and Research Unit, which has conducted several important studies, giving some insight into viewing habits. But as time went by, and as political pressure was intensified, the results of the research have been ignored. The following section is indicative of the issues that are sponsored and which private research has addressed in recent years in Sri Lanka.

Research on Sri Lankan television can be grouped into five categories. First, there are general surveys of audience sizes and their profiles, e.g., ETV Audience Profile Study, Island Wide Audience Surveys, ITN Audience Surveys, all of which give reasonably accurate pictures of the extent of television viewing in Sri Lanka. Second, there are appreciation studies, where particular programmes are singled out and audience evaluation is gauged, e.g., a study of the popularity of *Savasangita* (a monthly musical variety show), a study of the popularity of development programmes, responses to *Subha Prarthana* (a television drama), and responses to *News at 5*. A third category of research focuses on particular audience sections, e.g., studies of the television viewing habits of children and adolescents, and more particularly, a study of children's response patterns to locally-produced children's programmes. A fourth category is that of content analysis of particular programmes. Here analysis of the news has figured prominently, e.g., content analysis of *Rupavahini News*. Another study has focused on the portrayal of women in Rupavahini. Finally, there are comprehension and use studies. These tend to focus on educational broadcasting, e.g., studies on ETV programme utilisation and on the comprehensibility of ETV programmes. It is noticeable how similar this profile is to the audience research carried out by more developed public service broadcasting organisations.

Change and Development

By and large television in Sri Lanka is notable in three respects. First, the existing pattern of SLRC and ITN programme output is being challenged by new private local television services. Maharaja Television (MTV) began transmission in August 1992 and as a consequence quite a large number of western films were introduced. Another television service, Teleshan, also introduced on the same lines, commenced transmission in April 1993.

The country, therefore, now boasts four television channels, two public and two private, the latter financed by advertising and sponsorship. However, there is no subscription television. Between them the four channels provide up to 31 hours of broadcasting each day, with ITN surprisingly the most at 11 hours per day and Teleshan the least at five hours. Television reach in Sri Lanka is very high (SLR 98 per cent, ITN 95 per cent, Teleshan 90 per cent, and MTV 70 per cent) compared with some of its near neighbours, e.g., 35 per cent on average in Pakistan and 63 per cent for Doordarshan in India. (*Screen Digest*, 1994).

Second, a substantial amount of state propaganda is allowed to creep into programme formats, resulting in monotony and biases. Third, with the introduction of severe censorship, creative standards are restricted. For example, opposition views have generally been broadcast only immediately prior to elections, as required by election law when all parties have a right to equal broadcasting time. News items unfavourable to thc government regularly tend to be cut out. In 1987, a bomb blast killed hundreds less than a mile from the SLBC studios. But SLBC failed to cover it until confirmation by the official National News Agency, despite confirmation in the meantime from the BBC World Service.

Conclusion

Television in Sri Lanka could be considered as either still born or ill conceived. For a Third World country like Sri Lanka, radio and the press are still important, especially with an increase in literacy rates. However, the commercial money-making attitude prevalent in television has, by and large, produced adverse effects. For example, there is hardly any news coverage, either from home or abroad; however, the English language news bulletins bought from foreign agencies have created a certain degree of interest, but they too are subject to censorship. Nonetheless, television in Sri Lanka has a long way to go if it is to provide the quality of service and range of programmes enjoyed by some of its neighbours in developing Asia.

Notes

1. This paper was commissioned to help provide some awareness of television in Sri Lanka. Very little writing of substance is available on this subject, either to Sri Lankans themselves or to foreign students of mass media, and some of the reasons for that are indicated in this chapter. Nevertheless, this chapter seeks to give readers an opportunity to compare the Sri Lankan situation with those of its immediate neighbouring countries and thus it goes some way towards achieving that goal. As the author makes clear, research findings do not easily enter the public domain in Sri Lanka and many of the empirical studies referred to, towards the end of the paper, have not been published. Nonetheless it is important to include this sketch which serves to stimulate questions about the future of television and television research in Sri Lanka. It is clearly easier to arrive at a full picture of the structure of and practice in television in countries with fully developed media industry and media education sectors, but countries like Sri Lanka which do not as yet have these institutions embedded into their national fabric are nonetheless important when considering the future of television in Asia. And so, in the absence of full information, the value of any insight is particularly strong.
2. The figures are drawn from SLRC documents.
3. See Radio and Television Parliamentary Acts.
4. Television in Sri Lanka was to be linked to radio broadcasting in the 1960s, but plans were changed due to the change of government in 1970.
5. The pioneer authors were the radio playwrights like Dharmasri Munasinghe. The pioneer directors were D.B. Nihalsinghe and Dhamma Jagoda, a veteran stage playwright and director.
6. *Ceylon Daily News* (Supplement), 15 February 1985.

References

Mahendra, S. (1983). 'Comprehensibility of Educational Television (ETV) Programmes'. A research project undertaken on behalf of the Department of Mass Communication, University of Kelaniya, Dalugama, Sri Lanka.

III

Studies of National Issues and Experiences

12

Rip Van Winkle: A Story of Indian Television

Usha Vyasulu Reddi

Suddenly, the somnolent world of Indian television came to an abrupt end. From Monday, 14 October 1991, the air waves in India were awhirl with four different television channels in flagrant violation of Indian broadcasting laws. The predictions of many communication scholars that whoever controls the conduit also controls the content had become a reality (Gerbner et al., 1973; Reddi, 1982, 1985; Schiller, 1986), but both Doordarshan (India's television system) and the Government of India remained in total confusion as to their response. With the intrusion of the Satellite Television Asian Region TV (Star TV), in effect every lane and bylane in Indian cities has a cable system, making a mockery of all attempts by government to regulate the content of television.

The speed of change is so great that even the most foresighted decision-maker will never be able to keep up; and while the Government of India drags its feet, the de facto privatisation of Indian media continues to take place.

This chapter examines what these momentous changes in Indian media are, what these changes mean to Indian society and audiences, what policy options the government faces, what it has tried to do so far, and what potential exists for positively utilising these changing media scenarios for developmental and information purposes.

Some Background

Historians of Indian broadcasting have often commented upon the strange dichotomy in Indian media, where the print and film media have grown and flourished and have jealously protected their freedom from encroachment by government, while the electronic media have been possessed, controlled, and eventually emasculated by politicians and government rules. The fault, argue historians, lies in the birth and growth of these media in the pre- and early post-independence era.

If the earliest of Indián newspapers were started by social reformers and nationalists in the nineteenth century, Indian broadcasting had its origins in the radio clubs operated by the Indian Broadcasting Company in the 1920s and operated by government licences rooted in the Indian Telegraphic Act, 1885. As the then Viceroy, Lord Irwin, said at the opening of the Bombay radio station in 1927 and as has been parroted by Indians ever since, 'Both for entertainment and for education its possibilities are great, as yet we perhaps scarcely realise how great they are'.

Television's birth and growth in India is not too different. From a humble beginning as a UNESCO promoted educational experiment in 1959, India's television system grew, not as a medium in its own right, but as a response to events and decisions around it. Being an essentially entertainment medium-service, it grew with an onerous burden in a nation dogged by developmental and educational problems. Its birth was a result of increased worldwide awareness of the promise of television to fulfil these developmental needs, as pronounced by scholars such as Schramm (1964) and promoted by technologists such as Sarabhai (1969).

Without any recognition of television's special characteristics or of its potential, every milestone in Doordarshan's growth has been dogged by ad hocism, without any conscious planning for the future. It has grown into one of the world's largest networks—all this while faced with being the cynosure of Indian politicians and public alike.

To understand how all this came about we have to return to the pages of history, to the Constitution, to enacted laws, and the ideology with which Indian television has operated all these years. It is in the definition of the term 'freedom of the press' that much of the controversy lies. While in other nations, this freedom and its operating conditions have been laid down in constitutional provisions, the Indian Constitution gives no such statement. Article 19(1)(a) guarantees the fundamental right to freedom of speech. Media thus enjoy an implied right. But the Constitution also lays down, in the Preamble, that India is a 'sovereign, secular, socialist, democratic society': where all religions and races must live in harmony protected by the laws of the country. Still, the Indian Constitution is unique in that Part IV of the constitutional document deals with the Directive Principles of State Policy. These principles reflect the aspirations of the Indian society to work towards an equitable society with special attention and care being given to the depressed and backward sections of the country.

Broadcast media are further governed by Article 246 of the Indian Constitution, by which Parliament has exclusive powers to make laws with respect to 'post and telegraphs, telephones, wireless broadcasts, and other forms of communications'. This makes broadcasting a central subject and all laws relating to radio and television originate directly from the central government. Further, under the Telegraphic Act, 1885, the Government of India has the exclusive right to establish, maintain, and work 'wireless apparatus'. The monopoly of broadcasting by the government rests on this act.

The Ministry of Information and Broadcasting is the policy-making body for the broadcasting system today. All India Radio (AIR or Akashvani) and Doordarshan are the two most important departments attached to the Ministry, accounting for nearly two-thirds of the Ministry's budget. As a general rule, the Ministry is headed by a Minister for Information and Broadcasting (a political appointee) and a Secretary to the Government of India. The Secretary is normally drawn from the Indian Administrative Service; the position of Director-General may also be held by high ranking civil servants rather than by specialised broadcasters.

Broadcasting is financed by the government, although accounts of commercial departments (those earning commercial revenues) are maintained separately. The budget is prepared, presented, and operated in accordance with the norms and procedures laid down by the government for its departments, and government maintains a tight control on the expenditure of AIR and Doordarshan and the powers of the Director-General. While the heads of AIR and Doordarshan have substantial power to incur expenditure on the purchase of equipment, recruitment of staff, and other day-to-day management decisions, the full powers required for the specialised nature of broadcasting are denied to them. Despite being money spinning organisations, funds for programmes at these two agencies remain abysmally low, affecting the overall functioning of the two media in the country.

Television started in India as an experimental service in 1959, and commenced educational broadcasts in 1961. This was followed by agricultural programmes in 1966 and by 1975, there were six television centres in the country. The real breakthrough, however, came with the Satellite Instructional Television Experiment (SITE) in 1975 (discussed elsewhere in this volume) and television in India became a medium entirely carried by satellite, supported by a few microwave links. With the introduction of colour in 1982, and coverage of major national and international events, television rapidly grew from its humble beginnings in 1959 to a commercially viable and strong medium by 1984 (when commercial television started).

The foundation of Indian broadcasting is the network of radio and television stations in the country which contribute the bulk of the programmes broadcast. Specifically, the satellite based television network of high and low power transmitters located all over the country and the more than 20 production centres form part of one of the largest television systems in the world, with programmes broadcast for about 12 hours on weekdays and 15 hours on Sundays. Doordarshan's structure is at present two tier, with national and regional television stations and a network service which is the base for its commercial services.

Constitutional and structural provisions aside, there is an economic aspect to the ideology of broadcasting which cannot be reiterated enough. Implicitly, in a technological world, where those who control the technology also share the power, ownership and control of media determine the capacity of the media to pursue their goals with responsibility and dedication.

The Indian economic system, a mixed economy with both the private and public sectors operating and competing with each other, is a major factor influencing media in India. Within broadcasting, this is seen in the fact that while the electronic and telecommunications systems have grown as a result of direct government intervention (the stations being controlled by government), private companies form the bulk of the suppliers of telecommunications equipment, from switching equipment to small connectors, computers, and other hardware. The picture for software production is not very different. Production of programmes is undertaken in-house by television stations and also by private producers, who supply the programmes both on a programme to programme basis and on contract.

Space does not permit an analysis of the roles of Indira Gandhi in changing the perspective of government on television and of Rajiv Gandhi in deciding on its expansion. Nor should we forget the linkage between the Rajiv government's economic and social perspectives, a liberal policy aimed at pleasing the middle classes and a policy of expanding television availability.

The purpose of this brief outline of the history of Doordarshan has been to highlight the relationship between the ideology and structure of this medium, to have a glimpse at its growth and its place in Indian society. Keeping such a context in mind, we can now turn our attention to the forces which have led to the present media scene in India.

The Present

Ideally, with its rapid growth, protected status as a government monopoly, vast network of transmitters and stations, and its production capabilities, the present and future should look very rosy for Doordarshan. But something is wrong—fundamentally wrong—since no one is satisfied with the service offered by this organisation. If the urban population is unhappy with the poor quality of the entertainment content, equally so are the rural folk. Academics berate the structure and functioning of the system, politicians and bureaucrats criticise and ridicule it with contempt, but without giving up their control. In the meantime, Doordarshan staff continue stoically and silently to make programmes, plodding on even though every government in power since 1947 has established a committee to examine the policy, structure, and functioning of television; and every committee, including the Public Accounts Committee of Parliament (*Deccan Chronicle*, July 7 1992) has pointed out the growing gap between potential and performance.

Perhaps it is, as Ninan (1992) has argued, that the growth of Doordarshan was a reaction to extraneous developments. This led to its unplanned growth, to ad hocism, to being shackled by government, to the accumulation of mediocrity, and to politicisation. The extraneous developments which affected its growth were the transmissions from across the border in the 1960s, the SITE experiment (which was essentially a technology applications experiment) in 1975, the demand of the Asian Games in 1982, the introduction of commercialism with its subsequent demand for an increase in the quantity and quality of entertainment, today's invasion of Indian skies by Star TV and other such satellite based systems, and the invasion of terrestrial communications by cable television.

It is even more unfortunate that no government of free India has had the political will to address the issues of media ownership, control, operation, development and content squarely; and this, despite repeated recommendations of various committees—Chanda Committee, 1966; Verghese Committee, 1978; Joshi Committee, 1985; and Varadan Committee, 1991—to grant autonomy in structure and functioning and so empower Doordarshan to become an efficient organisation.

Even the Prasar Bharati Act of 1990 has remained largely unimplemented, with the result that when faced with the technological changes in communication, Doordarshan has seemed unable to respond.

A significant challenge from within India has come from the video and cable operators. Even while television was struggling to find its place in the media preferences of Indian audiences, video appeared in a big way, boosted by the policies of the Indian government and the aggressive marketing strategies of multinational electronics companies. In less than five years, from 1984 to 1989, the penetration of video moved from the capitals down to the districts and villages (Agrawal, 1991). The National Television Survey (NTS IV), conducted in November and December 1991 (Sehgal, 1992), estimated that video reached 13.08 million viewers (10.5 per cent of Doordarshan viewers) and the penetration of videos increases as we move up from the lower income groups to the highest. What is more, government has found it hard to legislate and enforce laws relating to video and video piracy (Gopal, 1986).

In contrast to video's steady growth over a five year period, cable came to India with a bang. Until 1990 cable systems were restricted to very few metropolitan cities and to places of luxury like five-star hotels. Since 1991, and particularly since the beginning of Star TV services over India, the inroads made by cable operators have been considerable.

While video viewing needs access to a VCR (still an expensive proposition), cable television requires a different but smaller investment by both operators and viewers. Cable needs a concentration of TV owners, already a reality in dense urban locations, and can be installed relatively cheaply with moderate monthly subscriptions, partly because only 150 connections are needed for an individual cable operator to break even, and on offer are four Star TV channels (BBC, Prime Sports, Channel V, and Star Plus) and a fifth or sixth channel for Hindi and regional language films. It is through cable that international satellite television has entered the Indian home, offering the viewers five to six alternative channels of programming to choose from. An analysis of cable television viewing shows that in absolute number terms, the middle classes have greater access than lower classes, as with video. Penetration of cable TV increases as we move from the lower income groups (7.6 per cent) to the highest income groups (15.8 per cent) (Bhatia, 1992).

Sinha (1992), quoting an Admar Cable View 1991 survey report, forecasts that 150–200 homes get 'cabled' every day. This works out to about 6,000 per month or 72,000 new connections per annum. Thus, the growth of cable, supported by direct broadcast satellite and direct reception sets, provides both a channel for Doordarshan and also an alternative. Supported by the coverage of international events captured by satellite dishes and distributed by cable, and helped by the lacunae in Indian laws in regulating and monitoring cable, Indian audiences have a plethora of programmes to choose from. Cable has grown unchecked and unregulated, because strictly speaking, cable is not a wireless medium coming under the Indian Telegraphic Act, and as long as the activity is confined to premises and does not require crossing of public right of ways/roads, it will not be deemed a telegraphic activity. The Ministry of Telecommunications, further, allows the installation of dish antennas for private viewing. The licence so granted to the cable operator is expected to be used for private viewing. But between the laws and the licences, the ambiguity in legislation, lack of standardisation of various activities, and the resultant inability of the authority to control cable operators, the path for the rapid proliferation of this medium as a viable alternative for the Indian viewer has grown rapidly.

Hence, the changing scenario in broadcasting, which presents both a challenge and competition to Doordarshan, comes from a coupling of satellite and cable television, for without the latter, satellite television has limited scope in India. At present, the challenge is limited and restricted to the urban areas; Doordarshan's audiences in rural India are marginally affected. While it is too early to forecast the impact that these technologies will have on Indian broadcasting, it is time to examine the Indian response to the challenge posed by them.

The Response

For years governments in power have ruled the airwaves—the survival of the two broadcast media has been dependent upon their status as government monopolies. For years governments have been talking about granting 'autonomy' in structure and functioning. All the various committees have recommended it and have repeatedly been browbeaten by politicians, who have subjugated the two media to overt political interests. But within a period of two years, the advent of satellite and cable has superseded the debate on autonomy. It has created a de facto deregulation of control of the airwaves. It has broken the monopoly of these two media in a very real and fundamental sense. The debate no longer rests around 'autonomy', but around 'what should we do' in response.

The atmosphere of economic liberalisation which has set in since 1991 has added to the confusion. Liberalisation of the Indian economy has had its impact upon the media. 'Change and the need for change' are the new norms by which Doordarshan has to function. It is no longer autonomy, but an opening up to private and public institutions for both hardware and software that is the issue. From the hardware angle, the decisions of the Ministry of Telecommunications to allow the installation of dish antennas, to grant licences to cable operators, to call for quotations to lease transponders on INSAT—are all indicative of the overall decision to open up the skies. All this will increase competition.

But such decisions taken by the hardware people are not balanced by parallel actions concerning the content of Indian television. The Indian response to the challenge has been conflicting. There are reports that the Prime Minister has instructed 'in no uncertain terms' that the way to counter the invasion of the skies is to open up Doordarshan to private companies (Sehgal, 1992, p. 1). Such an announcement paved the way for the establishment of the K.A. Varadan Committee to study various aspects of this proposal. The following Quotes are some excerpts from the Committee's report which reflect on the nature of governmental responses to the challenge of cable and satellite (*Seminar*, 1992, pp. 37–40):

> . . . . No country in the world . . . can afford to ignore the crucial part played by radio and television on the minds and feelings of its people.
> . . . [However] broadcasting in India has essentially been informed by developmental and public interest objectives. . . . In the Indian context, broadcasting rights in the hands of unscrupulous elements could lead to very undesirable effects upon the society . . .
> . . . . The next important question is as to what type of non-governmental agency should be set up to run the new channel . . . . The intention is that the management of the non-governmental agency should be broadbased to represent a wide spectrum of stake-holding and its share holding made fully accessible to the public . . .
> Another desirable safeguard . . . is to have cross media restrictions, so that owners of newspapers and magazines having circulation and influence within their specified geographical area or across the length and breadth of the country are not given licences . . .

The Committee reported several routes through which the present system could be changed: (*a*) leasing out time chunks in the existing channel; (*b*) leasing out an existing channel; (*c*) operation of transmitters on a regional basis; (*d*) licencing TV/radio transmitters for local transmitting infrastructure; and (*e*) leasing out of a transponder.

Based upon these possibilities which were examined the Varadan Committee recommended that:

1. subject to the viability of operations, preference should be given to setting up new TV/radio channels in different parts of the country for regional broadcasts;
2. the second Doordarshan channel in the four metro cities can be leased out to suitable licencees; additionally FM and other additional channels could be leased out;

3. the option to permit one agency or consortium to set up a series of transponders will rank only second to the option of permitting a number of *licencees*;
4. the option of licence/leasing a transponder on a satellite for direct broadcast would perhaps be appropriate for developmental or educational broadcasts;
5. the Committee does not recommend leasing out a particular chunk of time from an existing TV/radio channel.

A central authority to own the various infrastructure for leasing out to various licencees, including Prasar Bharati (current Doordarshan or AIR), was conceived in the context of the planned development of hardware for broadcasting purposes. This central authority, tentatively called the Broadcasting Council of India (BCI), would have as its members 'eminent public men of unimpeachable probity'.

The Varadan Committee also recommended that broadcasting rights could be given to public bodies such as universities, and well managed co-operative institutions with primary objectives in the areas of education, culture, or communication.

Coming on the heels of the Varadan report and as a response to adverse remarks by the Public Accounts Committee of Parliament, an internal committee was established within Doordarshan and the Ministry of Information and Broadcasting to suggest ways of improving advertisement revenues. This committee's report also considered the threat posed by satellite and cable television, and recommended an increase in the entertainment content of Doordarshan telecasts by increasing the time for afternoon transmissions, changing prime-time slots for increased entertainment, and a revised advertising policy (*Deccan Chronicle*, 7 July 1992). Increased entertainment programmes would be a mix of feature films, teleserials and reruns of old programmes.

If we take these committees' reports as representing the major responses to the challenge posed by satellite and cable, several ways of approaching the issue emerge.

One way of facing the challenge is to not take it seriously. After all, Doordarshan's audiences are estimated at 124 million, while satellite and cable together reach only about 14.5 million (11.7 per cent of Doordarshan's reach). A complacent position, which is so reassuring to the Government of India that its official handout containing the summary of the Varadan Committee report did not even contain a passing reference to the challenge posed by satellite television (Gill, 1991). The flaw in this approach is the assumption of a stagnant position in cable and satellite growth and it is also contradicted by the findings of satellite and cable connections in lower-middle class and slum areas of cities (installed on a cost-sharing basis) and in semi-urban and rural areas, perceived both as target audiences for Doordarshan and as its stronghold. In the time that committees submit their reports and the wheels of government move, the penetration of satellite and cable will be complete, with Doordarshan's audience substantially eroded.

Another way of approaching the challenge is to recognise Doordarshan's strength in regional language transmission catering to linguistically diverse audiences. Audiences in different states want programmes (both entertainment and information) in their own languages. In several parts of the country, neither English nor Hindi programmes can transcend the language barrier. Findings from research in educational television have repeatedly thrown up this demand for programmes in regional languages. Before cable operators, who have the potential for offering relevant and requested content in the regional language wake up to this reality, Doordarshan can and must improve the quality of content and production of its regional programmes.

Governmental instructions to Doordarshan to increase substantially its entertainment content during the prime evening slots, by making changes in schedules and by reducing the time devoted to news, is a follow up to the Mahalilk Committee report. One or two feature films a day, and two to four serials for entertainment is one way of countering the satellite and cable challenge. Such a decision takes Doordarshan further away from its stated goals of giving support to development programming for which it was created. It also does not address the fundamental question of the quality of content.

Another policy option before the government is the licensing of new television/radio channels in different parts of the country, i.e., opening up of the electronic media without disturbing the existing channel through privatisation. The hesitation to do so until now has rested partly on the realisation of the very high start-up cost of television.

Bhartia (1992) has questioned the economic viability of privately owned and operated local and regional channels. If these channels are to be based on advertising as a major source of revenue and are to operate as programme originating centres, she argues that it is inconceivable that a station with an estimated audience of about 500,000 could earn as much as Rs. 2 million per day on a continuing basis from local advertising to maintain itself. Networking these stations to make them financially viable faces major hurdles because of the prohibitive cost of accessing satellite transponders on the one hand, and the large gaps in microwave links on the other.

Even the consortium approach (as in the UK) has major pitfalls for India—from the character of Indian industry to the problems of concentration of ownership, from the need for locally relevant programming to the multiplication and duplication of capital and management costs.

A third option recommended by the Varadan Committee is to open up the second metro channel to private licencees. Towards this end, and in response to queries from Doordarshan, a group of well-known and established television producers proposed to the government that they could produce five hours of programming every day within three months' time. The telecast time of 35 hours a week could be increased to 120 hours per week within nine months and could generate an advertising revenue 50 times greater than in 1992 (Dharker, 1992).

What is worth noting about this proposal is that the potential within private media exists, both for programme production and for income generation, to make private television viable.

Effective utilisation of cable as a form of narrowcasting is another alternative which could be considered seriously. In the absence of any coherent action so far, cable operators have been using inferior quality cable, tapoffs, and splitters, among other devices. They have been drawing cables from house to house in a crude manner, leading to distortion and leakage of signals, etc. Such a situation could be corrected with regulation.

Cable has several tangible benefits to offer. It is local in nature, giving small advertisers an opportunity to advertise products and services, and in turn provides revenue to the cable operator. It is a low cost network which could generate employment while not having high start-up costs. The quality of coverage on cable is better, and it can prove to be an important source of revenue for government. Cable capacity can be increased and the needs of different target audiences can be met at the same time. It can draw from an already existing pool of programmes (royalty payments being much less than original programme production) and can be networked through satellite at a national level, especially since many cable operators are already showing Doordarshan programmes along with other channels.

A Future Scenario

The Indian ethos has included apprehension of change as one of its major characteristics, along with the notion of a paternalistic government benevolently looking after the needs of its people. So much so that the oft repeated remark is that 'government should do this or that . . .'.

Satellite based broadcasting, coupled with cable narrowcasting, has demonstrated that government inaction is the best condition for private enterprises to flourish, and they are now unstoppable. What is more, with the propensity for democratising access to media, they have become the vehicles by which the media literate citizenry can say 'we have grown up and want media content suited to our tastes and needs. We no longer believe that Doordarshan knows best'; and it is this demand, expressed in changing patterns of media exposure, which will change India's audio-visual landscape.

In addition to Doordarshan, India will have at least one national channel, privately owned and financed out of advertising, and offering a mixed fare of news, current affairs and culture based programming. Several regional channels in response to India's linguistic diversity will also emerge. Satellite based foreign sources—Star, CNN, BBC, and others—will also provide channels of television programming, as will India's own satellite based additional channels. An estimate of the number of channels which Indians will be able to access is about 50 by the end of 1994. While urban centres will be the first beneficiaries, these changes will percolate down rapidly to India's villages, as rural demand is the fastest growing segment in the Indian market. One can only hypothesise at the size of India's potential audiences, and video and cable will lose none of their importance.

The Indian ethos of apprehension to change will protect its society from 'evil foreign influences'. No medium, foreign or Indian, will be in an advantageous position to influence the Indian viewer's opinion or to manipulate it. Viewers will switch to a different channel if they do not like what they see, just as they have been switching off the television set at present.

The myth of the power of broadcasting to bring about a more educated and enlightened democracy has already been exploded several times in different societies. What is important is the power of media to democratise, to give access to information, to give expression to what V.S. Naipaul has called India's 'million mutinies' (Naipaul, 1990), and to provide access to express one's views—for this is what democracy is all about. Only a state monopoly could be afraid of that.

A Post Script

Many of the predictions which have been made when this paper was first written in 1991 have come true. Since late 1995, it is possible for an Indian home to receive two main Doordarshan channels, coupled with any of the 14 regional networks set up by Doordarshan for direct reception through satellite and cable. In addition, there are likely to be more than 60 channels available in India alone (when INSAT 2C becomes operational in January 1996). An exclusive 24-hour educational channel, a dedicated educational channel on extended C Band, an enrichment/educational channel called Doordarshan III or Plus channel, and a compressed video satellite to cable channel are part of the emerging scenario.

However, what remains of concern is not the availability of numerous channels but their content. Except for the now established Doordarshan channels (whose response has been promisingly fresh) and the Star TV system, content on private national and regional channels is of apallingly poor quality. Content remains predominantly focused on the Bombay film industry with little or no original programming, and production and technical quality leaves much to be desired. As with all systems, a clearer picture is likely to emerge after another two years by which time the media scenario in India will have undergone a total transformation.

References

Agrawal, Binod C. (1991). 'Passive pleasures of video: The technology intervention in the leisure of media rich'. *ICCTR Journal*, III (1–2), 14–32.

Bhartia, Shobana (1992). 'An independent channel'. *Seminar*, 390 (February), 29–32.

Bhatia, Rajan (1992). 'Television's new avtar is a hit'. *The Independent*, 25 July.

Dharker, Anil (1992). 'Television is like octroi'. *The Independent*, 11 July.

Doordarshan (1986). *Television India*. Prepared by Audience Research Unit. New Delhi: Doordarshan Directorate General.

Gerbner, George, Gross, L. and **Melody, William N.** (1973). *Communication in technology and social policy*. New York: John Wiley and Sons.

Gill, S.S. (1991). 'Satellite television: New Delhi sleeps as threats gather in the sky'. *Indian Express*, 8 December.

Gopal, B.V. (1986). *Video piracy and the law*. New Delhi: Deep and Deep Publications.

Government of India (1966). *Radio and Television: Report of the Committee on broadcasting and information media*. New Delhi: Government of India. (Also known as Chanda Committee Report).

——— (1978). *Akash Bharati: Report of the working group on autonomy for Akashvani and Doordarshan*. New Delhi: Government of India. (Also known as Verghese Committee Report).

——— (1985). *An Indian personality for television: Report of the working group on software for Doordarshan*. New Delhi: Government of India. (Also called Joshi Committee Report).

Naipaul, V.S. (1990). *India, a million mutinies now*. London: Minerva.

Ninan, Sevanthi (1992). 'Plodding On'. *Seminar*, 390 (February), 15–17.

Reddi, U.V. (1982). 'Some perspectives on the flow of world news'. *Media Asia*, 8 (2), 82–89.

——— (1985). 'Of the appropriateness of communication technology: A discussion'. *The Third Channel*, 1 (1), July, 75–88.

Sarabhai, Vikram (1969). 'Television for development'. Paper presented at in the Society for International Development Conference, New Delhi: India International Centre.

Schiller, Herbert I. (1986). 'The erosion of national sovereignty by the world business system'. In Traber, Michael. *The myth of the information revolution*. London: Sage.

Schramm, Wilbur (1964). *Mass media and national development*. Paris: UNESCO.

Seghal, Rashmi (1992). 'Rao sets the ball rolling for privatisation of Doordarshan'. *The Independent*, 10 March.

Seminar (1992). 'Extracts from the report on introducing competition in the electronic media' (Varadan Committee Report). 390 (February), 37–40.

Sinha, Tara (1992). 'Television comes of age'. *Seminar*, 390 (February), 27–28.

13

Pictured Realities and Pictures of Reality: Cross-cultural Intelligibility of the Visual in Television

Raghavachari Amritavalli

Like all popular sayings, the one that a picture is worth a thousand words is both right and wrong; for not all pictures speak the same language. How exactly do pictures speak to a viewer, and what do they say? It is suggested in this chapter that the answers are to be sought from works in cognitive psychology of human perceptual systems, as well as from investigations into the representative and symbolic dimensions of art. The paper begins by considering the problem of picture-perception, a problem with a tradition of investigation in cross-cultural psychology and anthropology, and moves on to the particular problem posed by film and television of integration, by the viewer, of a series of images.

There has been a fair amount of research on how viewers perceive television, which focuses on the reception and interpretation of the content, or the message of television, e.g., arguments for effects of the cultural context of the viewer on the interpretation of a programme, or effects of viewer bias in the selection and assimilation of information. Such research assumes that the medium itself is transparent to the viewer. It does not address the question of the perception of the television image per se, i.e., the issue of television as a picture, or a string of pictures, to be made sense of. Some evidence is available from responses to films, which suggest that the latter may be an area of interest; such as the alleged comment, 'we do not have such big mosquitoes', on a documentary about malaria which showed magnificently enlarged mosquitoes. But there has been little systematic attempt to build into audience research in television, insights from work on picture-perception, or visual perception, in general.

It is commonplace in film theory that images must be 'read' (cf. Monaco, 1981), with the corollary that some kind of 'learning' is involved in television viewing. However, there appears to be a lack of clarity of conceptualisation as regards the boundary conditions of this claim. It cannot be the case that the very necessity for the mental processing of a visual image automatically entails a kind of 'reading' that is 'learnt'. From the point of view of cognitive psychology, all seeing, including looking at what we perceive as the 'real' world—'veridical perception'—arguably involves a mental act, a mediation by the human conceptual system of the world of 'pure' visual sensation. In real life, the optical image on the retina is inverted, two-dimensional, and constantly shifting (to say nothing of its size!); whereas we perceive, via this information from the visual sensor, a world that is upright, three-dimensional, and stable (and of the 'right' size). Such is presumably the perceptual experience of all human beings. Moreover, our minds transform the sensation of a retinal image growing smaller or larger into the perception of an object retreating or approaching (the so-called 'constancy of size'); the sensation of a change in colour of the 'same' object into a perceived difference in its level of illumination (the 'constancy of colour'); and a kaleidoscopic variety of form for the 'same' object into a perception of changes in orientation of the viewer with respect to that object (the 'constancy of shape').

This paper would like to claim that such processing is part of the mental apparatus brought to bear on any visual stimulus by any human being. Then, if it is true that 'we search the television image as we search fields of vision' (Andrew, 1984, p. 28), we would not expect to find culture-specific differences in the way viewers experience the television image in terms of three-dimensionality, movement of objects on the screen towards or away from them, and (perhaps) inference of intended time of day as indicated by level of illumination.

This claim is not entirely vacuous, in light of the research on the perception of pictures across cultures, in the tradition of Hudson (1960). Briefly, this cross-cultural work argues for variance attributable to learning (or environmental influences) in the perception of pictures, specifically with respect to three-dimensionality and depth. Fairly typical of the way the ostensible results of the Hudson research paradigm are integrated into a discussion of the semiotics of cinema is the following observation by Monaco (1981, p. 121): '. . . there are cultural differences in the perception of images. In one famous 1920s test, anthropologist William Hudson set out to examine whether rural Africans who had had little contact with Western culture perceived depth in two dimensional images the same way that Europeans do. He found, unequivocally, that they do not'. How now do we reconcile our claim of universal characteristics in the human mental processing of visual stimuli with such results?

Critical analysis of the materials and methodology of Hudson-type testing apart (see, for an excellent review, Hagen and Jones, 1978), it is useful at the outset to draw a larger parallel here with a similar dilemma concerning human linguistic knowledge, addressed by contemporary linguistic theory. All human beings can learn a language, 'their' language; and all are equally adapted to learn any language—a British baby who chances to be adopted into a community of Bantu speakers will turn out to be a speaker of the Bantu language, rather than English. This argues the point that all languages are fundamentally 'similar' in some pretheoretical sense; a human being has as his birthright the gift of tongue—any tongue. Yet, it is immediately apparent that the languages of the world are wonderfully dissimilar; that languages other than one's 'own' have to be learnt, with varying degrees of success. No language exists today, in the post-Babel world, which is universally understood, after all.

Linguistic theory explains this by claiming that every language is simultaneously universal and particular. Every language has elements that come to us 'for free', these are the 'universal' elements. But every language has, in addition, elements that are the result of its particular choices in the universal linguistic system or of its history, culture-specific elements, if you will. The latter set of elements accounts for the diversity and mutual non-intelligibility of languages, while the former set ensures that all human languages are in principle learnable (by any human).

It seems to me that a similar dual perspective, a recognition of the simultaneous existence of the universal and the particular, is necessary to arrive at a 'grammar' of the perception of pictures (and by extension, of film and television). Suppose we grant that human beings see the world 'out there' in fundamentally similar ways, according to the principles of visual perception such as the constancies and invariances mentioned earlier. This much is universal, common to humankind. Then, insofar as a picture approximates 'reality', it must evoke perceptual responses common to all mankind; whereas insofar as a picture attempts to depict reality in conventionalised ways, it must evoke perceptual responses that vary across cultures.[1]

This might appear to be an oversimplification.[2] Moreover, as a theoretical perspective on pictures and picture-perception, it might appear confused, straddling as it does the rival approaches of Gibson (1966) and Goodman (1968). Gibson argues from the basic premise of a physical resemblance of some sort between a picture and its subject, whereas Goodman 'rejects any attempt to root pictorial labels in an objective analysis of the structure of the visible world . . . . All pictures must be read according to a culturally standardized system' (Hagen and Jones, 1978, p. 172). However, this paper takes the position of Hagen and Jones (1978); who point out that 'one may agree with Gibson that fully coloured and textured, geometrically accurate pictures contain the same kind of information as that found in the non-pictorial world, and still question the informational equivalence and perceptual effectiveness of impoverished or modified pictures' (p. 173). In other words, there are pictures and pictures.

That the picture itself is a crucial variable in any cross-cultural test of picture-perception is a fact not usually appreciated by the authors of these studies. Reviewing the literature on cross-cultural picture-perception, Hagen and Jones (1978) make this point, and conclude 'fairly confidently' that 'the perception of fully coloured and textured pictures is relatively independent of culture' (p. 206). But what strikes them is the rarity of studies using such pictures—coloured pictures, or pictures rich in realistic detail. Hagen and Jones (1978) quote Deregowski (1976) as symptomatic of an attitude to research that might account for this lacuna; the context is Deregowski's citing of a prior finding about the (apparently) 'immediate response of unsophisticated viewers to richly detailed photographic transparencies':

> . . . Deregowski goes so far as to say, 'I shall not concern myself with pictures, such as the above transparency, which approximate to reality so closely as to be mistaken for it, but

> with pictures that depict reality showing sufficient clarity to be readily recognizable in one culture and yet present difficulties in another, since only such pictures can tell us what happens when we see a *picture* for the first time' (p. 174, emphasis in the original).

In other words, pictures which 'look real' are, by definition, not pictures at all, and (therefore) picture-perception is to be tested cross-culturally, solely with culturally 'loaded' pictures![3]

But now, with the recognition that there are pictures that approximate to reality so closely as to be capable of being mistaken for it, one might argue that the putative problem of the television picture, or the film image, disappears: for surely the television picture—essentially a richly detailed photograph originating in a sophisticated camera—is so much like the 'real thing' that it may create problems for members of different cultures. But is this really the case?

In fact, the television image takes photographic reality merely as its point of departure. It is interesting here to draw a parallel with the development of Western art. Gardner (1982, p. 65) observes that what began as 'schematic and unrealistic' artwork tended increasingly towards 'realism' or 'retinal fidelity', until (in the early nineteenth century) 'audiences had begun to encounter landscapes and scenes that rivalled photographs in their degree of depicted realism'. But the achievement of such heights of realism was immediately succeeded by the plunge into periods (post-impressionist, cubist, expressionist) in which 'there was the rapid and near total collapse of any effort at depicting the world as it appears to the naked eye' (Gardner, 1982, p. 65). Whatever the explanation for this pattern of history in art (one might argue, with Hagen and Jones [1978, p. 195], that since even 'Western "snapshot" art . . . may be regarded as a choice of convention by a particular culture', it is as susceptible to change as any other convention), the point of interest to us is that the televised image appears to undergo a similar history, or a series of transformations in its evolution. The medium of television rapidly outgrows the allegiance to photographic reality characteristic of its period of infancy, and proceeds to create a visual world which is an alternative to, rather than a mere reflection of, the real world. Thus, the visual world of much of contemporary television is a bewildering mix of what is universal ('looks real') and what is particular, conventional, stylised.[4]

The impetus for this arises from a variety of sources. It is not merely from an effort to be creative or 'arty', or the imperative to attract and hold attention by resorting to novelty, although these factors do have their part. It is, rather, that the psychological distinction, thin at best, between the 'real', objective world out there, and the mental world of our visualisations, is blurred and obliterated by any programme which hopes to convey ideas. A science-awareness programme on the hole in the ozone layer, for example, juxtaposes and overlaps shots of the real world with simulations, perhaps computer-generated, of what might be happening in the upper atmosphere. Or let us take a simpler example, and return to our original problem of magnified mosquitoes. It is now apparent that this is a visual that is rooted in its cultural context. Magnification presupposes the microscope, and encapsulates a world-view which attempts to understand the structure of reality through the mediation of technology. It not merely hypothesises unseen worlds, but works on the premise that such worlds are not in principle unseeable. A viewer of such a visual on the television screen is really being asked to look through an imaginary microscope; it is not enough for him to have encountered real mosquitoes.

There are even humbler examples of culture-specific visuals which may bewilder the uninitiated. Consider the widespread use, in educational television especially, of flow-charts, diagrams and graphs, or the use of maps in newscasts and weather reports. These symbolic visual representations are drawn from an educational tradition predating television, synonymous with literacy and print. Crucially, they represent in visual form ideas and verbal descriptions, rather than 'raw' reality. They need to be 'read'. It is interesting, in this context, to consider the implications of such visuals when considering the view (to which the author personally subscribes) that television is an alternative route to adult education, as against adult literacy. It is perhaps difficult for the literate and educated producer to appreciate how deeply his visual experiences are embedded in his educational tradition.[5,6]

And what (further afield) would an illiterate, novice television viewer make of the visual pun, generated by a computer, which 'turns the page' of the screen, making-believe that the screen is a book? How is he to differentiate the pure fantasy of mere attention-capturing manipulations of the image—the bra which turns into a bird and flies away, the dancing child in her newly-washed frock who twirls and freezes into the photograph on the package of the nation's favourite detergent—from the claimed 'reality' of images showing the cross-section of a flower or a limb, images involving the transformation of time as in slow-motion or time-lapse photography, or the transformation of colour as in infra-red photography? Perhaps even 'literate' or 'cinemate' viewers do not fully make the requisite distinctions; and perhaps this is one kind of explanation for why television is so often felt to be a seductive medium, a medium which distances all experience and encapsulates it into a box which can be made to go dark at will.

From the production point of view, the need to capture and retain attention ensures that as the audience matures in viewing experience, the visuals keep moving just enough out of the range of the audience's 'experiential visual world' (which now includes over-familiar television techniques!) to remain intriguing. Thus, one way to compare television programmes across cultures is purely in terms of their visual inventiveness; and this, the paper suggests, is a function of those cultures' experiences with the medium. An early BBC production on magnetism is in the form of a lecture–demonstration of its basic properties by Sir Lawrence Bragg, set in a typical laboratory, with all the standard objects at hand. Such a 'realistic' use of the medium for a basic programme on magnetism is probably not an option any more for a BBC production, notwithstanding the personal magnetism of the programme presenter. A more trivial example is the evolution of title and credit graphics. Starting out simply as 'enlarged pages' on the screen, currently these are exercises in creating a visual display wherein letters and words appear, disappear, move together or apart, or dance on and off the screen; the information carried by the credits is no longer sufficient to sustain the visual in its own right.

In television, as in the comic strip, a series of pictures presented sequentially in time or in space have to be integrated into a meaningful 'story' by the viewer, who has to hypothesise the links in between. In a sense, then, all television is montage; the artistic use of montage merely develops the logic inherent to television, and indeed to all visual experience. For it is in the nature of visual experience to connect. Discussions of the psychology of vision begin by observing that our experience of panoramic vision, or of a continuous environment, is a construction of the mind, an illusion aided by memory.[7] We mentally integrate a succession of separate glances of limited scope when we 'see' a view, or a room and its occupants; much as, at a cognitive level, we put together a 'mental map' of a house or a neighbourhood that we have never seen all at once in a single glance. It is because we cope with the jigsaw of our real visual environment that we are able to make sense of the jigsaw of television.

Film theorists have sometimes considered the 'cut' (as against the 'pan') as a manipulation of reality, an interruption and a remodelling of reality (Monaco, 1981). In fact, the eye 'cuts' in real life from, for example, the face to the hand of an interlocutor, with no consciousness of either the eye movement or the intervening space. As Monaco (1981, p. 143) remarks, 'Psychologically, the cut is the truer approximation of our natural perception'. Yet we know from the history of film that it was some years before early film makers found the courage to tell a story in a sequence of cuts rather than in a single long shot or in a continuously moving shot; for they were not sure that the audience would understand.[8] Indeed, there is some evidence that preliminary exposure to the narrative technique of cinema is necessary in order to 'trigger' the extension of a naturally-available integrative cognitive skill. Arnheim (1969, p. 309) cites the following story, which (as he observes), whether 'authentic or not, makes a valid point':

> In one of the early books on film theory, Bela Balazs tells the story of a Ukranian gentleman-farmer, who, disowned after the Soviet revolution, lived as the administrator of his estate, hundreds of miles away from the nearest railroad station. For fifteen years he had not been in the city. A highly educated intellectual, he received newspapers, magazines and books and owned a radio. He was up to date, but he had never seen a film. One day he traveled to Kiev and at that occasion saw his first movie, one of the early Douglas Fairbanks features. Around him in the theatre, children followed the story with ease, having a good time. The country gentleman sat staring at the screen with the utmost concentration, trembling of excitement and effort. 'How did you like it?' asked a friend afterwards. 'Enormously interesting,' he replied, 'but what was going on in the picture?' He had been unable to understand.

Anecdotal and introspective evidence suggests that some adults remember vividly the moment when, as children, they discovered that the visual images on the screen in the darkened theatre cohered into a story, after all. These are experiences predating television; psychologically, they are the viewer-centred complement of the discovery, from the producer's point of view, of the principle of montage.

The insight into the interconnectedness of the separate visuals on the film and television screen, which came relatively late to children of an earlier era who were exposed only occasionally to films, appears to come much quicker to children today who are regularly exposed to television. The following amusing personal anecdote bears this out. A two-and-a-half year old girl was watching a regional language magazine-type programme about the promotion of small entrepreneurs by friendly nationalised banks (which provided the necessary capital). The programme featured different entrepreneurs, the first three being a flower seller, a dairyman who had acquired a herd of buffalo, and a tailor. A series of images appeared on the screen showing each of these people at work; there was no visual indication of the shift from one entrepreneur to the next, this being achieved by the voice-over.

The voice-over was in a language the child was unfamiliar with. At the moment when the camera cut from a last loving shot of the buffalo herd to a close-up of the next entrepreneur, the tailor at her machine, the child exclaimed with wonder: 'Look, they are stitching clothes for the buffaloes!'

This child had understood the principle of montage and of television. Or we might say, in the words of Harvard's Project Zero team, that she had grasped the 'narrative nature' of television (Gardner and Jaglom, 1982, p. 243):

> [a] fundamental challenge facing the child during his first years of viewing is an appreciation of the narrative nature of much of television. For the one- and two-year-old, television presents an army of isolated images that bear no connection to one another. Any image could appear at any time . . . . By the age of three or four, the child begins to sense that television presents narratives . . . . However, even when the narrative purpose of television has been grasped, the understanding of individual narratives may remain extremely meager.

The Project Zero team's observation was made in the context of studying 'a small group of first-born, primarily middle-class youngsters between the ages of two and five' (Gardner and Jaglom, 1982, p. 242) in the United States. It is significant that their remarks appear equally pertinent to a middle-class Indian urban child. Equally significant, and intriguing, is their choice of title for the chapter quoted from here: '. . . The Child as Anthropologist'. The title suggests the possibility of extending the research techniques for studying the response to television of children in a particular culture, not merely to children in other cultures, but also to adults in cultures which are in their infancy as regards television production and viewing. As Gardner and Jaglom (1982, p. 241) observe, 'in being placed in front of a television set and being asked, in effect, to make sense of the innumerable fleeting images it presents, the young child of two, four, or eight years of age is a kind of anthropologist'.

The major argument in this paper has been that insofar as television and films call into play the universal human cognitive capacity to make 'visual sense' out of a retinal impression, or a series of retinal impressions, of the 'real world out there', these media transcend cultural barriers. However, it appears that there may be very few pictures that can be said to be entirely 'culturally neutral' in this way; for a picture is not a slice of the real world, neither does it purport to be one (except, perhaps, in the artistic tradition of *trompe l'oeil*!). Rather, the paper suggests that the visual world created by man is the outcome of his visualisations, however trivial; it thus necessarily reflects a world-view, rather than simple visual verisimilitude.

In saying this the paper tends more towards the Goodmanian theory of pictures than the Gibsonian one. However, we retain the possibility of particular pictures being more 'Gibsonian' than 'Goodmanian', or vice-versa; thus it is suggested, following Hagen and Jones, that a componential analysis of pictures aimed at separating universal elements from conventional cues is a prerequisite to any meaningful anthropological study of picture-perception

The paper has presupposed without argument the ability of all humans to recognise a picture *qua* picture (as opposed to regarding it as an object in its own right). The literature records isolated instances, in older subjects with no prior exposure to pictures, of puzzlement; but such puzzlement appears to arise as much from the strangeness of the material medium presented (e.g., paper) as from the central fact of object-representation. We take picture-creation and picture-recognition to be part of the human cognitive capacity for symbolic representation, viz., the 'stand for' relation, which is arguably a cognitive prerequisite for language as well.

This is not to deny that there are developmental factors in picture-recognition, which are well worth exploring. For instance, there appears to be a stage at which the perceiver is unable to separate a picture from the larger environment in which the picture occurs. This effect is not culturally specific, in that very similar phenomena are reported from Africa and from North America. Hagen and Jones (1978, p. 194) quote a study by Deregowski (in Africa) which showed:

> a very interesting effect of vertical vs. horizontal presentation of a picture of a profiled standing buck. When the picture was presented lying flat on the ground, nine subjects reported that the buck was 'lying down'. Six of these subjects were then shown the picture vertically and all reported that the buck was then 'standing up'. This result is suggestive of similar findings with children . . . which imply that there is a stage in the development of pictorial perception in which the space behind the picture plane is not completely separated from the space of the ordinary environment which surrounds the picture. For the sophisticated observer, a picture is not simply a window to the world; it is a window to a rigidly constructed tunnel which encloses a self-contained world independent of the surround. The simple window concept may well precede the tunnel concept.

Compare the above with the following observations of the Project Zero group (Gardner and Jaglom, 1982, p. 243):

> To the extent that a one- or two-year-old child attends to television, . . . these youngsters accept the material presented on television as a natural part of everyday life . . . [t]here is essentially no appreciation of television as a distanced medium, one whose content represents rather than constitutes the daily flux of experience. Thus, at twenty-five months one of our subjects . . . sees a broken egg on television and runs to fetch a paper towel to clean up the egg . . . . Not until the child is four

or five does he understand that what is presented on television exists in a world apart from his immediate life space.

And finally, the question of the cross-cultural validity of a television visual, here considered from the point of view of the perceiver, is of vital interest to the producer as well. The paper has tangentially suggested how the inquiry into picture-perception leads on naturally into an inquiry about the nature of representation in art, and cultural variables in art styles. The question thus arises whether the television visual, having progressed beyond verisimilitude, needs to adhere to the Western 'realist' style of representation ('snapshot art' as Hagen and Jones term it), or to other options in style intrinsic to that culture. The realistic, single-perspective drawing is not found in all cultures, nor is it the kind of drawing that children first spontaneously produce. One style 'common not just in primitive people but in children everywhere', according to an opinion quoted by Hagen and Jones (1978, p. 202) is the cultural option known as 'split' or 'chain-style' depiction. (This is 'essentially the simultaneous depiction of several points of view or object aspects on the same picture plane' [Hagen and Jones, 1978, p. 203].)

I remember a chain-style drawing of a south Indian musical instrument, a veena, by a girl aged about ten.[9] This is a child with almost no formal education, currently attending an informal single-teacher school. Being a child of the urban poor, she is not unexposed to films and television, as also hoardings and pictorial labels on products in the Western realistic style. Yet her drawing of the instrument, done after listening to a musician visiting the school, was clearly multi-dimensional. She had drawn parts of the veena that could not have been visible from her perspective, but which are essential to the production of music by the instrument. (The body of the instrument consists of a long column of wood, indicated in the drawing by fine 'grain' lines, with a circular resonating chamber at one end. The widely spaced thick vertical black bars in her drawing, above the wooden column, are actually the frets in the instrument, which are on the horizontal plane, and would be at a ninety-degree angle to the body of the instrument as she drew it. Additionally two fine black lines at the very top stood for the minor strings, which actually occur 'on the other side' of the wooden column, so to speak.)

The question arises how chain-style representations compare with 'realistic' representations in terms of information content, communicative efficacy, and audience preferences. Deregowski is cited by Hagen and Jones (1978, p. 202) as arguing that:

> in all societies there is, in children, an aesthetic preference for chain-type drawings and if this preference is not destroyed it persists into adulthood. In most societies this preference is suppressed; this is done because the preferred drawings are worse at conveying information about the depicted objects than are the non-preferred representative drawings. Thus aesthetic preference is sacrificed at the altar of communicative efficiency.

However, Hagen and Jones (1978) rightly point out that 'chain-style art is essentially the simultaneous depiction of several points of view or object aspects on the same picture plane, and there is no a priori reason of which we are aware for rejecting the possibility of successful information depiction with such a style' (p. 203).

It is to be hoped that systematic work aimed at investigating such questions might open up the visual world of television to a wide range of cultural styles in art and in other forms, other than those indigenous to the cultures that produced the technology of television. Much work remains to be done on cross-cultural readings of television and there is danger in presuming that 'Eastern' audiences read television uniformly and that they read it in 'Western' ways, with 'Western' style consequences.

Notes

1. The point being made here regarding universal and particular features of visual stimuli is prefigured, though not precisely in these terms, in theories of film communication which adopt a perceptual psychological approach to the subject. Thus, Andrew (1984, p. 25) writes:

> When Metz declared that we must 'go beyond analogy' he meant that . . . [w]e must examine not just the codes that add themselves to the image, cultural codes . . . we must examine first and foremost those codes which permit an image to appear at all, the codes of resemblance . . . . The labor involved in bringing film stimuli into recognizable images is not a unique or special labor. Something like it must happen in every perceptual case.

2. Thus, Sless (1981, p. 114, ff.) develops a theory of drawings according to their perceived function: 'description' vs. 'explanation' of the pictured object. He argues that while 'a description of something assumes it to be intelligible, an explanation assumes that in some respect the phenomenon is unintelligible' (1981, p. 123). In our terms, a picture aiming at description would be immediately recognisable, whereas the explanatory picture would more likely have abstract or conventional characteristics.
3. Hagen and Jones report that outline drawings are the category of pictures which are the best studied in the Hudsonian tradition. These pictures retain 'edge information', while dispensing with colour, texture and shadows. Although outline drawings are not 'arbitrarily conventional pictures', it is nevertheless argued that 'such pictures present naive observers with a very unnatural optic array' (1978, pp. 178–79). More serious is the charge of 'a certain lack of systematicity in task analysis and control' in this research paradigm. Thus, subjects are reported to have been classified as 'two-dimensional perceivers' who in fact seemed to see both 2D and 3D possibilities, and asked the experimenter for 'guidance in their perceptual choice' (*ibid*, p. 183). The accuracy of the size cues in the drawings for Hudson's pictorial depth perception test is also called into question by these authors.
4. Cross-cultural picture work appears to deny, or to fail to recognise, the possibility of a 'mix' in a single picture of the conventional or arbitrary, and the 'real' or the 'duplication of three-dimensional visual experiences'. Hagen and Jones (1978) argue forcefully against the position that 'all picture components have essentially the same status', i.e., that all pictorial information is classifiable as 'cue', 'convention', or 'technique' (p. 195):

   > Superposition, linear perspective, shading and texture are not conventions. They are present on the ambient optic array of the ordinary environment; they are present on the retina; they are present on the film plane of a pinhole camera. They are present by virtue of optical, logical, and geometric necessity, and not by virtue of arbitrary custom. To confuse these sources of ordinary environmental information with arbitrary symbols is to hopelessly entangle the multiple components of pictures beyond the reach of systematic analysis.

   In one Hudsonian outline-figures study, an 'implied motion' picture (which uses the convention of lines to suggest movement) was regarded as essentially 'of the same order of difficulty' as one using overlapping lines to show depth. These authors also point out that the origin of 'the present flood of work in South Africa on picture-perception' lies in the [mis]perception of pictures requiring knowledge of such conventions as 'prototypical identity', 'pain stars, rain dashes, shock waves, speed lines, left-right sequencing, etc.'. (Hagen and Jones, 1978, p. 198). They conclude: 'It is quite obvious . . . that more careful attention to the various classes of pictorial elements is critical not only to forwarding understanding pictorial perception but also to successful utilization of pictorial materials as didactic aids' (p. 198).
5. There is of course the larger question of how well such visual material is understood in the general educational setting. Arnheim (1969, p. 309) asks

'what exactly children and other learners see when they look at a text book illustration, a film, a television programme', mentioning in particular the problem of interpreting maps: 'children sometimes assume a country to end where the map ends . . . border lines are often so neat as to give a misleading impression of completeness . . . . Avoidable difficulties arise frequently in the use of colors'. He concludes that 'what holds for maps is equally true for every sort of visual presentation in textbooks, models, charts, films, etc.'.

6. 'In the conventional growth theory the vast masses must first cross the illiteracy barrier before they can participate in growth . . . electronic media like radio and television have the potential of transcending the literacy barrier and therefore also the class barrier. They make it possible for the non-literate masses to have access to information and, consequently, to the fruits of development without first crossing the literacy barrier. People belonging to the pre-industrial oral culture, therefore, can take a leap into the post industrial world . . .' (Joshi et al., 1985, p. 16).
7. Hooper (n.d.) provides an excellent introduction to this topic.
8. 'Before the turn of the century, most movies consisted of short events photographed in long shot in a single take . . . . Filmmakers of this period were worried that audiences wouldn't see the continuity between one segment (shot) of the story and another' (Giannetti, 1987, p. 110). The innovation of breaking up a single scene into a sequence of shots is credited to various directors (and narratives) by various authors. Giannetti ascribes it to the American Edwin S. Porter, who directed a multi-shot final scene in *The Life of an American Fireman* (1903).
9. My thanks to Mrs. Janaki Iyer and K.G. Vijayakrishnan for making this drawing available to me.

References

Andrew, J.D. (1984). *Concepts in film theory*. Oxford: Oxford University Press.

Arnheim, R. (1969). *Visual thinking*. Berkeley: University of California Press.

Deregowski, J.B. (1976). 'On seeing a picture for the first time'. *Leonardo*, 9 (1), 19–23.

Gardner, H. (1982). *Art, mind and brain: A cognitive approach to creativity*. New York: Basic Books.

Gardner, H., and **Jaglom, L.** (1982). 'Cracking the codes of television: The Child as Anthropologist'. In Gardner H. *Art, mind and brain: A cognitive approach to creativity*. New York: Basic Books.

Giannetti, L. (1987). *Understanding movies*. Englewood Cliffs, NJ: Prentice-Hall (Fourth edition).

Gibson, J.J. (1966). *The senses considered as perceptual systems*. Boston: Houghton Mifflin.

Goodman, N. (1968). *Languages of art: An approach to a theory of symbols*. Indianapolis: Bobbs-Merrill.

Hagen, M.A. and **Jones, R.K.** (1978). 'Cultural effects on picture perception: How many words is one picture really worth?' In Walk, R.D. and Pick, H.L. (eds.). *Perception and experience*. London: Plenum Press.

Hooper, K. (n.d.). *Imaging and visual thinking*. Unit 5 of the Second Level Interdisciplinary Course on Art and Environment. Milton Keynes: The Open University Press.

Hudson, W. (1960). 'Pictorial depth perception in sub-cultural groups in Africa'. *Journal of Social Psychology*, 52 (October–December), 183–208.

Joshi, P.C. et al. (1985). *An Indian personality for television*. Report of the Working Group on Software for Doordarshan, vol. 1. New Delhi: Publications Division, Ministry of Information and Broadcasting.

Monaco, J. (1981). *How to read a film*. Oxford: Oxford University Press.

Sless, D. (1981). *Learning and visual communication*. London: Croom Helm.

14

Aspects of Ethnicity and Gender in Malaysian Television

Mustafa K. Anuar and *Wang Lay Kim*

Television in Malaysia is not only the most important medium (Shukla, 1992)[1] for the dissemination of information and entertainment, but is also regarded—particularly by the State—as an important tool for facilitating or encouraging socio-economic development and for fostering national integration amongst the country's multi-ethnic peoples.

In addition, Malaysian television, in particular, and the mass media, in general, need to be seen and studied in the context of a national politics that is easily influenced by ethnic sentiments and considerations. In this connection, public policies such as the National Culture Policy, the New Economic Policy, and the Privatisation Policy also need be analysed as they have, by and large, influenced the form and content of most of the television programmes in the country. It is thus within this social context that this paper attempts to examine the role and position of television in Malaysia vis-à-vis ethnicity and gender.

The Malaysian Setting

This Southeast Asian country consists of various ethnic groups, the main ones being the Malays, Chinese and Indians.[2] Needless to say, while the multi-ethnic nature of the Malaysian population is a source of cultural celebration, it can also be—and has been on a number of occasions—a real potential source for inter-ethnic conflicts of varying degrees. The contributory factors to ethnic frictions range from the political to the socio-economic to the cultural. One significant factor that needs to be mentioned here is the coincidence, to a certain extent, of ethnicity with socio-economic status, which really has its origins in the colonial days. In particular, many Malays and Bumiputeras—especially in the period immediately after the country's independence—are by and large economically backward compared to the non-Bumiputeras as a group. This has inevitably created ethnic dissatisfaction and tension, and intense inter-ethnic competition for economic and political power. Such a socio-political situation is further complicated by the fact that most political parties, the ruling coalition Barisan Nasional (BN)[3] and the Opposition[4] alike, are to a large extent ethnic based. This has resulted in many of them flirting with the temptation to manipulate and exploit ethnic sentiments, if and when opportunity prevails.

Given these ethnic, political, cultural and economic complexities, it is therefore little wonder that the overriding concern of Malaysians in general, and the professed objective of the government in particular, has been to deal with inter-ethnic conflict and resolution. In this connection, the mass media have been identified by the State as being a useful and effective instrument in bringing about the desired national integration and unity. Furthermore, the effort to achieve this objective of national unity is normally made in the name of promoting and maintaining political stability and security, and eventually fostering socio-economic prosperity in the country. It is also in this context that laws—undemocratic in essence—such as the powerful Internal Security Act, Official Secrets Act, Broadcasting Act, Printing Presses and Publications Act, and Societies Act, are legitimised and utilised.

Seeking National Unity and Prosperity

The period after Malaysia's bloody ethnic riots of 1969 made the pursuit for national identity and unity all the more urgent. As a demonstration of this professed concern, the Malaysian government spelled out in the *Third Malaysia Plan 1976–1980* (Government of Malaysia, 1976), the country's five-year socio-economic programme, what 'national identity' entailed, in an effort to hasten the process of national integration.[5] It was hoped that a 'national identity' would achieve political saliency and recognition, particularly in a social context where, as in Malaysia, there is clearly a need to make such an identity reign supreme over other competing loyalties or 'primordial' ethnic attachments (Smith, 1988), in the ultimate desire to achieve some measure of ethnic unity and goodwill in the society concerned.

In the project to create a 'national identity', it is crucial that Malaysians be given the encouragement and opportunity to possess a sense of belonging to the Malaysian nation. In fact Anderson (1983) defines a nation as 'an imagined political community'. This sense of belonging to a nation, he asserts, is not artificially manufactured nor false, but it is a sense born out of ideological construction. Thus, Anderson argues that 'It is imagined because the members of even the smallest nation will never know most of their fellow-members, meet them, or even hear of them, yet in the minds of each lives the image of their communion' (1983, p. 15). And 'print-capitalism'—that which led to printing technology and mass publication of books and newspapers—he adds, facilitates this imagination of communal belonging as people are brought together, or given a strong sense of togetherness, by these mass media.

This nationalist and cultural pursuit relates closely to the notion of hegemony as a lived process. For such an hegemony, argued Williams (1978, p. 112), needs to be continually 'renewed, recreated, defended, and modified. It is also continually resisted, limited, altered, challenged by pressures not at all its own'. And the images that are constructed and transmitted 'through the education system and media become the often unconscious assumptions of later generations in whose social consciousness they form a kind of rich sediment . . .' (Smith, 1988, p. 207).

In other words, social institutions such as the mass media become the ideological 'sites' where the State can continuously attempt to disseminate its own version of the historical and cultural 'past' that has been reinterpreted and reconstituted for the consumption of the public in general. This practice of selecting certain segments of the past is very much part and parcel of hegemony. Williams, in this connection, introduced the notion of 'selective tradition', which means that the selection of a certain segment of the past is passed off as 'the tradition' or 'the significant past', and this particular past is then used—through institutions—'to ratify the present and to indicate directions for the future' (1978, p. 116).

The above argument only reinforces Stuart Hall's (1986, p. 9) contention about media representation:

> . . . it matters profoundly what and who gets represented, *what* and *who* regularly and routinely gets left out; and *how* things, people, events, relationships are represented. What we know of society depends on how things are represented to us and that knowledge in turn informs what we do and what policies we are prepared to accept.
>
> Some things, people, events, relationships always get represented: always centre-stage, always in the position to define, to set the agenda, to establish the terms of the conversation. Some others sometimes get represented—but always at the margin, always responding to a question whose terms and conditions have been defined elsewhere: never 'centred'. Still others are always 'represented' only by their eloquent absence, their silences: or refracted through the glance or the gaze of others (emphases in the original).

Pressed by the need to forge a 'national identity' and to provide an intellectual leadership in this area of concern, the government sponsored a National Culture Congress in 1971 at the University of Malaya, Kuala Lumpur, where at the end of this meeting a National Culture Policy was promulgated. The Congress was in essence an attempt to seek, to borrow Williams's concept, 'the significant past' of Malaysia.[6]

This policy has in general somc implications on the ethnic cultures and their representations on television. For one thing, the 'Malay thrust' or emphasis of the cultural policy means that there is a likelihood that ethnic cultures, other than the Malay's, become marginalised in the electronic medium.

Furthermore, it is also highly likely that these male-dominant ethnic cultures ensure that the values promoted through this cultural policy are largely male-biased, and hence discriminatory against women. Thus, for example, what sounds like a genuine concern for the welfare of women can ironically work against them. In her speech during a National Women's Day celebration, the Prime Minister's wife, Dr. Siti Hasmah Mohamed Ali, cautioned women not to neglect their families in the quest to advance themselves and also reminded them to maintain a caring attitude for the family in order to sustain a well balanced human and economic development in the country (*The Star*, 30 August 1992). It thus appears here that men have been excluded, consciously or otherwise, from this vital familial responsibility.

Television and the State

Television Malaysia started its operation on 28 December 1963, with an on-air period of 24 hours weekly. This channel, now called TV1, is by and large the primary channel that promotes government policies. A second television channel, now known as TV2, commenced on 17 November 1969. Radio-Television Malaysia (RTM), which handles public broadcasting (i.e., radio and television), is owned and operated by the government.

RTM, given its close relationship with the government, has objectives that are very supportive of the government and of the latter's major policies.[7] It is not surprising, therefore, that the government disallows opposition political parties to use broadcasting stations to propagate their political ideologies. In addition, the social responsibility (such as fostering good ethnic relations) of the Malaysian mass media, like the RTM, has always been promoted by political leaders in the government. An example of this is a speech made by the late Prime Minister Tun Abdul Razak in 1974 to a group of newspaper editors and publishers.

> The press and other mass media act as [an] intermediary between the Government and the people. Their functions and responsibilities are more important and complex in a multi-racial country like Malaysia. All those concerned should take heed to ensure that whatever is published for the general public should not cause misunderstanding or be detrimental to certain groups. In this way the press and the mass media could help the Government foster the spirit of understanding and strengthen the friendship among the people . . . . The press should also avoid publishing materials which will give rise to tension among . . . various parties (cited in Grenfell, 1979, p. 7).

Television in Privatised Malaysia

Sistem Televisyen (M) Berhad (STMB), or TV3 as it is popularly known, is to date the only private television station in Malaysia.

Fleet Group, the dominant partner in this broadcasting joint venture, was awarded the operating licence by the government in August 1983.[8] The birth and continued existence of TV3 is a living testimony to the government's serious pursuit and implementation of its Privatisation Policy and the New Economic Policy.[9] The first policy is based on the philosophy that the private sector should play a leading role in the socio-economic development of the country, while the second strives to narrow what the government perceives as the socio-economic gap between the Bumiputeras and non-Bumiputeras, and also to promote Bumiputera corporate ownership and participation in the private sector.

TV3 burst onto the airwaves with the promise of a 'better choice' of entertainment for Malaysian viewers (Asiah, 1991). Although 'private' and commercial in nature, TV3 is nonetheless expected to operate within the political parameters prescribed by the ruling coalition. This was confirmed by the then chairman of TV3, Mohamed Tawfik Ismail, the son of a former deputy prime minister, who said that his company would comply with all the conditions imposed by the government (Karthigesu, 1987).

It is undeniable that TV3 has in many ways changed the overall cultural landscape of Malaysian television. Soon after its launch, TV3 pursued an aggressive policy of buying expensive imported programmes which were then scheduled against TV Malaysia's normal fare. This, in turn, triggered TV Malaysia to clean up its act, so to speak, and embark on a buying spree, importing more televisual products with the aim of attracting more viewers such as the urban Chinese viewers, and consequently earning huge advertising revenues. Competition between the two television stations has since become intense.

Another private television station company, City Television Sdn. Bhd., also a benefactor of the Privatisation Policy, is expected to operate the country's fourth television network by the beginning of 1995 (*The Star*, 24 June 1994). The major shareholder of this commercial enterprise is Melewar Corporation Bhd. (50 per cent), a company that is closely associated with the Negeri Sembilan royalty, while the other three shareholders are Utusan Melayu (M) Sdn. Bhd. (30 per cent), Medan Mas Sdn. Bhd. (10 per cent) and Diversified System Sdn. Bhd. (10 per cent) (*New Straits Times*, 24 June 1994).

Media organisations that are owned and controlled by elites and which are situated within a dominant culture that espouses patriarchal values, tend to encourage male-dominated values and ideas.[10] Fernandez (1992), for instance, points out that the commodification and stereotyping of women in the media not only help capitalists in their accumulation of wealth but also inevitably perpetuate the domination of men over women within the dominant culture.

A newspaper interview with a male advertiser brings home the point about this unhealthy tendency: 'Men like cars, men like women, cars and women together are just a way of putting subjects which work well together. Ads sell lifestyle. If I am talking to a group of men who like to drink and chat up women just to boost their own silly egos, then using a woman would give them inspirations' (*The Star*, 16 November 1991). Female sexuality, it appears here, is sorely needed to boost a man's ego.

The Privatisation Policy has also resulted in both the RTM and TV3 stations privatising certain slots or programmes. The policy has witnessed the mushrooming of predominantly Malay production houses that produce Malay dramas and musical programmes, many of which eventually get broadcast over RTM and TV3. As a consequence of this structural change, and also due to the heavy emphasis on Malay-based 'National Culture', more dramas have been produced by private companies.

Not that there aren't any dramas, movies or entertainment programmes broadcast over television that cater to the Chinese and Indian audiences. These, however, normally take the form of imports from Hong Kong, Taiwan and India. Only lately have both television stations started buying and showing Chinese dramas and Tamil entertainment programmes produced by local production houses. In addition, many of these and other popular programmes, local and imported alike, receive sponsorships from big companies manufacturing and selling, for instance, cigarettes like Dunhill, More, Salem, and Benson and Hedges; detergent like Breeze; and beauty care like Kao; a corporate move that is welcomed by the television stations. It is also noteworthy that the strategy of market segmentation employed by the advertisers and corporate sponsors has made it necessary that certain popular television programmes be selected and scheduled according to ethnic and, to a certain degree, gender requirements.

As intimated earlier, only certain television programmes are selected for privatisation. Programmes like news and documentaries, which are considered as essential information items and having a vital social and ideological role to play, are still produced and controlled by both television stations—and not left in the hands of the private producers.

Analysis of Selected Television Programmes

Three different television genres were identified, namely, drama, situation comedies (sitcom), and news. From this, several television programmes were selected for analysis. It should be noted, however, that while these selections are in no way representative of all the programmes that are broadcast by the television stations, they nonetheless can provide us with some idea of the general pattern of television programming and the dominant manner in which ethnic groups, women, and men are depicted.

Drama and sitcoms were chosen because the ways in which they present us with 'real' people in 'real' situations can help us understand how they fit into our perception of the society we live in (Bowes, 1990). News, on the other hand, was selected for analysis because it is generally perceived by the audience as being 'real' and 'factual', thereby reporting and constructing a 'true' account of events that are unfolding before our very eyes.

Privatised Malay Dramas

Spurred by the government's policy to encourage local, and particularly Malay, television productions, and at the same time to promote the core elements of the proposed 'National Culture', many local Malay dramas have been broadcast almost daily by TV1 and TV3. Malay dramas have at least one common characteristic, i.e., they use the Malay language which is the national language, or commonly referred to as the Bahasa Malaysia.

Another characteristic is that most of these dramas revolve around themes and social issues that in the main concern members of the Malay/Bumiputera and Muslim community. Hence, it is no surprise that many of these dramas normally have a 100 per cent Malay cast with the location of the shooting in, say, a Malay village, a Malay neighbourhood or a Malay business premise.

The issues often touched upon by these Malay dramas are the socio-cultural implications of modernisation upon certain members of the Malay community; over-zealous material pursuit that is portrayed as conflicting with religious (i.e., Islamic) and traditional values; love affairs involving Malay couples; family and marital problems within a Malay family; the trials and tribulations of successful Malay entrepreneurs in the context of industrial development of the country; and a re-enactment of certain 'historically and culturally significant' incidents during the glorious Malacca Sultanate, etc.

These Malay dramas have titles such as *Drama Swasta* (TV1), *Dramaneka* (TV1), *Primarama* (TV1), *Sandiwara Semasa Breeze* (TV1), *Pentas Jumaat* (TV1), *Layar Mutiara* (TV1), *Drama Pilihan* (TV1), *Cerekarama* (TV3), *Cereka Istimewa* (TV2), and *Cerekapilihan* (TV3). RTM's TV2 generally shows very little Malay dramas as it basically caters to the tastes of the urban middle-class and non-Malay viewers.

Take the example of a Malay drama, *Perkahwinan* (Marriage), which was shown on TV3. The plot is about a married Malay couple who were undergoing the strains and stresses of their respective professions and of hurried modern living. The husband was a committed dramatist whilst the wife a dedicated copywriter. This problem, in turn, affected their marital relationship as well as their expected role as parents of their two children. Alienated and feeling uncared for, the son soon found himself involved in unsocial activities in school, such as stealing a friend's money. After having realised the urgency and seriousness of their family problems, the couple eventually came to a compromise and made adjustments, so as to ensure that communication and love were still intact between them.

What can be said of this drama is that, like most other Malay television dramas, it projects characters such as architects, engineers, doctors and other professionals. This suggests an inherent desire among writers to match their ideas with those of the government, i.e., to situate Malay professionals (in the dramas) in the context of a Malaysia that is commercially and industrially developing. *Perkahwinan*, however, does raise the need to question certain values of a modernised society. In other Malay dramas with similar plots (i.e., the main characters having conflicts with modern lifestyle), Islamic values are injected, partly as an indirect response to the government's desire to instil Islamic values into the administration and wider society.

Perkahwinan also reveals that many Malay drama producers tend to offer a narrow interpretation of the government's major policies, such as the National Culture Policy, resulting in most of them having failed to take cognisance of the fact that Malaysia is indeed multi-ethnic and thus requires, to a large degree, a multi-ethnic treatment. In other words, there are times when the plot will have to expand beyond the social, cultural, economic and political boundaries of a particular ethnic community. Thus, the plot of *Perkahwinan*, for instance, could have included a few main non-Malay charactérs who are perhaps equally nervous, troubled and trapped by modern lifestyles.

Malay dramas need not necessarily always use Malay characters in their stories. Since Bahasa Malaysia is the national language, Malay dramas should have the capacity to even depict the social life of some non-Malay characters in a multi-ethnic setting. This would go a long way towards creating a dynamic ethnic interaction in many of the Malay dramas. As O'Shaughnessy (1990, p. 94) argues, 'Television must connect with people's actual experiences, both in terms of our real lives and our fantasy lives; unless we can recognise ourselves, our desires, and our dreams in television it will mean nothing to us. Television must be relevant . . .'. In short, viewers from certain ethnic groups will not feel displaced and marginalised by a television fare that does take them into consideration. Besides, this could be one creative way of enabling Malaysians to visually and culturally share a certain 'significant past'.

In three other Malay dramas that were analysed—*Ceraian–ceraian Harapan* (Fragments of hope), *Dr. Sim*, and *Tuhan Sayang Padamu* (God loves you)—women were mostly portrayed as wives and mothers. If they were depicted as business persons, they had either failed in their businesses or had become utterly hopeless mothers who were incapable of blending careers and families, thereby ending up with delinquent children. Or, worse still, transforming into bitches who stole husbands from other seemingly dependable wives.

In the case of *Tuhan Sayang Padamu*, for instance, the main female character was depicted as a career woman, being chauffeured around and making important decisions. But she was invariably characterised as a 'bitch' and hopeless mother. The son was so pressured by the mother to do well in studies that he dropped out of school and turned to drugs. The failure in the son is again attributed to the failure of the woman as a mother. It appears that the script writer did not see the necessity to apportion some blame to the father as well.

Locally-produced Chinese Dramas

Apart from showing Cantonese movies under slots like *Jade Theatre*, the television stations, as has been suggested earlier, also broadcast locally-produced Chinese drama serials such as *The Single Family*, *Everybody Loves Somebody*, and *Fatt Choy Special*. Like their Malay cousins, these Chinese dramas generally revolve around issues and themes that are basically relevant to Chinese viewers as a whole. The cast is usually made up of Chinese actors and actresses. The social setting is often Chinese, thereby giving little or no possibility of inter-ethnic communication in these dramas. The usual format and plots of many of these dramas give the impression that one ethnic group is really living separately from the others in Malaysia. Should there be a creation of a 'significant past' via these cultural products, it is highly likely that it would be selective. In short, a past that is treasured and promoted by one particular community to the exclusion of others.

Like the Malay dramas, the Chinese ones too give emphasis to the stereotyped portrayal of women as wives and mothers. It needs to be said here, though, that television female stereotypes may not necessarily be a product of conscious effort or conspiracy amongst producers and script writers. One reason is that these female characterisations do appeal to a large audience for, as one producer commented, it is easier to show characters that people can identify with rather than experiment with new styles that are unacceptable to many. Moreover, the fact that patriarchal values are dominant in the society makes it less possible for producers to demolish female myths and stereotypes. Fernandez (1992) contends that the media generally subvert women's positions and act to preserve the dominant values of society. Anyone going against the grain of accepted 'givens' is seen as a threat to the comfortable patriarchal order of which media persons, men and women alike, are themselves a part of.

Local Situation Comedy

2 + 1 constitutes one of the most popular sitcoms produced locally. The story normally centres around the major characters of Sara (Eurasian), Rajeswary (Indian) and Cindy (Chinese). They normally find themselves in a situation where they interact with Sam (Malay), their fashion-designer neighbour. Sam is the 'live wire' of the whole sitcom as his effeminate behaviour is fully exploited by the script writer.[11] The result is that the multi-ethnic female characters are at times eclipsed and are given less opportunity to develop, especially when almost all the attention is given to the butt of the joke, Sam.

Two episodes of *2 + 1*—'Tangkap Cintan' and 'Mr. Right'—showed the women characters being incessantly obsessed with the notion that women, no matter how successful they were, could only find security in the arms of handsome and physically strong men. In short, women in many ways are still dependent on men. Sam was not represented as the right person for the women simply because he was not 'man enough'.

Sitcoms normally thrive on stereotypes, be they gender or ethnic, and *2 + 1* is no exception. Many a time, the manner in which Indian or Chinese characters speak and the subjects that they talk about, for instance, are exaggerated (and laughed at) so as to associate it with the popular, but distorted, image of the ethnic community and gender represented. The danger of using stereotypes is that 'they often present a one-sided viewpoint (generally that of the dominant culture), which fails to challenge the way in which we perceive groups and individuals' (Susan Boyd-Bowman quoted in Bowes, 1990, p. 134). Thus, while this sitcom makes an attempt to provide a multi-ethnic cast and setting, the portrayal of the characters concerned may not necessarily go a long way towards creating an overall sense of 'Malaysian-ness'. Furthermore, the 'narrative closure' of this sitcom—like most other sitcoms—does not allow for the female characters to really develop over a long period of time.

News

News is broadcast daily in four languages, namely, the national language (Malay), English, Mandarin and Tamil. The prime-time news (i.e., 8:00 PM–8:30 PM) slot on TV1, TV2 and TV3 is in Malay. In general, the news normally gives emphasis and prominence to matters concerning government pronouncements, and social and political activities of the parties in the BN—apart from items like sports, foreign news, disasters, and crimes. News on the local Opposition is usually few (and negative) and far between.

As mentioned earlier, mass media are considered by the government as an important instrument in propagating messages that can help unite the diverse ethnic groups in Malaysia. News slots, particularly the ones on television, are indeed utilised by the ruling party to project its stated concern for national unity. Thus, from time to time via the electronic medium, ministers would make it a point, in their public speeches, to exhort and remind Malaysians of the importance of working consciously towards achieving ethnic harmony and prosperity in the country.

But such pious concern for inter-ethnic understanding and harmony can be conveniently pushed aside or crushed particularly when the factor of political survival comes to the fore—as was the case of the 1990 Malaysian general election.[12] At that time, the Malay-based UMNO Baru party (the dominant partner of the ruling coalition) had on one particular occasion, created and exploited ethnic and religious fears in its attempt to wrest the much needed political support of the ethnic Malay community away from its political foes, the newly established Malay-based opposition party Semangat '46, and the Islamic Pas Party.

The leader of the Malay-based Semangat '46, Tengku Razaleigh Hamzah, was not spared the savage criticisms and damning allegations of the ruling coalition and, in addition, became a victim of the somewhat 'predatory instincts' of much of the mainstream media. The attack came to a climax when the mainstream media highlighted the event where Razaleigh, as leader of the Opposition coalition Gagasan Rakyat, when he visited Sabah (after the ruling Partia Bersatu Sabah [PBS] left the BN to join the Gagasan Rakyat), was seen wearing an ethnic Kadazan headgear, the 'sigah', that was given to him by PBS leader, Datuk Joseph Pairin Kitingan. The mainstream media coverage was slanted in such a way as to make the traditional headgear appear to have a cross on it, thereby giving the Malaysian public, particularly the Malay-Muslim voters, the impression that Razaleigh was then in league with a political party whose members were predominantly Christian. In short, Razaleigh's 'ethnic-Malay commitment' and (Islamic) religiosity were being questioned.[13]

The implication of this incident is that the emotive element of 'race' was constantly brought into Malaysian political discourse and the consciousness of most Malaysians. In other words, the politics of 'race' and ethnic divisions was, and remains, utilised by certain politicians and political parties for their own ends, irrespective of its grave social and political repercussions.

This episode shows that the electronic media can also be utilised (especially when the ruling party faces a crisis of hegemony) as a weapon to sow seeds of ethnic fear and hatred—all this for the self-serving purpose of ensuring political survival. Malaysia can do without a 'significant past' that is basically composed of communal anxiety, insecurity and antagonism.

In another news segment that concerns an official signing ceremony, men were shown clinching a deal whilst women were depicted as assistants drying up the wet signatures on the documents. These shots have the effect of marginalising women and getting trivialised by 'men of action', in other words, they are there simply to play supportive roles.

It would of course be fallacious to claim that women do not get coverage in the news. But many a time such coverage revolves around the traditional role of women. For example, there was a news item on a food fair which was 'graced' by female participants, but this invariably reinforces stereotyped notions of women's 'natural' inclination and expertise.

What seemed to further strengthen this stereotype was the subsequent juxtapositioning of an advertisement with this news item. An advertisement from Malaysian Telecoms showed a businessman making a call that eventually enabled him to clinch a business deal. This mix of the news item and advertisement seems to underscore the established notion of men and women in their so-called allotted roles—women's traditional part in the kitchen and men's in the business world. This is indeed a myth, for many Malaysian women have joined the work force and have become successful in many professions and businesses. This example indeed illustrates an interesting use of production codes and conventions, such as the juxtapositioning of news items and advertisements, that result in the reinforcement of stereotypes of women and men.

Television news normally ends up with a sports round-up. What is evident here is that women, who are active in sport, are given little coverage. For example, in the game of badminton, much attention has been given to the Thomas Cup events where male players are involved, whilst little coverage has been given to the Uber Cup competition for women players.

Conclusion

The mass media, it is often said, do not operate in a social vacuum. It thus follows that Malaysian television is subject to the push and pull of social forces in the country. While Malaysian television is given a social responsibility to promote ethnic harmony and understanding, this noble aim can go wrong as long as broadcasting institutions are expected unswervingly to serve the 'general interests' of the government. This official role of Malaysian television (of fostering national unity) can become problematic, particularly when the thrust of the dominant political culture is ethnic. In this connection, political parties and interest groups must have the crucial political will to change the communal/ethnic character of Malaysia's party politics.

Furthermore, as we can see from the analysis, major ethnic groups, particularly the Malays and the Chinese to a certain extent, get highlighted in Malaysian television whilst other ethnic minorities are marginalised from the small screen. Nicholas (1992), for instance, argues that the Orang Asli (aborigines) as a group not only receive scant television coverage but also, when covered, get 'negative and unfair' coverage. It is not surprising, therefore, that women of the Orang Asli community are doubly disadvantaged.

As for the Chinese community, for instance, although there is some degree of television coverage, many still feel that it is not sufficient. For example, the Malaysian Chinese Association Deputy President Lim Kim Sai claimed that 'The lack of television coverage on government efforts to help the Chinese community is among reasons for poor support for the government among urban Chinese. The current practice of highlighting government projects for

Bumiputeras had given non-Bumiputeras the impression that their interests were not taken care of' (*New Straits Times*, 29 July 1992).

This raises important questions about the place of 'national identity' and 'National Culture' in the official quest to create a distinct Malaysian nation. While there is some basis to the assertion that Malaysia's 'National Culture' should be grounded in the indigenous (i.e., Malay) culture and the incorporation of elements of other cultures as well, the present political setting can make the attaining of this objective difficult, if not impossible. As shown by a few examples in this paper, over-zealousness in promoting certain government policies on the part of (Malay) television producers and other creative people, corporate sponsorships, lucrative advertisements and market segmentation of television audiences, and political expediency, can result in television alienating and marginalising certain sections of the Malaysian population.

Certain ethnic minorities and social groups—particularly women—in Malaysia are seldom covered, let along highlighted and discussed, by broadcasting stations. Put another way, there is rarely an opportunity for minority ethnic groups and women as a whole to seek and share a 'significant past' through popular cultural forms like television. As far as gender is concerned, the earlier mentioned programmes show that women are being marginalised and trivialised and, in some instances, undergoing a media process of, to borrow Tuchman et al.'s (1978) term, symbolic annihilation. It is noteworthy that this gender distortion occurs in local as well as in imported television programmes.

It is imperative, therefore, that the Malaysian government and other influential groups consider seriously the importance and urgency of democratising the access to mainstream mass media in the country, television in particular, if they are really concerned about national unity and social justice. The Malaysian people—both females and males alike—must be given equal opportunity to express publicly their ideas, and anxieties and fears even, so as to provide them with a sense of being part of a nation. Also, in order to maintain and promote this notion of the people's legitimate right to political and cultural participation and expression, Malaysians on their part should also seek and use alternative media of communication that exist in the country, ranging from alternative theatre, to folk theatre to popular music (Tan, 1992).

Notes

1. One indication of television's popularity in Malaysia is the fact that television's advertising expenditure had reached a M $410.4 million mark in 1991 *New Straits Times*, 16 June 1992, a level that is considerably high by Malaysian standards.
2. According to the *Fifth Malaysia Plan 1986–1990* (Government of Malaysia 1986, p. 128), Malays and other Bumiputeras (indigenous people) in 1985 constituted an estimated 56.5 per cent of the population of Peninsular Malaysia, Chinese 32.8 per cent, Indians 10.1 per cent, and Others 0.6 per cent; the corresponding proportions in 1980 were 55.1 per cent, 33.9 per cent, 10.3 per cent, and 0.7 per cent. In Sabah, Bumiputeras formed 84.2 per cent of the population in 1985, Chinese 14.9 per cent, Indians 0.6 per cent, and Others 0.3 per cent; compared with 82.9 per cent, 16.2 per cent, 0.6 per cent and 0.3 per cent respectively in 1980. In Sarawak, 70.1 per cent of the 1985 population were Bumiputera, while 28.7 per cent were Chinese, 0.2 per cent Indian, and Others 1.0 per cent; compared with 69.6 per cent, 29.2 per cent, 0.2 per cent and 1.0 per cent respectively in 1980.

   The Malays constitute the major ethnic group in the Peninsula, and their numerical and political dominance explains, in part, where the name 'Malaya' ('land of the Malays') was derived from.

   'Bumiputera' is a term whose meaning originally was restricted to the Malays who considered themselves to be literally 'sons of the soil'. However, with the formation of the Malaysian Federation (which includes Sabah and Sarawak) the term was enlarged so as to encompass those ethnic groups that are also considered indigenous, and thus making 'Bumiputeras' the single largest ethnic group in the country.

   The 'non-Bumiputera' (or 'non-Malay') group, on the other hand, comprises chiefly the Chinese and the Indians, with minority communities of Arabs, Eurasians, Europeans and Sinhalese. It needs to be said here that the dichotomisation of Bumiputera/non-Bumiputera in present day Malaysia provides a constant source of ethnic irritation in the nation's politics, economy, culture, and daily social intercourse.

   The ethnic divisions in Malaysian society are, at least in popular perception, reinforced and complicated by religious differences. Since all Malays are Muslims, at least nominally (and they constitute the majority of the country's Muslim population), it follows that Islam can be easily 'ethnicised'.
3. The coalition consists of United Malays National Organisation (UMNO) Baru, Malaysian Chinese Association (MCA), Malaysian Indian Congress (MIC), Parti Gerakan Rakyat Malaysia (Gerakan), United Sabah National Organisation (USNO), Parti Bersatu Rakyat Jelata Sabah (Berjaya), Parti Pesaka Bumiputera Bersatu Sarawak (PBB), Parti Bansa Dayak Sarawak (PBDS), Sarawak United People's Party (SUPP), and Sarawak National Party (SNAP).
4. There are two broad groupings of the Opposition coalition: one, the Angkatan Perpaduan Ummah (APU), consists of Semangat '46, Pas, Berjasa and Hamim, whose guiding principles essentially derive from Islam. The other, the Gagasan Rakyat (People's Might), is composed of Semangat '46 and its 'secular partners': Democratic Action Party (DAP), Parti Rakyat Malaysia (PRM), All Malaysian

Indian Progressive Front (AMIPF), and Malaysian Solidarity Party (MSP). Parti Bersatu Sabah (PBS) joined towards the end of the election campaign period. Semangat '46 functions as the vital link between these two large groupings.

5. 'A national identity is born out of a common set of social norms and values evolved over a period of time. This plurality of race and the fact that Malaysia is a relatively young nation present a great challenge to the moulding of a national identity within the time-frame of the present generation. The effort calls for greater determination and sacrifice on the part of all Malaysians. It calls for (*i*) a full identification [with] and commitment to the national goals and ideals; (*ii*) viewing emergent problems of whatever nature in terms of a challenge to Malaysia's capability as a nation and a people; (*iii*) accepting the country's socio-cultural diversity as a source of pride in regard to the nation's uniqueness; and (*iv*) treating internal differences and conflicts as a natural process of consensus seeking in the pursuit of the most satisfying compromises and alternatives. A common national identity lies in the willingness of the people to accept the above as guidelines for action . . . . The evolution of a Malaysian national identity will be based on an integration of all the virtues from the various cultures in Malaysia, with the Malay culture forming its core'. (Government of Malaysia, 1976, p. 93–94)
6. The National Culture Policy is based on three major principles: (*a*) The National Culture must be based on the indigenous culture of this region. (*b*) The suitable elements from other cultures can be accepted as part of the National Culture. (*c*) Islam is an important component in the moulding of the National Culture. In addition, the policy stipulates that the second principle must be seen only in the context of the first and third principles 'and not from other values' (Malaysia, 1973, p. vii).
7. RTM's objectives are: (*a*) to explain in depth and with the widest possible coverage the policies and programmes of the government in order to ensure maximum understanding by the public; (*b*) to stimulate public interest and opinion in order to achieve changes in line with the requirement of the government; (*c*) to assist in fostering national unity in our multiracial society through the extensive use of Bahasa Malaysia; (*d*) to assist in promoting civic consciousness and fostering the development of Malaysian arts and culture; and (*e*) to provide suitable elements of popular education, general information and entertainment (Karthigesu, 1990).
8. The initial shareholders, when the station began its operation, were Fleet Group (40 per cent), Syed Kechik Foundation (20 per cent), Utusan Melayu (20 per cent), Maika Holdings (10 per cent), and former Finance Minister Daim Zainuddin (10 per cent) (Gomez, 1990). Fleet Group is now owned by its holding company, Renong, an UMNO Baru giant investment arm.
9. The New Economic Policy expired in 1990. A new economic strategy, called National Development Policy, generally with somewhat similar objectives, subsequently replaced it.
10. The notion of patriarchy is defined by Hartmann (1981) as a hierarchy in which particular people fill particular places where one sees a set of inter-relationships among men to allow men to dominate women.

11. This sitcom was discontinued as a result of the Malaysian Censorship Board's decision to terminate it (*New Straits Times*, 24 July 1992).
12. Malaysia's 1990 general election was, for the ruling BN coalition in general, a contest that had transformed into what was perceived—at least in the initial phase of the election campaign period (11–21 October 1990)—as a fierce battle, especially after the otherwise disparate opposition parties successfully managed to form a viable opposition coalition. And for UMNO Baru, the ruling coalition's dominant partner—and especially its president (and, by tradition, Malaysia's prime minister), Dr. Mahathir Mohamed—this was one vital electoral competition that would put to the test its popularity and political strength since its recent creation (after the old UMNO was declared illegal by the High Court on 4 February 1988). But, more importantly, this political test was especially significant to UMNO Baru as it would confirm or refute the fear that Tengku Razaleigh Hamzah and his breakaway Semangat '46 party were strong and influential enough to pose a serious threat and challenge to UMNO Baru's and, by extension, Mahathir's claim to being the only credible and powerful champion of the Malay community and its interests. In other words, the hegemonic position that was hitherto held by the ruling BN seemed to have been variously undermined by the opposition parties and other groups outside the formal political arena, at a point when the whole nation was about to vote for the next government.
13. The *Watan* (20 October 1990) reported that many Sabahans expressed amazement at the way certain members and supporters of the ruling BN made an issue out of Razaleigh's wearing of the Kadazan headgear, given the fact that Mahathir, too, was given similar headgear to wear—without much fuss and controversy—during his state visit a week before this incident.

References

Anderson, B. (1983). *Imagined communities. Reflections on the origin and spread of nationalism*. London: Verso.

Asiah, S. (1991). *Penyiaran dan Masyarakat* (Broadcasting and society). Kuala Lumpur: Dewan Bahasa dan Pustaka.

Bowes, M. (1990). 'Only when I laugh'. In Goodwin, A. and Whannel, G. (eds.). *Understanding television*. London: Routledge.

Fernandez, I. (1992). 'Who calls the shots? The ideology of control by the media on women'. A paper presented at the Seminar on The Mass Media and Women in Malaysia, Penang, Malaysia, 27–29 July.

Gomez, E.T. (1990). *Politics in business: UMNO's corporate investments*. Kuala Lumpur: Forum.

Government of Malaysia (1976). *Third Malaysia Plan 1976–1980*. Kuala Lumpur: Government Printers.

——— (1986). *Fifth Malaysia Plan 1986–1990*. Kuala Lumpur: National Printing Department.

Grenfell, N. (1979). *Switch on: Switch off*. Kuala Lumpur: Oxford University Press.

Hall, S. (1986). 'Media power and class power'. In Curran, J. et al. (eds.). *Bending reality. The state of the media*. London: Pluto Press.

Hartmann, H. (1981). 'The unhappy marriage of marxism and feminism: Towards a more progressive union'. In Sargent, L. (ed.). The unhappy marriage of marxism and feminism. London: Pluto Press.

Karthigesu, R. (1987). 'Commercial competition to government monopoly in television: Implications of the Malaysian experience'. *Kajian Malaysia* (Malaysian Studies), V(2), 19.

———. (1990). 'Television in Malaysia: An examination of policy formation'. *Media Asia*, 17(3), 134–35.

Malaysia (1973). *Asas Kebudayaan Kebangsaan* (The Basis of National Culture). Kuala Lumpur: Kementerian Kebudayaan, Belia dan Sukan.

Nicholas, C. (1992). 'Orang Asli women and media empathy'. A paper presented at the Seminar on The Mass Media and Women in Malaysia, Penang, Malaysia, 27–29 July.

O'Shaughnessy, M. (1990). 'Box pop: Popular television and hegemony'. In Goodwin, A. and Whannel, G. (eds.). *Understanding television*. London: Routledge.

Shukla, S. K. (1992). 'Understanding the medium—Television. Understanding the image—Women'. A paper presented at the Seminar on the Mass Media and Women in Malaysia, Penang, Malaysia, 27–29 July.

Smith, A.D. (1988). *The ethnic origins of nations*. Oxford: Basil Blackwell.

Tan, S. B. (1992). 'Counterpoints in the performing arts in Malaysia'. In Kahn, Joel S. and Wah, Francis Loh Kok (eds.). *Fragmented vision: Culture and politics in contemporary Malaysia*. North Sydney: Allen & Unwin.

Tuchman, G., Daniels, A.K. and **Benet, J.** (eds.). (1978). *Hearth and home*. New York: Oxford University Press.

Williams, R. (1978). *Marxism and literature*. Oxford: Oxford University Press.

15

International News on Indian Television: A Critical Analysis of *The World This Week*

Keval J. Kumar

Introduction

Though India has been in the vanguard of non-aligned nations in their struggle for a New World Information and Communication Order (NWICO), its national communication policy (as reflected in its broadcasting practices, for instance) does not help promote regional co-operation or independence from transnational enterprises in the area of news and information exchange. Not only in its news programmes but also in its commercially sponsored and independently produced current affairs programmes, Doordarshan (Indian Television)—a media unit of the Ministry of Information and Broadcasting—makes little effort in gathering and processing international news. All that it does is to subscribe to transnational news agencies like Visnews, World Television News (WTN), and other agencies, and transmit the actuality and archival footage received, though in a slightly edited form. In most cases the commentary is its own. As a consequence, the 'images' transmitted are those that are of political, economic and cultural interest to the transnational agencies, and to the countries that support their global activities. Thus, we do not ever see or hear the stories of non-aligned countries, such as those in Africa, Asia and Latin America, as they would like to have them told. The Anglo-American perspective acquires widespread validity, no matter what the subject, and vitiates our understanding of international affairs.

Review of International News Research

Research on international news 'flows' and 'coverage' in the area of television is still in its infancy, especially in India. The late Kyoon Hur (1984) found that over 400 studies had been conducted, though mostly related to the print media. Further, majority of the studies were limited to quantitative examinations of the volume and direction of flows. Hur noted that the distinctions between 'flows' and 'coverage' were not given due weightage in these studies. He pointed out that international news flow analysis deals primarily with the volume and direction of news flows between and among countries. News coverage analysis, on the other hand, is content analysis, which deals not only with the amount but also with the nature and type of international news disseminated across international boundaries. What was needed, he stressed, was a combination of quantitative and qualitative methods to understand the structures and processes of news flows more completely.

Communication research on Indian television, and particularly on international news on Indian television, has yet to take off. But international news in the Indian press has been surveyed by a number of researchers. Yadava (1984), for instance, has compared foreign news coverage in five 'national' English newspapers (*The Times of India, The Hindu, The Indian Express, The Hindustan Times*, and *The Statesman*). His sample comprised of issues of these dailies for two weeks (one continuous week and one composite week) in 1979 and 1984. He concluded that 'there is a noticeable decline in the foreign news space in Indian newspapers' (p. 120) and 'the dependence upon the four major western news agencies for foreign news coverage is somewhat less now' (p. 119). Yet, 'nearly one third of the foreign news is from and about the United States of America, and Western Europe accounts for nearly four per cent of the foreign news items' (p. 119). Interestingly, 'the image of the western developed countries especially the United States that gets portrayed to Indian readers is that of a major nuclear power, prosperous and making tremendous progress in science and technology' (p. 119). Most of the news of the Third World, however, is conflict and disaster-oriented, 'thereby portraying them in a rather poor light to Indian readers' (p. 120).

There has been no parallel study of the coverage of foreign news on Indian television. The few television studies that have been carried out in recent years relate to the Satellite Instructional Television Experiment (SITE) (Agrawal, 1988), the Kheda Television Project (Agrawal and Malek, 1981), the representation of women on Doordarshan's news and current affairs programmes, serials and commercials (Krishnan and Dighe, 1990; Media Advocacy Group, 1994; Prasad, 1994; Rao and Vani, 1988), the portrayal of violence on television (Rao, 1990), and an 'impact' study of the first soap opera on Indian television, *Hum Log* (Singhal and Rogers, 1989). Narayanan (1989) conducted a study of the 'impact' of television on the families of Bombay. The Krishnan and Dighe (1990) study did look at foreign news as well as domestic news but only in terms of 'representation', and not in terms of sources, news flows and coverage.

This study attempts a close critical analysis of the sources of international news on Indian television, the nations whose images dominate the small screen, and the kinds of professional news values at work. International news figures prominently in the daily news programmes (in English, Hindi, and the regional languages) and also on a weekly current affairs programme called *The World This Week* (*TWTW*). This paper focuses on *TWTW*, the only independently produced foreign news programme commissioned for Doordarshan. (Since early 1994, video news magazines such as *Newstrack*, *Eyewitness* and *Parakh* have also been shown on Doordarshan.) Both quantitative and qualitative research methods are employed to examine the extent of dependence on transnational news agencies such as Visnews and WTN, the nature of the coverage, and the political economy of international news in an Indian context. The larger macro context in which this study is set is the two-decade old UNESCO debate on NWICO and the 'new' UNESCO strategy on 'Communication in the Service of Humanity'.

UNESCO and the Non-aligned Demand for NWICO

Since January 1985, when the United States, followed by Britain and Singapore, walked out of UNESCO, NWICO has been off the agenda for the Western media. The hostility to the demand of non-aligned countries for a fair and balanced flow of international news, information, and data, continues. Indeed, the attempts by non-aligned countries to set up their own national and regional news 'exchanges' (rather than unidirectional 'news agencies') have been derided or pronounced as failures on the ground that they are all 'government-controlled' and, therefore, lacking in credibility. Transnational news agencies which are run solely as commercial enterprises are purported to be free of government, or even commercial, influences; hence, their news reporting is perceived to be more objective, more balanced and more credible.

Genesis of the Demand

The demand for a more just and more equitable 'flow' of information and news across international borders had its roots in the struggle of the nations of Asia, Africa, and Latin America to break free of colonial chains. Already, early in their freedom movements, defiant efforts were made to counter the information disseminated by colonial governments through news agencies, the press and other media. The development of the vernacular press and 'alternative' forms of news distribution, such as small magazines, pamphlets, handwritten letters, street plays, and public meetings, played a vital role in spreading the message of independence. Several leading nationalist leaders were active journalists.

Once independence was won, the struggle became part of the effort to follow the path of non-alignment and self-reliance. Indeed, information was valued from the beginning as a public resource and a social good linked to development. The transnational agencies were, therefore, replaced by national agencies, not all of them under direct government control. Many transnational agencies like Reuters did not leave gracefully.

During the late 1960s and early 1970s, the non-aligned nations banded together to fight the international economic order which offered unfair and unequal trade advantages to the industrialised nations. They argued that 'free trade' was in reality a 'one-way' trade from the North to the South, and that 'free flow' of information as espoused by the United Nations was in reality a 'one-way flow' of news and information, again from the North to the South.

They further argued that political freedom without economic and cultural freedom was meaningless: a de facto colonialism prevailed; their national and cultural identities were under threat.

Their mass media were dominated by the West: films from Hollywood, TV serials from Western networks, popular music from the multinational record companies, and news in all media from the transnational news agencies. They, therefore, sought to re-write the United Nations Charter which had been adopted at a time when most of the developing world was under colonial rule. They felt, and many still do feel, that the Charter reflected colonial interests and values which are repugnant to the non-aligned free world.

With their growing numerical strength in the United Nations, the non-aligned countries made their demand for a New International Economic Order (NIEO) and NWICO at several meetings of UNESCO. The setting up of the McBride Commission was a direct consequence of such demands. The United States and her allies, now reduced to a minority in the world body, perceived this as a 'crisis', for it challenged the very principles of Western-type liberal democracies, the concept of laissez faire, and the Western 'images' of Third World reality. Indeed, the debate was not simply between the proponents of 'free flow' and those arguing for a 'free and balanced' flow. Rather, it was between two radically different approaches to news and news values, which have their roots in distinct social philosophies and cultures.

UNESCO's 'New' Strategy for International Communication

In November 1989, at its Twenty-fifth General Conference, UNESCO adopted a new strategy in the field of communication. Its supposed aim was 'to improve the organisation's effectiveness in ensuring the free flow of information on national and international levels, and its wider and better balanced dissemination, without any obstacle to the freedom of expression' (Media Development, 1990, p. 6). This Major Programme Area IV of UNESCO's Third Medium Term Plan (1990–95) has been termed 'Communication in the Service of Humanity'. In reality, it was a strategy to woo the United States, Britain, and Singapore back into UNESCO's fold, now that the outcry against the 'old' information order had died down.

The emphasis in the new strategy is the need for the free flow of information globally, rather than on setting right the imbalance in one-way information flows—the primary demand of the non-aligned countries. The 'new' strategy proposes, besides the strengthening of the International Programme for Development Communication (IPDC), 'a media education that would lay emphasis on the development of critical acumen among users and the capacity of individuals and communities to react to any kind of manipulation and would at the same time, promote a better understanding of the means available to users to defend their rights' (Media Development, 1990, p. 7).

However, it does not address itself to the crucial issue of the restructuring of the one-way international news flows, and the need for a strict regulation of the practices of transnational news agencies. Also, glaringly missing from the document is any reference to power: who exercises it and how it is employed, or what is the character of the 'development' it sees as the goal of communication (Schiller, 1990).

International News on Indian Television

International news on Indian television is largely news of the Western nations as seen from an Anglo-American perspective; news of developing countries too is reported on occasion by the transnational agencies, but from the same perspective and interest. Both Doordarshan and privately sponsored channels depend heavily on the actuality and archival footage supplied by the transnational television news agencies

During the years preceding the proliferation of cross-border channels, Indian television was largely indigenous. Except for an occasional series like *The Guinness Book of World Records* presented by David Frost, there was hardly any imported programme at prime-time. Children's programmes, however, continue to depend on imports, such as Walt Disney Cartoons, serials like *He Man and the Masters of the Universe*, *Glow Friends*, and *GI Joe*, which are palmed off as 'entertainment programmes' when in reality they are feature-length commercials made by the toy manufacturers themselves. Disney films like *Jungle Book*, are now dubbed in Hindi.

International news figures prominently on Indian television. Doordarshan's national channel transmits six 10 to 15 minute news bulletins daily, three of them in English and three in Hindi. A daily morning bulletin on 'International News' follows the main bulletin in English. Besides, regional stations in major cities broadcast at least one news bulletin every day in the regional languages. All these news bulletins carry international news with actuality footage taken from the transnational news agencies.

The news bulletins are structured in the manner of British TV news bulletins. They begin with political news, events, and personalities of the nation, then move on to those from abroad, ending with news items of regional and local interest. Then follows a sports segment which gives extensive coverage of national and international sports events. The international sports events are profusely illustrated with footage, again from the transnational agencies. The weather segment is a totally indigenous effort, and (until recently) the weather person was only heard off-screen, and was never 'nominated'. The bulletin winds up occasionally with a light hearted human interest story, with footage again from the transnationals.

Besides the news bulletins on the national and regional channels there are other programmes, mainly sports series like *The World of Sport, Matchpoint, Sportgame, Badminton with Padukone*, which also use extensive footage from the transnational agencies. The location of most sports events telecast is North America and Europe. Advertisements figure conspicuously in the footage, on sports gear, athletes' clothes, and on strategically placed parts of the playground or the racing track. Each of these series is sponsored by advertisers and is preceded and followed by spot advertisements. Several multinational companies with subsidiaries in India advertise in and sponsor such series. About the only thing 'Indian' in these series is the anchor person and the accent of the animated 'readers' (by no stretch of the imagination could they be termed 'commentators') of a script which accompanies the footage obtained from the transnationals.

The Transnational Television News Agencies

In the early 1980s, two transnational news agencies, Visnews and the smaller United Press International/Independent Television News (UPITN) serviced the national television networks of most nations. Their domination of the international news film market has been compared to that of the 'big four' (Reuters, AP, UPI and

AFP) in the news text market. More recently, they have faced challenges from other sources, notably Cable News Network (CNN). Regional alternatives have also been appearing, such as Eurovision, which chiefly serves Europe and also parts of Africa and Asia, and Intervision, serving Eastern Europe and the Soviet Union. Moscow Television, Chinese Central Television (CCTV) and NHK International also have widespread international distribution networks. In Asia, the AsiaVision news exchange has been established under the auspices of the Asia Broadcasting Union (ABU).

The Visnews Monopoly

Visnews was established in 1957 by the BBC in an attempt to block American film syndicates from gaining a monopoly in Britain and the Continent. By creating this highly successful 'profit-retaining trust' in which revenue was ploughed back into the organisation to finance further development, the BBC gave birth to a global monopoly far greater than anything seen before in TV news (King, 1981). By 1981, it was sending 40–50 stories per day by satellite, terrestrial electronic circuits, or airfreight to almost every country that had television.

Lord Radcliffe, the first chairman of Visnews, set out its goal thus: 'to create a service of pictorial television news clear of political control by anybody, impartial in its presentation, seeking to collect and distribute news on a worldwide basis, and organized so that it should not fall under the control of any one group, or influence, or person' (King, 1981, p. 284). Besides the BBC, the original owners were Reuters, the Canadian Broadcasting Corporation, the Australian Broadcasting Commission and the Rank Organisation. In 1968, Rank was forced out and was replaced by the New Zealand Broadcasting Commission. In 1984, Reuters tried to seek a controlling stake in Visnews but was opposed by the BBC and other shareholders. Reuters then developed a trans-Atlantic partnership with UPI (Kumar and Biernatzki, 1990).

Today, Visnews is the largest enterprise in the world specialising in the gathering and distribution of television news for broadcasting companies. Its head office is in London, for both Visnews Ltd. and VisCentre; for the American continent its head office is in New

York (Visnews International USA), and the Far East office is in Hong Kong (Visnews Far East Ltd.). Visnews distributes television news stories to 409 television networks in 83 countries around the world, and the agency's daily services are broadcast on approximately 650 million television sets (UNESCO, 1989). The agency covers all kinds of events: lead stories and miscellaneous events world-wide; political and economic news; social, cultural and scientific events; major arts and entertainment events; and sports.

Visnews does not stop at gathering and distributing news stories. It supplies transparencies and footage of newsmakers and places; leases camera crews for special location work; provides archival footage to clients from its library—one of the world's largest collections of visual material covering events since the last century. Its most controversial activity is making 'public relations' and 'promotional' films for countries and companies, as well as 'sponsored' documentaries and sales promotion films. The Visnews subsidiary, BrightStar, is a leading provider of satellite television transmission capacity between North America and Europe. Visnews Ltd. is a subsidiary of Reuters Holdings PLC, with the BBC having a minority holding in its equity. (In 1994, Visnews Ltd. was transformed into 'Reuters' to reflect the majority equity stake [51 per cent] by the news agency; NBC's share is 38 per cent and BBC's 11 per cent.)

World Television News

Visnews' main competitor in the international television was market is WTN (formerly UPITN), a transnational communication enterprise which combines the resources of its principal shareholder, American Broadcasting Company (ABC) and the British television network, Independent Television News (ITN). Until 1984, the transnational American news agency UPI was ITN's main partner, but huge losses incurred due to expenditure on coverage of the elections and the 1984 Olympics, led UPI to withdraw support.

Though WTN is now based in the United States, its main servicing centre is in London, where a 45-minute news package is put together at ITN House and then beamed by satellite to subscribers.

Cable News Network (CNN)

Its live coverage of the Gulf War has turned CNN, a cable network headquartered in Atlanta, Georgia, into a transnational agency. Nearly world-wide reception of its 24-hour news transmission and *World Report* has been made possible because of its direct uncoded broadcasting on five satellites, one of the most important of which is the Soviet-built and controlled Stationer 12, which has a footprint covering all of Europe and Africa and most of Asia (quoted in Kumar and Biernatzki, 1990).

New Delhi TV and The World This Week

New Delhi TV (NDTV) is a private-enterprise video production venture established in 1988 by Dr Prannoy Roy, a renowned psephologist (and a former World Bank consultant), and his wife Radhika (a former journalist with *India Today* and *The Indian Express*). It has a small team of researchers, producers and technicians. Dr Roy is the sole presenter of the current affairs series *TWTW* which (until 1994) was broadcast once a week on Fridays immediately after Doordarshan's English news at 9:30 PM. *NDTV* operates from a small but well-equipped studio in a residential neighbourhood of the capital. It has developed its own graphics software, and does all its editing with the aid of computers. NDTV produces *TWTW* for Doordarshan, which is paid a 'telecast fee' by the sponsors. Doordarshan in its turn offers the sponsors free commercial time prior to and following the programme.

TWTW had no sponsors and hardly any advertisement support when it was launched. Doordarshan authorities then requested NDTV to look for sponsors, since the production costs for *TWTW* were cutting into its limited budget for news and current affairs.

Three multinational companies, Nestle, BPL-India and Dunlop, were persuaded to sponsor the series. Later, Dunlop was replaced by an Indian company, Godrej, the makers of soaps and consumer durables like refrigerators and steel cupboards. *TWTW* proved such a commercial success that in August 1990, Doordarshan's advertising revenue from 35 commercials screened prior to the series rose to Rs. 3.30 million. From 1 June 1990, *TWTW* was shifted from Category A to Category A Special by Doordarshan.

This meant that higher advertising rates had to be paid for commercials preceding the programme. In March 1991, 15–20 commercials were being screened each week on *TWTW*. Advertising support has declined considerably since the arrival of 24-hour pan-Asian news channels like BBC and CNN.

Until early 1994, *TWTW* was the only independently produced and commercially sponsored current affairs series on international news granted telecast facilities on Doordarshan. Such an exclusive privilege was contested by other private video enterprises such as PTI-TV, Times TV, ITV and HTV—all based in New Delhi. It has been debated in the press and questions have been raised about NDTV's 'arrangements' with Doordarshan, as also its arrangement with the three commercial sponsors, Nestle, BPL-India, and Godrej. 'Confidentiality' marks these arrangements, and this raises suspicions about its credibility. (The relevance of *TWTW* after the launch of the Star TV network in 1992 continues to be questioned by media critics.)

The Sample and the Methodology

In order to obtain an insight into the trends of reporting on *TWTW*, as well as of the process of selection of nations and people that are deemed newsworthy, a sample of 20 programmes stretching over a period of two years, 1989 and 1990, was randomly selected. This represents 20 to 25 per cent of the total number of programmes telecast over a two-year duration. *TWTW* was broadcast fairly regularly once a week in 1990, but in the previous year there were short breaks, especially in the months during which national and state assembly elections were held, i.e., at the end of 1989. Each of the 20 programmes was either watched at the time of telecast, or a recorded version was watched at a time convenient to the researcher. Each time, a written record was made of the headlines, the various news items, and the location of the items. In addition, some jottings were made of the kind of actuality and archival footage used, as well as of snatches of phrases and comments in the commentary. Finally, the sources where they were mentioned (quite rarely, in fact), in the credits or on the footage, was noted down.

It was soon evident that a clear and definite pattern was being followed: that three to four 'segments' demarcated by the signature tune and insignia was the norm. The first segment dealt with 'hard' news items, mainly political and economic stories located in elite nations, but one needed to check this over a longer period in order to come to any conclusion about a deliberate or even unconscious value system at work. Four to six news items usually made up this segment. It was also noticed that stand-up spot reports were not included unless they were exclusive stories for *TWTW*, which were few and far between.

The second 'segment' focused on sports items. Here again, no more than five to six items were taken up for presentation. But the pace was speeded up, and the commentary more excited and animated, presumably to match the action on the screen. The impression gained initially was that sports and games of interest to Western audiences predominated, such as soccer, tennis, boxing and car racing. But this initial impression too had to be checked out through a longitudinal analysis.

The third and usually the concluding 'segment' entitled 'Newsmakers' focused attention on people from the world of culture and technology. Occasionally, the programme concluded with a miscellaneous item or two, or with a music video, or even a montage. This broad structure persisted till late 1994.

Stories/items in each of the three or four segments were classified into meaningful categories. This could be easily done with sports; each sport or game came readymade with a label like soccer, tennis, boxing, etc. But the first segment comprising 'hard' news could not be so easily pigeon-holed. This was equally true of the third segment 'Newsmakers', and the occasional fourth segment which could be termed 'Miscellaneous'. Accordingly, the 'hard' news stories were categorised into the following: political, economic, technological, developmental, cultural, human interest, disasters, sports, and others. Since the majority of stories in the 'Newsmakers' segment were from the world of culture, the following classification was determined to be appropriate: popular music, theatre, art, cinema, sports, politics, science, and others. For the 'Miscellaneous' segment the categorisation followed was similar to that employed for the first 'hard' news segment. Obviously, there is some overlapping in the categories enumerated. They are not totally exclusive categories and the interpretation of the researcher does enter the picture. However, the critical researcher, unlike the empirical or positivistic researcher, is not unduly concerned about this, for he sees himself as an interpreter of the social scene.

The World This Week: *An Analysis*

A close examination of the 240 news items broadcast in 20 programmes over a period of two years suggests that 'hard' news stories (38 per cent) and sports stories (39 per cent) from the main thrust of the programme (see Table 15.1). It must be stated though that the time allocated to 'hard' news stories generally exceeds that given to the sports segment. The kind of stories that take top priority relate to politics, science and technology, economics, the world of sports and Western culture. Development stories are rare.

Table 15.1: Segments and News Stories in *TWTW*

Segments	*1989*	*1990*	*Total*	*%*
1. Current Affairs	43	48	91	38.0
2. Sports	50	43	93	39.0
3. Newsmakers	21	28	49	20.0
4. Miscellaneous	4	3	7	3.0
Total	118	122	240	100.0

There is no significant difference in the breakdown of items in the segments for 1989 and 1990. This is a 'pattern' that appears to have become fixed. It is a pattern that corresponds to a variety show where several items are packed in, in a businesslike and rapid pace. On average, each week's programme comprised four items on current affairs, six on sports, and two on newsmakers; an average of 12 items per week. The 'Miscellaneous' segment found place only once in a way and told stories usually related to the environment (deforestation in Malaysia); technology (high definition TV in Japan, the invention of a new tractor by a British farmer); or a public service ad campaign (California's campaign against smoking). Six out of the seven 'Miscellaneous' items were located in industrialised countries (three in the United States, two in Britain, and one each in Japan and Malaysia).

The 'Hard' News Stories Segment

Out of a total of 91 news stories in the first segment on current affairs, as many as 37 (40 per cent) were located in Western countries. The United States with 13 (14 per cent) stories, West Europe with 13 (14 per cent) stories, and Great Britain with 11 (12 per cent) stories ranked as the high priority nations for *TWTW*. Of the developing world, only the Latin American region (with 10 stories) was represented quite well. Latin American stories related to elections, the drug mafia, terrorism, and of course soccer. The USSR and its former East European allies got as many stories as the United States. The 50 countries of Africa were represented by a mere six stories, three of which were located in South Africa and two in Namibia. These related mainly to the release of Nelson Mandela and apartheid, and to elections in Namibia (see Table 15.2).

Table 15.2: Location of 'Hard' News Stories

Country/Region	*1989*	*1990*	*Total*	*% of Total*
1. United States	7	6	13	14.3
2. Great Britain	4	7	11	12.0
3. West Europe	6	7	13	14.3
4. USSR	5	2	7	7.7
5. East Europe	3	3	6	6.6
6. South Asia	4	4	8	8.8
7. West Asia	2	6	8	8.8
8. Asia–Pacific	2	2	4	4.4
9. Australia	–	2	2	2.2
10. Africa	5	1	6	6.6
11. China	1	1	2	2.2
12. Latin America	3	7	10	11.0
13. Canada	1	–	1	1.1
Total	43	48	91	100.0

Asia got 16 stories but West Asia (what the West terms as Middle East) got half of them. The Indian sub-continent (including Pakistan, Sri Lanka, Burma, Bangladesh, Nepal, Tibet and Afghanistan) figured only in eight stories, three of which were special features on medicine. While the discussion was about developments in medicine which related to India, the footage used showed doctors at work in hospitals either in the United States or Britain.

The Sports Segment

In the sports segment a total of 93 news stories were presented during the two years of our sample. Of these, an overwhelming majority (52 per cent) were located in Western Europe and the United States, and only ten (10.8 per cent)—mostly on soccer—were from the countries of Latin America and the Carribean. Seven (7.5 per cent) sports stories were set in Australia and an equal number in the Asia–Pacific region. However, South Asia, the whole of Africa, and China did not merit a single mention, while East Europe and West Asia were represented by three and one story respectively (See Table 15.3).

Table 15.3: Location of Sports Stories

Country/Region	*1989*	*1990*	*Total*	*% of Total*
1. United States	13	12	25	26.9
2. West Europe	10	13	23	24.7
3. Great Britain	9	3	12	12.9
4. Latin America	5	5	10	10.8
5. Asia–Pacific	4	4	8	8.6
6. Australia	4	3	7	7.5
7. USSR	3	1	4	4.3
8. East Europe	2	1	3	3.2
9. West Asia	–	1	1	1.1
10. Africa	–	–	–	–
11. China	–	–	–	–
12. South Asia	–	–	–	–
Total	50	43	93	100.0

Top Ranking Sports and Games

The sports and games stories that headed the second segment on sports were those that were popular in Western countries. At the top of the frequency list was soccer with 14 (15 per cent) stories, followed by tennis and car/bike racing, each with 10 (10.8 per cent) stories. Boxing and athletics were represented by nine (9.7 per cent) of the total number of sports stories. Other stories that received fairly good coverage included powerboat racing (with five stories), horse racing/riding (with four stories), and cricket (with three stories). Bull-fighting, ice hockey and skiing were the other sports that got some coverage. But field hockey, an extremely popular Indian sport, received no coverage at all in the 20 programmes of our sample (see Table 15.4).

Table 15.4: Sports and Games Featured in *TWTW*

Sports/Games	*1989*	*1990*	*Total*	%
1. Soccer	6	8	14	15.0
2. Tennis	6	4	10	10.8
3. Car/bike racing	7	3	10	10.8
4. Boxing	4	5	9	9.7
5. Athletics	5	4	9	9.7
6. Powerboat racing	2	3	5	5.3
7. Horse racing	3	1	4	4.3
8. Cricket	1	2	3	3.2
9. Bull-fighting	1	1	2	2.2
10. Skiing	–	2	2	2.2
11. Ice Hockey	1	–	1	1.0
12. Others	14	10	24	25.8
Total	50	43	93	98.4

The 'Newsmakers' Segment

Who is a 'newsmaker' for the NDTV team? Our analysis suggests that he/she is a Britisher or an American (from the United States, not from Canada or Latin America), white of course, and most likely a pop star or pop singer, rich and famous, and sometimes powerful. Out of the 49 'newsmakers' that made it to *TWTW* in 1989 and 1990, as many as 21 (42.9 per cent) were from the United States and 14 (28.6 per cent) were from Britain. There were no 'newsmakers' at all from the erstwhile Soviet Union, East Europe, West Asia, China, or the whole of Africa. Australia had five, the Asia-Pacific region two, and South Asia just three. These three were Indians who were a success in Britain. Other successful Indians settled in Britain who also figured as 'newsmakers' included Pamela Bordes, Salman Rushdie, and Peter Singh ('the rocking Sikh of Southall', according to the commentary) (see Table 15.5).

Pop groups of the United States and Britain were featured prominently in this segment on 'Newsmakers'. Michael Jackson was featured twice in 1989, and the Rolling Stones, Paul McCartney, Boy George, Eric Clapton, Chuck Berry, and the Everley Brothers,

Table 15.5: Countries of Location of 'Newsmakers'

Country/Region	*1989*	*1990*	*Total*	*%*
1. United States	14	7	21	42.9
2. Great Britain	2	12	14	28.6
3. Australia	2	3	5	10.2
4. West Europe	1	2	3	6.1
5. South Asia	–	3	3	6.1
6. Asia–Pacific	1	1	2	4.1
7. Africa	1	–	1	2.0
8. Latin America	–	–	–	–
9. China	–	–	–	–
10. West Asia	–	–	–	–
11. USSR	–	–	–	–
Total	21	28	49	100.0

once during 1989 and 1990. A children's brass band of Australia and a new group from Massachusetts (that did not touch alcohol or drugs) also found a place. Among the film stars were Bette Davies, Greta Garbo, and Lawrence Olivier. Among politicians were Margaret Thatcher, Yasser Arafat (his wax form at Madame Toussad's), Prince Charles ('the environment friendly prince'). Ronald Reagan, the arms dealer Khasshogi, and the son of Emperor Hirohito. But no list of 'newsmakers' would be complete without the presence of McDonalds (in Moscow), women (WRENS) in the British Navy, and New York's children in bullet-proof vests.

Conclusion

Our quantitative and qualitative analysis of *TWTW* suggests that in all three segments pride of place is given to the United States and Western Europe. Where there is a fourth segment (which we have termed 'miscellaneous') the number of stories about happenings in these two regions exceeds those in other parts of the world. There appears to be a clear relationship between the country where the news agency has its headquarters and the volume and kind of reporting on international news. NDTV (and Doordarshan too) does not have much of a choice as footage about events in other countries does not find a place in the daily or weekly satellite feeds. Neither can it request for 'special footage' because of the enormous costs involved (about £200 for a minute's footage).

International news on Indian television is thus determined by the satellite feeds Doordarshan receives from transnational news agencies. It is not very clear whether NDTV obtains its actuality and archival footage from Doordarshan or directly from the transnational news agencies. However, since much of the footage used by NDTV is earlier seen on Doordarshan's news bulletins, it seems likely that Doordarshan makes the footage available to the independent video company. The main agencies which both Doordarshan and NDTV subscribe to are Visnews and WTN, though one occasionally sees footage from other agencies such as CNN, CCTV, Moscow TV, NHK International, and news exchnages like Asia-Vision and ArabVision. Since neither Doordarshan nor NDTV have full-time correspondents abroad, their dependence on the news agencies is total.

However, there is a careful selection process at work, especially where 'hard' news is concerned. Sports, and cultural and human interest stories are in most cases carried with the agency's footage and commentary, but editing of footage and re-writing of the commentary accompanying 'hard' news stories is more the norm than the exception. NDTV officials claim that they hardly ever look at the commentary on 'hard' news stories; that they do their own research and write their own commentaries. NDTV is 'banned' from reporting on Indian news, and its reporting on political stories focusing on India's neighbours has to be handled with care, because of Doordarshan's overseeing eye.

An 'original' commentary, however, does not radically alter the messages conveyed by the vivid images. For Indian viewers do not view *TWTW* for the news (this has already been provided by Doordarshan's six daily bulletins), but for the extended visual coverage of current affairs. Further, even with an independently written commentary, the visual footage tells its own story, which is as it were 'inscribed' into its every warp and woof. We do not know of course how Indian audiences read these 'inscribed' messages; it is more than likely that some groups would accept them, others would reject them, and still others 'negotiate' them in terms of their own experiences. But for a good number of viewers (according to some estimates, *TWTW* has about 20 million viewers) these images are the only ones they are exposed to about international affairs. (This situation has changed dramatically with the introduction of cross-border TV channels.) How audiences deal with such images and incorporate them in their views and opinions about elite nations (which dominate the news) and the developing world is an area of communication research that needs to be carried out in the Indian context.

Communication researchers like Roach (1993) and Hamelink (1985) have argued for a 'delinkage' and 'disassociation' by the non-aligned world transnational news agencies. But such a radical step will not suffice. What is needed rather is the development of professional practices and news values that have their roots in the needs and experiences of the peoples of the developing world. The universalism of professional practices and news values is what has led to 'homogenisation' and 'transnationalisation'. The debate about the need for NWICO continues to be relevant, but beyond fairness and balance is the need for a new kind of journalism that is development and liberation-oriented, that stands for peace and understanding rather than for war and conflict; for the needy and the marginalised rather than for the rich and the powerful; and for meaningful issues rather than exceptional events. NWICO will dawn only when there is a deliberate break with the professional practices and news values represented by the transnational news agencies and Western-style journalism, and the adoption of styles of journalism relevant to the information needs of different cultures.

References

Agrawal, B. (1988). 'Television studies in India'. *ICCTR Journal*, 1(1).

Agrawal, B. and **Malek, M.R.** (1981). *Television in Kheda: A social evaluation of SITE*. Ahmedabad: Space Applications Centre.

Hamelink, C. (1985). *Global communiation and Cultural Autonomy*. London: Sage.

King, J. (1981). 'Visnews and UPITN: News film supermarkets in the sky'. In Richstad, J. and Anderson, M. (eds.). *Crisis in international news: Policies and prospects*. New York: New York University Press.

Krishnan, P. and **Dighe, A.** (1990). *Affirmation and denial: Construction of femininity on Indian television*. New Delhi: Sage.

Kumar, K.J. (1988). 'Communication and development'. *Communication Research Trends*, 9(3), 1–16.

Kumar, K.J. and **Biernatzki, W.** (1990). 'International news flows'. *Communication Research Trends*, 10(4), 1–30.

Kyoon Hur, K. (1984). 'A critical perspective of international news flow research'. *Critical Studies in Mass Communication*, 1(4), 365–78.

Lansiparo, Y. (1987). 'Asiavision news exchange'. *Media Asia*, 14(1), 46–52.

Media Advocacy Group (1994). *Doordarshan news*. New Delhi: Friedrich Ebert Foundation.

Media Development (1990). Excerpts from the UNESCO document 'Communication in the service of humanity'. 37(3), 5–7.

Narayanan, A. (1989). *The impact of TV on Indian families*. Bombay: Somaiya Publishers.

Prasad, N. (1994). *A vision unveiled*. New Delhi: Friedrich Ebert Foundation.

Rao, L. (1990). 'Portrayal of violence on Indian television'. Singapore: Asian Mass Communication and Information Centre (AMIC).

Rao, L. and **Vani, M.N.** (1988). 'A cultural enigma: Portrayal of woman on Indian television'. Paper presented at ITSC Conference, London.

Roach, R. (ed.). (1993). *Communication and culture in war and peace*. Thousand Oaks: Sage.

Schiller, H. (1990). 'Forgetful and short-sighted: What hope for the future?' *Media Development*, 37(3).

Singhal, A. and **Rogers, E.** (1989). *India's information revolution*. New Delhi: Sage.

Sparks, C. and **Roach, C.** (eds.). (1990). 'Farewell to NWICO'? Special issue of *Media, Culture and Society*, 12(3).

UNESCO (1974). *Television traffic—A one-way street*. Paris: UNESCO.

——— (1989). *World Communication Report*. Paris: UNESCO.

Yadava, J.S. (1984). *Politics of news: Third World Perspective*. New Delhi: Concept.

16

Development Dilemmas for Indian Television

Arbind Sinha

Introduction

Sitting in a small living room of a middle or upper-middle class Indian family with a black and white television set,[1] one can try to observe the viewing behaviour of television audiences and often wonder about the fate of development programmes transmitted on television—local, regional or national. On local channels the development programmes start early in the evening, i.e., between 5:30 PM to 6:30 PM. It is not a particularly good time for the target audiences of these programmes. Children come home from school and play outside. Parents who work have hardly come back from their jobs at that time, and those working in the field do not find the time to watch these programmes. Housewives often complain that this is the time when they have to prepare the evening meal for the other members of the family. So whom do these development programmes target?

Moving to another viewing situation in a slightly bigger living room, well furnished with expensive furniture, a colour television, a video cassette recorder placed in one corner making it convenient for all the occupants of the room to view programmes, and a cable connection attached to the television to receive four other channels through satellite, the pictures on the screen are invariably music or popular Hindi films.

Other than spill-over programmes, which viewers residing in bordering areas receive from a neighbouring countries' transmission, there are six additional channels, apart from Doordarshan, available to Indian viewers. These are Zee TV, ATN, Star Plus, Prime Sports, V Channel (music channel), Jain TV, and BBC. An obvious question is—where are we headed? What expectations does the nation have from television and what does it offer to the people of India?

Let us examine the role and responsibility of Indian television. When India was masterminding the gigantic plan to acquire television, it was basically conceived as a mass medium and a mass educator for its large population scattered in remote and culturally diverse areas. It was realised that the development of communications infrastructure, especially mass media, could accelerate the process of dissemination of development information and thereby help in improving the quality of life.

Television is supposed to disseminate the message of development and modernisation and create awareness for generating public participation. It should support government plans and programmes for bringing about social and economic change and to protect national security, as well as advance the cause of national integration. To perform this task, India planned a major expansion in television.

Expansion of Television

The growth in television—both in technology and reach—in the last three decades has been phenomenal. From the first appearance of television in India as a pilot project under All India Radio on 15 September 1959, which aimed to transmit educational and developmental programmes on an experimental basis to the population in the capital city and surrounding areas, it remained confined to a few cities for almost 15 years. Expansion plans were drawn up after India's one year Satellite Instructional Television Experiment (SITE), conducted in 1975–76, to promote socio-economic development through intensive communication. The technological constraints which had limited signals reaching remote areas have been overcome and with the help of the Indian satellite system (INSAT) the number of television transmitters and sets in the country have grown considerably. From a total number of 20 transmitters until 1982, presently the number of transmitters of all kinds—high power transmitters, medium power transmitters, low power transmitters and transposers—in the country is 564 (Audience Research Unit, 1994).

The expansion of television technology in terms of its reach, by installing transmitters, has not been haphazard or unplanned. The government wanted it to serve the decision-makers or policy-planners sitting in Delhi to communicate their views to large numbers of the population. Interestingly, during 1984, there was a special drive to install as many transmitters as the Ministry of Information and Broadcasting could, and the figure shows that one transmitter was installed in the country almost every third day. After 1984, the process slowed down. Again the process geared up and a record number of transmitters were installed in the year 1989 (see Figure 16.1), when India was preparing for its Lok Sabha (parliamentary) election to form its federal government.

Figure 16.1: Year-wise Installation of Television Transmitters in India

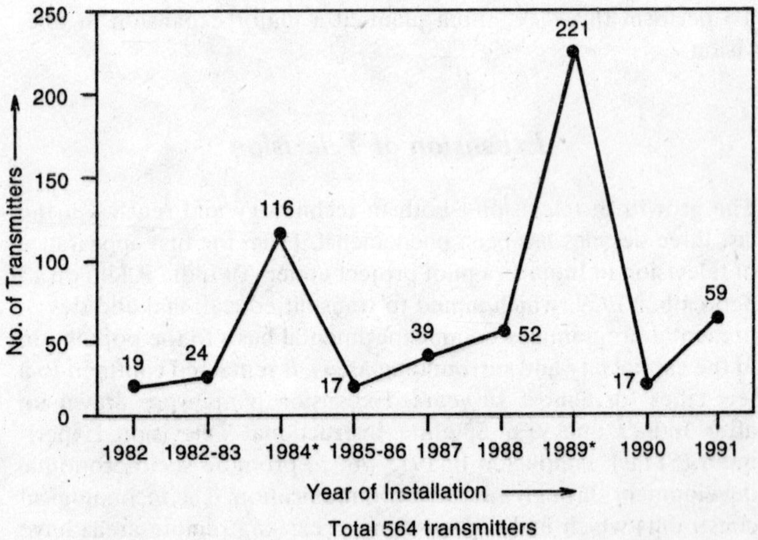

But why was there a priority given to installation in these two particular years? Satellite technology was available to India in the year 1983 and after that there were no serious technological problems. There was also no shortage of technical staff to install the transmitters.

With the technological revolution, television signals can reach up to two-thirds of the 3.3 million square kilometre geographical area of India and 84.5 per cent of its 850 million population (Audience Research Unit, 1991). A rough estimation is that more than three-quarters of these sets are in urban areas or their immediate vicinity. The remaining population and geographical areas to be covered are the deserts, the hilly areas, and the dense forests. Due to difficult geographical terrain, communication in such areas is not smooth and establishing continuous contact with the people of some of these areas is difficult. This failure to reach these parts of the population undermines the goal of Vikram Sarabhai, who initiated ideas of using satellite television for development in India. He wanted television to reach the most difficult and least developed areas of the country and because of their condition he believed that it should have reached them quickly. They should have been covered first, if the country's media had concern for developing the countryside. Very little of this had been done before the middle of the 1990s, and little is planned for the near future. A special plan is required to cover these areas, perhaps by providing direct reception sets.

As a result of developments in satellite communication Indian viewers can receive programmes originating in other Indian states or from across its national borders. If these programmes were watched they might have implications for India's sense of national identity, but as yet no firm data exists on this.

Community Television

The figures given earlier only indicate the reach of the television signal to the people. But covering them under the reach of the signal is not enough. The fact remains that the common masses in India are not in a position to afford private sets of their own. Community viewing sets are the only hope for them. Since mid-1975, when India had only four television transmitters feeding approximately 0.25 million private television sets and 900 community viewing sets, there has been an expansion in television. Under the SITE programme, 2,400 community sets in six SITE clusters and another 600 in the Kheda district of Gujarat were added.

Today, in less than two decades, even though the number of television transmitters has gone up a 160 times and the number of private sets has multiplied by a 120 times, no more than 64,000 community sets (Audience Research Unit, 1994) are available for India's half a million villages. Obviously, it requires more media planning to accelerate the development of the countryside. Curiously, even in advanced countries with expensive television systems, community television does not get much support from the state. Where market forces predominate, community television is perceived to be of little commercial importance and, therefore, is not widely supported. This lack of development of community television is partly the result of the non-adoption, at the operational level, of a 'participatory development' paradigm.

Programme Reach

Analysis of recent figures provided by official sources (Audience Research Unit, 1994, p. 13) shows that only 15 per cent of television time is used for education, 33 per cent for information including news, and the largest chunk (52 per cent) is used for entertainment programmes on national transmission. The proportion for regional and local transmissions are 32, 37, and 31, and 52, 28, and 20 per cent respectively. However, the overall share of regional and local transmissions is only 24 per cent and 4 per cent respectively. Joshi and Parmar (1992) found that over 92 per cent of programmes, including local and national news, on Indian television were of Indian origin. Foreign programmes have actually made few inroads into Indian television.

Based on a large scale survey of 17 urban centres, Doordarshan's study demonstrates that the reach of transmission (the percentage who watched TV yesterday) varies by time of day as well as by day of the week. The reach of morning as well as evening transmission on Sunday is the highest—88 per cent. There is little difference in the reach of TV between adults and children. It is followed by nearly 20 per cent of each category for morning programmes and by 84 per cent for evening programmes during the week. The amount of time spent on Sunday watching television forms about 42 per cent of the time spent during the entire week (Audience Research Unit, 1990). However, the reach of afternoon programmes is higher on weekdays (25 per cent) compared to that of Saturday (19 per cent).

A cross-sectional survey of viewers (those who viewed television at least three days in a week) by Joshi and Parmar (1992) conducted in four cities and their vicinities, shows that viewers spend a little less than 90 minutes in front of their television sets every day. The viewing time is much higher on Sundays as compared to other days. Women watch more programmes than men. According to the study (*ibid*, p. 63), women watch TV for 93 minutes per day as against 85 minutes by men. Although the viewing behaviour of different groups in society differs, the next section offers an attempt to present a general scenario of typical viewing.

Viewing Behaviour

Research shows that during the morning there is little serious viewing. While reading the morning newspaper a viewer may switch on the television and sometimes wait for the morning news bulletin at 8:15 AM. If some interesting programme is announced, it may also be viewed. In the afternoon, senior citizens or housewives view the afternoon transmissions, specially designed for housewives. This is the time when the programmes are seen in a leisurely manner; the content is often about housekeeping, preparation of different types of food, and child-rearing. The author's own observations of different viewing situations indicated that housewives often take note of the suggestions given during this transmission (Sinha et al., 1990).

Television audiences differ according to programme content. Children prefer sports and fantasy programmes, whereas their elders prefer news, serials, films, and film based programmes. For households with satellite channels, the same situation prevails but they have other choices too. But, one wonders, what place has development communication created for itself in the 20 years of its life span in India? Some understanding of programme content provides a perspective on the present situation.

Transmission Content

The sudden growth of television in the last decade demanded a lot of programming of various types, in various languages. This was not synchronised with equally planned software; so the programme production side remained weak. Although more than 30 programme production centres are operational, lack of good programmes, manpower, and expertise available in the country meant that many 'quick and easy to make' type of programme were produced, although efforts are now being made to improve the quality. A quick look at the programme content indicates the possible implications they may have for society and the different agendas we can expect from powerful and influential sources.

National programmes try to emphasise national integration, communal harmony, family welfare, and India's cultural heritage, including dance, music, drama, literature, science, news, and current affairs. Although content varies each week and month, a cursory look at the content of Doordarshan's programmes indicates that the objective of gearing up the pace of development is lost in the considerable increase in commercial advertisements, sponsored programmes, and feature films and film based items introduced from the early days of 'regular television' in Delhi and Bombay.

Two sets of arguments are presented for and against the increased broadcasting of sponsored films and film based items. Those who are opposed to the idea are worried about the adverse impact that films have on society. It is not uncommon to hear from people in general, or even from the police and administration, the assertion that films have contributed to the deterioration of social values and have increased crime rates. Before television started transmitting films, they were shown only in urban cinemas and viewership was restricted to very few. Broadcasting has taken them to mass audiences. But few of these films highlight social, cultural, and political issues of the country. The selection of films for broadcasting is supposed to be carefully done. The screening of films for television is decided by a committee, but the committee members do not necessarily represent the country at large.

Some television serials have been very popular and through these serials subtle messages on important national issues such as education, family planning, and national integration have been given. Television serials have also touched upon topics like social values, superstition, the cultural mosaic of the country, the problems created by the division of India and Pakistan, and the day-to-day difficulties faced by society. Serials like *Bharat Ek Khoj*, *Race to*

Save the Planet, and *Turning Point* merit special mention, not least because viewers may have faced language problems for the latter two as they were broadcast in English. In addition *Janvani* (People's voice), a periodical feature broadcast for quite some time, put Cabinet Ministers and the general public face to face in front of the camera and the responses of Ministers to sometimes difficult questions were viewed by millions of people.

Other developing nations like Niger, El Salvador, the Ivory Coast, Guatemala, and Indonesia, who have used television for education and development in the recent past, have had similar experiences. Indonesia in particular suffered from philosophical dilemmas when, like in any other developed or developing nation, foreign items and commercials started dominating development communication. The undesirability and unintended effects of commercial items were strongly felt and a number of times programmes were rescheduled to minimise their effects on rural lives. But India, as a developing nation, needs her own rationale.

Television News

One of the important tasks television has to perform is to inform the viewers about what is happening in the surrounding region and in the world. In spite of the fact that television is controlled by the federal government in India, the viewing figures as well as the credibility of television as a source of information remains high, both in urban as well as in rural settings. A survey conducted by the Audience Research Unit of Doordarshan claims that in the 17 selected cities the viewership of evening programmes is as high as 68 per cent of the total audience (Doordarshan, 1990, p. 34). The report indicates that regional news viewing in the cities is 51 per cent. The study by Sinha et al. (1990, p. 34) conducted in the rural areas for news on local television claims it to be almost 90 per cent. The study also reports that those who were watching other programmes on other channels did switch back to local news. A study by Joshi and Parmar (1992) suggests that 12.3 per cent of the total viewing time of television viewers is devoted to national as well as local news.

The World This Week, a sponsored weekly news magazine, is popular among those who understand English. On more or less similar lines, *Parakh*, another weekly news magazine in Hindi, started recently. It is getting popular but has yet to establish its viewership.

Private entrepreneurs have launched parallel video news magazines on cassettes for non-transmission mode, such as *Kalchakra* (Hindi), *Newstrack*, *Eye Witness*, *Business Plus*, *People Plus*, and a few more, to feed the information needs of the people who want to know more than what government media reports. These video magazines try to cover exclusive stories relating to important national issues and sometimes, as with *Newstrack* and *Eyewitness*, they achieve an appeal broad enough for them to be taken up by Doordarshan. But normally their circulation is limited to the better-off institutions and to the more affluent.

Television news, although very popular, has been threatened by the introduction of satellite television. BBC has become both a status symbol and a reference point for objective reporting, especially when viewers believe that Indian television, being a government medium, censors the news. At a national level, this number is insignificant. But this is the layer of Indian society that has always been vocal and successful in mobilising public opinion. They are the ones who have access to all channels of information—newspapers, magazines, radio, television, and satellite channels. They also watch local broadcasts. However, the situation in general, and particularly in rural areas, is different. Joshi and Parmar (1992) report that only a negligible percentage of radio owners tune their sets for BBC news, though it also broadcasts news in Hindi, the national language of India.

People hold divergent views about censorship of television news items. Some blame the government for not allowing the truth to be told. They strongly feel that withholding footage is neither professional nor serves any purpose. For them, there is nothing like an eye witness account to discourage rumours. Another view is that censorship is necessary, bearing in mind the social situation of the country. The coverage of television news items as well as the footage of sensitive video magazines is carefully monitored using the argument that one careless mistake can lead to riots and bloodshed. They criticise video magazine producers for trying to stay outside the purview of censorship and not behaving responsibly. They do not see censorship as a step towards trivialising the visual media. The government thinks that unlike satellite channel news, which is limited to educated viewers, television news reaches a large population. Thus, the medium can only show contentious footage when a majority of the country is educated (Mullick, 1993). Moreover, it is argued that international news agencies do not have any social responsibility for what happens in a country as a result of their news items. The debate goes on.

Educational Programmes

One other major responsibility of Indian television is to provide support for the education system in the country. Since its inception the medium has played this role conscientiously, ever since the first transmitter in Delhi, School Television (STV), was launched on 24 October 1961. At the moment three kinds of educational broadcasts are available for students in primary education, higher education and distance education.

The success of SITE paved the way for using INSAT for educational programmes between 9:00 AM and 12:00 NOON on all working days for schools. It has 45 minute slots for each of the five languages—Gujarati, Hindi, Oriya, Marathi, and Telugu. The services in Hindi basically meant for Bihar and Uttar Pradesh are also being broadcast by all the TV transmitters in these states as well as in other Hindi speaking states.[2] The Central Institute of Educational Technology in Delhi and six state Institutes of Educational Technology in the states of Andhra Pradesh, Bihar, Gujarat, Maharashtra, Orissa, and Uttar Pradesh have been set up to produce educational programmes for 22.5 hours of transmission every week.

Educational Television programmes (ETV), transmitted from Delhi, are not curriculum based and are targeted at children in the age group 5–8 years and 9–11 years; Saturday broadcasts are aimed at primary school teachers. Other STV programmes are curriculum based and are broadcast from Delhi, Bombay, Madras, and Srinagar. These programmes are received by schools which have television sets specially provided by the state government for educational uses. Not all schools have such sets and it could be claimed that adequate educational support has not been given to the primary education system.

Since 1984, Indian television has broadcast 11.5 hours of programmes every week for higher education. A one hour programme is transmitted between 1:00 PM to 2:00 PM and the same schedule is repeated between 4:00 PM to 5:00 PM on all working days. It aims primarily at the under-graduate level. Fourteen Educational Media Research Centres and Audio Visual Research Centres have been set up by the University Grants Commission (UGC) for programme production. Around 2,000 colleges, out of nearly 4,500 colleges in the country, have been given television sets for students to see these programmes and some of the colleges have provided television sets out of their own funds.

Since 20 May 1991, the programmes produced by the Indira Gandhi National Open University (IGNOU), the apex body for distance education in the country, have provided television support to its registered students for some courses. A half-hour broadcast, three days a week—on Mondays, Wednesdays and Fridays—is carried on the national network. The possibilities for a dedicated satellite based channel for educational programmes or even an educational satellite to cater to all sectors of education are being explored.

No comprehensive study has yet been conducted of the use made of the information carried by either primary or higher education broadcasts, although there have been sporadic attempts by in-house researchers in various institutes.

The question which bothers students of communication, particularly those who are familiar with the rural situation, is the benefit derived from these technologies or even the actual use it has been put to. In the last 20 years, more educational institutions have been created to accommodate the growing number of students, but few facilities, such as electronic and audio visual equipment and laboratories, have been provided.

Expenditure on educational institutions is the responsibility of the state and the federal governments who provide large sums of money as grants, which of course come from tax payers. The question remains as to whether providing technology to a few, places an unreasonable burden on the population at large.

Experiments in Development Television

From its inception, Doordarshan has been given the crucial responsibility of providing a fillip to the forces of socio-economic development, particularly in rural areas. (Audience Research Unit, 1986). However, the only example of using television exclusively for development communication was the Kheda Communication Project (KCP), popularly known as 'Kheda' or the 'Kheda project'. An account of 'Kheda', from its inception as a part of SITE from 1975–76 till it ceased functioning at the end of 1991, removes any doubts communication practitioners might have about the contribution that television can make to socio-economic development, despite the fact that SITE had already indicated that the success of television as a means to accelerate the pace of development depends upon various, often complicated, factors (Agrawal, 1981; Sinha, 1985).

Kheda Experiences

Kheda[3] was identified as an exception to the six SITE clusters selected on the basis of underdevelopment. A 1 KW transmitter was set up in Pij village in Kheda to serve community TV sets in the villages within a radius of 35 . Unlike the other SITE target areas, where the continuity projects became 'orphans' in the hands of unwilling and unprepared state departments once the one year SITE was over, Kheda was the responsibility of the Space Applications Centre's managers and programme producers and researchers who had learned valuable lessons from their involvement with SITE. They continued their rural broadcasting experiment with clearer perceptions of the strengths and limitations of television. KCP, after SITE, became an entirely local project and no national or regional network provided programmes. It covered some 607 community television sets in 443 villages.

One of the features of the credo developed for KCP was to 'educate the community—particularly the deprived—about their rights, including minimum wages, etc.' 'Kheda' was an experiment within the experiment of SITE using the approach of a 'centralised medium' based on satellite signals feeding national level programmes and a 'localised medium' with a low power transmitter transmitting local programmes specially produced for the local audiences based on their own development problems and in their own dialect. Mayo and Sarvaes (1992) write that KCP emphasised decentralised and participatory broadcasting from the start, especially in the production of programmes addressing social problems. Villagers were involved to a great extent, not only as actors but also as writers and even producers and directors of programmes.

For Bhatia and Karnik (1989) the effort was not only to develop and demonstrate a new approach to the use of television for development and education but also to try and chart a more meaningful direction for Indian television. They also claimed that 'Kheda' had succeeded in demonstrating effectively that TV could be used for development and for social change (*ibid*). KCP received world-wide recognition and it was awarded a UNESCO prize for rural communication effectiveness.

But, by the end of 1982, when INSAT became operational and the whole country was linked through a national network and colour transmission was started, the communication scenario began to change. A 10 KW transmitter was commissioned at Ahmedabad and its output overshadowed Kheda's development communication. There was a spurt in individually owned television sets and the pressure to maintain the community sets was correspondingly reduced; and as feared the Pij transmitter was closed down with the justification that Kheda viewers would be served along with Ahmedabad city by the high power transmitter there (Pal, 1978).

There was no transmission from Pij between 25 August 1985 and 21 May 1988. By that time Kheda villagers had realised the importance of having local television. They protested, wanting their 'Kheda television' back. The pressure worked and the Pij transmitter restarted on 22 May 1988; but it was not the same 'Kheda'. There was less enthusiasm and no large viewership. Only about 30 per cent of the community sets were operational and only 10 per cent of the total sets were used for viewing Kheda programmes. There was some viewing of Kheda programmes on individual sets but most people switched over to the Ahmedabad Channel for the local Gujarati news at 7:30 PM, and not many of them switched back to the Pij (Kheda) channel after the local news. Sinha et al. (1990, p. ii) reported 'Viewers have taken television more as a source of information and entertainment. It is not establishing its development role fully. Sponsored serials are preferred to development programmes'. The transmission time for Kheda programmes was changed, which did not help. More government guidelines were to be followed for programme-making. Programme quality had deteriorated, and the commercial pressures on professionals adversely affected those who had been working in development communication. Finally, by October 1991, the Ministry of Information and Broadcasting decided not to renew the Memorandum of

Understanding under which KCP was operated by the Department of Space, resulting in the end of the 'Kheda project'. Neither the people of Kheda district nor the programme-makers put up a fight this time.

The premature death of this development communication experiment leaves many unanswered questions. Those who believe that television can play a meaningful role in developing the community at large must carry out a post mortem on the successes, the failures, and the lessons to be learned from the demise of this model of development communication.

Development Communication

The role and responsibilities of television are largely defined by the priorities and strategies of the state. The expectations of television in India 'to develop the mass through education, information and enlightenment, to improve the quality of life of the largest masses of the people, to bring communities and societies, regions the States together as one nation through mutual awareness and sympathy while preserving, consolidating and enriching their unique ways of life, culture, customs and traditions' (NAMEDIA, 1986, p. 13) limit the scope of our discussion of development communication.

Not much is said about the entertainment values of the medium. Television tries to highlight the folk art, music, and dances of different cultural pockets of India but fills as much as it can with films and film based programmes which are popular among the masses. Increasingly larger numbers are catered for by video and satellite channel availability. But entertainment is not the greatest concern to this author except to say that it should be positive and not harmful in any way.

The second commitment of Indian television is to support the education system. However, the impact of television transmission for primary school students, for higher education, and for distance education is being questioned by society at large and by educational policy-makers. The challenge lies in better organisation of programmes, in ensuring the safe custody of sets, in the provision of regular electric or battery supplies to run them, and in guaranteeing the opportunity to view. But research also has to be carried out to make software more effective. Although software aspects of broadcasting are being taken care of by the Institutes of Educational Technology and by Audio Visual and Media Research Centres, the problem of creating an environment for better production and consumption remains.

Development Dilemma

The medium stands at a crossroads in the role it has to play in improving the quality of life. However, the increasing dependence on sponsored commercials—a source of revenue required for its functioning and growth—and the competition it faces from other open channels attracting audiences with entertainment programmes, have presented considerable threats to national television. In the beginning it was successful in its role of development communication to the deprived masses, but slowly the nature of its role as an agent of change seems to have disappeared. Srivastava (1986, p. 151) writes '. . . if one objectively reviews the performance of TV during this period (25 years of television in India), it becomes quite evident that there has been a shift from the original intention of using it as a medium for education and development since it has been dominated by poor quality entertainment aimed at pleasing urban viewers'.

This is not what was expected. Television, as a medium for development, was supposed to disseminate development information. For many of us it was there to help modernisation, to create awareness for generating public participation and support for the government's plans and programmes for bringing about social and economic change, to protect national security, as well as to advance the cause of national integration. Perhaps we have ascribed inappropriate expectations to the medium, or perhaps the medium has its own limitations.

SITE evaluation has clearly indicated that television as a medium plays a limited role in taking information to the people. Information through television is capable of arousing expectations which are difficult to meet, unless there are wider structural changes in the social system. Innovative ideas are only information inputs and the consumption of information is very closely associated with the receiver's socio-economic position. For village India, development communication might remain a high sounding idea and might result in indifference towards the message as well as to the medium itself (Sinha, 1985). Sinha (*ibid*) also warned that the wide gap between the communication the masses receive, the way they are expected to respond to the communication, and the actual reality of their lives, might lead either to a state of apathy or to serious tension. Development messages have to be planned and communicated carefully.

The SITE and KCP experiences demonstrate that development is not a linear process initiated and executed by particular agencies. Rather it is a multi-faceted process, dependent on many factors and many players. Television can disseminate information supportive of development, but unless a development project has strong support from powerful groups who understand its value, and unless the infrastructure is in place to match the demands generated by that information, such information soon becomes superfluous. This is not a problem for India alone. Mayo and Sarvaes (1992, p. 1) write 'The euphoria and naive optimism about the role of communication technologies and institutions in the developmental process have diminished in the past two decades. The theories of modernisation that defined the process and method of progress have been discredited as ethnocentric, functionalist and individualistic that have failed to bring about equitable improvement in the quality of life. Communication technologies failed in their predicted role as powerful tools for creating the "climate for development" by changing unscientific attitudes in traditional societies'.

It is unfortunate that despite the best intentions, development communication projects with a participatory approach rarely get beyond an experimental status because of social, political, and economic constraints. Development communication cannot be treated as 'normal' television and probably requires separate training for those who produce rural media and separate standards for judging its quality and success. The social use of development communication in India is not only lopsided in terms of distribution between the rural and the urban, but is also grossly inadequate to meet even the needs that exist in the metropolitan sector. It will be a long time before even a semblance of equitable access for the Indian population is available.

At the moment, the media in order to earn revenue through advertising are implicated in creating a market for consumer goods. Though it is largely an urban phenomenon, the same commercial advertisements on television reach rural areas and can have disturbing effects on rural people, whose wants are encouraged, whose appetite for luxury goods and services is whetted, but which can lead to a sense of frustration among those who cannot afford them.

Those who are concerned about development communication, particularly for the deprived masses, have been calling for alternatives to privatisation and commercialisation, and their social, cultural, and political consequences. Time and again voices are raised for more autonomy to television. Political parties include this in their election manifestos, but to date nothing concrete has been proposed. As a result of the growing sponsorship of radio and television programmes, particularly entertainment programmes, and of the lobbying by private channel operators, the call to privatise all television gets louder.

Others claim that a state-owned system, at least in principle, has to take care of all sections of society. But, the private sector works on different principles. It has to earn revenue. No Government can afford both—to both pay for the running of the system and to lose control over it. The obvious compromise is sponsorship. Whilst the sponsoring agencies may finance television to promote their products, their target would be better-off people. The sponsoring agencies who invest large sums on advertisements will seek a return on their investment. So, who will take care of the information needs of the deprived masses of the country? This large portion of India's population live with huge constraints and for them product advertisements have little relevance. They have little choice, the overwhelming criterion is affordability. Thus, there would be two types of marketing; social marketing and commercial marketing, leaving the first one as the responsibility of the state. The first would be resourced by directly taxing people in general, and the latter by earning revenue from the commercials and taxing those who buy consumer goods. So, do we need separate television for achieving rural development? If so Doordarshan, which is not a private medium, could be financed for this from the national budget. Thus, high cost entertainment TV could earn its revenue while low cost development communication could be the state's responsibility.

In sum, Indian television is at a crossroads in relation to development. On one side are the market forces pumping more and more money to increase consumerism. On the other side is the changing hi-tech scene demanding more resources whilst constraining programme quality. On another side are the Indian masses expecting television to help them escape from their present plight; and on still another side is the resource constraint, a State helplessly watching the dilemma and not in a position to empower the medium to take up its development role wholeheartedly.

Thus, the real dilemma is—should Indian television keep to its original commitment to development or join the entertainment marathon?

Notes

1. Approximately three-quarters of the total estimated 30 million sets in the country are black and white sets.
2. India has 15 major languages and States are identified on the basis of the spoken language.
3. Kheda is the name of an administrative district in the State of Gujarat in Western India, approximately 60 KM from Ahmedabad, the main city of the State. The 1 KW low power transmitter was installed in one of the villages of Kheda, hence it is known as 'Kheda'.

References

Agrawal, Binod C. (1981). *SITE social evaluation: Results, experiences and implications*. Ahmedabad: Space Applications Centre.

Audience Research Unit (1986). *Television India*. New Delhi: Directorate General Doordarshan.

——— (1990). *Facts and figures about Doordarshan*. New Delhi: Directorate General Doordarshan.

——— (1991). *Television India*. New Delhi: Directorate General Doordarshan.

——— (1994). *Doordarshan–1994: An update*. New Delhi: Directorate General Doordarshan.

Bhatia, B.S. and **Karnik, K.S.** (1989). *Kheda communication project*. Ahmedabad: Development and Educational Communication Unit.

Doordarshan (1990). *Television viewership*. New Delhi: Directorate General Doordarshan.

Joshi, S.R. and **Parmar, K.M.** (1992). *International television and video flow in India: A case study*. Ahmedabad: Development and Educational Communication Unit.

Mayo, J.K. and **Sarvaes, J.** (1992). *Kheda communication project: An Indian experiment in participatory broadcasting*. UNESCO's orientation kit on Development Communication (Draft). Miami: Florida State University.

Mullick, A. (1993). No news isn't good news'. *Indian Express*, 3 January 1993, p. 3 (Ahmedabad edition).

NAMEDIA (1986). *A vision for Indian television*. Report of the feedback project 'Indian Television: Today and Tomorrow'. New Delhi: Media Foundation of the Non-Aligned.

Pal, Y. (1978). 'The crucial decision'. *Seminar*, 232 (December), pp. 12–15.

Sinha, A. (1985). *Mass media and rural development*. New Delhi: Concept Publishing Co.

Sinha, A., Parmar, K.M., Joshi, H. and Trivedi, B. (1990). *Kheda viewership study*. Ahmedabad. Development and Educational Communication Unit.

Srivastava, J.S. (1986). 'Rural India is not in the picture'. In Agrawal, Binod C. and Sinha, Arbind (eds.). *SITE to INSAT*. New Delhi: Concept Publishing Co.

17

No News is Bad News: 4 June and Individualism in Hong Kong

Terence Lo

Immense social energies were generated in Hong Kong in response to the announcement of martial law in Beijing on Saturday, 20 May 1989. This was two weeks preceding what became variedly known as the 'June 4 massacre' or the 'Tiananmen incident'—the military crackdown on the protesting university students in Tiananmen Square. Roughly seven hours after the midnight announcement on China Central Television was relayed to television in Hong Kong, a two-hour radio phone-in programme starting at 8:00 AM that Saturday was inundated with calls from angry individuals, and was extended to six hours.

In the meantime, a severe tropical storm—Typhoon Brenda—started to affect Hong Kong. Following established practice, radio stations kept blasting their typhoon warnings advising people to stay indoors and away from windows. They also announced cancellation of public events, usually following regular news bulletins. In the afternoon, the Hong Kong Professional Teachers Union, the body calling for a protest march to be held that evening, received at least one call from a member of the public asking them to confirm, through radio, whether the march would go ahead if the weather conditions got worse. The confirmation appeared to be presented as a news item on a radio news bulletin fifteen minutes later, and was repeated in several subsequent half-hourly news bulletins.

That early weekend evening, a large number of young people, mostly on their own and some in pairs or very small groups, found themselves travelling on various means of public transport. It was extremely unusual, considering that it was well past the early

Saturday afternoon rush hours, that a severe typhoon was threatening Hong Kong, and that most shops were closed due to the weather. The young people were unusually quiet, and seemed to know they were heading in the same direction. Their numbers grew as they quietly got nearer Victoria Park (a spot acquiring some of the images associated with Speakers' Corner in London's Hyde Park). There, a brief rally was held with the participants standing in heavy rain and ankle-deep muddy water. They then marched to the New China News Agency, China's de facto consulate in Hong Kong, where another rally was held. Following a request from a rally organiser, they closed their umbrellas to confirm that they were willing to expose their bodies to the heavy rain as a gesture to show their support for the Beijing students on hunger strike. When the rally ended, they left, as quietly as they had come. They learnt through their walkman radios on their way home, on the late night TV news when they arrived home, and in the morning papers the next day, that they had made history.

The *Sunday Morning Post* of 21 May 1989 reported on its front page that more than 50,000 people had taken part in the rally, and described it as 'the biggest pro-democracy event the territory has ever seen'. The *Sunday Standard* of the same day quoted a witness saying that it was 'as if the whole under-30s population had turned up'. But it was nothing when compared to the protest march held later that same Sunday. About one million people (out of Hong Kong's population of six million) took part in the march, which began at 2:00 PM and finished in a rally that ended at 10:30 PM. According to the *Hongkong Standard* of Monday, 22 May 1989, the

> marchers came from all walks of life: students mingled with workers; teachers marched alongside the elderly; priests mixed with popstars; parents took their children. For most of them it was the first time that they had ever attended a political rally. They were attracted to the march by press advertisements, radio broadcasts and the urgings of fellow demonstrators. The further the procession went the larger it grew. Builders climbed down from their scaffolding to join the march, clerks left their offices, shoppers fled department stores.

And of course the mammoth size of the procession was seen on TV during news bulletins and updates throughout the day, attracting more people to join.

Some commentators attributed the massive turnout in the protest marches to the power of the media to stir up public emotions. Typhoon Brenda was also blamed for keeping people indoors. Bored, frustrated, and continuously exposed to the news media which played up the drama of the Beijing situation, people were driven to vent their anger in public. Other commentators disagreed, and argued that the media only reflected, rather than created, public sentiments. And of course many of those who had, for the first time in their lives, participated in protest actions would not accept that their strong feelings were the result of their having been duped by the news media.

This paper will approach the question of the power of the news media, in particular television news, during this period of social upheaval in Hong Kong by, first, analysing news as a discourse of truth, as an institutional apparatus in the production of social knowledge permeating everyday life; and, second, by studying the role of the news media in the articulation, at a particular historical moment in the development of Hong Kong, of the collective experience of oneself as a more or less autonomous individual driven by one's conscience to take socially responsible actions, that personal experience encapsulated in the liberal notion of 'individualism'.

To do this, the power of the news media will be analysed not as originating and flowing unidirectionally from the news media to their audiences, but as something that circulates in the social network of news as everyday experience, something that exists through the social practice of news as a discourse of truth, in the process of which people recognise themselves as individuals able to have genuine feelings, enjoy independence in thinking, and exercise autonomy in action. In this paper power will be analysed in 'its capillary form of existence, the point where power reaches into the very grain of individuals, touches their bodies and inserts itself into their actions and attitudes, their discourse, learning processes and everyday lives' (Foucault, 1980, p. 39). Individualism as concretely materialised in the human experience of genuine emotion, independent thought, and autonomous action will be analysed not as opposed to power imposed from above, but as an effect of power with individualised actors as its vehicle:

> The individual is not to be conceived as a sort of elementary nucleus, a primitive atom, a multiple and inert material on

> which power comes to fasten or against which it happens to strike, and in so doing subdues or crushes individuals. In fact, it is already one of the prime effects of power that certain bodies, certain gestures, certain discourses, certain desires, come to be identified and constituted as individuals (*ibid*., p. 98).

TV news as an institutional practice will be analysed as a discursive arena, a social space in which individuals exercise their power and experience empowerment in the pursuit of truth. This will involve analysing the formal association of the notion of TV news with the notion of truth, and the circulation of these notions in the personal enactment and experience of individualism.

This paper focuses on the social upheaval within Hong Kong during the week after the television relay of the announcement of martial law in Beijing on 20 May 1989. It will examine the upheaval as a cultural phenomenon associated with the news media in Hong Kong. As such, the still ongoing debate on whether there was any shooting at all in Tiananmen Square on 4 June 1989 is irrelevant. What is experienced as 'June 4' in Hong Kong is very much a distinct cultural phenomenon of Hong Kong, and will be studied as such in this paper.

News as Everyday Discourse of Truth

News is first and foremost a discourse of truth. As a media genre distinct from more entertainment-oriented media products, news is conventionally understood as serving to provide up-to-date factual information about society. Many people in Hong Kong give formal recognition to the importance of news, mainly because they perceive that the information provided about the larger social trends may have significant bearing upon their everyday life, or because they feel that it is their civic duty to keep themselves informed about current social issues. To the average Hong Kong person, however, news is likely to be a personally significant experience in his everyday life only to the extent that particular news items appear immediately relevant to the quality of his life, usually after those news items have been interpreted by local experts in their specialist fields as relevant to immediate local concerns.

The bulk of these interpretations tend to appear in the less prominent parts of the media. They may be published in the press as special feature articles or contributor items in the pages not devoted to the main news of the day; or they may be broadcast on TV in regularly scheduled current affairs programmes or special news magazine programmes. This is especially so when the complexity of the arguments require extended space or time to be put forward clearly, or when the issues in question are so controversial that several conflicting viewpoints have to be set alongside one another and discussed in detail. Over time people in Hong Kong have developed the expectation that these relative peripheral parts of the 'news' media will offer in-depth analyses of the most important and the most locally relevant issues, including those reported in the more central parts of the 'news' media due to their importance as well as those not reported due to their complexity. This has generated the paradox that it is precisely the more peripheral news products that play a central role in the popular experience of 'news' as an everyday media category. In such popular experience, the central parts of the news media function precisely to legitimise the peripheral parts of the news media.

It is, therefore, not surprising that a relatively large number of Chinese dailies published in Hong Kong attempt to establish their individual identities through those pages not devoted to the main news, as the main news pages in most of the local dailies tend to give the same information, and do not contribute to attracting additional readership. Also, TV stations in Hong Kong have identified a significant sector of the local population who do not normally watch prime-time television, and yet are consistent news-watchers. This situation is normal in Hong Kong where Cantonese television has always been associated with light entertainment for the average person on the street. However, due to fierce competition, the TV stations have been trying to attract the 'non-TV watchers' to their prime-time broadcast by strengthening prime-time current affairs programming on their Cantonese channels, especially since the mid-1980s. These current affairs programmes focus on current issues of local concern, especially those directly related to the livelihood of the average Hong Kong person. The programmes appeal to people interested in viewing a broader range of local news topics as well as more in-depth handling of the topics than normally available in regular news bulletins.

It seems, therefore, useful to adopt a broadened definition of news to give full recognition to 'news' as a popular social practice, as a significant social experience in the audience's attempt to monitor social reality. In such a broadened definition, 'news' as a media category will go beyond the main news pages of the printed press, and also beyond the main news bulletins on the broadcasting media, to include any media materials that provide commentaries on, or in-depth analysis of, current social issues. It will also include the various forms of promotions and previews of important news items to be published or broadcast in the more central parts of the 'news' media.

Truth through 'Claw-back'

This broadened definition of 'news' as a media discourse of truth is particularly relevant when analysing the experience of televised 'news'. Because of its conventional identity as a predominantly visual medium, television seems particularly adept at handling news as a discourse of truth. The popular view of television as literally a 'window to the world', through which one can observe social reality in its most immediate, truest form, is based on an empiricist theory of reality, sometimes negatively termed the 'transparency fallacy'

Still, to the average TV viewer, seeing is believing. And the most visible strength of television is its apparent ability to bring the social reality 'out there' onto the television screen in the living room. Whatever evidence there may be to support a particular viewpoint, the TV camera seems perfectly capable of capturing it from the widest possible range of physical as well as discursive angles, a capability that has been popularly seen to strengthen the accuracy and objectivity of TV news, and ultimately serve to validate the truth of TV news. TV news in Hong Kong has indeed acquired such a pivotal importance in the popular mind that some newspaper editors are known to have made use of evening TV news programmes as a reference to decide on the priority to be given to news items in their papers to be published the following morning, with some reporters even going as far as copying directly from the news stories aired on television.

Fiske and Hartley (1978) introduce the term 'claw-back' to refer to the formal structure of reporting in TV news bulletins. The 'claw-back' mechanism operates to place interpretive constraints on events that may disrupt society's dominant value system, by clawing elements with potentially deviant meanings back into socio-centrality. It does this while at the same time producing the impression of authenticity and objectivity, and, therefore, the truth of the news report. The 'claw-back' mechanism operates on the basis of a visible distribution of functional roles over geographical as well as discursive spaces and consists of three stages.

The first stage is located at the individual figure of the news reader, or the anchor-person, in the TV studio. Visibly situated safely behind the news counter, he occupies the highest rank in the hierarchy in this discourse of truth. He reminds the audience that he is not the real author of the news discourse when the offers the audience a report produced by a reporter, the 'real' author of the news discourse. But his physical distance and discursive detachment from the real author ensures his objectivity in handling the information based on the inevitably more 'subjective', though 'authentic', experience outside the TV studio. Speaking in an impersonal, authoritative manner, the news reader expresses the institutional objectivity of news, and impresses on the audience the truth of the news report.

Lower down the hierarchy is the individual figure of the reporter who is seen, or at least heard, reporting from the scene. He is the one supposedly having followed professional procedures to collect and integrate all the relevant information available in producing his report. He may or may not make use of his personal visibility to authenticate the truth provided in the actuality film, but he invariably puts his personal signature on the report to confirm that he is the individual authoring the report. At this second stage of the 'claw-back' mechanism, the reporter mediates between the institutionally guaranteed objectivity of news on the one hand, and his individual subjective experience of the social reality 'out there' as a professional witness, or even more 'subjective' and, therefore, more 'authentic' accounts provided by other eyewitnesses, on the other.

At the third stage of the 'claw-back' mechanism are the actual people speaking their feelings and knowledge about the news event in their roles as eyewitnesses, spokespersons, or participants of one kind or another in the event being reported. The truth of their discourse is limited by their personal positions in the news event, making their experience appear excessively subjective, but their discourses are essential for the authentication of the 'final truth' delivered by the news reader.

In news bulletins on Hong Kong's two Cantonese TV channels, the 'claw-back' mechanism tends to be used when the news event reported upon is complex, and involves a number of different, or even conflicting, voices. In such a news report, the news reader provides a brief summary of the event and then passes the reporting role to the reporter, whose name he pronounces. The reporter may or may not appear personally in the actuality film, but when he finishes his report, he invariably signs off by pronouncing his job title and his name. If he does appear on the screen, his name is also given as a subtitle on the screen for a few seconds.

The news reader is, on the other hand, introduced only once at the beginning of the news bulletin by having his name flashed onto the bottom part of the screen for a few seconds. Audience members who prefer to concentrate on his face while listening to the news headlines can easily miss it. This differential naming practice reflects the play between nomination and exnomination, which expresses and reinforces the contrast between subjective experience and impersonal truth: 'That which is exnominated appears to have no alternative and is thus granted the status of the natural, the universal, or that-which-cannot-be-challenged' (Fiske, 1987, p. 290). The under-nomination of the news reader on the two Cantonese channels appears to produce the effect of reinforcing the objectivity of the news reader's discourse as unchallengeable, whereas the explicit or even excessive nomination of the reporter tends to emphasise his personal and more subjective, yet more authentic role in this discourse.

Depending on the news event being reported, the reporter may also be seen to be wearing more casual clothes or special clothing suitable for particular types of weather or outdoor situations. He is also more likely to speak with an emotive tone, as if to emphasise the authenticity of his experience at the scene of the report. On the other hand, the news reader is invariably seen to be dressed formally, signalling his institutional impersonality, although people who have visited the local TV news studio during news broadcasts are always ready to point out that the formal dress code applies only to the top half of the news reader's body. In contrast to the reporter, he also tends to speak more formally, with an authoritative and emotionally neutral tone.

However, there are occasions when the news reader doubles up to play the role of the reporter. He may be heard narrating for an actuality film. He may even be shown, usually very briefly, to be present at the scene of the news event. Rather than generating doubts about the objectivity of the information provided, it seems to increase its authenticity and accuracy. So, rather than emphasising institutional impersonality and discursive detachment, occasionally collapsing the top two stages of the 'claw-back' operation seems to give priority to authenticity and context-specific accuracy as guarantees for the objectivity and truth of the news discourse.

As noted earlier, the conventional news bulletin on Hong Kong TV, covering both local and international news, serves to represent the paradigm case of 'news' as a media genre, giving legitimacy to a whole array of news magazines and current affairs programmes covering, in the vast majority of cases, local issues only. In a similar way, the full 'claw-back' mechanism in its three stages seems to be a paradigm case of news reporting as the discourse of truth, giving legitimacy to news reports whose truth presumably does not need to be underwritten with the 'claw-back' mechanism due to the inherent transparency of the truth in the actuality film provided. This arrangement is particularly noticeable in current affairs programmes, which are not 'official news' as the news bulletins are, but as has been pointed out earlier, play a much more significant role in the popular experience of that media category classified as 'news' in the Hong Kong community.

This is not to say that conventional TV news bulletins are less powerful than news magazines and current affairs programmes, or that news items reported through the full 'claw-back' mechanism are less powerful than those not reported through it. On the contrary, the power of TV news works through: (*a*) the common sense views of the conventional TV news bulletin as the ideal-typical case of news; (*b*) the 'claw-back' mechanism as the ideal-typical case of news reporting operation; (*c*) news magazine and current affairs programmes being experienced as legitimate variations at the periphery of the media category of 'news' as a discourse of truth; and (*d*) reporting practices not strictly adhering to the 'claw-back' mechanism as legitimate strategies in the production of the discourse of truth. Moreover, just as news magazine and current affairs programmes induce the 'truth effect' of 'news'—the 'power effect' of 'news' as a discourse of truth—by foregrounding their authenticity and contextual accuracy, the presentation of non-scheduled previews of specific items to be covered in news bulletins and updates on specific news items already covered also induce 'truth effects' through foregrounding the immediacy and relevancy of these news items.

News, Knowledge and the Intellectual

'News' as a discursive formation on Hong Kong TV intersects with the public discourse of the academic as an increasingly important discourse of truth in local everyday life. Commentaries by local academics on controversial social issues have been used with increasing frequency in TV news and current affairs programmes. The person of the academic symbolises expert knowledge. His institutionally validated expertise in a specialised field of learning ensures that his gaze on society is broad enough to encompass most, if not all, the relevant perspectives. Being able to integrate potentially conflicting opinions from different perspectives in a single, individual mind, the academic speaks with a particularly truthful authority. The institutional position of the academic also symbolises his freedom from commercial or political interests that may distort his understanding of a particular issue. As an intellectual, he is assumed to be engaged in the most relentless pursuit of truth for its own sake rather than for more tangible rewards.

Foucault has pointed out that 'the intellectual . . . is linked . . . to the general functioning of an apparatus of truth' (Foucault, 1986, p. 73), and that the university hierarchies constitute the most visible form of the production of knowledge as a discourse of truth, articulating power, constantly inducing the effects of power: '. . . knowledge functions as a form of power and disseminates the effects of power' (Foucault, 1980, p. 69). Knowledge and power are always articulated through each other; one always implies the other: 'It is not possible for power to be exercised without knowledge, it is impossible for knowledge not to engender power' (Foucault, 1980, p. 52).

As a perfect individual embodiment of intellectual expertise and personal autonomy, the academic is invested with the power to be an author in the discourse of truth, a power that he, as a human body imbued with intellectual conscience, cannot refuse without giving up his individual identity as an academic. With TV's technical advantage, the academic as an embodiment of truth is brought face to face with the audience. The person already socially authorised to speak the truth is brought under the gaze of the audience to discourse on truth in the most truthful manner by offering intellectual illumination on complex social issues so that there is no question of the academic being misunderstood and misquoted by an inexperienced journalist. The observable practice of editing an interview so that the same academic is seen in separate parts of a current affairs programme, juxtaposed with excerpts of other interviews, does not alter this impression. If anything, it only shows the professionalism of the editor in making the issue more 'illuminating' to the audience, enabling each individual audience member to make use of the information provided to formulate his own judgement.

Foucault has noted that journalism represents a specific application of the Rousseauist dream of an open society, in which there are provisions to enable each and every individual to be fully informed about the whole society, and to communicate their opinions about society to everyone else. With the assumption that individually formed collective opinion will inherently lead to justice, it is believed that the subjection of every part of society to observation and evaluative discourse by all will discourage people from socially harmful behaviour. Journalism is one such instrument functioning to keep society under democratic surveillance. It is a material practice embodying a form of power that is 'exercised by virtue of the mere fact of things being known and people seen in a sort of immediate collective and anonymous gaze . . . [a] form of power . . . that . . . refuse[s] . . . to tolerate areas of darkness (Foucault, 1980, p. 154). Foucault terms this 'a politics of the gaze', a network of power relations which requires that everyone in society takes part as an autonomous individual in the network of democratic surveillance and personally experience 'the will to know'.

This network provides spaces for the emergence of autonomous, conscientious individuals, whose function is to carry out journalism's mission to subject society to ever more pervasive democratic surveillance, to generate and disseminate the truth about society, and who in the process of doing so become subjects of truth:

> We are subjected to the production of truth through power and we cannot exercise power except through the production of truth . . . we are forced to produce the truth of power that our society demands, of which it has need, in order to function: we *must* speak the truth; we are constrained or condemned to confess or to discover the truth (Foucault, 1980, p. 93, emphasis in original).

The academic, as an individual in the university hierarchies, is only the most visible embodiment of this process, with individuals associated with various forms of intellectualism and the production of knowledge occupying less visible positions.

TV News as Panoptic

Imagine the following scenario: the typical Hong Kong TV news watcher finishes work, goes back to his small flat in a high-rise block of 30 storeys, and the first thing he does is switch on the television set to watch the early evening news. He does this almost automatically as he goes through the same drill every day, receiving his daily dose of TV news at the same time of the day. He may perform this ritual on his own, or he may partake in the ritual with one or two of his family members. In any case, he is unlikely to be watching the news with any large number of people, as the average household size in Hong Kong has been dwindling.

He is even likely to be sitting at roughly the same spot facing the same direction as his counterparts in other flats in the same block, as the average flat in Hong Kong is small and the feed-in socket from the communal antenna serving the entire block of flats is fixed on the wall on the same side of the living room. The small size of the living room and the standard position of the antenna feed-in socket leave virtually no room for innovation in the positioning of the television set and the chairs to watch it from. Thus, the average early evening TV news watcher is likely to be going through very similar motions with a large number of similar people in separate physical locations. Although he is not fully aware of this, he nonetheless knows somewhere at the back of his mind that many other people are watching the same news bulletin, and most important of all he is doing the right thing in keeping himself informed about society, just like everybody else.

Compare this scenario with Bentham's ideal model of the Panopticon, discussed extensively in Foucault's study of the emergence of the modern disciplinary society. Designed to be a prison, it is an annular architectural structure consisting of a perimeter building in the form of a ring and a watch-tower in its centre. On the watch-tower there are large windows opening on to the inner face of the ring. The perimeter building is divided into cells, each traversing the whole thickness of the building. Each cell has two windows, one facing outward from the ring allowing daylight to pass through and illuminate the entire cell, the other facing inward allowing all activities in the cell to be visible from the watch-tower.

Whereas the watch-tower is so designed that anyone positioned there can fully monitor the behaviour of the inmates in their cells, the inmates have no way of ascertaining whether there is anyone in the watch-tower observing them at any particular moment. As such, they have no choice but to assume that their activities are monitored at all times, and that they have to behave properly in order to avoid punishment. Kept in their separate cells without any means of communication, the inmates will have to assume that the inmates in other cells are behaving in an identical manner. The rationale of the design is that in time the inmates will get trained to be their own watchers. Whether they are on their own or in small groups, they will keep themselves under constant surveillance to ensure their own proper behaviour without having to depend on the inspecting gaze of the authority. The watch-tower remains the symbolic centre of power, but the real effects of power are induced through the individual bodies situated in isolation at the periphery.

Foucault sees Bentham's ideal model of Panopticon as a graphic instance epitomising the rise of a 'surveillance' model of discipline that has gradually infiltrated every aspect of social life. He sees a 'swarming of disciplinary mechanisms' in the formation of the modern disciplinary society, as evidenced in the proliferation of disciplinary institutions on the one hand, and in the increasing number of existing institutions being subjected to the disciplinary principle of Panopticism on the other. There is such a continuous 'de-institutionalisation' of disciplinary mechanisms that eventually one 'sees . . . the spread of disciplinary procedures, not in the form of enclosed institutions, but as centres of observation disseminated throughout society' (Foucault, 1979, p. 212).

The principle of Panopticism operates through isolation, visibility, and constant surveillance, including the surveillance of the self by the self. Power is exercised in the generation of knowledge, including the generation of the objects of knowledge, in the perpetual process of surveillance of others and the self: '. . . the exercise of power itself creates and causes to emerge new objects of knowledge and accumulates new bodies of information' (Foucault, 1980, p. 51). Knowledge and the objects of knowledge are therefore the articulation of power, the vehicles through which power is exercised, the embodiments of power. As embodied in a myriad of practices in contemporary society, the Panopticon is 'a machine in which everyone is caught, those who exercise power just as much as those over whom it is exercised . . . . In the Panopticon each person, depending on his place, is watched by all or certain of the others' (*ibid.*, pp. 156–58).

To Foucault, Bentham's principle of Panopticism complements the Rousseauist dream on the sacred mission of journalism (Foucault, 1980). It is through the ongoing subjugation of disciplinary mechanisms that power works through individual bodies, subjecting them to surveillance, to knowledge, turning them into objects of knowledge while at the same time investing them with power, constituting them as autonomous subjects as possessing a distinct individuality with the desire to know about and to discipline others and the self through knowledge:

> . . . the individual is not a pre-given entity which is seized on by the exercise of power. The individual, with his identity and characteristics, is the product of a relation of power exercised over bodies, multiplicities, movements, desires, forces' (Foucault, 1980, p. 73–74);
>
> power relations can materially penetrate the body in depth, without depending even on the mediation of the subject's own representations. If power takes hold on the body, this isn't through its having first to be interiorised in people's consciousness. There is a network or circuit of bio-power, or somato-power, which acts as the formative matrix of . . . [the personal

experience of] . . . the historical and cultural phenomenon within which we seem at once to recognise and lose ourselves (Foucault, 1980, p. 186).

TV News Blackout as Annihilation

For a few hours on the evening of Friday, 19 May 1989, there were constant reminders on TV that an important policy speech on the Beijing student movement would be made by the Chinese Communist leadership and that the speech would be transmitted on TV around midnight. To many audience members, in particular those who had for several weeks greatly intensified their use of the 'news' media to monitor the Beijing situation, including Hong Kong students who had been using television sets provided temporarily at various public spots round their campuses, it appeared that the speech would be an extremely important moment in the latest development of the Beijing situation. So it was, but in Hong Kong.

Soon after midnight, Premier Li Peng was shown on TV speaking to Chinese Communist Party cadres in the Great Hall of the People announcing firm measures to crackdown on the student demonstrators in Tiananmen Square. His hardline stand was apparent both verbally and non-verbally. Indeed, the visual climax of the televised speech was when Premier Li showed his determination on the crackdown by raising his right arm with a tight fist and swinging it downwards as if symbolising the use of physical force to clear the students from Tiananmen Square. This sequence showing him swinging his fist was repeated on TV over and over again in the next couple of days, in regularly scheduled news bulletins as well as frequent unscheduled news updates.

The martial law order announced included a part specifying a foreign news blackout. The announcement of the news blackout produced the impression in Hong Kong that the student demonstrators in Tiananmen Square would soon be confronted with potential physical violence threatening annihilation of their lives. The deep worry in Hong Kong was that something terrible was going to happen while the outside world was not watching. The news updates shown frequently on Hong Kong TV about the news ban was visibly annihilating. In the unusually frequent news updates on the martial law order, the news ban was constantly emphasised with actuality film showing Western journalists crowded in a small room putting video tapes into satellite-linked transmitters, described as trying to beat the deadline when satellite transmission services for the foreign press would be suspended. To the Hong Kong TV audience, the Western faces symbolised the watching eyes from the outside world, and seeing them 'live' on TV over and over again in the process of being excluded did nothing but confirm that the gaze from outside was to be obstructed, annihilated.

The news blackout was in itself symbolically annihilating to the audiences in Hong Kong who had kept the TV on all day, and for many all night, to monitor the development of the Beijing situation. Banning information from Beijing meant the annihilation of the discursive existence of the Beijing students, and to those who had developed an intense discursive relationship with the Beijing students through various communication media in Hong Kong, it was like the violent destruction of a life-line.

Unscheduled TV news updates normally bring the most updated information on important issues and are closely identified with the notions of immediacy and urgency, much more than regular news bulletins. Yet, these 'news' updates following the announcement of the martial law order constantly reminded the audience that there was no news, that the professional journalists were losing control, and that nobody, not even the academics invited to appear on special magazine programmes to speculate on the situation, were sure what was going to happen. And they did this supported with visual evidence that they were really losing control, which was why they had no new actuality material. The repeated showing of Primier Li's fist-waving motions, and the repeated use of the same actuality film on the students' activities already broadcast earlier, did nothing but confirm that the news ban had stopped news from coming through, which only served to intensify the sense of urgency.

To the deeply anxious Hong Kong person keeping the TV on all night and all day, and often with the radio on at the same time, hoping to catch the latest information on the development of the student movement in Beijing, it was only too obvious that the news institution was losing control of truth. In regular news bulletins and special news updates, the news reader in the studio repeatedly confirmed verbally that there was no news. The reporter sent to Beijing was not available to help contain the disruption of the discourse of truth; his discursivity had been annihilated. The absence of the second stage of the 'claw-back' mechanism emphasised the authenticity and contextual accuracy of the actuality film. What the actuality film confirmed visibly was that there was no news.

The academics in Hong Kong had also lost control of truth, and the understanding was that the young intellectuals in Tiananmen Square were confronted with tanks and machine guns. The loyal news-watchers suffering from intense anxiety felt strongly that they had to reappropriate truth and let it speak freely. They did this by 'reclaiming' the media. They demanded that the media's surveillance capability be restored, with as many individuals as possible visibly participating in the surveillance operation, in person (see Figure 17.1).

They inundated radio phone-in programmes with highly emotional calls. They created public spectacles through massive turnouts in protest rallies: they exposed themselves to Typhoon Brenda pitting their bodies against natural forces, and later simply offered their bodies to be counted on the street. These visibly powerful spectacles 'forced' the media to speak their truth: reporters, editors, commentators, and publishers gave them spaces. They also occupied paid advertising space in newspapers with personal and institutional names: from 23 May to 27 May, there were in local Chinese newspapers an average of 125 declarations per day bearing signatories of groups of individuals and organisations expressing solidarity with the Beijing students and demanding that the news ban be lifted. Radio music programmes repeatedly played the song 'For Freedom', specially written for that historical moment in Hong Kong, and sung by a large number of local pop singers, who were repeatedly shown on TV crowded together in a recording studio singing their hearts out.

Taking part in these processes, the people of Hong Kong recognised that their bodies were invested with power, that their bodies counted. Power demands that truth be spoken. In exercising the power invested in their bodies, to restore news as a discourse of truth, they recognised themselves as subjects in truth, and acted out their subjection to truth. They were compelled by truth to exercise the power already invested in their bodies, making them individual centres of the dissemination of truth. Substantial human and financial resources in Hong Kong were mobilised to send news clippings to Mainland China through the post, and through every

Figure 17.1: A Model of the Surveillance Process

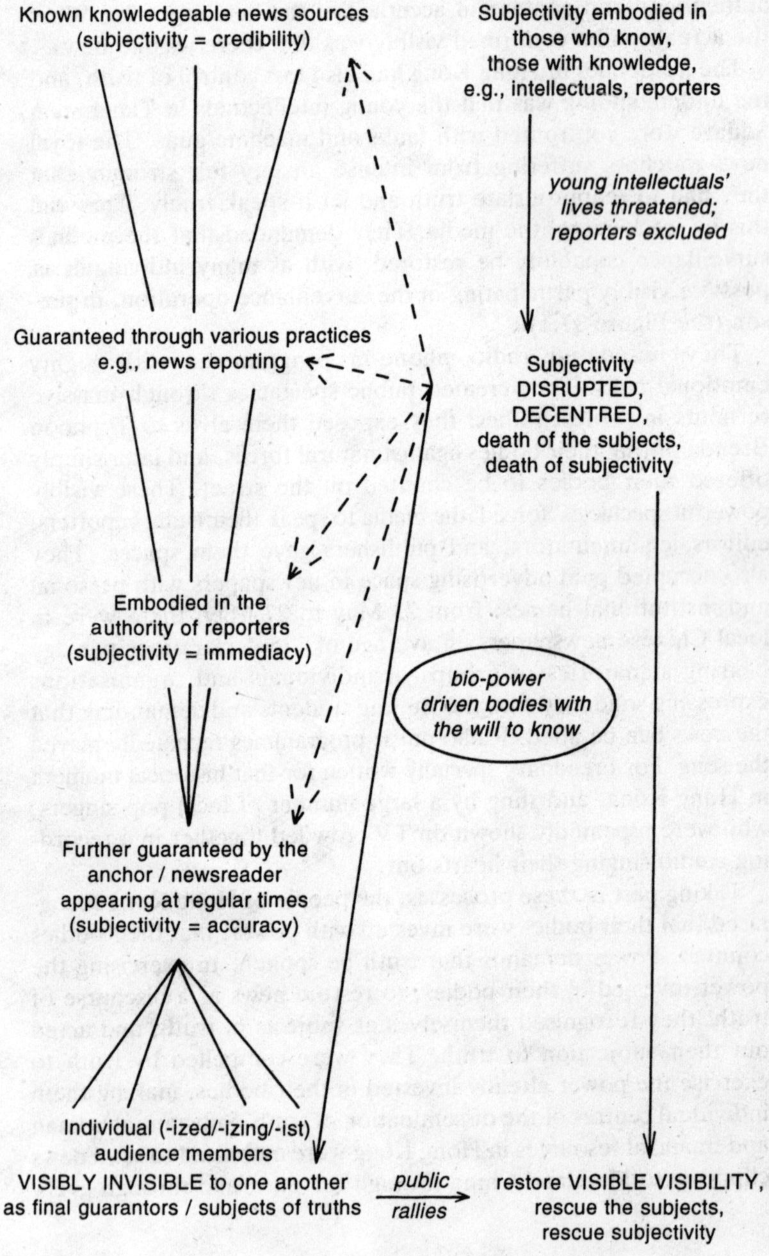
Known knowledgeable news sources
(subjectivity = credibility)
Guaranteed through various practices
e.g., news reporting
Embodied in the
authority of reporters
(subjectivity = immediacy)
Further guaranteed by the
anchor / newsreader
appearing at regular times
(subjectivity = accuracy)
Individual (-ized/-izing/-ist)
audience members
VISIBLY INVISIBLE to one another
as final guarantors / subjects of truths
public
rallies
Subjectivity embodied in
those who know,
those with knowledge,
e.g., intellectuals, reporters
young intellectuals'
lives threatened;
reporters excluded
Subjectivity
DISRUPTED,
DECENTRED,
death of the subjects,
death of subjectivity
bio-power
driven bodies with
the will to know
restore VISIBLE VISIBILITY,
rescue the subjects,
rescue subjectivity

single facsimile number available. Even though truth was not coming from China, it had to go to China. No one could ascertain whether those news clippings ever reached their destinations. But to Hong Kong, truth was saying that the Hong Konger was a full-grown individual capable of independent thinking, genuine feeling, and autonomous action, and that Hong Kong was watching. One million individual bodies of a community of six million offered themselves on the streets in Hong Kong on Sunday, 21 May 1989 to prove it, in and through TV news.

References

Fiske, J. (1987). *Television culture*. London: Methuen.

Fiske, J. and **Hartley, J.** (1978). *Reading television*. London: Methuen.

Foucault, M. (1979). *Discipline and punish: The birth of the prison*. (Translated by Alan Sheridan). Harmondsworth, UK: Peregrine Books.

———. (1980). *Power/knowledge: Selected interviews & other writings 1972–1977*. (Ed. Colin Gordon). New York: Pantheon Books.

———. (1986). *The foucault reader*. (Ed. Paul Rabinow). Harmondsworth, UK: Peregrine Books.

IV

Emerging Issues

18

Open Markets and the Future of Television—Fiction and Fact: GATT, GATS and the World Trade Organisation

David French and *Michael Richards*

The conclusion of the long process of international trade negotiations known as the 'Uruguay Round' of the General Agreement on Tariffs and Trade (GATT) has thrown a long shadow over the preparation of this book. The main sections of this book address a variety of individual national experiences but at times the GATT process has seemed to render out of date any attempt to consider the future of television within the boundaries of any single country. GATT sometimes appears to have ushered in an era in which television will become a commercial commodity, divorced from any special cultural significance and to be traded internationally[1] like, to quote a former chairman of the American Federal Communications Commission, 'toasters with pictures' (in Brown, 1994, p. 260; see also, Foster, 1992; Fowler and Brenner, 1982; Veljanovski [ed.], 1989).

An important aspect of this change is of course the role of the large, multinational media conglomerates in selling their wares through satellite systems, for whom national frontiers present no obstacle. Such cross-frontier broadcasting has in the past often been resisted by national governments struggling to retain some autonomy in television policy. But the Uruguay Round of GATT, with the inclusion in the free-trade process of audio-visual services, and thus of international trade in television programmes, marks a change in this position. The negotiations reached their successful conclusion through the joint efforts of 111 governments and this represents a radical shift in the balance of forces. From being the key defenders of national televisual independence through the use of import quotas and other similar restrictive trade practices, the world's governments seem *themselves* to have conspired to demolish these barriers, the very instruments of their previous policies.

For this reason it is important that this concluding chapter should examine the GATT process, the pressures that have encouraged and enabled it to come to eventual agreement, the nature of the trade regime that it establishes and the degree to which any element of national autonomy will survive. Inevitably this is to some extent an exercise in futurology, always a risky enterprise and one that is particularly difficult when the subject changes as fast as does television.

Accordingly, we do not set out to make concrete propositions about particular countries or dare to risk anything as concrete as specific dates. Some major events are only now in the process of intellectual digestion. A crucial element in this difficult diet is the conclusion of the Uruguay Round itself.

Other developments have also proceeded very fast, in line with the imperatives of commercial competition. One current example at the time of writing is the change in popular music provision on satellite television associated with the dispute between Star and MTV, leading to the creation of Channel [V] by a consortium of major media conglomerates, including, in addition to Star, Time Warner, Sony, Thorn-EMI and Bertelsman. Newspaper coverage (Rawsthorn, 1995) suggests that this example is a key indicator of the central importance of the Southeast Asian market to the major world media interests (*Screen Digest*, 1995). Similarly, the destruction of the Apstar satellite in the 26 January 1995 launch explosion of the Chinese Long March rocket (Poole, 1995) may be of crucial significance for the state of television competition in the region in the medium term future. But in both cases it is difficult to predict how the stories will unfold and it is important to resist the temptation to share the instant, sometimes sensational, reactions of newspaper journalists.

The purpose of this chapter is more modest; it is to reflect on the processes currently in train in an attempt to sort out some of the realities which may lie behind the high-flown rhetoric in which discussions sometimes take place.

Television, the Audio-visual Sector and World Free-trade Negotiations

The process of negotiating towards the GATT agreement, for most of its long drawn-out history, was associated with trade in goods, whether manufactured products or raw materials. Under the same umbrella, but for our purposes more important, is the associated General Agreement on Trade in Services (GATS). Together, these agreements led to the creation of the World Trade Organisation (WTO) as of 1 January 1995. The purpose of the whole process was to remove trade barriers, whether in terms of government-imposed quotas, discrimination in the form of tariffs on imports that were not charged on domestically produced goods, or 'invisible' barriers, such as unnecessary health tests or labelling requirements, which made the task of the importer difficult. Behind this lay the view that, first, world consumers would get a better deal if they had available to them the maximum range of choice, enabling them to choose freely on the basis of price and quality, rather than in terms of that which happens to be produced locally. Second, producers would be encouraged to supply goods with maximum efficiency in order to compete with alternative sources from all over the world and would be assisted in doing so by virtue of not having to pay the costs associated with negotiating local frontier taxes and so on (see, for examples of positive views of the free market model, *Economist*, 1993; OECD, 1993).

In the final 10 years of the GATT negotiations, trade in services became an important new focus of negotiation. The major protagonists in the GATT negotiations were the representatives of the major world economies, with USA the most important of all; for them freedom of trade in services was of particular commercial importance. As Broadman (1994, p. 289) puts it: 'The United States, as the largest services provider, has much to gain from the liberalisation of services markets around the world'.

In this respect GATS, which reached through conventional negotiations an outcome favourable to USA, provides an interesting contrast to the dispute over the New World Information and Communication Order (NWICO), when the then American government was 'forced' to resort to the crude exercise of political and economic muscle in order to frustrate agreements which it feared would block its access to world media markets.

The inclusion of cultural services has by no means been a constant or unproblematic feature of other free-trade agreements. Some examples will show the need to be cautious in building expectations about how the position with GATS may develop. Broadman (1994) points out that, within the North American Free Trade Agreement (NAFTA) framework, Canada and the USA have excluded trade between them in audio-visual services. In contrast in the European Union (EU) television has been seen as appropriate for inclusion in the single market, alongside all other commercial products (see Aldridge and Hewitt [eds.], 1994; and particularly for background, Collins, 1994a). But even within Europe there has been intense argument about the appropriateness of quotas for imports from outside the Union and about various forms of support from particular countries for their own television and film industries (see London Economics, 1994; *Screen Digest*, 1994b; and earlier European Commission, 1989).

In late 1993, the GATT and GATS negotiations reached a conclusion. Among the important factors leading to the agreements was the simplification of negotiations, particularly with the joining together of the vociferous European powers into the single EU negotiating bloc and the effective disappearance of communism as an alternative economic power and ideological pole. Paradoxically, given the late extension of the negotiations to include the service sector, it was a disagreement over audio-visual trade between two of the world's largest producers, USA and the EU, that came closest to finally disrupting the agreements.

After the final acts of negotiating brinkmanship, the eventual GATS resolution saw the inclusion of the culture industries. But it would be quite wrong to imply that the concerns which earlier found expression in the struggle for NWICO have in any way receded.[2] But what are the factors that seem to have given such an important place to the new discourse on market freedom, rather than emphasising the need to foster the interests of those who may find themselves damaged by such competition? Is it really the case that the rhetoric of GATT, GATS and the WTO will lead to a relaxation of trade barriers as they apply to television and how do such formal procedures relate to other changes in the direction towards free markets in television?

Television and the Information Society: Cultural Form, Commodity, or Both?

In its traditional status as a cultural form, television has been protected from the rigours of the marketplace by conventions such as those captured by the term 'public service'. But, in the sense that its output has always been produced at a real cash cost and that television programmes have long been commercially traded, any claim that the growth of the Information Society is uniquely the factor which has transformed television from the status of culture to commodity is absurd. When the current Pope has figured in the top 20 record releases of some countries for his reading of the Ave Maria, it is increasingly difficult to think of any form of culture that does not have commodity value. But whatever is made of this curiosity, it is quite clear that television has always had a dual status; it has been a cultural commodity, vigorously sold across the world's growing audio-visual markets.

At the same time there have been other very important changes which have led to the commercial importance of television becoming increasingly recognised. Partly, this is a function of the increasing importance of the service sector within the major industrialised economies. As illustration, Broadman (1994, p. 283) notes that roughly 19 per cent of world trade is in services and that, for the United States, this constitutes 52 per cent of GDP, employing 79 per cent of the workforce.

These particular factors will become acutely relevant when we come to discuss the implications of GATS and the WTO; it is easy to understand USA's special concern with the service sector when one realises that in 1993 the country 'ran a *merchandise trade deficit* of $96.3 billion, but ran a *services trade surplus* of $55.1 billion' (Broadman, 1994, p. 283, our emphases). The point becomes still more obvious when we consider the importance in the overall American trade position of audio-visual products. As Collins reports (1994b, p. 100) the cultural industries, of which television and film are the major parts, are 'second only to the aerospace industry' in terms of their contribution to American exports.

It can readily be seen, therefore, that television and the audio-visual sector as a whole are increasingly central to some of the main world economies. Furthermore, a crucial step in the argument, one that will be vital to the discussion later in this chapter about regulation and its relationship to the market, is that governments may increasingly be perceiving that they have to make domestic sacrifices in order to achieve international competitiveness. In other words, just as in the case of airlines where many governments have abandoned competitiveness between domestic providers in order to build big national companies able to compete in the international marketplace, so perhaps governments will be tempted to relax the regulatory conditions within domestic television in order to boost the competitive resources of the national supplier in the wider world audio-visual market.

This is, of course, a market in which very large profits are anticipated and, in some cases, already being made. To give two recent examples, the latest results for BSkyB, the British part of Rupert Murdoch's satellite empire shows an operating profit of £170 million and the growth potential is only at the very beginning of its upswing (Snoddy, 1994); and in the Middle East, local entrepreneurs are quoted as investing $900 million on new satellite services (Khalaf, 1994). In this connection, *Screen Digest* (1994a) gives useful statistical background on the pace of television development across the continent of Asia.

But there is more to the changed perception than scale alone. The process of *technological convergence* has engendered critical changes in the nature of the subject under discussion. As noted in Chapter 1 of this book, broadcasting in general, and television in particular, have been crucially defined by the technology of their transmission and reception. The transmission of visual images from source to receiver was very largely restricted to the domain of television and, similarly, television programmes were, in most countries, almost always received off-air. When data was transmitted, it was often in hard copy and sometimes by land line. With the growth of new ways of conveying television pictures, through satellite and cable[3] and, in reverse, the use of what used to be exclusively 'television technology' for the transmission of information of all kinds, this distinction has broken down. The increasing sophistication and power of digital technologies have moved the networking of information to centre-stage in debates about world trade. A recent editorial in *Media Development* (1994, p. 4) put it as follows: 'As the world moves towards a new millenium we are assured that the new world order, assisted by the "information highway" will bring about global development, new solidarities and an era of plenty'.

Most of the governments of the world share this view of the prominence in the economic future of the new information industries. But what also seems to be very largely shared is an assumption that the motor of such expansion should be private capital and, therefore, that commercial businesses should be the key institutions. To quote *Media Development* (1994, p. 4) once more:

> The scramble for the media and information market is reminiscent of the scramble for territory in colonial times. Except that this war is being won and lost in corporate board-rooms, on the stock market, in the financial corridors of the world and finally in the hyper-saturated media environments of our lives.

Challenges to Traditional Assumptions about Broadcasting

Broadcasting policies have varied radically around the world. But there are four main reasons which have recurred as explanations for the widespread rejection of pure free market solutions to the organisation of television. These are: first, spectrum scarcity, which has normally been assumed to preclude the fundamental free market principle of open access to the market for newcomers willing to risk their capital in order to offer new services, or old services at new prices, to potential consumers; second, is the legacy transmitted to broadcasting from the press, of the priority of freedom of speech and the need, frequently abused in political systems which claim to be pluralistic, to take special measures to preserve it in a situation of spectrum scarcity; third, is the perceived power of broadcasting over its viewers, both in terms of alleged immediate effects and in the longer process of building cultural solidarity, neither of which are governments normally happy to turn over to commercial operators; fourth, and finally, is the simple difficulty of introducing an effective pricing mechanism by which consumers will be required to pay an appropriate fee for the services they use.

These concerns have been strong enough to ensure that in most countries other than USA, exceptional by virtue of its dominant position in the world market, governments have attempted to insulate broadcasting from market forces. The multiplicity of channels and the now well-understood practical viability of encryption technology, together with academic media research which has, over many years, cast doubt upon simple views of the 'power' of television, seriously undermine the assumptions which legitimated such efforts at control. The earlier chapters illustrate this and show the limitations of the capacity of national governments to continue to intervene in an era of increasing cross-frontier, satellite delivered television.

Satellite television, with its ownership in the hands of buccaneering capitalists, has then been a crucial factor in this process of change. The earlier parts of this book illustrate this in a variety of ways. But it is crucial to understand that the process of technological convergence has not just been a matter of changing technology but also of the importation into the domain of television of vigorously commercial approaches. If satellites are associated with names such as Ted Turner and Rupert Murdoch, then the business of computing and digital technology resonates as strongly with those of Bill Gates and his younger contemporaries. Crucially, the industries and technologies with which broadcasting is converging have always been led by private capital and have only in aberrant national circumstances been subject to regulation for the public good. In other words, if countries wish to jump on the broadband highway, collectively to ride the Internet and the Worldwide Web, then they have, superficially at least, to speak its language and that is the language of private capital and of the free market.

If this change is to be fully understood, then it needs to be set against the assumptions of the previously most important model of international organisation, the 'public service cartel' known as the European Broadcasting Union (EBU). The EBU, based on a core of national broadcasters of Western Europe, but extending in a web which covers most of the Western world, continues to provide its members with a variety of services from shared facilities at major sporting events, international exchange of news coverage, some joint production of programmes to joint, monopolistic, negotiations of rights to world events such as the Olympics. The services the EBU provides gives the viewers of its constituent television organisations far more than their national providers could by themselves deliver, a benefit particularly important to those in smaller countries with restricted televisual infrastructures. The financial structure of the EBU is complicated, involving membership fees which relate to the size of the national television market and the agreed ability of the member organisation to pay (Eugster, 1983). Only associate members pay a fee which is related to the use they make of EBU services and there is little evidence of any pricing mechanism linking supply to demand in the EBU's financial transactions. Looking at it now, organisations like the EBU seem like hang-overs from a previous generation. To bewail their passing may be simply naive. But one very quick way of recognising the degree of change in the international climate in broadcasting is to consider the furore that would certainly ensue among the free marketeers of current television were they to confront, for the first time, the prospect of an equivalent to the EBU being set up now.

The switch in approach is crucially one of perception—of the future of television and the practicalities of controlling it. For the most part, governments have been used to taking the lead in this and if governments lose faith in their future ability to control, then their frame of reference will change. Instead of trying to restrain the tiger of domestic and international capital, they may well feel compelled to choose between riding it or being consumed by it.

GATS and Reality of Free-trade in Television

The conclusion of the Uruguay Round of GATT marks an important step in the structure of world televisual trade and in the move to centre-stage of free-trade ideologies. But the operation of GATT is less straightforward than is sometimes assumed. In their discussion of the earlier stages of the GATT process, in which a relatively limited group of countries agreed to a core of free-trade practices, Hoekman and Mavroidis (1994) discuss a number of areas of trade restrictions where GATT proved difficult to enforce. One very revealing example is the long history of conflict between what is now the EU and Japan. While Japan has had striking success in import penetration of European markets, the reverse has not been the case. According to the Japanese authorities, this is a matter of local taste and consumption patterns, which potential European exporters have failed to address. But for the EU it is a question of hidden trade barriers in the form of a series of unfair practices within the Japanese market. So how has the elaborate machinery of GATT addressed the issue? As Hoekman and Mavroidis (1994, p. 139) delicately put it: 'The discussion that followed in the GATT Council failed to shed light on this case and ultimately the [then] EC decided to refrain from pursuing it'.

From the European side at least this was a major episode and for neither party was resolution in the form of a stalemate satisfactory. It provides a good indicator of the difficulties in translating international trade agreements into agreed trading practices, even in the relatively simple form of trade in goods. How much more difficult will it be with regard to trade in services and, in particular, trade in audio-visual services and software? Claims to be objective about qualitative issues such as cultural taste are bound to be extremely difficult to substantiate, but it is precisely these matters which will be at the heart of any future conflicts about televisual trade barriers.

One important factor is that completely free-trade in the near future is not even envisaged by the GATS negotiators. Countries are able to claim exemptions from the GATS procedures for an initial 10 year period. In other words, they can avoid having to conform to free-trade conventions in the audio-visual sector if they make an appropriate indication that they intend to do so. Among others, the EU, Canada and Australia have already taken this action. (Broadman, 1994).

Another important issue which makes the implications of GATS for broadcasting even more complex than for other areas is the special position that the parent GATT process allows for 'state trading enterprises'. 'The right of contracting parties [i.e., governments] to maintain or establish state-trading enterprises or to offer exclusive privileges is *not at all* prejudged by the General Agreement' (Hoekman and Mavroidis, 1994, p. 133, their emphasis). State-trading enterprises are particularly important in television and their practices normally operate very much against the principles of the free market. Government subsidies and licence fee-based revenues, for example, not only remove the broadcasters themselves from commercial pressures, they also give them a favoured position in competition with 'business' rivals. Technically, there is no doubt that this privileged position amounts to a restraint of free-trade. Similarly, in television systems with an important public sector it is very common to have careful mechanisms for the selection of 'suitable' commercial competitors. In the language of 'public service', this is about the positive virtue of protecting 'quality'. But, in the language of classical economics it is quite the opposite, being clearly a negative act—denying the principle that the interests of consumers will best be served by open access to a market for those willing to try to sell new, maybe better, services.

Now it is quite clear from the discussion provided by Hoekman and Mavroidis (1994) that the special position ascribed to state-trading enterprises is not intended to allow them to operate in complete freedom from rules about fair competition. But it is also quite clearly recognised that their position is particularly difficult and sensitive. Given the overall importance attached by governments to the communication media in general, and to television in particular, it is not to be expected that the treatment of public sector television will be an easy issue for the WTO adjudicators to unravel, particularly since so much of the context of television regulation is governed by discretion and historic understanding rather than formal rules (see Michael, 1989). The powerful and entrenched position of public broadcasting is neatly revealed by the divided loyalties of those who might be expected to be its strongest enemies. Mark Fowler, the Chairman of the Federal Communication Commission referred to earlier for his 'toasters with pictures' comment, is a strong enthusiast for the free market, but is noted by Duncan Brown (1994, p. 262) as supporting the retention of public service programming in order to provide those ingredients which 'the nation might wish from its broadcasting' but which the market will not provide. Alan Peacock, who headed a British enquiry about the feasibility of opening broadcasting to market forces, in the end supported a Public Service Broadcasting Council (Peacock, 1986) with much the same objectives in view.

The full complexities of the new international regulatory apparatus which GATS represents will emerge over a longer period than the 12 months between the conclusion of the agreement and the time of writing. But it can be seen that it would be quite wrong to assume that the whole complex, heavyweight apparatus of GATT, GATS and the WTO together and by themselves will necessarily imply a simple and straightforward transition to a free world market in audio-visual trade. The following quotation encapsulates another important area of difficulty which will continue intermittently to stall the process. This is the existence of inevitable and recurrent differences of national interest:

> While a case can be made that there will be *global* efficiency gains from multilateralisation of anti-trust, and that each country will share in such gains as long as governments cooperate . . ., the problem from a practical perspective is that the distribution and magnitude of such gains are uncertain (Hoekman and Mavroidis, 1994, p. 129, their emphasis).

It can be assumed that Hoekman, who works for the World Bank, and Mavroidis, then employed by GATT, are enthusiasts for the process. How much stronger will be the doubts of those more sceptical and, in particular, those who fear that their national interest may suffer in a wholly free international market? There are plenty who hold this view, whether from developing economies or enthusiasts for economic isolationism in USA, of whom Batra (1993) is a strident representative. It is essential to any understanding of the outcome of the Uruguay Round to recognise that the new apparatus it sets up for international free-trade is one based upon voluntary commitment on the part of governments and upon continuing co-operation between them. As an authoritative article in the British *Financial Times* (de Jonquieres, 1995, p. 19) put it:

> . . . the WTO, like GATT, has no powers to force through decisions, which will mostly be reached by consensus. Ultimately, its effectiveness will depend upon how readily members co-operate in liberalisation by making reciprocal concessions based upon a calculation of self-interest.

Free-trade: Nevertheless a Dominant Ideology?

If it is misleading to think that GATS will lead to the immediate dismantling of trade barriers in broadcasting, it would of course be just as wrong to assume that all will continue as before. The earlier chapters of this book show above all the existence of a sequence of change that cannot be reversed, but one in which governments and other cultural interest groups remain active players.

Chapter 2 sets out to show some of the complexities in national reactions to change in global media patterns. The global trade in media products is not a process to which governments will be willing to sacrifice dearly held goals of nation-building, and protection of the national culture and sensitive interest groups such as religion and the young. Behind all this may also be the view that a strong national hand in broadcasting is a good way of ensuring the retention of a strong hand in the control of the state. Furthermore, governments are also not unaware of the possibility that to enter a world free market in a position of weakness may not be the best way to build a position of strength and that, conversely, it may actually be a very good way of ensuring continued weakness. See the chapter in this volume by Mark Hukill for an example in this respect.

It is a constant theme throughout the book that national and local media markets continue to display strong resilience, with strong appetites for programmes relevant to their particular concerns and interests. Commercial operators will have to address such differences of consumer demand and this may limit the disruptive effect of international suppliers. But, on the other hand, it is also evident how vulnerable protective policies are on the part of governments when confronted by factors favourable to the liberalisation of the market. These include: the demands of parts of their publics, and often some of the most affluent and most vocal are most oriented to their role as consumers, to become eager customers for new satellite television services; the pressures of local industry to link to new international information networks; the willy-nilly arrival from the skies of satellite delivered services; and the demands of local suppliers to be free to compete on the same programming terms as their new rivals.

In reality there will be no clear-cut global resolutions on the struggle between national restraints and world competition. The GATT negotiations have moved the balance towards the side of free-trade, but not decisively so. They have very forcefully increased the prominence of free-trade assumptions in the consideration of world trade and the inclusion in GATS of the audio-visual sector has attracted a great deal of attention. But the nature of the negotiating process and, in particular, the importance in it of the good will of governments, calls for considerable caution in assessing the future significance of the WTO in isolation from wider processes.

It would, however, be wrong to leave the issue without considering a range of other, less tangible factors which strongly, and perhaps decisively, push the process of ideological change in the same direction. It is a very overt policy of the world economic institutions, notably the World Bank, the International Monetary

Fund and the various policy groupings of the major world trading powers, that their financial support to developing economies is dependent upon the adoption of market principles in the management of those economies. The pressure is reflected and reinforced in the imposition of the same policies by many of the providers of bilateral aid. An implication of this is that governments across the world, whatever their political complexions, are being encouraged and required to incorporate into the heart of their decision-making processes economic managers who are committed to free market approaches. All these processes also have to be seen in the light of the collapse of communism and its replacement often by a particularly evangelical capitalism in the Soviet Union and many of its allies, removing an alternative source of material and ideological support.

In final conclusion the verdict on the world trade position has to remain unproven. There is plenty of evidence that local demand and local cultural resistance to global forces will remain powerful. To put a previous argument more strongly, there is limited sense in positing the operation of free markets in television. More normally the discussion should be of the conditions of constraint within which some market forces are allowed partially to operate. But such resistances have to be seen in the context of some major shifts of dominant ideologies which will work very powerfully against them to maximise market freedom. In considering the place of the GATT process in the rise of free market ideologies in world television, it is probably best to see it not as an independent variable but as a powerful symbol of the degree to which such positions have come to hold centre-stage. Its future will provide an important test-bed, showing quite how far individual nations will be able to stand against the tide of free world trade.

Notes

1. This is particularly clear when looking from the narrow viewpoint of the United Kingdom, a country which claims a particular role in the creation of the 'public service' tradition but which has adopted a policy which is overtly very committed to commercial success in international markets. Even here, however, the change to free market approaches are somewhat inconsistent. See Department of National Heritage (1994) for illustration. For a basic general background to GATT and the Uruguay Round see Greenaway (1994).

2. See *Media Development* (1994, p. 2) again, for example: 'All available indices point to the fact that the free market privileges those sectors of society that are already advantaged . . . . It seems that the only freedom on offer is the freedom to consume, for the few, not the many'.
3. The authors are well aware of the very long history of cable as a means of transmitting television, but the point here is that cable networks have moved from the background to central prominence within the relatively recent past.

References

Aldridge, M. and **Hewitt, N.** (eds.). (1994). *Controlling broadcasting: Access policy and practice in North America and Europe*. (Fulbright Papers 13) Manchester: Manchester University Press.

Batra, R. (1993). *The myth of free trade: A plan for America's revival*. New York: Charles Scribner's Sons.

Broadman, H.G. (1994). 'GATS: The Uruguay Round Accord on international trade and investment in services'. *The World Economy*, 17(3) May, 281–92.

Brown, D.H. (1994). 'The academy's response to the call for a marketplace approach to broadcasting regulation'. *Critical Studies in Mass Communication*. 11 (September), 257–73.

Collins, R. (1994a). *Broadcasting and audiovisual policy in the European Single Market*. London: John Libbey.

———. (1994b). 'Unity in diversity? The European Single Market in broadcasting and the audiovisual, 1982–1992'. *Journal of Common Market Studies*. 32(1) March, 89–102.

de Jonquieres, G. (1995). 'Dreams behind the scenes'. *Financial Times*, London. 5 January, p. 19.

Department of National Heritage (1994). *The future of the BBC: Serving the nation; competing worldwide*. Cm 2621. London: HMSO.

Economist (1993). 'For richer, for poorer: No, developing countries do not lose from the GATT deal'. 18 December, p. 82.

Eugster, E. (1983). *Television programming across national boundaries: The EBU and OIRT experience*. Dedham, MA: Artech House Inc.

European Commission (1989). *Broadcasting directive: Television without frontiers*. 89/552/EEC. Luxembourg: Office of the European Communities.

Foster, R. (1992). *Public broadcasters: Accountability and efficiency*. Edinburgh: David Hume Institute and Edinburgh University Press (Hume Paper 18).

Fowler, M.S. and **Brenner, D.L.** (1982). 'A marketplace approach to broadcasting regulation'. *Texas Law Review*. 60, 207–57. Reprinted in Wartella, E., Whitney, D.C. and Windahl, S. (eds.). (1983). *Mass communication review yearbook. Volume 4*. Beverley Hills, CA: Sage.

Greenaway, D. (1994). 'The Uruguay Round of trade negotiations'. *Economic Review*, 12(2) November, 31–34.

Hoekman, B.M. and **Mavroidis, P.C.** (1994). 'Competition, competition policy and the GATT'. *The World Economy*, 17(2) March, 121–50.

Khalaf, R. (1994). 'Saudi businessmen reach for the media stars'. *Financial Times*, 16 November, p. 6.

London Economics (1994). *The economic impact of television quotas in the European Union: A report for Sony Entertainment*. London: London Economics.

Media Development (1994). 'Public communication–Superhighway or one-way street' (Editorial), XLI(4), 2.

Michael, J. (1989). 'Regulating the communications media: From the discretion of sound chaps to the arguments of lawyers'. In Ferguson, M. (ed.). *Public* communication—The new imperatives: Future directions for media research. London: Sage.

OECD (1993). *Assessing the effects of the Uruguay Round*. Trade Policy Issues 2. Paris: OECD.

Peacock, A. (1986). *Report of the Committee on Financing the BBC*. Cmnd. 9824. London: Home Office/HMSO.

Poole, T. (1995). 'Rocket blast boosts Murdoch'. *The Independent*, 27 January, p. 15.

Rawsthorn, A. (1995). 'MTV faces challenge for Asian music market'. *Financial Times*, 9 January, p. 2.

Screen Digest (1994a). 'Asian television: Massive growth but uncertain opportunity' April, pp. 81–88.

——— (1994b). 'European directives: Seeking harmony in the media'. June, pp. 129–36.

——— (1995). 'Worldwide television market base; the global set count'. February, pp. 33–35.

Snoddy, R. (1994). 'The audiences are spoilt for choice'. Survey of Broadcast and Communication Media. *Financial Times*, 4 October, p. 1.

Veljanovski, C. (ed.). (1989). *Freedom in broadcasting*. London: Institute of Economic Affairs (Hobart Paperback 29).

Contributors

Raghavachari Amritavalli is Professor in the Department of Radio, Television and Cinematography, Central Institute of English and Foreign Languages, Hyderabad, India. Her main research interests are in theoretical linguistics and the psychology of language and perception.

Mustafa K. Anuar is Lecturer in Communication Studies in the School of Communication, Universiti Sains Malaysia, Penang, Malaysia. His main interests are politics and the media and youth sub-cultures in Malaysia.

David French is Director of the Centre for Communication Studies, Coventry University, Coventry, United Kingdom. He has considerable experience in teaching and research in media policy and a particular interest in pan-European dimensions in media education. He chairs the European Communication Group.

Mark A. Hukill is Senior Lecturer and Head of the Electronic and Broadcast Media Division, School of Communication Studies, Nanyang Technological University, Singapore. His current interests include telecommunications policy, and broadcast and information systems development in Southeast Asia. He has wide experience of government consultancy, including TV work for the Republic of Niger.

Shin Dong Kim is visiting scholar at the Universities of Chicago and Indiana, USA. Previously he has taught and researched at Korea University, Seoul, and has particular interests in the relationship between global capital and the Korean media industry.

Wang Lay Kim is Lecturer in Communication Studies in the School of Communication, Universiti Sains Malaysia, Penang, Malaysia. Her main research interests lie in the study of gender and the media. With Zaharom Nain and Mustafa K. Anuar she is working on a textbook on media studies.

Keval J. Kumar is Reader and Visiting Professor in the Department of Communication and Journalism, University of Poona, Pune, India. He is author of *Mass communication in India* and *Media education, communication and public policy: An Indian perspective*.

Terence Lo lectures on cultural studies, gender studies and critical language studies in the Department of English, Hong Kong Polytechnic University, Hong Kong. His research interests include the formation of identity in post-industrial Hong Kong, critical discourse analysis and literacy development in postmodernity.

Sunanda Mahendra is a senior member of the Mass Communication Department, University of Kelaniya Dalugama, Sri Lanka, and is Vice President of the Commonwealth Association for Education in Journalism and Communication for Sri Lanka.

Zaharom Nain is Lecturer in Communication Studies in the School of Communication, Universiti Sains Malaysia, Penang, Malaysia. His current areas of research are the political economy of the Malaysian media and the implications of cultural studies in a development context. He is currently co-editing a collection on Communication and Development with Michael Richards.

Chung-bong Ng lectures on cinema and television in the School of Communication, Hong Kong Baptist University, Hong Kong. He is a veteran TV production executive, film critic and an active researcher in the history of Hong Kong. His books include a study of Hong Kong cinema and many publications about Hong Kong history.

Usha Vyasulu Reddi is currently Professor of Mass Communication and Director of the Audio-visual Research Centre, Osmania University, Hyderabad, India. In addition to her involvement in educational television, she is a specialist in communication policy and has published widely on media and society.

Michael Richards is Professor and Chair of the Consumer Culture Research Centre, Southampton Institute of Higher Education, Southampton, United Kingdom. Among his research interests are television and national identity, and television and children. With David French he has edited *Media education across Europe*.

Arbind Sinha is a senior scientist with the Indian Space Research Centre, Ahmedabad, India, and co-ordinates its Development Communication Research Unit. He has published *Mass media and rural development* and has subsequently worked on the link between new broadcasting services and their audiences.

Ubonrat Siriyuvasak is Lecturer in Broadcasting at the Department of Mass Communication, Chulalongkorn University, Bangkok, Thailand. Her interests include popular culture, gender and media, communication and media structure.

Seemi Naghmana Tahir is Associate Professor and Chairperson of the Department of Mass Communication, University of Baluchistan, Quetta, Pakistan. Seemi Tahir has interests in media policy in Pakistan and in the field of journalism education.

John V. Vilanilam is Vice Chancellor, University of Kerala, Thiruvananthapuram, India. Previously he was head of its Department of Communication and Journalism and concurrently Dean of Mass Communication, University of Calicut, Calicut, India. He has published widely in international journals and his most recent books include *Science, communication and development* and two collections of poems and light essays.

Index